BOUNTIES TO BLACK SOLDIERS

Wm. W. Belknap

HERITAGE BOOKS
2009

HERITAGE BOOKS
AN IMPRINT OF HERITAGE BOOKS, INC.

Books, CDs, and more—Worldwide

For our listing of thousands of titles see our website
at
www.HeritageBooks.com

Published 2009 by
HERITAGE BOOKS, INC.
Publishing Division
100 Railroad Ave. #104
Westminster, Maryland 21157

Copyright © 1870 Wm. W. Belknap

All rights reserved. No part of this book may be reproduced or transmitted in any form or by any means, electronic or mechanical, including photocopying, recording or by any information storage and retrieval system without written permission from the author, except for the inclusion of brief quotations in a review.

International Standard Book Numbers
Paperbound: 978-0-7884-4822-5
Clothbound: 978-0-7884-7625-9

41ST CONGRESS, } HOUSE OF REPRESENTATIVES. { Ex. Doc.
2d Session.   { No. 241.

BOUNTIES TO COLORED SOLDIERS.

LETTER

FROM

THE SECRETARY OF WAR

IN ANSWER TO

A resolution of the House, of the 7th ultimo, relative to collection and payment of bounties to colored soldiers.

APRIL 8, 1870.—Referred to the Committee on Military Affairs and ordered to be printed.

WAR DEPARTMENT, *April 6*, 1870.

The Secretary of War has the honor to submit to the House of Representatives, in obedience to the resolution of March 7, 1870, the report of a board of army officers, of which Brevet Brigadier General B. P. Runkle, United States Army, was president, upon the facts connected with the collection and payment of bounties to colored soldiers.

WM. W. BELKNAP,
Secretary of War.

WAR DEPARTMENT,
BUREAU REFUGEES, FREEDMEN AND ABANDONED LANDS,
Washington, March 31, 1870.

GENERAL: In compliance with indorsement of the 9th instant from the War Department, Adjutant General's Office, transmitting resolution of the House of Representatives, dated March 7, 1870, I have the honor to forward herewith a copy of the report of the commission, of which Colonel Ben. P. Runkle, United States Army, was chairman, as called for in said resolution and indorsement. Together with this report the original record of the proceedings of the commission is transmitted. To copy this record would involve the employment of a large clerical force, and cause considerable delay. The original is, therefore, forwarded, with the request that, when no longer required, it be returned to this office, to be filed as part of the permanent records of this bureau.

Very respectfully, your obedient servant,

O. O. HOWARD,
Brevet Major General U. S. A., Commissioner.

Brevet Major General E. D. TOWNSEND,
Adjutant General U. S. A., Washington, D. C.

BOUNTIES TO COLORED SOLDIERS.

REPORT OF COMMISSION APPOINTED BY SPECIAL ORDERS NO. 189, DECEMBER 17, 1869, BUREAU OF REFUGEES, FREEDMEN AND ABANDONED LANDS.

WASHINGTON, D. C., *March* 5, 1870.

GENERAL: We have the honor to report that, in obedience to Special Orders No. 189, dated War Department, Bureau Refugees, Freedmen and Abandoned Lands, December 17, 1869, the commission appointed by said order met at Nashville, Tennessee, and proceeded with the discharge of its duty.

This commission was, by the terms of the order, assembled for the purpose of a careful hearing of complaints of claimants for government bounty, made against officers or agents of this bureau, or other persons concerned in the payment of bounties to colored soldiers, sailors, and marines. And the commission proceeded, accordingly, (in part without reference to the charges set forth in certain papers referred to them,) thoroughly to investigate the subject of the payment of bounties, in order to ascertain, if possible, not only whether the charges preferred, but also whether any charges whatever could be substantiated.

The commission conceived it to be their duty fully to investigate and make clear the nature and extent of the frauds committed upon claimants, as well as the causes which had given rise to rumors of fraud which the commission might discover to be without foundation.

PROCEEDINGS AT NASHVILLE TENNESSEE.

At this point the commission summoned and examined the leading colored men of the city, including nine ministers of the gospel, one physician, and one lawyer. These gentlemen, without exception, stated that they had each lived in Nashville from one to five-and-thirty years, and that, though they had heard complaints against claim agents, they had never heard any against bureau officers.

Mr. N. B. Merry, a very prominent and intelligent colored minister, stated that he heard hundreds of complaints, but could not give the name of a complainant.

None of these gentlemen being able to give any names of persons who had been cheated by claim agents, bureau officers, or others, the commission directed them to notify, through their pulpits, and otherwise, all colored soldiers who had, or supposed they had, any grounds of complaint against claim agents or agents of the bureau, to present themselves before the commission.

In response to this notice, eighty-seven colored claimants appeared and were examined.

The commission have ascertained from the records of the Second Auditor of the United States Treasury, and the records of the chief disbursing officer and of the claim division of the bureau, and from the statements of the claimants themselves, that sixty-seven of them had no cause of complaint whatever. Twenty-seven of the above-mentioned sixty-seven have been paid in full all bounty and arrears of pay due them from the United States. (See third, fourth, fifth, and sixth days' proceedings, cases Nos. 9, 15, 16, 26, 29, 31, 32, 33½, 35, 36, 37, 40, 41, 42, 46, 54, 55, 56, 57, 59, 61, 63, 70, 73, 77, 82, 86.) It appears that the claims of sixteen of them have not been filed in the office of the Second Auditor, although each stated positively that his claim had been placed in the hands of a claim agent. (See third, fourth, fifth, and sixth days' proceedings, cases 2, 5, 8½, 14, 19, 25, 33, 39, 43, 44, 45, 51, 52, 75, 80, 85.) Four have failed to furnish evidence required by the Auditor to substantiate their claims. (See third, fourth, fifth, and sixth days' proceedings, Nos. 10, 11, 22, 68.) Two were not entitled to bounty. (See third and sixth days' proceedings, cases Nos. 18, 76.) The claims of seven have been disallowed. (See third, fourth, fifth, and sixth days' proceedings, Nos. 3, 7, 8, 24, 34, 49, 71.) The claims of eight are still awaiting settlement in the office of the Second Auditor. (See first, third, and sixth days' proceedings, Nos. 1, 13, 17, 28, 48, 74, 84, 87.) The claim of one is contested. (See No. 30, fourth day's proceedings.) The claims of two are awaiting information in the office of the Adjutant General of the United States Army. (See Nos. 4, 12, fourth day's proceedings.) In regard to the remaining twenty-six cases it appears that one, (see case 72, sixth day's proceedings,) having been settled, has been paid since investigation. The money of one (see case 78, sixth day's proceedings) is in the hands of the chief disbursing officer of the bureau.

William Thomas (see case 64, sixth day's proceedings) states that after he had been paid by the bureau officer, Mr. G. W. Glassie, a claim agent, took up the check for $190, which he had received from the bureau agent, and gave him his (Glassie's) own check for $170, and then charged him $10 for going to the bank with him.

For a report on case 79, Dallas Webster, see report in the case of Eastman, bureau agent, where the facts are fully set forth.

In one case, (see No. 81, sixth day's proceedings,) which comprises a statement of four cases, the treasury certificates in favor of the claimants were issued before the passage of the act approved March 29, 1867, making General Howard responsible for the payment of bounties, and sent to Wolf, Hart & Co., of Washington City, who failed to pay over the amount to the claimants. The soldiers appealed to the bureau authorities in Washington, whereupon the authorities recovered the money from Wolf, Hart & Co., and paid it to the proper claimants. This case was brought to the notice of the commission by a prominent Union citizen of Tennessee as a specimen case showing the manner in which claimants were paid before the passing of said act, and as such the commission have recorded it, and will refer to it under another head.

Among the eighty-seven complainants who appeared before the commission were eight men who stated that they had been employed by the United States military authorities to work on fortifications constructed for the defense of Nashville and other places in Tennessee; that they were promised pay for their labor, which they never received. (See fourth, fifth, and sixth day's proceedings, cases Nos. 23, 53, 58, 54, 62, 66, 67, 83.) The commission have no comments to make on the truth or falsity of these statements further than this: we were not ordered to investigate this class of complaints, nor did we, even after hearing the statements, intend to mention the same until we took the evidence of D. W. Glassie, a citizen and claim agent of Nashville, Tennessee.

Mr. Glassie was asked the question why, if there has been no fraud on the part of bureau officers or claim agents in the payment of bounties, are there so many rumors of frauds, and has the alleged non-payment of laborers employed on fortifications during the war had any effect in causing these rumors? He replied: "When they (*i. e.*, the laborers on fortifications) were first employed on these works there were no provisions made for compensating them. They were taken by general orders, as one would take a house in war times, by confiscation or discovery; consequently no record was kept of their service for many months. After provisions were made for employing them and paying them, their time was kept and the service paid for by Colonel Burrows, who was sent here for that purpose. There are, I suppose, about ten thousand laborers in this country, who were employed as first stated, who have not been paid for their services."

Upon learning this, and believing that there were a large number of this class of claimants who, knowing that the bureau had paid certain other men money after they (said men) had put in their claims with claim agents, and being ignorant of the difference between their own claims and the claims of those who had been paid, concluded that they had been swindled either by claim agents or bureau agents, and consequently made continual complaint of fraud, while in all probability there was no foundation for such complaints. The commission determined to report these cases as one of the causes which have given rise to rumors of fraud.

J. B. Coons, bureau agent at Nashville, Tennessee, stated to the commission that he had collected a large number of this class of claims, which had been paid by an officer stationed at Nashville by the Engineer Department, United States Army, who paid the claims of all men whose names appeared upon the rolls, and who could substantiate their claims; and it would accordingly seem that full justice has been done these people, as far as is possible without further legislation.

There also appeared a large number of men and women, who stated that they had performed services in the United States hospitals at Nashville, Tennessee, under promise of payment, and although they signed pay-rolls, they were never paid. The commission recorded the statements of five (see Nos. 20, 21, 60, 65, fourth, fifth, and sixth day's proceedings) of these complaints. In regard to this class Mr. Glassie stated as follows:

The persons claiming for services in hospital come under several heads, viz: Those who were employed to assist in and about the hospitals, and who were borne properly on the rolls—they signed the rolls every two months, and some one got the money; those who were pressed for a day or two, as on the fortifications, when a large number of hands were required—of those no record was kept; and a third class, who, like flies about a kitchen, swarmed about hospitals to find something to eat without working for it. This class are most numerous and loud-mouthed. They were always in the way, and would steal everything they could lay their hands on, carry it off, and sell it to citizens, and buy whisky, smuggle it to the soldiers, &c., and now claim pay for having been supported by the government.

Judging from the above, and from general reports, we are of the opinion that in a great majority of these cases there is no cause for complaint, and though there may be persons who have not received their past dues, it is not probable that such is the fact. Claim agents, however, have filed the claims of these persons, and they have been led by this to expect payment, and not receiving it, have imagined themselves defrauded—by whom they know not, and therefore entered complaint. "It appears" (again referring to the evidence of Mr. Glassie) "that there is a large class of claims seldom heard of. I refer to the thousands of colored men who were pressed in as teamsters, and who, if ever borne on the rolls, were never paid. Here was actual service performed and not paid for."

It seems clear to the commission that there are sufficient causes, or supposed causes, for complaint to account for charges and rumors of frauds, and no matter how energetic, faithful, and honest the bureau agents may have been, charges would still be made, and rumors of fraud still exist, and this from the very nature of things, and not from the fault of any one.

Of the cases remaining to be accounted for, one complained that his claim agent never returned his discharge. (See No. 50, fifth day's proceedings.)

Elvis Key, private Company F Fourteenth United States colored troops, (see No. 47, Nashville, Tennessee,) claims to have received only $120, while the amount of his certificate is $176. If this claimant has been defrauded, the commission are unable to discover by whom. The Second Auditor's certificate shows that the amount of his bounty was $176, from which was deducted the sum of $12 50, for legal and notarial fees. An examination of the books of the disbursing officer at Nashville shows that he was paid the amount he was entitled to, and a certified copy of the original check, on which this claimant was paid, was furnished the commission by General George W. Balloch, chief disbursing officer, Bureau Refugees, Freedmen and Abandoned Lands, and is hereto attached. (See also Drew's Statement A, No. 9, and C.)

No. 1381.] NASHVILLE, *Tennessee, October* 13, 1868.
First National Bank pay to Elvis Key, or order, one hundred and sixty-three dollars and fifty cents, in current funds.
$163 50. GEO. W. BALLOCH,
Brevet Brigadier General and Chief Disbursing Officer.

Official copy:
GEO. W. BALLOCH.

Indorsed:
his
ELVIS × KEYS.
mark.

Attest:
J. B. COONS.

Official copy:
GEO. W. BALLOCH.

There are three cases concerning which we have been unable to gain any information. (See cases Nos. 6, 27, 38, proceedings at Nashville.) The claimants probably gave us the wrong names. If they gave us their right names they have never filed any claims.

CASE OF D. W. GLASSIE.

It appears by the evidence taken by the commission at Nashville, that colored soldiers had been in the habit of borrowing money from different claim agents at exorbitant rates of interest; that payment had, in some cases, been extorted from them after they had received their bounty from the bureau agents.

The statement of D. W. Glassie, the principal party charged with so loaning money and extorting payment, makes it unnecessary to look further. He boldly pleads guilty to the specification that he did so loan money, but denies the charge of fraud. He says, (see affidavit, seventh day's proceedings,) "I have loaned money to colored soldiers to buy homes, farms, wagons, teams, cows, to take them home from Nashville, to buy medicines, pay doctor's bills, to bury the dead, to pay lawyer's fees, fees in account, and to keep them out of the penitentiary;" and, in fact, it would seem that but for these loans by Mr. Glassie, the ex-colored soldiers would have had a serious time. He says when a claimant applied for a loan, he would ascertain what he was willing to pay for it; draw his check payable to his order for the full amount, (including interest;) send him to the bureau where he could make the acknowledgment, showing the check if necessary; and, when he returned with papers properly acknowledged, send some one to the bank to identify him and collect the premium. This was the mode of procedure where he was attorney of record. The money was generally paid back to Mr. Glassie in Washington. All this Mr. Glassie seems to regard as a fair commercial transaction, of course including the making out, swearing to, and forwarding the affidavit (that he had advanced the full amount) necessary to substantiate the claims before the claim division of the bureau. He then explains his manner of collecting loans made to claimants in cases where he was not attorney of record, and could not collect advances. "I took (he says) his (the claimant's) notes, one for the principal, and one for the interest; took up the soldier's receipts from claim agents, and gave him mine; saw attorney of record, and agreed with him to notify me when the claim was allowed, and certificate sent to General Howard; hunted up the claimant and sent him to the bureau, and in about seven days placed a lookout over him, and was at the bank through a trusty man, who (on payment) presented the note and collected the money." "I relied (he says) on my own vigilance in these cases," and finally offers $1,000 to any one who would reimburse him the principal of his advances.

Now the above proves, in the opinion of the commission—

1. That in cases where he was the attorney of record he made advances to colored soldiers, and collected far more than he so advanced; taking advantage of the necessities of claimants, he made a commercial transaction greatly to his own gain and to their loss.

2. Where he was not attorney of record, he, with such attorney's aid, made loans at high rates of interest, and, through a system of runners, collected the same.

It does not appear from any statement made by a witness that any bureau agent was in collusion with Mr. Glassie in his business, and Mr. Glassie states that J. B. Coons not only refused to aid him, but advised claimants that the fees of agents had been deducted, and not to pay any further sum.

J. B. COONS, DISBURSING AGENT AT NASHVILLE, TENNESSEE.

The commission made diligent inquiry with a view of ascertaining if there was any cause of complaint against this gentleman, but, to Mr. Coon's credit it must be said, succeeded in finding very little against him. The witnesses generally stated that not only they had no complaints to make against Mr. Coons, or any other bureau agent or officer, but that they had never heard of such complaints. The following special complaints were, however, made:

Ann McClellan, who states that she filed two claims, one on account of services of her brother, (this claim has been disallowed,) and one on account of her husband, (this claim is not on file in the Second Auditor's office,) declared that Mr. Coons sent her to Glassie; Glassie sent her back, when Coons told her to "get out," or he would kill her.

Ann Barrow, who claimed pay for work which she alleged she had performed in hospital No. 13, states that Mr. Coons treated her so spitefully that she would not go to him again.

Robert Smith, corporal Company F Seventeenth United States colored troops, stated that he had heard reports about Judge Coons, to the effect that he did not pay all he should pay.

Edas Brown, widow of Philip Brown, One hundred and tenth United States colored infantry, and Mary Chambers, widow of Martin Chambers, Company G, Thirteenth United States colored troops, both of whom have failed to furnish evidence necessary to substantiate their claims, complained that Mr. Coons required them to furnish witnesses to marriage who could write their names, which was impossible.

Isaac Maxwell, Company H Fifteenth United States colored troops, and Sorrow Goff, Company C One hundred and first United States colored troops, (whose claim is pending,) and Henry McKay, Company A Twelfth United States colored troops, (whose claim has been disallowed,) all stated that Mr. Coons would give them no satisfaction, but sent them to claim agents for information. To sum up, the burden of all this seems to be—

1. That Mr. Coons was in some instances rude and abrupt in his official intercourse with claimants. This, to any one who knows how certain claimants will, hoping against hope, continue to annoy an agent after he has done all in his power for them, does not appear serious; yet no annoyance of this kind is an excuse for rudeness on the part of a government official, especially when the ignorance of the applicant is the cause of the frequent application.

2. That Mr. Coons, refusing to furnish information, sent them to claim agents, which would seem to imply a neglect of duty. This it was impossible for Mr. Coons to avoid. Certificates were, until April 21, 1869, sent direct to the claim agent, who transmitted them to General Howard. The bureau agent was not informed of the settlement of the claim until it was sent to him for payment or he wrote to Washington asking that it be sent to him. It would require weeks to write to Washington for the information and receive an answer. Accordingly the claimants were told, "Go to your claim agent, and if he says your claim has been allowed I will write for it." The claim agents, in case the claim was not allowed, would reply that they knew nothing about it, or that it had been disallowed, or was pending, &c., when the impatient and dissatisfied claimant would return to the bureau, and probably from time to time renew his travel and investigations. After April 21, 1869, the date above mentioned, the certificates were sent direct to the Commissioner. Mr. Coons stated that both before and after the aforesaid date he had experienced great difficulty in procuring information for claimants, and that he was generally forced to rely on the claim agents. He further said that letters written to Washington by claimants are returned to him with the information, but that he is unable to find the writer. There appears to be some cause of complaint on the part of the claimant in this matter, but Mr. Coons does not seem to be at fault; and as the same thing is referred to elsewhere, we will consider it hereafter and suggest a remedy for consideration.

3. One witness also stated that he had heard Mr. Coons made short payment.

The commission examined Mr. Coons's records, and inquired carefully concerning his character for honesty and integrity, and, notwithstanding the eulogy (?) of Mr. Glassie, we believe him to be an honest and upright man.

MR. COONS'S MANNER OF PAYMENT.

The commission is of the opinion that Mr. Coons has not fully discharged his duty in the manner of payment of amounts due claimants, and this rather through a failure to appreciate the necessity for greater care than through any intention to neglect his duty. The law makes bounties payable in currency, and not in checks or drafts. A check for the full amount due each claimant, and payable to his order, signed George W. Balloch, brevet brigadier general, chief disbursing officer, drawn on the First National Bank of Nashville, (United States depository,) is sent to Mr. Coons. It is Mr. Coons's duty, and he is so instructed, (see circular letter, War Department, Bureau Refugees, Freedmen and Abandoned Lands, office of chief disbursing officer, Washington, D. C., November 20, 1868,) to cause claimants to indorse said checks, and see them draw the money on the same. Such is a fair construction of the circular. This, as appears by Mr. Coons's statement as well as Glassie's evidence, (see seventh day's proceedings,) Mr. Coons has failed to do, though it is averred that he invariably sent his messenger to the bank with claimant. It nowhere appears (save in one instance, where claimant paid a soldier five dollars to identify him) that any claimant has suffered loss by this course of Mr. Coons; but it would be well to instruct him to obey literally the terms of the circular, and thus conform to the requirements of the law.

In conclusion, the commission is of the opinion that there has been no acts of the bureau officers at Nashville, Tennessee, to warrant charges or give rise to rumors of fraud.

The commission next proceeded to Columbia, Tennessee, to investigate charges preferred against John L. Wilson, bureau agent at that place. We pursued the same course there as at Nashville; called together the colored ministers and prominent men, examined them, caused the former to give notice to their congregations, and examined all who came. We also took the evidence of the cashier of the bank where Wilson cashed his checks for bounty, as well as other prominent and influential citizens, in order to ascertain his (Wilson's) general character and manner of doing business. The following is a summary of his case:

CASE OF JOHN L. WILSON.

In the communication of J. M. Cloon of November 29, 1869, referred to this commission, he charges J. L. Wilson, disbursing officer for Bureau of Refugees, Freedmen and Abandoned Lands at Columbia and Pulaski, Tennessee, with being in connection with Messrs. Hickey, at Columbia, and Messrs. Jones, at Pulaski, engaged in swindling colored claimants out of bounty, &c., due them. This commission gave said Cloon notice that they would be at Pulaski, and invited him to present such witnesses as he might desire. Said Cloon did not appear before the commission at Columbia, and such witnesses as could be found were examined without finding any evidence whatever criminating John L. Wilson.

Mr. L. Frierson, cashier of the bank at Columbia, who cashed all checks sent to Major Wilson, was examined, (see eighth day's proceedings,) by which it appears that Wilson's payments are in compliance with regulations. His evidence is also very damaging to Cloon, who makes the charges against Wilson.

The testimony of J. L. Bullock, attorney-at-law, (see eighth day's proceedings,) and William Vance Thompson, attorney-at-law, (see ninth day's proceedings,) exonerate Major Wilson so far as to general character and reputation, and give said Cloon a bad character.

The Messrs. Hickey were examined, (see eighth and ninth days' proceedings,) and positively deny all the charges made by Cloon relative to criminal connection between them and Wilson. They avow having done business for claimants, for which they charged a fee, but collected the same after the claimants were paid, and without the knowledge of, or any arrangement with, Major Wilson. The commission are satisfied that no criminal arrangement existed between Messrs. Hickey and Wilson, and found no one who complained of personal injustice or fraud committed on them by these parties.

On reaching Pulaski, Cloon was notified of the presence of the commission, and appeared in person, with a large number of witnesses, all of whom were examined. Indeed, nearly every witness examined had been requested to appear by Cloon, or had been notified by some of Cloon's witnesses, except such as were summoned by the commission to elucidate questions raised by such witnesses.

Stephen Sloss, colored, testified (see eleventh day's proceedings) that he had paid Mr. Jones $15 fees after he had received his bounty from Major Wilson.

Richard Harris, colored, testifies (see eleventh day's proceedings) to many complaints being made of fees collected by Jones with the connivance of Wilson, but can give no particular case.

J. T. Fisher, colored, testifies (see eleventh day's proceedings) that George Fogg paid Jones $10 in Jones's office immediately after he (Fogg) was paid by Major Wilson; also two others, whose names he could not give, after they had left Major Wilson's presence.

Green Turner, colored, testified (see 12th case, eleventh day's proceedings) that he paid Jones $20, but not in the presence of Wilson, or with his knowledge.

Theodore M. Greed, colored, testified (see 21st case, twelfth day's proceedings) that he paid Jones $15 after he had been paid by Major Wilson in the back room; that he thought it was too much, although willing to pay a fee for services Jones had rendered him.

James H. Jackson testifies (see 27th case, twelfth day's proceedings) that he paid Jones $15 fee for Katie Gardner in Wilson's presence.

Katie Gardner, colored, testifies (see 36th case, twelfth day's proceedings) that she had agreed to pay Jones for services, and that she gave her money to Jackson to count and pay Jones.

W. I. Parkes testifies (see twelfth day's proceedings) that only in two or three cases were checks brought by others (Jones) than Wilson to be cashed.

Of the above seven cases, where fees were paid to Jones, it appears that some kind of service was rendered by Jones, and that he obtained such fee after the claimants were paid by Wilson—there was no evidence to induce the commission to believe that Major Wilson had any arrangement with either Jones or Messrs. Hickey by which they or Major Wilson were to obtain unjust or illegal fees from the parties paid by Wilson.

Stephen Sloss, J. T. Fisher, Green Turner, and others had testified before the United States commissioner, when Wilson was held for trial for the very offense charged here, and it appears from statement of Mr. Smith, United States district attorney, (see second day's proceedings,) that the grand jury failed to find an indictment, though Cloon, his accuser, stands indicted for a similar offense.

The testimony of Sloss is, therefore, much impaired by this fact and testimony of Hall, (see 16th case, eleventh day.) The testimony of Fisher is impaired by that of John Young (see 11th case, eleventh day's proceedings) and Charles Hall, (see 15th case, eleventh day.) The testimony of Jackson is rendered unworthy of credit by that of A. R. Richardson, (see case 28, twelfth day's proceedings,) and that of Katie Gardner herself, as also the record from court. (See twelfth day's proceedings.) The Messrs. Jones are given an excellent reputation by D. A. Wellborn, clerk of court, (see case 30, twelfth day,) James T. McKissick, (see twelfth day,) and many others of whom the commission inquired.

The statements of C. P. Jones and John L. Wilson are appended to the twelfth day's proceedings.

The commission are satisfied that no criminal or improper arrangement existed between Major Wilson and Messrs. Jones, and that even if the service rendered claimants by Jones was of no great value, they were importuned by the claimants to do the work, and were legally entitled to fees for the same. They are further well satisfied that through the efforts of Jones, claimants were protected from fraud by Cloon. With reference to the charge that Major J. L. Wilson was arraigned before the United States courts, and "there punished for nefarious practices," it appears that on the testimony of Cloon and several colored witnesses to facts relative to the payment of fees to Jones by them, said Wilson was held for trial by J. J. Noah, United States commissioner, but when the case came before the grand jury they failed to find an indictment, and the case was thrown out of court. Said Cloon has since been indicted by the grand jury for forgery, &c. The commission are satisfied that the prosecution of Wilson was a base fraud on the part of Cloon, and gotten up by him to get Wilson out of the way, and to cover up his own misdeeds. The commission are satisfied that John L. Wilson has taken great care to see that all the money due claimants was paid into their hands, and to prevent their being swindled out of it after such payment.

The commission have been inclined to think Major Wilson somewhat careless and negligent in looking after and making up claims yet pending, but from their observations believe it to be difficult for him to do his whole duty in this regard. The various claim agents have taken the discharges and papers of most of the claimants in the country, and as they do not hesitate to promise much more and speedier action than any bureau agent can, the claimants still go to them, wandering from one to another, as shown by the whole body of evidence, as the flattery or promises of one or the other agent may be most powerful.

Coupled with charges against John L. Wilson, bureau agent at Columbia, the commission find charges preferred by Cloon against the Messrs. Hickey, attorneys-at-law at Columbia, and Jones & Sons, attorneys-at-law at Pulaski.

HICKEYS AND JONESES.

In M. M. Cloon's letter to the Second Auditor, dated November 29, 1869, he says on page 13: "Again four correspondents of the said firm," (supposed to refer to Chipman, Hosmer & Co.,) "namely, J. M. Hickey and A. M. Hickey, of Columbia, Tennessee, and Calvin and Charles A. Jones, of Pulaski, Tennessee, are associated with the aforesaid John L. Wilson, the bureau agent (for several counties of Middle Tennessee) previously named, in his swindling scheme, which is carried on as follows: The claimant goes to the office of the said Wilson and asks if his claim is ready for settlement. Wilson says 'No.' The claimant tells him that his claim agent told him that it was settled. Wilson says, 'If you depend upon your claim agent you will never get it,' in the mean time telling claimant to go and see the Hickeys or Joneses, assuring him that they will promptly receive his money. The claimant complies, and goes forthwith to said parties, who tell him that they must get fifteen per cent. for getting his bounty. Of course the poor illiterate negro would give twenty-five or fifty per cent. as quick as he would fifteen, and complies at once to their proposition, when he is ordered to report at their office in about ten days, at which time he will get his money. Claimant accordingly appears back at the appointed time, and is taken to Wilson's office; after which, Wilson goes to the bank with claimant's check for bounty, it having been previously indorsed by claimant, and draws the amount of said check; returns and pays to the claimant the amount of the same in the presence of the Hickeys, who take the money out of their claimant's hands and deducts his fifteen per cent., and the balance he returns to claimant. Now, when that poor claimant first went to Wilson, he had his check in his possession, but denies it, that the Hickeys or Joneses, who are his coadjutors, may rob him out of fifteen per cent. of it, and who, of course, divide with Wilson."

The facts of the case as developed by the commission are as follows: The Messrs. Hickey, of Columbia, and Joneses, of Pulaski, Tennessee, have taken up claims for bounty and pension, and have prosecuted the same, not as claim agents, but, as they allege, as attorneys. They have, according to their own statement, charged a fee of ten per cent. on their amount of bounty collected; that they did this on the statement of Judge Trigg, of the United States district court, who told them (see affidavit of C. P. Jones, twelfth day's proceedings) that they had a legal and perfect right to inquire into and investigate said claims when solicited by claimants, as lawyers, and to charge a reasonable fee for services.

J. M. Hickey also states in his affidavit (see ninth day's proceedings) that they were presenting these claims with the hearty approval of the Hon. Samuel Arnell, member of Congress from that district, who had informed him that he was very glad these claims were being taken up by honest men, and out of the hands of swindling claim agents like Cloon, and that he would facilitate the collection of these claims to the extent of his ability; that he approved of their action in charging ten per cent., and recommended that they send him lists of the claims they had taken up, and he would put them through as soon as possible. He moreover states that the only correspondence he has ever had with Chipman, Hosmer & Co. was asking for information in certain old cases of claims for bounty or pension. The Hickeys and Joneses acted as one firm in the prosecution of these claims.

With regard to the preceding statements quoted from Cloon's letter, both the Hickeys swore that it was false so far as they were concerned, and that if Major Wilson had ever sent claimants to them they had no knowledge of it.

Both the Hickeys and Joneses claim that in every case where they have collected these fees they had previously made a direct contract with the party for the amount of their fees. This was supported by all witnesses except one, Stephen Sloss, who (see eleventh day's proceedings) swears that he never made any contract with the above firms, but that Major Wilson paid him in the back room of Jones' office, at Pulaski, and that when he came through the front room Mr. C. P. Jones asked him for $15 as his fee; that he protested against paying it, and that he went back and asked Major Wilson if it was right he should pay it, when Major Wilson told him all legal fees had been paid, but he finally paid it.

Mr. C. P. Jones swears positively that the contract was made in the presence of these witnesses, and that Sloss came back to him and demanded the return of the fee, saying that Cloon had sent him, and that the fee belonged to him, (Cloon.) Sloss's claim amounted to $301.

Charles A. Hall swears that he heard Stephen Sloss acknowledge his willingness to pay C. P. Jones the fee. (See his affidavit, eleventh day's proceedings.)

All the witnesses before the commission who testify that they paid a fee to the Joneses or Hickeys, swear that it was not done in the presence of Major Wilson.

There was not one particle of evidence brought before the commission to show that Major Wilson had ever sent a single claimant to any member of this firm or firms, or that there ever was the slightest understanding between them and Major Wilson. The only statement in Cloon's letter above quoted, supported by evidence before the commission, is, that

BOUNTIES TO COLORED SOLDIERS.

Major Wilson did pay claimants in the back room of Jones's office at Pulaski, while members of these firms were in the front room, and there collected their fees. Testimony of prominent gentlemen in Columbia and Pulaski shows these firms to be old established ones of the highest standing and strictest integrity.

J. M. CLOON.

We have now the unpleasant task of introducing to your special notice Mr. Cloon, a distinguished (?) character from foreign parts, who figures conspicuously in connection with the greater part of our proceedings. A large number of Mr. Cloon's letters have been referred to us, and a still further number have fallen into our possession from other sources. June 15, 1869, Cloon writes from Pulaski, Tennessee, a letter in which he charges Mr. Drew with swindling colored people. This letter is signed M. M. Cloon. Mr. Drew replied to this letter June 25, 1869, and expressed "the earnest hope that success may attend your (Mr. Cloon's) laudable exertions to punish and expose dishonesty, whether perpetrated by private persons or by officials." Again, November 20, 1869, Cloon writes a letter to General Samuel Breck, assistant adjutant general United States Army, abusing bureau officials generally, charging them with crimes and misdemeanors, and stating that General Howard has covered up and concealed their rascality. This letter is from Huntsville, Alabama, and signed James M. M. Cloon. In the meantime another letter, dated July 3, 1869, comes from Pulaski, Tennessee, addressed to W. P. Drew. In this letter the following sentence occurs: "I have learned a few days ago that Mr. Wager, your representative at Huntsville, Alabama, reported me through headquarters, which has affected a friend of mine named James Cloon, who has nothing to do with me, nor I with him." This letter is signed M. M. Cloon. Finally, another actor appearing upon the stage, in a seventeen page letter dated Huntsville, Alabama, November 29, 1869, addressed to Hon. E. B. French, Second Auditor United States Treasury, and signed James Cloon, pours out all the charges against bureau officials, claim agents, and citizens which have been investigated by this commission, and are referred to in this report. It appeared upon the face of these papers that these charges were preferred by three persons, residing at three different places. They were, however, preferred by one and the same party. His different signatures are only the shallow trick of an intriguing rascal, whose cunning has overreached itself. We repeat, this is apparent upon the face of the papers, but the proof "makes assurance doubly sure." In his testimony before the commission Cloon states that his name is James Michael McGinnis Cloon, and that he sometimes signed his name James M. M. Cloon, sometimes M. M., and sometimes James, and in reply to the question, "Have you ever, in writing over the signature of M. M. Cloon, said or intimated that you had no connection with a person named James Cloon?" says: "I do not propose to answer any question tending to criminate myself;" and finally, in his letter to the Second Auditor, under date January 18, 1870, gives the following lucid explanation of his different styles of signing his name: "The Hon. Commissioner of Pensions has seemingly suspended me from further practice in his office, for what cause I know not, other than he writes to the firm of O'Neill & Dufour, claim agents of your city, saying that my name is one thing to-day and another to-morrow. My name in full is James M. M. Cloon. I sometimes contract my name by using only the M. M., and sometimes the J.; the name being rather copious, I find it often essential to contract the same for which reason." In fine, Cloon lies in his letter to Drew of July

3d; shields himself behind a technicality (thereby acknowledging his guilt) in his evidence, and finally writes himself down a rascal in his letter to the Second Auditor. It would not, therefore, have appeared strange if this commission had declined to hear Mr. Cloon's testimony. We nevertheless determined to examine him. Your attention is invited to the following extract from the record, (see twelfth day's proceedings:)

Question. Do you know anything further tending to criminate General Balloch?— Answer. (I know nothing further criminating General Balloch,) but I know that General Balloch has been informed of this matter. I wish to make a further statement criminating this man Mr. Wilson with the grossest fraud.

Mr. Cloon here called for the reading of the testimony which the recorder had taken down, and when the sentence inclosed in parentheses had been read, he objected to it, and wanted it entirely stricken out. This the commission refused to do, but gave him the privilege of making any statement regarding it he might choose. He declined, however, to proceed unless the whole was stricken out, but the commission again declining to comply with his request, he left the room.

It was evident that Mr. Cloon only wanted an excuse to refuse to testify. The commission were willing to record any statement that he might make, but were determined that he should not make statements and retract them unless both statement and retraction should appear upon the record. In other words, that all that passed should appear upon the record. Cloon's conduct during the examination was insulting; he attempted to dictate to the commission, to prescribe what questions they should ask, and made himself generally offensive. We endeavored to treat him with courtesy, but it had the effect of rendering him still more impudent. The following extract from the record is given as a specimen of his conduct:

At the close of the examination of Mr. A. R. Richardson, the witness stated to the court that if Mr. M. M. Cloon would like to ask any questions he would be glad to answer them. Permission having been given, Mr. Cloon turned to the commission and said: "I can show by evidence that the statements made by Mr. Richardson are incorrect," (or words to that effect.) Mr. Richardson said to him: "Do you mean to say that the statements I have just made are incorrect?" (or words to that effect.) Mr. Cloon replied, "I do, sir." Mr. Richardson then said, "Do you mean to say that I lie?" (or words to that effect.) Mr. Cloon replied, "I do, sir." Here Mr. Richardson reached to the floor, and laid hold of the tongs, when Mr. Cloon drew from his pocket a pistol with motions as if he intended to point it at Mr. Richardson, when the commission interfered, and Mr. Cloon was ordered to leave the room, and told that when he was wanted by the commission he would be sent for. He did so, but protested against the whole manner of procedure on the part of the commission, and was told to reduce his protest to writing. He again returned without having been sent for by the commission. He was then informed that he must leave the room, or apologize to the commission for his conduct. He then said he had nothing to apologize for, and would not apologize; *that he was armed at all times, and would use them if necessary*. He was informed that he had drawn arms in the presence of the commission, which was contemptuous and insulting. He was again ordered to leave the room, when he laid his protest in writing before the commission and asked if the commission desired to examine him as a witness. The commission then decided to examine him at once, Colonel Runkle voting against his examination on the ground that he had insulted the commission, and that he was, from evidence already before the commission, not entitled to credit under oath. Mr. Richardson left the room at the time of the difficulty, but returned and apologized to the commission for his part in the affair, stating that it was his intention, when he picked up the tongs, to request the commission to protect him from insult, or he should feel obliged to protect himself.

Mr. Cloon, finding himself getting into deep water, seized the opportunity, when the commission refused to strike out any of his statements, and declined to testify further.

The commission now invite attention to the evidence of fraud on the part of James M. M., or M. M. Cloon, claim agent, operating in Middle Tennessee and Northern Alabama:

Lucas Goodman, Company I United States colored troops, testifies

14   BOUNTIES TO COLORED SOLDIERS.

(see case 2, eighth day's proceedings) that Cloon said he was employed and paid by the government.

Brown Leftwick, Company C Forty-fourth United States colored troops, and James Workman, Company D Fifteenth United States colored troops, testify (see case 3, eighth day) that they filed claims with Cloon for commutation of rations while prisoners of war, and have never got anything.

Richard Harris testifies (see eleventh day's proceedings) that Green Trother was defrauded by Cloon out of between $100 and $200; also, (see eleventh day,) that he took up check of Nathan Holt for $193 40, and gave him only $140, thus defrauding him out of $53 40; also, (see same day,) Cloon took up a check of Robert Alexander for $219 30 and gave him only $140, thus defrauding him of $79 30.

Thomas Upshur, Company K One hundred and tenth United States colored troops, testifies (see case 10, eleventh day) that Cloon took up his check for $135 70 and gave him only $120, thus defrauding him of $15 70.

Green Turner, Company A First United States colored heavy artillery, testifies (see eleventh day) that Cloon told him he was a government agent, and he and all the colored people thought he was sent out by the government.

James Brown, Company I One hundred and tenth United States colored troops, testifies (see case 14, eleventh day) that he carried his check to Cloon, which was for $203 20, and received from him only $140, thus defrauding him of $63 20.

Reuben P. Clark testifies (see eleventh day) that Cloon made advances of magic oil, and took receipts as of money, and that Cloon tried to induce pensioners not to go before the commission.

Sallie Tynham, mother of Calvin Tynham, Company B One hundred and tenth United States colored troops, testifies (see case 20, twelfth day) that Cloon took up her check for $250 and paid her only $240.

Anderson Sloss, Company B One hundred and eleventh United States colored troops, testifies (see case 25, twelfth day) that Cloon represented himself as a government agent; that Cloon loaned him $40; that he carried his check, which Captain Simpson gave him, to Cloon, who gave him a sum of money which, with the $40 he had loaned him, made $100; (said check is hereto attached, it having been furnished this commission by John L. Wilson, to whom it was sent by General George W. Balloch for investigation of the case:)

No. 571.]   NASHVILLE, TENN., *June* 5, 1868.

First National Bank pay to Anderson Sloss, or order, three hundred and one dollars in current funds.
$301.

       (Signed,)   GEO. W. BALLOCH,
                                                             Bvt. Brig. Gen. and C. D. O.

Official copy:
                                                           GEO. W. BALLOCH,
                                                             Bvt. Brig. Gen. and C. D. O.

Indorsed:
                                                                his
                                                       ANDERSON + SLOSS.
                                                                mark.
Witness:
                                                           M. M. CLOON,
                                                             Southern Ex. Co.,
                                                           per D. C. PIERCE.

Official copy:
                                                           GEO. W. BALLOCH,
                                                             Bvt. Brig. Gen. and C. D. O.

BOUNTIES TO COLORED SOLDIERS. 15

That he never put his mark or name on the above check; that he afterward received of Cloon $15, which Cloon said was for pension. The above sums deducted from amount of check show that Cloon fraudulently retained $186, besides forging the indorsement of Sloss on the check. Sloss further testifies that Cloon prevented him from going before the pension commission.

Burrell Reedus, Company I One hundred and tenth United States colored troops, testifies (see case 32, twelfth day) that Cloon loaned him $60; that Captain Judd gave him a check for $305 84, for which Cloon only gave him $194 80; he was therefore defrauded of $51 04. He further testifies that he did not sign or put his mark to his check.

Katie Gardner, mother of Alexander Gardner, testifies (see case 36, twelfth day) that Cloon sent her $160 about the first of last year, saying it was bounty money. As she afterward received her bounty from Major Wilson, this money must have been pension money, and is all she has received. Her name does not appear on pension books at Nashville. It is very probable her pension has been paid.

- Winnie, or Winey Roberts, widow of Henry Roberts, Company A One hundred and eleventh United States colored troops, testifies (see case 38, twelfth day) that she received her bounty, but has never received any pension; also, that Cloon tried to keep her and others from going before the pension commission. The pension records at Nashville show that her pension was paid by check 1,247, dated October 14, 1868, to W. W. Ingersoll, attorney, for $357 47. By list attached to testimony of J. M. Dufour, it appears that her pension certificate, No. 119,091, was sent to Cloon, September 25, 1868. (See also Pension Office, A.)

Sophia Parkeson, widow of Henry Parkeson, Company C Twelfth United States colored troops, testifies (see case 39, twelfth day) that she never had any pension money, and that Cloon tried to keep her from going before the pension commission, offering her $50 to go away. It appears from list attached to J. M. Dufour's testimony that her pension certificate, No. 115,913, was sent to Cloon, July 14, 1868. It further appears from pension records at Nashville that it was paid by check 993, dated September 16, 1868, to W. W. Ingersoll, for $64 40. It appears from records of Pension Office (see Pension Office, A) that this certificate was issued at rate of $8 per month, from January 18, 1865, and $2 additional for each of three children, from July 25, 1866, paid to September 4, 1868, to W. W. Ingersoll, attorney Nashville agency. By computing the amount it will appear that about $499 59 has been paid on this claim, of which the woman has received nothing.

It also appears from affidavit of J. M. Hickey (see ninth day) also, (see Pension Office, B,) and see affidavit of J. M. Dufour,) that pension certificates have been issued in the following cases, which were sent to O'Neil and Dufour, and by them sent to M. M. Cloon, who still holds them, thus keeping the parties out of their money, viz: Mary Roundtree, widow of Albert Roundtree, Company C Seventeenth United States colored troops; Bidda English, widow of Franklin English; Amanda Grimes, widow of Alfred Grimes; Rachael Crofford, widow of Henderson Crofford, Company K Twelfth United States colored troops; Ruthie Fox, widow of Benjamin Fox, Company A Thirteenth United States colored troops; Rhoda Jones, widow of ———.

It does not appear that any money has been paid on the above certificates. The parties were prevented from appearing before the pension commission by M. M. Cloon, who caused Hickey's arrest, and notified these parties they were not wanted. There is no doubt these certificates are held by Cloon for fraudulent purposes. Doubtless there are many more in the same condition among those contained in the long list of pension certificates sent to Cloon by O'Neil and Dufour, attached to J. M. Dufour's affidavit.

William Reedus, Company I One hundred and tenth United States colored troops, testifies (see case 6, eleventh day's proceedings) that he sold his claim for commutation of rations while a prisoner of war to M. M. Cloon, for $20. There was allowed and sent to Cloon $45 25. (See affidavit and list of J. M. Dufour.)

From the testimony of Richard Harris (see eleventh day) it appears that Horace Braden or Bradey, Company E One hundred and tenth United States colored troops, sold his claim for commutation to Cloon for $20. There was allowed and sent to Cloon $54 75. (See list of Dufour.)

Also from same (see eleventh day) it appears that Turner Harville, Company K One hundred and tenth United States colored troops, sold his claim for commutation to Cloon for $25. There was allowed and sent to Cloon $57 50. (See list of Dufour.)

Thomas Upshur, Company K One hundred and tenth United States colored troops, testifies (see case 10, eleventh day) that Cloon gave him his check for $37 20, which he said was for commutation of rations. There was allowed and sent to Cloon $54 25. (See list of Dufour.)

James Vance, first, Company I One hundred and tenth United States colored troops, testifies (see case 13, eleventh day) that he sold his claim for commutation for $25. There was allowed and sent to Cloon $54 75. (See list of Dufour.)

Alexander Ceaden, Company F One hundred and tenth United States colored troops, testifies (see twelfth day) that he sold his claim for commutation to Cloon for $25. There was allowed and sent to Cloon $58. (See list of Dufour.)

Anderson Sloss, Company B One hundred and eleventh United States colored troops, testifies (see case 25, twelfth day) that he got *nothing* for his claim for commutation. There was allowed and sent to Cloon $78 25. (See list of Dufour.)

Joseph or George W. Green, Company K One hundred and tenth United States colored troops, testifies that he sold his claim for commutation to Cloon for $15. There was allowed and sent to Cloon $50. (See list of Dufour.)

Burrell Reedus, first, Company I One hundred and tenth United States colored troops, testifies (see case 32, twelfth day) that Cloon offered to buy his claim for $25, but he refused to sell; *got nothing*. There was allowed and sent to Cloon $58. (See list of Dufour.)

Albert Harney, Company K One hundred and tenth United States colored troops, testifies (see case 33, twelfth day) that Cloon gave him $20 for his claim for commutation. There was allowed and sent to Cloon $57 50 (See list of Dufour.)

James Brown, Company I One hundred and tenth United States colored troops, testified (see case 14, twelfth day) that he got *nothing* on his claim for commutation. There was allowed and sent to Cloon $54 75. (See list of Dufour.)

There are doubtless many more cases of this character among the long list of commutation claims prosecuted by Cloon, and for which certificates were sent to him by O'Neill & Dufour. It is very probable that in many of them Cloon committed forgery in order to collect them, and perjury or subornation of perjury in making up the claims. This is evident also in the cases of Harry Robinson, (see case 2, fourteenth day;) Martha Drake, (see case 3, fourteenth day, and No. 6, Drew, E;) William Love, (see case 4, fourteenth day;) Louisa Funnell, (see case 7, fifteenth day;) Elizabeth Funnell, (see case 8, fifteenth day;) William Finlay, (see case 9, fifteenth day, &c.;) for whom he has made up claims for bounty, &c., or pension.

It would seem unnecessary to present evidence of Cloon's bad character after reciting the above frauds. Attention is invited, however, to the evidence of Mr. L. Frierson, cashier, Bank of Columbia, (see eighth day,) A. C. Hickey, (see eighth day,) W. V. Thompson, (see ninth day,) J. M. Hickey, (see ninth day,) Richard Harris, (see eleventh day,) Reuben P. Clark, (see eleventh day,) D. A. Welborn, clerk county court, Giles County, Tennessee, who testifies to Cloon passing under two names, (see twelfth day,) William Rhodes, (see twelfth day,) James T. McKissick, (see twelfth day,) D. G. Anderson, justice of the peace, (see twelfth day,) C. P. Jones, (see twelfth day,) John L. Wilson, (see twelfth day, and letter of Cloon attached,) and Lewis M. Douglass, (see case 6, fifteenth day's proceedings,) who testifies that Cloon sent parties before him to testify to papers by which they would have perjured themselves, (see fifteenth day.)

In addition to the above, it appears (see record, nineteenth day) that M. M. Cloon now stands indicted by the grand jury of the United States circuit court for the middle district of Tennessee, for forging a power of attorney for the collection of pension money due one Lucy Chambers, widow of Philip Chambers. Attention is also invited to the application forwarded by M. M. Cloon, purporting to come from Lina Ballentine, for bounty, &c., of her deceased husband, (see papers referred by General Balloch attached to twenty-eighth day's proceedings.) The whole thing is evidently a fraud from beginning to end. The applications and most of the signatures are in Cloon's own handwriting, as also the letter signed Lina Ballentine, as per J. M. Clark. Another indictment for forgery and fraud may be founded upon it.

The forgoing evidence clearly shows:

First. That M. M. Cloon, either in connection with, and by the consent and direction of, the local bureau agents at Pulaski, Tennessee, or through some intrigue of his own, cashed checks delivered by some bureau officers to claimants in payment of bounty, and that he paid such checks short, thus swindling the claimants out of various sums, from $10 to $100. (See cases of Nathan Holt, Robert Alexander, Thomas Upshur, Green Turner, James Brown, Sallie Tynham, Alexander Sloss, and Burrell Reedus.)

Second. That M. M. Cloon forged the names of claimants on their check for bounty. (See cases of Alexander Sloss and Burrell Reedus.)

Third. That M. Cloon had, either alone or in connection with another claim agent, swindled widows out of the whole amount of their pensions. (See cases of Sophia Parkeson and Winnie Roberts.)

Fourth. That he has held in his possession the pension certificate of a large number of widows and orphans, thus depriving them of their just dues for a great length of time, and causing much suffering. (See cases of Kate Gardner, Mary Roundtree, Bidda English, Amanda Grimes, Rachael Crofford, Ruthie Fox, and Rhoda Jones.)

Fifth. That he has swindled a large number of soldiers out of a large portion of their commutation for rations while prisoners of war, by buying the same after the check had come into his possession. (See cases of William Reedus, Horace Braden, Turner Harville, Thomas Upshur, James Vance 1st, Alexander Cerden, Anderson Sloss, Joseph or George W. Green, Burrell Reedus, Albert Harney, and James Brown.)

Sixth. That he gave out a false and fraudulent notice to claimants for pensions, to prevent them from going before the pension commission,

18   BOUNTIES TO COLORED SOLDIERS.

thus exposing his rascality. And further, he caused the arrest of the Messrs. Hickey to prevent their bringing the parties whom he had swindled before the commission.

Seventh. That he threatened and endeavored to bribe witnesses to prevent their appearing and testifying before the pension commission.

Eighth. That he made advances of "magic oil," and took receipts calling it money.

Ninth. A letter hereto attached marked "Exhibit," dated Nashville, Tennessee, October 8, 1869, signed M. M. Cloon, shows that he went before the pension commission, representing himself as a newspaper reporter, and thereby obtained information which enabled him to issue his fraudulent notices, and cause him to threaten and endeavor to bribe witnesses.

[Exhibit.]

LAW OFFICE OF L. I. NOAH & F. W. SALMONSON,
No. 63½ Cedar street, Nashville, October 8, 1869.

GENTLEMEN: On yesterday I wrote you, asking you that you forward me immediately the names of the different witnesses in our pension cases. Since then I have determined that it would be rather difficult for you to furnish the names of the witnesses in all the cases; therefore you will please give the names of all witnesses in as many Giles County cases as possible—that is, those cases executed before "Welborn." I don't intend having any of my Maury County cases brought before the commission. Remember that you must show what each and every witness *proved.*

This is a matter of vital importance, but less to you than to myself. It will in future determine what attorneys ought to command the respect of the department. So you will please give the matter your immediate attention.

I have gone before the committee as a reporter, and have got a full and complete history of their proceedings. I have been shown many a document and application which was forwarded from my office through you, as well as many which were forwarded through others. I shall go before them to-day again in a new *rôle*, and take with me some officers of the garrison at this place, together with Judge Trigg, of the United States circuit court, and some other United States officers.

Truly yours,

M. M. CLOON.

Messrs. O'NEILL & DUFOUR,
Washington, D. C.

You should give the names and dates of births of the children, when and by whom married, &c.

Tenth. That he has filed fraudulent claims against the government, well knowing them to be fraudulent. (See cases of Martha Drake and William Findley.) Particular attention is in this connection invited to the case of Lina Ballentine, the original paper in which cases are filed herewith.

Eleventh. That he has falsely represented himself to be an agent of the government of the United States for the collection and payment of bounties.

CHIPMAN, HOSMER & CO.

In a letter dated Florence, Alabama, June 15, 1869, Cloon, over the signature of M. M. Cloon, charges thus:

I have not forgotten the swindling arrangement entered into some time ago between Chipman, Hosmer & Co. and some of you gentlemen who figured rather conspicuously in the bureau at Washington. I have not forgotten the conduct of Mann, who came down here some time ago on a swindling expedition, and I suppose you have not forgotten it. Then why don't you use your influence with the Second Auditor, or try and have Chipman, Hosmer & Co. suspended, whose rascality is known all over the United States?

Mr. Cloon, having received about ten days' notice, produced his witnesses, and they were examined at Pulaski, Tennessee, on the 10th and 11th days of January, 1870. The following is a synopsis of their testimony:

Henry Hargrove, Company K One hundred and tenth United States colored troops, put in his claim with C. A. Beckert, two years ago. Received $50 advances, and signed a receipt in presence of Squire Baugh. (Schedule marked Drew, A No. 4, shows certificate No. 366,706, amount $203 20, and advances collected by Chipman, Hosmer & Co. $100 paid the 7th January, 1868.)

Jerry Jenkins, Company K One hundred and tenth United States colored troops, filed claim with Beckert. Received from Beckert $20, advanced. Signed a paper. Never received any other money from Beckert, save $40 for commutation of rations. (Drew, A No. 8, shows certificate No. 356,730 for $203 20. Advances collected by Chipman, Hosmer & Co., and paid on the 31st day of January, 1868, $40.)

James Vance, 1st, Company I One hundred and tenth United States colored troops, filed claim with Beckert. Received from Beckert $50, advanced. (Drew, A No. 33, shows certificate No. 366,681 for $300 20. Advances collected by Chipman, Hosmer & Co., and paid on the 7th day of January, 1868, $150.)

Thomas Upshur, Company K One hundred and tenth United States colored troops, filed claim with Beckert. Received from Beckert $25, advanced. (Drew, A 32, shows certificate No. 366,726 for $203 20. Advances collected by Chipman, Hosmer & Co., and paid on the 3d day of January, 1868, $50.)

Poldo Bailey, Company K One hundred and tenth United States colored troops, filed claim with Beckert. Received from Beckert $50, advanced. (Drew, A No. 36, shows certificate No. 366,693 for $203 20. Advances collected by Chipman, Hosmer & Co., and paid on the 7th day of January, 1868, $100.)

William Reedus, Company I One hundred and tenth United States colored troops, filed claim with Beckert. Received from Beckert $100, advanced. (Drew, D, shows treasury certificate No. 366,677 for $300 20. Advances collected by Chipman, Hosmer & Co.; paid on the 9th day of December, 1867, $200.)

James Brown, Company I One hundred and tenth United States colored troops, filed claim with Beckert. Received from Beckert $35, advanced. (Drew, A No. 37, shows certificate No. 336,665 for $300 20. Advances collected by Chipman, Hosmer & Co., and paid on the 3d day of February, 1868, $80.)

Albert Harney, Company K One hundred and tenth United States colored troops, filed claim with Beckert. Received from Beckert $50, advanced. (Drew, A No. 6, shows certificate No. 366,704 for $203 20. Advances collected by Chipman, Hosmer & Co., and paid on the 7th day of January, 1868, $100.)

Henry Hines, Company H One hundred and tenth United States colored troops, received from one Goldsmith $80, advanced. (Drew, A No. 5, shows certificate No. 363,225 for $204 20. Advances collected by Chipman, Hosmer & Co., and paid on the — day of ——, 1868, $188 20.)

Now by reference to the affidavit of W. H. Baugh, justice of the peace, it will be seen that Charles A. Beckert and D. A. Mann, in January or February, 1868, advanced money and took receipts therefor at the house of said Baugh; he does not know the amount set forth in the receipt, whether it corresponded with the amount advanced or not. He took no official acknowledgment of the advances, nor did any one else; that William Reedus received $50, James Vance 1st, and James

BOUNTIES TO COLORED SOLDIERS.

Vance 2d, each $50, Paul Harney, $50, and fifteen or twenty others got $50 each; and that he was paid $20 over and above his legal fees for his services.

The commission are therefore of the opinion that Charles A. Beckert and D. A. Mann did advance to the colored soldiers heretofore named the amounts testified to by the said soldiers, and that they collected a far greater amount, as shown by the schedules " Drew, A & B," furnished by the Bureau of Refugees, Freedmen and Abandoned Lands. The following table shows the amount of advances, &c.

Names.	Company.	Regiment.	Amount advanced.	Amount collected.	Loss to soldiers.
Henry Hargrave	K	110th United States colored troops	$50	$100	$50
Jerry Jenkins	K	do	20	40	20
James Vance	I	do	50	150	100
Thomas Upshur	K	do	25	50	25
Poldo Bailey	K	do	50	100	50
William Reedus	I	do	100	200	100
James Brown	I	do	35	80	45
Albert Harney	K	do	50	100	50
Henry Hines	H	do	80	188	108

The commission is strengthened in this opinion by the fact that it does not seem to them possible that men would travel about the southern States, paying their own expenses, paying extra fees (hush money) to magistrates, advancing money, lying out of the use of it for a considerable length of time, unless they found it a very profitable investment. Doubtless they did.

It now remains to trace the connection between C. A. Beckert and D. A. Mann, and Chipman, Hosmer & Co.

The following appears in the evidence of members of this firm:

Charles A. Beckert was our correspondent at Decatur. I first met Beckert about one year ago. He was employed as our correspondent in the usual way, by applying to us and sending us cases. I never saw him before he was our correspondent.

Major Mann was a correspondent, but neither agent nor partner of ours; he was what might be termed an itinerant correspondent—that is, he was constantly traveling and collecting cases which he forwarded to us. We first employed Major Mann as a clerk immediately after his muster out of the volunteer service in 1866, on the strength of previous friendship between him and me. He was at one time our book-keeper, during the absence of our regular book-keeper. He had been an officer on the staff of General Ullman, and had had considerable experience in the organization of colored troops. He grew restive in our office as a clerk, and he arranged to do business as correspondent. When he left our office and his situation as clerk, he severed all business relations existing between the firm and himself, except such as existed between any other correspondent and the firm. Do not know whether he was ever authorized to make advances, and refer you to General Gilmore. Major Mann at any rate was governed by the same arrangement made by us with other correspondents. To my knowledge, we have not furnished any money to correspondents previous to the time the advances were made, but it may possibly so have been furnished. It is possible, though I am not aware of it, that checks signed by our firm, or drafts procured by the firm, were furnished Major Mann before he went out, or in his absence; but do not think it probable. (See affidavit of A. A. Hosmer.)

Mr. Hosmer further states, Beckert is still a correspondent of our firm. Major Mann is not to my knowledge, only in the closing up of all old cases. We still do business with Major Mann in the settlement of old cases. He ceased to be a clerk in our office on his own motion. He ceased to send us cases on his own motion, and the only trouble we ever had with him was with regard to his signing the name of General Gilmore. (See affidavit of A. A. Hosmer.)

Evidence of CHARLES D. GILMORE:

Question. Have you had charge of the colored bounty claims division of Chipman, Hosmer & Co.'s business?—Answer. I have had more charge of it than any other member of our firm. (See Gilmore's affidavit.)

Q. Did the firm of Chipman, Hosmer & Co. ever, directly or through agents or correspondents, make advances to colored soldiers?—A. Yes, in a very few cases; directly in three or four cases ; indirectly in, I think, not over fifty or sixty cases.

Q. Through what correspondents or agents did you make these advances?—A. The indirect advances were made in this way: Correspondents had in their possession money belonging to us, the same being fees due white cases, accumulated in their hands; asked permission to make advances, which was granted, and these advances were collected. Upshaw, of Norfolk, drew on us once for money we honored his draft, and the only remuneration we received for the use of the money, was his business. We had advanced money through D. S. Mann, Charles A. Beckert, and a man named Goldsmith, and I think these were all.

Q. Did the firm of Chipman, Hosmer & Co., or any member of said firm, ever furnish D. S. Mann or Charles A. Beckert with checks, or drafts, or money, in any way, directly or indirectly, to advance to colored soldiers?—A. In no way, except as stated above. (See Gilmore's affidavit.)

It appears from the foregoing that Chipman, Hosmer & Co. admit that D. S. Mann and Charles A. Beckert were their correspondents, and that they (Chipman, Hosmer & Co.) made advances through them; and although they deny that Mann and Beckert were their general agents, there can be no doubt that they (Mann and Beckert) were their special agents to make advances in these cases., As to their responsibility, Mr. Gilmore says:

Question. What per cent., if any, of the profits on the advances made by Mann and Beckert, or any other correspondent, did your firm receive?—Answer. Not anything; we simply collected these advances in order to retain the business of these men, who were doing business through us, and being responsible for these advances, we were anxious that such safeguards should be thrown around the advances by the bureau as would secure us.

Mr. Gilmore says further:

Question. Do you admit your responsibility in cases of advances made by Mann and Beckert, or other correspondents?—Answer. Yes, if they were not properly made, we hold ourselves ready to pay the amount.

But in addition to the admissions of Chipman, Hosmer & Co., we find (see following schedule) on every voucher on which the chief disbursing officer of the bureau paid Chipman, Hosmer & Co. these advances, a receipt of which the following is a copy :

Received of Chipman, Hosmer & Co., attorneys at Washington, D. C., this 20th day of January, 1868, forty dollars and — cents, being for money ―――――――
Paid on the 17th day of October, 1867, to Jerry Jenkins, of K company, 110th regiment United States colored troops.

D. S. MANN.

And on the reverse of said receipt, the following affidavit:

DISTRICT OF COLUMBIA, *County of Washington, ss :*

On this 29th day of January, 1868, personally appeared before me the undersigned, a notary public within and for the District aforesaid, C. D. Gilmore, who, being duly sworn, declares and says that he is a member of the firm of Chipman, Hosmer & Co.; that the money cited in the within receipt was paid as therein stated in good faith by D. S. Mann as agent of the firm, and not on his personal account.

C. D. GILMORE.

Sworn and subscribed before me the day and year first above written.
T. J. GARDNER,
Justice of the Peace.

There is therefore no question in this matter, either as to the facts, or as to the parties legally responsible. It is therefore recommended that demand be made upon Chipman, Hosmer & Co. for the amount lost by the soldier in each case, and that the same, when collected, be paid to said soldiers through the bureau agents.

The schedule which appears in the affidavit of Charles D. Gilmore shows that the firm of Chipman, Hosmer & Co. have collected advances made by Mann and Beckert, to the amount of over seven thousand dollars, in fifty-four cases, in addition to the cases already reported upon. It is fair to presume that Mann & Beckert pursued the same course with all. It is therefore recommended that the cases of the soldiers whose names appear on the said schedule be investigated, and such action taken as the facts may warrant.

As to the question of complicity on the part of Chipman, Hosmer & Co. in these frauds, they state that they collected the advances, described their manner of doing business, deny that they received any portion of the profits, and declare that they collected these advances for Beckert and Mann, in order to retain their general business. They have furnished a list of cases, and an additional list later, in which they have collected advances, and state, under oath, (see affidavit of Gilmore,) that it contains the names of all soldiers to whom they have made and collected advances, and the commission having examined their books and compared the said list with the records of the bureau, are of the opinion that it is correct, so far as their books show.

This is a small number when compared with ten thousand cases in which they have acted as agents, and it seemed reasonable to suppose that if they had entered into an arrangement to swindle their clients, they would have carried it on to a far greater extent. But it is hardly probable that men of high standing and good character, doing an immense claim business in all its branches, and whose success depends greatly on their reputation for honesty and integrity, would involve themselves in such petty business, or even go into it to a greater extent, for the reason that to do so they must place themselves, fortune, and character at the mercy of hundreds of men—local agents through the country, through whom they are forced to do business, and over whom they have little or no control. In fine, while we question the propriety of Chipman, Hosmer & Co. (or any other claim agents, attorneys in fact) making the affidavit required to substantiate the advances, which they did not make in person, and for the truth of which they must rely on uncertain receipts and acknowledgments of claimants, taken by irresponsible parties, and although we believe them to have been culpably careless in this regard, we are not prepared to say that D. A. Mann or Charles A. Beckert and Chipman, Hosmer & Co. ever entered into a conspiracy to defraud colored soldiers. Now, while we say this, we simply give Chipman, Hosmer & Co. the benefit of the doubt. We cannot understand the statement of the affidavit herein set forth, that the advances were made by Daniel S. Mann, as agent of the firm, and not on his personal account, and reconcile this with the statements of Hosmer and Gilmore, (see affidavits,) that they regarded all these parties with whom they did business, as correspondents and not as agents, nor their defective style of bookkeeping. Omitting many transactions, yet looking at all the facts fairly, we consider it possible that Chipman, Hosmer & Co. have, as well as the claimants, been swindled by Beckert and Mann, and restitution by Chipman, Hosmer & Co. of the amount taken by Mann and Beckert, will go far toward making amends for their (Chipman, Hosmer & Co.'s) carelessness, or, to put it mildly, too great confidence in the integrity of these men, Mann and Beckert.

GENERAL GEORGE W. BALLOCH AND W. P. DREW.

The next question which arises, is: Has William P. Drew, George W. Balloch, or any other officer of the Freedmen's Bureau at Washington City, ever at any time, or under any circumstances, been connected with any claim agent, or other person whomsoever, in any arrangement or attempt to swindle colored soldiers?

The commission has earnestly and diligently, in view of the repeated assertions of M. M. Cloon, sought for some evidence tending to criminate these officers. The only evidence we succeeded in obtaining was the assertion of M. M. Cloon, which is as follows:

About eighteen months ago I was approached by Captain Charles A. Beckert, who informed me that Chipman, Hosmer & Co., for whom he was acting as sub-agent, had sent out a man named Major Mann, whose object it was to loan money to colored claimants, who did so loan to colored claimants, certificates for whose bounty the said Chipman, Hosmer & Co. was possessed of at that time. The money was to be advanced in proportion to the amount of each party's certificate; that is to say, if the certificate called for $300 or upward, the sum of $75 or $100 was advanced to said claimant, whose note was to be taken for double the amount advanced; on the other hand, if the certificate called for $200, more or less, the sum of $25 was to be advanced, and notes to be taken for double the amount of advances. Said notes were to be acknowledged before a justice of the peace, paid for the purpose. These notes were to be presented with each party's certificate to General Balloch, who was to deduct the amount from each note from each certificate to which it applied, to be paid over to Chipman, Hosmer & Co., and he (General Balloch) was to receive twenty-five per cent. of the net profit.

The commission endeavored to bring Beckert before them, but he failed to come, (although we sent a messenger seventy miles after him.) Beckert, however, sent an affidavit, in which he tells a different story. He states:

That he was approached by Cloon at two different times; that he (Cloon) proposed to him to advance money on claims; that he (Cloon) had already made $6,000 at the business; and he says, as to the remarks I should have made to the said M. M Cloon, that General Balloch was implicated in the advancing of money to colored soldiers on their claims, that I had said to the¶ said Cloon General Balloch did receive twenty-five per cent. profit on said advances, is untrue and false, and without any foundation, as I only knew that the advances were made by D. S. Mann on his own responsibility, and in accordance with a circular issued by General O. O. Howard, regulating advances on said colored claims.

Such are the statements of these two worthies, the one an unmitigated falsifier, the other an unprincipled swindler. It is hard to tell what two such men would say. It may be that each said what the other alleges. If so, it seems to us that nothing further is required to show that both statements are utterly false. Cloon has shown by his numerous letters and statements that he cannot tell the truth; and we do not believe that Beckert would hesitate to lie if it was necessary to cover up his conduct in these cases. In fine, in a matter like this, neither of them is entitled to credit, if, indeed, they could be believed under any circumstances. They were both engaged in swindling, and doubtless each one of them was anxious to make some show of authority for his nefarious proceedings. Aside from all this, it does not appear, from the manner of doing business at the bureau, that General Balloch would have been the person with whom such an arrangement could have been made. The certificates for bounty passed from the treasury into the claim division of the bureau, where the bills of the claim agents for fees and advances are audited and allowed or disallowed; the account then passes to General Balloch, chief disbursing officer, who simply pays the accounts of the claim agents, and sends the balance to the soldier. It would seem, therefore, that General Balloch could not have made such an arrangement, or carried it out if he had made it; and it is not possible that any one would have agreed to pay him large sums of money for doing that which it was his official duty to do, and for neglecting which he would have been discharged from office.

Referring to the evidence contained in the affidavits of Gilmore and Hosmer, of the firm of Chipman, Hosmer & Co., we find Mr. Gilmore says:

Question. Did you ever make any arrangements, verbal or written, with any officer of the Bureau of Refugees, Freedmen and Abandoned Lands, to the effect that Chipman, Hosmer & Co., or any member or agent thereof, should make advances to colored soldiers, and same to be settled and paid by said bureau? If so, please state the terms of such arrangements.—Answer. We never made any arrangement whatever with any bureau officer, or any one, before making or collecting advances; whatever we did, we so did under the laws and regulations.

Q. Did you ever have any conversation with Mr. Drew, or other officer or agent of the bureau, on the subject of advances; and if so, please state its terms.—A. I advised Mr. Drew to have an order issued, that advances should be paid through the bureau without its being acknowledged before some bureau officer, and before that order was issued we had several cases that were not acknowledged in that way, which we returned to our correspondents to be so acknowledged before we would collect the advances. Subsequently this order was issued by the bureau, and I went to see Mr. Drew often on the subject. I had conversation with Mr. Alvord on this subject, also with General Balloch. In some cases I desired General Balloch to send the whole amount to his local disbursing officer and let him decide whether the soldier had received the advances sent us to collect where we refused to collect the advances.

Mr. HOSMER. We had no arrangement here with the bureau with regard to advances, previous to the time they were given, or at any time. If there was any law or order authorizing the advances to be made, I read it, and knew of it at the time, and believe there was such a law or order. To the best of my knowledge, there was no understanding with any officer of the government as to how we should collect these advances. We were governed in these cases by the law or authority governing all persons alike.

As to the manner of making these advances and securing the proper evidence for their collection, I must refer you to General Gilmore, who had the matter in charge. I knew nothing about it of my own knowledge, and never had a private conversation with any bureau official on the subject. Any statement made by any person that we had any arrangement with any officer of the Bureau of Refugees, Freedmen and Abandoned Lands to make advances, collect the same, with certain interest, and to pay to said officers a per cent. of profit, is, to the best of my knowledge and belief, unqualifiedly false.

After making all due allowances for the fact that, if Chipman, Hosmer & Co. had made a swindling arrangement with any bureau official, they (Chipman, Hosmer & Co.) would be the last ones to tell it, we are of the opinion that no officer of the bureau in Washington ever entered into any arrangements with any claim agents or other persons to swindle soldiers. We do not believe that they have received or agreed to receive any sum of money whatever; we are of the opinion that they are honest men, and have discharged their duties under many difficulties in a manner deserving of credit, and accordingly acquit General Balloch and Mr. Drew of any suspicion of frauds whatever.

While at Columbia and Pulaski, Tennessee, the commission took testimony touching the official conduct of Henry A. Eastman, Brevet Lieutenant Colonel Reeves, Lieutenant George E. Judd, United States Army, and Messrs. Simpson and Carlin. At Huntsville, Alabama, testimony was taken concerning D. C. Rugg; and at Memphis, Tennessee, concerning Lieutenant Garritt. All the above gentlemen have been at one time or another agents of the bureau, and the following is a summary of their cases, as appears from evidence before the commission.

EX-BUREAU AGENTS.

Charges of fraud against ex-bureau agents are made in Mr. Cloon's letter of November 29, 1869, to the Second Auditor, before referred to. The evidence brought before the commission on this point is about as follows:

The bureau agents who had previously occupied about the same territory now in charge of Major John L. Wilson are H. A. Eastman, Captain George E. Judd, Messrs. C. R. Simpson, and G. W. Carlin, the last named being in the capacity of clerk to Simpson, and Colonel T. H. Reeves. Colonel Rugg, formerly bureau agent at Huntsville, was charged by one witness with defrauding him out of a portion of his bounty.

BOUNTIES TO COLORED SOLDIERS. 25

Reviewing the evidence against these agents *seriatim*, we take first the name of Mr. Eastman.

Dallas Webster, corporal Company F Thirteenth United States colored troops, (see No. 79, Nashville,) swears that he was paid by Mr. Eastman in July, 1868, the sum of $150; that his discharge was not returned; that he was paid by a check which he cashed at a bank at Nashville, being identified there by a colored soldier; that Mr. Eastman told him he should charge him $25 for paying him; that he went back to Columbia after cashing his check and paid Mr. Eastman $25. He states, further, that Mr. Eastman was in the habit of charging $25 to all the claimants whom he paid, and gives the names of several claimants who have paid this sum. He states, further, that one Felix Battle sold his claim to Eastman for $140. This man was sent to the bank where his check was cashed with a note from the commission asking for a transcript from their books of the number, date, and amount of the check paid to this man, with the name of the signer of the same. This note was returned by the hand of the claimant, with a pencil memorandum to the effect that the check was for $150, payable to Dallas Webster, and signed by Bullock, (Balloch.)

The commission called upon General Balloch for a certified copy of the check made payable to this man's order, and, as will be seen in reference to the same, hereto attached, the check calls for $216 70:

No. 878.] NASHVILLE, TENNESSEE, *June* 26, 1868.

First National Bank pay to Dallas Webster, or order, $216 70 in current funds.
$216 70.
GEO. W. BALLOCH,
Brevet Brigadier General and C. D. O.

Official copy:
GEO. W. BALLOCH,
Brevet Brigadier General and C. D. O.

Indorsed:
DALLAS + WEBSTER.
his
mark.

Witnesses:
H. A. EASTMAN.
C. A. DOUGLAS.

H. A. EASTMAN.

Offical copy:
GEO. W. BALLOCH,
Brevet Brigadier General and C. D. O.

In addition to this the commission called upon General Balloch and asked permission to see the original check, which was produced, and which agreed perfectly with the certified copy attached above.

Considerable doubt was thrown over this man's evidence by the fact that while he swears that one Martin Webster, Company B Thirteenth United States colored troops, paid Eastman $25 for obtaining his bounty, the records of the disbursing officer at Columbia show that he was paid by Major J. L. Wilson. The testimony of Marshall Dobynes, Company E Fourteenth United States colored troops, (see Columbia, No. 1,) is to the effect that when he was paid by Eastman the amount of $60, which he was owing to the firm of Noah & Fuller, was deducted by Eastman from the amount due him, and that Mr. Noah, of the above-mentioned firm, was present when he was paid, and that his brother was paid in the same way.

Mr. Vance Thompson, a citizen of Columbia, testifies that there were rumors prejudicial to Mr. Eastman after the latter left Columbia. The commission had before it many residents of Maury County, both white and colored, whose statements were not taken down, but whose testimony was to the effect that Mr. Eastman had not borne a good reputation for honesty and integrity; and the opinion of the commission is, founded on the evidence brought before it, that these statements are founded upon fact, and that, if it had remained in session in Maury County a sufficient length of time, numerous cases could have been found of similar character to that of Dallas Webster. While Colonel Reeves, the successor of Eastman, was stationed at Columbia the records of the office were destroyed by fire, nothing being saved except Colonel Reeves's own receipts, so that the commission were unable to refer to these to substantiate any statements of the above character brought before it. Not a single charge of any kind was brought before the commission against Mr. Eastman's successor, Brevet Lieutenant Colonel T. H. Reeves, United States Army. And the commission are of opinion that he was a faithful and honest government officer. Captain Judd, former agent at Pulaski, is charged by Richard Harris (see his affidavit, eleventh day's proceedings) with paying claimants by check, and sending them to Cloon to get them cashed; that although he (Harris) frequently called Judd's attention to the fact that claimants were being swindled, yet he would take no action in the matter, but rather winked at these irregularities.

Burt Reeder swears (see his affidavit No. 32, Pulaski) that when he was paid it was by Captain Judd; that Captain Judd gave him a check, which he said called for $305 84, and told him to go to Cloon and get him to cash it; that he did go to Cloon and got him to cash it; but he only paid him $194 80. From this and other evidence the commission are clearly of the opinion that, although Captain Judd must have been fully informed of the manner in which claimants were being swindled, not only in the matter of cashing checks but also in the matter of advances and fees, yet he seemed to have taken no steps to put a stop to it, and rather by his own action to have facilitated claim agents in their swindling schemes. If Captain Judd did not know that every time he paid a claimant by check, without carrying out instructions of circular, dated November 20, 1868, he was transgressing the law, he must have been very ignorant of his duties, and totally unfit for the position he held, and yet this excuse is the most charitable one we can give him. Captain Judd was succeeded by Mr. Eastman, who had a clerk, one Carlin. Carlin acted also for a short time as bureau agent. The reputation of these gentlemen seems to have been no better than their predecessor, Captain Judd.

Richard Harris, (an educated and very intelligent colored man, who seems to have the welfare of his race much at heart,) in his affidavit before referred to, says the same state of things existed during their stay at Pulaski, as had existed while Captain Judd was there. If there was not complicity in fraud on the part of one or both of these gentlemen, there was, judging from evidence, great ignorance of their duty as agents of the bureau. And attention is invited to the statements of James Brown, Company I One hundred and tenth United States colored troops, (see No. 14, Pulaski,) who was paid by check, and took to be cashed by Cloon by Simpson's directions. Refer also to statement of Reuben P. Clark, Company K Forty-fourth United States colored troops. (See No. 15, Pulaski.) See also statement of Thomas Upshur, Company K One hundred and tenth United States colored troops, (No. 10, Pulaski;) and also the case of Anderson Sloss, Company B One hundred and eleventh United States colored troops, who was sent with his check by Simpson to Cloon, and where the man was cheated out of all his bounty, forgery being resorted to in this case.

Colonel Rugg, who was for some time clerk to the bureau agent, and afterward disbursing officer at Huntsville, Alabama, is also charged by one claimant, Charles Ashwood, Company A One hundred and tenth United States colored troops, (see his affidavit, No. 9, Pulaski,) with defrauding him out of a portion of his bounty. Ashwood states that he placed his claim in the hands of Colonel Rugg; that he afterward borrowed $15 of Colonel Rugg; that at the time of borrowing the money he signed a paper; that he afterward went to Colonel Rugg to inquire about his money; that the colonel went with him to the bureau office; that he was then paid, Colonel Rugg taking possession of the money; that he went thence to Colonel Rugg's office, and that Colonel Rugg told him his bounty amounted to $160, and out of this he took the $15 he had previously loaned him. He further states that he knew more was coming to him, inasmuch as his discharge had been returned to him with the amount of his bounty indorsed thereon, viz: $248; and that Colonel Rugg told him he must not tell any one how much he had received. Another case of fraud, in which Colonel Rugg's name appears, is that of Cary Crenshaw, Company H One hundred and tenth United States colored troops. Crenshaw swears that he was paid by check in the presence of Colonel John B. Callis, bureau agent, Colonel Rugg, his clerk, and a gentleman whom he takes to be John W. Rames, then acting cashier of the Freedmen's Bank, which was then in Colonel Callis's office. The records show that he was paid by Colonel John B. Callis, witnessed or paid by D. C. Rugg, to the amount of $194 20. Crenshaw says, further, that he then handed the check to the bank officer, whom he takes to be Mr. Rames as before mentioned, and stated that he wanted to deposit it. The gentleman then asked how much cash he wanted, and he replied, "$50." That amount was then given him, and an entry made upon his bank-book, which at the time he supposed to be for the difference between $50 and $194. An examination of his bank-book showed that at that time he was credited with $79 20. This transaction shows that the claimant was cheated out of $64 80! Mr. Rames informed the commission that the entry was in his handwriting, but that he recollected nothing about it. Colonel Rugg said about the same thing. Lieutenant Garrett, some time agent of the bureau at Memphis, Tennessee, is accused of having turned over to Moyers & Dedrick, claim agents, claims for collection which came into his hands as an agent of the bureau.

James Cartman, corporal, Company G Third United States colored heavy artillery, testifies (see Memphis, No. 3) that he first filed his claim with Lieutenant Garrett, the bureau agent, and that he afterward found that it was in the possession of Moyers & Dedrick.

Madison Cartman, sergeant, Company G Third United States colored heavy artillery, testifies to the same thing. (See Memphis, No. 4.)

Thomas Branch, Company F Third United States colored heavy artillery, testifies to the same thing.

It was brought to the knowledge of the commission that Lieutenant Garrett, while agent of the bureau, had turned over to Moyers & Dedrick a very large number of these claims, and for which he had received compensation from them.

From Pulaski, Tennessee, the commission proceeded to Huntsville, Alabama. After a thorough examination of the records at Huntsville, and of the manner of payments and general operations of John H. Wager, disbursing officer, the commission are satisfied that he has carefully complied with the instructions and regulations of this bureau, and that there is no reasonable ground to question his honesty and faithfulness in the discharge of his duty. Moreover, the commission found no complaints or charges against him whatever, except the inferences to be drawn from the communication of M. M. Cloon.

From Huntsville the commission proceeded to Memphis, Tennessee. The commission remained in Memphis from Saturday evening, January 15, 1870, to Monday evening, January 17, 1870. We examined a number of witnesses and availed ourselves of the records and evidence on file in the office of Colonel F. S. Palmer, the very efficient and energetic officer on duty at that point. We find that swindling operations have been carried on to a considerable extent, and chiefly by two firms.

MOYERS & DEDRICK.

The acts of this firm are remarkable for their boldness, and the success which has attended them; and if any credit is due to men for being thorough masters of their business, without regard to the character of such business, then these men are certainly entitled to a crown. They had many different modes of operating, which we will take up in order; in so doing we do not propose to give all, but merely specimen cases.

Cases before passage of law making bounties payable through bureau.

Johnson Fusill, Company I Fifty-fifth United States colored troops. This case was settled by certificate No. 294,426, April 8, 1867, for two hundred and sixty-five dollars. Some time in August, 1867, Fusill went to Moyers & Dedrick's office, and they told him that his case had been settled, but thinking him dead they had sent his money back to Washington; and gave him then and there thirty dollars in clothing, and ten dollars in money. Giving up all hope of getting his money from Moyers & Dedrick, the claimant appealed to Colonel Palmer, bureau agent, in December, 1869. Palmer demanded an explanation from Moyers & Dedrick, who stated that they had paid the money to the wrong man, on April 19, 1867, previous to the date that they had told Fusill they had sent the money back to Washington, and paid him the forty dollars above stated. Finally, they paid Colonel Palmer, for Johnson Fusill, two hundred and six dollars and twenty cents, being the balance due after deducting fees and advances.

John Wiggins, Company I Fifty-fifth United States colored troops. This case was settled March 27, 1867, by certificate No. 294,430, payable to the order of claimant, and sent to Moyers & Dedrick. Moyers & Dedrick informed the claimant, February 1, 1868, that the claim had been allowed but no money received, and paid him twenty dollars, which they called advances; and about February 28 paid him twenty dollars more, for which two sums he agreed to pay seventy dollars. About three weeks thereafter, J. Moyers gave him a check for one hundred and fifty dollars, which he accepted in full for his claim. Upon this case being taken in hand by Colonel Palmer, Moyers & Dedrick settled and paid Wiggins a balance of sixty-three dollars and fifty-seven cents. It appears that Moyers & Dedrick had the receipt of claimant for full amount of his bounty; but this being signed by + mark, and as claimant, being able to write his name, never signed by mark, this defense failed, and they settled accordingly.

The above are specimen cases.

Cases after the passage of the bureau law.

Cases wherein Moyers & Dedrick collected a far greater sum than they advanced. We do not deem it necessary to enter into the partic-

BOUNTIES TO COLORED SOLDIERS.

ulars of each case. The following table will show at a glance the loss suffered by each soldier, as shown by his affidavit:

Name.	Co.	Regiment.	Amount advanced.	Amount collected.	Loss to soldiers.
William Moody	E	11th U. S. C. T	$20 00	$50 00	$30 00
William Dandridge	B	3d U. S. C. T	20 00	50 00	30 00
Cyrus Kimball	F	11th U. S. C. T	10 00	25 00	15 00
Green Johnson	B	3d U. S. C. T	100 00	172 50	72 50
John Dilliworth	H	55th U. S. C. T	30 00	60 00	20 00
Martha Hilton, widow of Matthew Hilton.	B	11th U. S. C. T	40 00	65 00	25 00
Mary Warren, widow of Joseph Warren.	B	11th U. S. C. T	40 00	60 00	20 00
Warren Brown	G	3d U. S. C. T	75 00	138 00	63 00
John Buchanan	G	11th U. S. C. T	10 00	30 00	20 00
Daniel Parsons	F	11th U. S. C. T	60 00	123 50	63 50
Vice Anna Tansil, widow of Moses Tansil.	B	11th U. S. C. T	100 00	164 50	64 50
Peter Canady	H	55th U. S. C. T	20 00	63 50	43 50

After the 14th day of March, 1868, it became necessary for parties advancing money to colored soldiers to procure the certificate of the bureau officers that the whole amount was actually advanced. This, however, did not stop the abuse. It appears that Moyers & Dedrick would advance a certain amount of money, and the claimant would, under their instruction, appear before Colonel Palmer and make oath that he had received a greater amount. The following are cases of this character:

Madison Cartman, sergeant G Third heavy artillery, received advances from Moyers & Dedrick, $90 in money and clothing, and made oath before Colonel Palmer to $104.

William Cannon, Company F Third United States colored heavy artillery, received of Moyers & Dedrick $77, ($42 thereof in clothing,) and swore to before Colonel Palmer, at Messrs. Moyers & Dedrick's direction, $100. This amount was drawn by Moyers & Dedrick from the bureau at Washington. The action as above, in both cases, has a legal name which it is superfluous for us to mention.

Not content with making advances and collecting double the amount from the bureau, Moyers & Dedrick have pretended to make advances, (in some cases they may have advanced something,) and have, after payment by the bureau officer, resorted to threats and intimidation in order to extort such pretended advances. In order clearly to understand these cases, it will be necessary to remember that Moyers & Dedrick had an arrangement with one Moyers, who kept a clothing store immediately under their office, by which said Moyers was to sell clothing to claimants, and Moyers & Dedrick advanced them money to pay for it.

Wilson Polk, Company F Sixty-fourth United States [colored troops. Moyers & Dedrick advanced him $20 in money, $40 in clothing. Colonel Palmer paid him $210. When he stepped out of his office, Captain Dean, Moyers & Dedrick's clerk, demanded $160, and threatened to put him in the station-house if he did not pay; and he paid.

Madison Cartman, Company G Third United States colored heavy artillery, paid Moyers & Dedrick $25 on being threatened with arrest and imprisonment. This they claimed as interest on $90 advanced, (see Drew, "A" No. 43,) and which had already been deducted and paid to them by the bureau.

John Small, Company H Third United States colored heavy artillery, received from Moyers & Dedrick, as advances, $75 in money and clothing, which was deducted by the bureau. After payment Moyers's brother demanded $24 interest on this advance. Paid Colonel Dedrick $10.

John McKinney, Company D Sixty-fourth United States colored troops, received of Moyers & Dedrick $89, $74 thereof in clothing. This amount, $89, was deducted by the bureau, (see Drew, "A" No. 46.) After payment G. G. Moyers met him outside Palmer's office and demanded $80 interest. Paid $35.

Thomas Branch, Company F Third heavy artillery, received advances from Moyers & Dedrick, $30 in clothing. This amount was deducted and paid to Moyers & Dedrick by bureau. After payment Moyers & Dedrick demanded, and he paid them, $7 interest (as they claimed) on said advances.

Henderson Thompson, Company B Third United States colored troops, received from Moyers & Dedrick $15. After payment by Colonel Palmer Mr. Ryan caught him outside of Palmer's office and demanded and received $73, and Captain Dean, Moyers & Dedrick's runner, took $25 more. Dean threatened him with arrest and imprisonment.

Alfred Fogg, Company F Eleventh United States colored troops, received from Moyers & Dedrick $80, advances, $15 in money, and balance in gun, pistol, and clothing. This amount was deducted and paid Moyers & Dedrick by the bureau, (see Drew, "A" 44.) After payment by Colonel Palmer J. C. Davis demanded for Moyers & Dedrick $17 50, which he paid.

But aside from the evidence above set forth, it was the fortune of the commission to witness some of the operations of this firm. Colonel Palmer paid to colored soldiers their bounty, and gave them full and explicit instructions to the extent that all fees had been paid, and that no one had any legal claim to any further fees or advances. No sooner had these men stepped outside of the door than they were pounced upon by the agents of Moyers & Dedrick, who carried them off, and, doubtless, fleeced them. There is no remedy for this; the streets are public; and when Colonel Palmer employed the police to clear the sidewalk, they guarded every street and alley with their runners, and there was no escape for the ex-colored soldiers. Sometimes such threats and intimidations failed; but this enterprising firm is never without a resource. Having entered suit before some magistrate, they would have constables present, who, in case the soldier deposited his money in the Freedmen's Bank, or with any third person, immediately "garnisheed" the same, and the suit, it seems, results invariably in a total loss of the amount to the soldier. It appears that they employed persons who induced the soldier to deposit his money with them, in order that they might "garnishee" the amount. (For specimen cases of this kind, see Madison Cartman, seventeenth day's proceedings, case No. 9.)

It has been alleged that this firm have filed claims against the government which they knew to be fraudulent. But one case of this kind came to our notice.

Marshall Johnson, who, it appears, is a horse thief, prosecuted two claims for bounty, on account of Richard and Logan Killick, Company A Fifty-fifth United States colored troops, through Moyers & Dedrick. On examination it was shown that Johnson was no kin to the Killicks, whose father and mother are still alive, and who are the proper claimants. We are not informed whether Moyers & Dedrick were aware of the above facts when they filed the claims, and we have, therefore, no opinion to offer in the premises.

The sum of $51,321 80 has been paid by the bureau, in advances, to Moyers & Dedrick. It would seem, from the cases heretofore mentioned, that Moyers & Dedrick never advanced more than fifty per cent. of the above amount. This amount has been paid on seven hundred and thirty-nine certificates. It appears that of this number, advances were paid on one hundred and fourteen certificates to the amount of $7,781, by the order of the honorable Secretary of War, October 26, 1869. In addition to the above order, circular dated War Department, Adjutant General's Office, Washington, was issued November 29, 1869. This circular states:

> That the officers appointed to hear the answers to charges against certain attorneys and claim agents, having reported that the complaints against the firm of Moyers & Dedrick relate exclusively to their dealings with their colored clients, and that from the nature of the evidence an examination of these cannot for some time be complete.
>
> It is ordered, further, by the Secretary of War, that Thomas Wilson, the attorney for the firm of Moyers & Dedrick, be permitted in conjunction with the proper officers of the Freedmen's Bureau, and subject to the further orders of the War Department, to adjust and settle all business for colored claimants in which the firm is concerned.
>
> E. D. TOWNSEND,
> *Adjutant General.*

Under the above circular, and an indorsement from the War Department, dated December 9, 1869, advances were paid on two hundred and ninety-six certificates. It therefore appears, that the authority for paying advances on four hundred and ten out of the seven hundred and thirty-nine certificates came from the War Department.

We learn from Thomas Wilson that the fees and advances are paid to Moyers & Dedrick after deducting the amount due said Wilson for collecting the same.

The commission are satisfied from the evidence taken, and from information which they obtained at Memphis, and from their own observation, (having witnessed the actions of the runners of this firm,) that Moyers & Dedrick, notwithstanding the leniency of the War Department, notwithstanding the very light punishment imposed upon them, still continue to swindle colored soldiers, and believing that this arrangement was made merely that justice might be done to claimants, and the amount due them no longer withheld, respectfully recommend that all pay and advances claimed by Moyers & Dedrick be stopped, and held to satisfy the claims of those they have undoubtedly defrauded, and that their claims be settled by the bureau, Mr. Wilson, or any agent designated by the department, and the balance due paid to the claimant.

If these charges against Moyers & Dedrick are true, and we believe they are, they ought not to be permitted to collect all their fees and advances by simply paying a third party a small per cent. for collecting the same. Nearly fifty per cent. of the whole amount of advances allowed and paid by the bureau have been allowed and paid this firm, and it is worthy of your serious consideration, whether or not they shall pocket their ill-gotten gains and continue the practices heretofore referred to, in defiance of right and justice, and notwithstanding the earnest and repeated efforts of one of the most faithful and energetic of your officers. There is an odium which attaches itself to the whole of this firm's operations, and it necessarily reflects upon the officers of the bureau. But it is our opinion that no officer or agent of this bureau is in the slightest manner connected with any of their acts, and it is due to these officers, as well as the claimants, that these men be held to a strict accountability.

The next party we are called upon to witness is—

M. COOMBS, JR.

From the evidence taken by this commission, as also the evidence furnished by Colonel Palmer, it would appear that M. Coombs, jr., & Co., have been engaged very extensively in defrauding colored claimants.

A. M. Sperry, cashier Freedmen's Bank, Memphis, testifies (see case 8, seventeenth day's proceedings) that Mrs. Oakley, who had received from M. Coombs the pension due America Tucker, mother of Isaac Tucker, had received only about $200, while the records of the Pension Office show a payment to Coombs of $446 22, thus defrauding this woman out of about $246. The commission sent for both Mrs. Oakley and America Tucker, but neither of them appeared.

Mary Buford, widow of Soloman Buford, Company G Eleventh United States colored troops, testifies (see case 13, seventeenth day's proceedings) that she had never received any pension money except $120, paid her by A. M. Sperry, while it appears from the pension records at Nashville, (see memorandum attached to her testimony,) that M. Coombs, jr., has collected $480, out of the whole of which she has been defrauded. From the same memorandum it appears that M. Coombs, jr., & Co., has collected the pension of Mary Ann Wright, amounting to $468 47. A. M. Sperry stated that this woman complained to him that she had only received about $200. This woman could not be found at the time the commission sought for her.

Julia Tucker, widow of Conger Tucker, Company E (?A) Fifty-ninth United States colored troops, testifies (see case 15, seventeenth day's proceedings) that she put in her claim with M. Coombs, jr., and has never received any money. The Second Auditor reports that this claim for bounty, &c., was settled January 12, 1867, by certificate No. 283,917, for $142 67, the same being sent to B. D. Hyam, of Washington, D. C. It appears (see case 1, Palmer, A) that this check was cashed for M. Coombs, jr., by the First National Bank, of Memphis, and there is no doubt she has been defrauded by said Coombs.

Hannah Booker, widow of Archibald Booker, late private Company D Fifty-third regiment United States colored troops, testifies (see case 17, seventeenth day's proceedings) that she was defrauded of $15 bounty money paid her by Colonel Palmer, by said M. Coombs, jr., being made to pay him April 1, 1869, $70 for $55 she had previously borrowed of him. Also that subsequently, April or May, 1869, he borrowed $75 of her which he has not paid. She also swears she was not aware said Coombs had put in a pension claim for her, and that he had never paid her any pension money. The Commissioner of Pensions reports that her claim has been presented and allowed by certificate 112,220 and paid at Nashville agency to September 4, 1868. The records of pension agency at Nashville, Tennessee, show that it was paid to M. Coombs, jr., as follows: by check No. 546, dated May 14, 1868, to order of Hannah Booker for $373 73, and in same manner September 12, 1868, for $47 60. It appearing, therefore, that at the very time he (Coombs) collected of her the money she had borrowed of him, and also borrowed of her $75 of her bounty money, he had in his hands $421 33 of her pension money which he had collected without her knowledge.

From report of Colonel F. S. Palmer (see case 2, Palmer, A) it appears that Orrin Harris, Company C Sixty-first United States colored troops, was paid $100 by M. Coombs, jr., in advance, which was all of the claim he ever received. It appears from the records of the Second Auditor that Orrin Harris's claim was allowed January 23, 1867, by certificate No. 285,264 for $300, which was sent to B. D. Hyam. It is, therefore, clear that Harris has been defrauded out of nearly $200 by M. Coombs, jr., or some one connected with the prosecution of his claim. Colonel Palmer's report would make it appear to be M. Coombs, jr.

From report of Colonel Palmer (see case 2, Palmer, A) it would seem that Dick Gregor, Company C Fifty-fifth United States colored troops,

BOUNTIES TO COLORED SOLDIERS. 33

was defrauded by M. Coombs, jr., out of $252, being amount of certificate No. 293,709 issued in settlement of Gregor's claim for bounty, &c.

From report of Colonel Palmer (see case 1, Palmer, B) it appears that Henry Grier, late corporal Company B Fifty-fifth United States colored troops, has been defrauded by M. Coombs, jr., out of $222 06. His claim having been allowed and paid March 25, 1867, by certificate No. 293,704 for $248 31, sent to B. D. Hyam and by him sent to M. Coombs, jr.; said Coombs having only paid in advance $26 25.

Henry Clay, late corporal Company A Sixty-first United States colored troops, (see case 1, Palmer, D,) swears that he had never received any advances whatever from M. Coombs, jr., or any other parties. It appears, however, that $100 advances was paid to B. D. Hyam, attorney of record. Also (see Palmer, D) that M. Coombs, jr., refunded $100, and admitted that he had advanced no money whatever to said Clay.

From report of Colonel Palmer (see case 2, Palmer, D) it appears that $200 was retained from the claim of William Young, Company A Fifty-fifth regiment United States colored troops, as advances, and that the amount was refunded by B. D. Hyam on account of M. Coombs, jr., he admitting that no advances had been made on the claim. From report of Colonel Palmer (see case 5, Palmer, D) it appears that $100 was paid to B. D. Hyam, attorney of record, for advances made by M. Coombs, jr., to Henry Bellamy, Company G Sixty-first United States colored troops, although it is evident that no such advance was made by said Coombs on this claim. The widow of Bellamy claims that amount is still due her in right of her deceased husband. (See also No. 15, Drew, A.)

From report of Colonel Palmer (see case 1, Palmer, F) it appears that the entire amount of the claim of Frank Key, Company B Fifty-fifth regiment United States colored troops, was retained as advances by M. Coombs, jr., through the attorney of record, B. D. Hyam, although Coombs afterward admitted that he had made no advances on this claim, but was only aiding one Brown to collect an old debt. The amount thus fraudulently retained was $38 81. (See No. 45, Drew, A.)

From the report of Colonel Palmer (see case 3, Palmer, F) it appears that M. Coombs, jr., & Co. were made to refund the sums set opposite to their names to the following soldiers, the same having been retained by authorities at Washington on misrepresentation that certain sums had been advanced to claimants:

Ruthy Curlie, widow of Pleasant Curlie, Company G Eleventh United States colored troops	$55 00
Simon Reynolds, Company E Fifty-fifth United States colored troops	40 00
Wesley Simmons, Company C Fifty-fifth United States colored troops	30 00
Reuben Hogan, Company B Fifty-fifth United States colored troops	56 00
Washington Lyons, Company A Sixty-first United States colored troops	20 00
George Holloway, Company —— United States colored troops	28 00
Abraham Horton, Company K Eleventh United States colored troops	25 00
David Weston, Company D Eleventh United States colored troops	68 00
Henry Branch, Company E Eleventh United States colored troops	25 00

H. Ex. Doc. 241——3

BOUNTIES TO COLORED SOLDIERS.

Lewis Horton, Company B Eleventh United States colored troops	$25 00
William Horton, Company F Eleventh United States colored troops	28 00
Nelson Adams, Company I Sixty-first United States colored troops	63 00
David Allen, Company D Fifty-fifth United States colored troops	30 00
Reuben Tickes, Company K Eleventh United States colored troops	15 00
Mary Wood, mother of Charles Wood, Company M Third United States heavy artillery	33 00
John Ingraham, Company C Fifty-fifth United States colored troops	30 00
Moses Pedan, Company A Fifty-fifth United States colored troops	65 00
Isam Strong, Company K Eleventh United States colored troops	30 00
	666 00

The above are given to show the multiplicity of frauds committed by M. Coombs, jr., & Co.

From report of Colonel Palmer (see case 7, Palmer, F) the following named soldiers had unjust charges for advances made by M. Coombs, jr.:

Alexander Alston, Company B Fifty-fifth United States colored troops	$58 00
Humphrey Means, Company E Sixty-first United States colored troops	114 00
Abraham Marsh, Company L Third United States colored heavy artillery	91 50
Abraham Polk, Company G Eleventh United States colored troops	86 50
	350 00

M. Coombs, jr., was also made to refund fees, &c., which he had fraudulently collected. (See Palmer, G.) Besides the above, there are numerous instances of fraud in making up claims, where it would appear that M. Coombs, jr., has been culpable. Doubtless the above recited cases are but a small part of the most infamous frauds committed by M. Coombs, jr., and the commission are of the opinion that, inasmuch as the attorney of record is responsible in many of the above cases, he ought to be held accountable for these losses, and all others of a similar character that may come to light. They are further of the opinion that all claims presented by the said Coombs should be investigated thoroughly by government agents before they are allowed and paid. He seems to have been guilty of forgery, perjury, and every other crime by which he could accomplish his dishonest ends.

DR. JOHN INGALLS.

Dr. John Ingalls, claim agent, of Memphis, Tennessee, appears to have been engaged in various swindling operations. He put in a claim for pension for Emily Elliott, widow of Jacob Stanley, knowing at the time that she had been married to Granville Elliott, (see case 2, seventeenth day; also, Palmer, G, case 4,) and has collected her pension

BOUNTIES TO COLORED SOLDIERS. 35

due up to September 4, 1868, retaining the entire amount, thus defrauding her of the pension due her up to the date of her marriage to Elliott, and defrauding the government of all paid for time subsequent to such marriage. It appears, further, (see case 11, seventeenth day,) that he defrauded William C. Lupee, Company E Fifty-ninth United States colored troops, out of $25, after he was paid by Colonel Palmer. There were rumors of other frauds on the part of Dr. Ingalls, but the above are all in which this commission obtained any evidence.

WILLIAM WALKER.

It appears that William Walker, claim agent, has defrauded a large number of claimants out of considerable sums, having fraudulently collected the same as advances. For history of his operations, see full report of the case by Colonel Palmer, (Palmer, C.)

The following is an exhibit of the amounts fraudulently collected:

1. William Black, sergeant Company E Fifty-fifth United States colored troops	$46 75
2. Edmund Barnett, private Company C Fifty-fifth United States colored troops	46 75
3. Austin Peterson	13 00
4. George Allen	24 00
5. Aaron Glass	26 25
6. Peter Connor	10 45
7. Henry Gaines	68 30
8. Nelson Burk	37 60
9. Meldon Miller	36 47
10. Green Hoffman	25 00
11. Ransom Wilbank	31 37
12. Lewis James	118 17
13. Duncan Benton	12 00
14. Philip Clark	12 00
15. James Dickson	17 00
16. Samuel Allen	81 25
17. Cora Williams	29 00
18. Charles Kirkpatrick	32 30
19. Osband Jones	31 80
20. Clayborne Thompson	24 00
21. George Washington	24 30
22. Perry Lindsley	5 36
23. Moses Douglass	6 15
	731 97

GENERAL OBSERVATIONS ON THE PAYMENT OF BOUNTIES THROUGH THE BUREAU—SUCCESS OF THE SYSTEM.

It would seem that, after so long and careful an examination, both of the testimony of a large number of witnesses, (inlcuding colored soldiers, claim agents, disinterested citizens, and bureau officials,) and a thorough search of the records of the departments for information, we should be able to render an opinion as to the general result of the payment of bounties through the agencies of the bureau.

Has the payment of bounties through the bureau been of advantage to the colored soldier? We have no hesitancy in saying that it is our conviction that these payments have resulted in very great advantage to the claimant.

BOUNTIES TO COLORED SOLDIERS.

We are of this opinion for the following reasons:

1. The conduct of certain claim agents who have, in cases of soldiers whose certificates were allowed before the passage of the bureau law, and passed into the hands of these claim agents, defrauded the claimant out of nearly the whole amount, convinces us that had no law been passed for the protection of these claimants, the frauds would have been enormous. It is no injustice to these claim agents to presume that they would, in the absence of the law, have acted with the whole number of their clients as they did with the few whose certificates fell into their hands before the passage of this law.

2. When we compare the frauds practiced upon colored soldiers in the payment of bounties with those practiced upon white soldiers, who are educated and intelligent, and far better able to take care of themselves, but had no special act for their protection, we must conclude that but for this law the colored claimants would have lost a very great portion of their bounty.

3. When we compare the fraud practiced upon colored claimants, in the matter of bounty, with those practiced upon the same class of claimants, in the collection and payment of pensions, notwithstanding the earnest and continued effort of all the officers of the Pension Bureau and the officers of the United States courts, the wisdom of the law and the energy, efficiency, and faithfulness of the officers who have executed it need no defense.

4. Forty thousand four hundred and forty-three certificates for bounty of colored soldiers, amounting to $7,937,985 37, have passed into the hands of the Commissioner of the bureau for payment. Of the above amount he has paid, through his agents, $6,700,427 76, and out of this latter sum he has allowed and paid to attorneys of records $125,224 70 advances. This has been paid upon the best of evidence, such as is satisfactory to the auditing officers of the Treasury. This is a small amount compared with the sum total paid to claimants; and if they were swindled out of the whole of this amount through false affidavits, still it would demonstrate the wisdom of the law and the efficiency of the bureau officers. Fifty-one thousand dollars of the above $125,000 was allowed and paid to one firm, not only under the sanction of the Treasury Department, but a large portion of it under the direct approval of the Department of War. Is it possible that this or any firm of claim agents would have taken a less amount from these clients in the absence of the law and the protection of the bureau officials? On the contrary, in our opinion, they would have taken well-nigh the whole amount. Therefore, every dollar which has been paid to claimants is a dollar saved by the operation of bureau officers under this law. But they have not been swindled out of all; on the contrary, the largest proportion of the sum total has actually been advanced, and in the case of the frauds practiced by the agents of Chipman, Hosmer & Co., which appear next to Meyers & Dedrick to be the heaviest, they, Chipman, Hosmer & Co., declare their readiness to refund the whole amount on the demand of the bureau. Beside this, the bureau has rejected claims for advances to the amount of $20,000. In fine, it seems very clear that the bureau officers have, in the matter of advances, done their whole duty under the law.

5. It may be claimed that soldiers have been swindled by claim agents and third parties, through collusion with local bureau agents, after the money has passed out of the hands of the commission. We made diligent endeavor to ascertain if this was a fact, but, as appears by the report and evidence, there has been great smoke and little fire. It is true that certain ex-bureau agents have been implicated in some such operations, but they do not appear to have carried out their designs to any very great extent;

BOUNTIES TO COLORED SOLDIERS. 37

in fact, there is little positive evidence on this point, and they have long since either resigned, or been discharged. Swindling is carried on, without a doubt, in the city of Memphis, Tennessee, but it is done in direct defiance of the officer of the bureau, and by the very men who, but for this law and the bureau, would have an opportunity to swindle the claimants out of the whole amount. This is done after the money is paid to claimants, and cannot be prevented by the bureau officers.

6. It may be said that the chief disbursing officer has not carried out the provisions of the law in sending checks payable to the order of the claimant. We are of a contrary opinion, for we consider payment by check under circular hereto attached—

[CIRCULAR LETTER.]

WAR DEPARTMENT,
BUREAU REFUGEES, FREEDMEN AND ABANDONED LANDS,
OFFICE CHIEF DISBURSING OFFICER,
Washington, D. C., November 20, 1868.

The following instructions are issued to guide agents in paying bounties to freedmen, (late soldiers :)
Whenever checks or drafts payable to the order of the claimants are sent to agents of this bureau, it is the duty of the agent to assist the claimant to convert the same into currency, and not leave him to do it himself, and thus put him in the power of sharpers and unprincipled men. The simple delivery of the check or draft to the claimant does not fulfill the terms of the law.
By order of the Commissioner.

GEO. W. BALLOCH,
Brevet Brigadier General and Chief Disbursing Officer.

which requires the money to be placed in the hands of the claimant, to be in conformity with the requirements of the law. It is necessary to send checks for the safety of the Commissioner. In case of fraud, the check makes a record against the party committing the same. It is safer for the local agent to pay; he is not in constant danger of his being robbed of his currency, (and to any one who has traveled through the South, paying bounties, danger is no myth.) Arrangements can be made to cash the checks at a trifling expense, and then both agent and claimant have the record of the bank for protection.

7. It is claimed that payments are unnecessarily delayed by officers of the bureau, and the claimants wronged by being kept out of their money. The charge is without any foundation whatever. The claimants are scattered over sixteen States in which slavery has existed; and beside this, numbers of the soldiers have emigrated and settled in the free States. The Commissioner makes payments from Boston, Massachusetts, to Galveston Texas, and from Mobile, Alabama, to Chicago, Illinois, and even to Canada. His agents are comparatively few in number, and are scattered over a vast extent of territory. Instead of being blamed for delay, he should be congratulated upon the rapidity and accuracy with which the payments have been made. Take a single State or district for instance. An agent has a large extent of country under his jurisdiction. He has in his possession from ten to fifty vouchers for payment, seldom over twenty at one time. These are scattered over his district. A, who lives at one end—probably one hundred miles away—through a party who calls himself disinterested, complains that the agent does not make a special trip to him, while B, who lives in another direction, complains that he does not go at the same time to pay him. The agent waits until he has three or four cases in the same locality, and in so doing does right, for it is wrong to put the government to a great expense in going a long distance to pay a single claim when it can be avoided. Again, the agent notifies A and B to come to his office and receive their money; and immediately the disinterested

party complains, saying it is an outrage that the claimant should be put to this expense, and insists that it is the duty of the agent to hunt up the parties and pay them, regardless of expense to the government. Now, if it is supposable that, in the absence of the law, and the agents appointed under it, these claim agents, or other parties into whose hands the certificates might pass, would, at their own expense, hunt up and pay the claimants, then there is sense in these objections; otherwise not. In fine, the very delay complained of is a sure indication that the payments have been, and are being, conducted in the mutual interest of the government and the claimant. Moreover, much of this delay is occasioned by the necessary examination in the departments, and investigations as to the validity of the claim, even after it has been allowed, as claims have been discovered to be fraudulent after settlement.

In making these observations, we do not wish to be understood as attacking all gentlemen who do business as claim agents. We believe the great majority of them to be honest men; but owing to the small fee allowed by the government, these men have not sought this class of claims, and they have accordingly fallen into the hands of the dishonest minority. It is to protect claimants against the latter and not the former that the law is required.

RECOMMENDATIONS.

From the preceding evidence and information attained by this commission, it seems clear that if the orders and regulations of the bureau are carried out thoroughly, there is very little opportunity for fraud upon colored claimants for bounty, &c. The money can certainly be put into the hands of those to whom it properly belongs. After it is received by them there will, of course, be all kinds of schemes devised and efforts made to defraud them of it; but no care or effort on the part of the government can entirely obviate this; the matter must necessarily be left to the intelligence of the claimants, and philanthropic efforts of their friends living among them. The commission are, however, impressed with the necessity for, and therefore recommend, a most *thorough* system of inspection direct from headquarters, by which every disbursing agent employed in the payment of all these claims shall be carefully instructed and overlooked, their books examined, the payments observed, and, in fact, vigilantly watched, so that every irregularity may be quickly corrected, every fraud investigated, and unworthy or incompetent officers removed, and dishonest ones punished. An officer thoroughly acquainted with the various schemes and plans for fraud, and well informed as to suspicious parties engaged in, and their manner of prosecuting them, can, doubtless, by careful supervision of every officer engaged in paying claims, construct such a net-work of protection as, in conjunction with excellent laws on the subject, will make frauds almost impossible. If it were possible, the commission would recommend that no claim agent or attorney whatever be allowed to prosecute these claims, but all the preparation and prosecution of them be done through government officers. This would seem impossible, however, because most of the claims have already been taken up, and the papers taken out of the hands of claimants, and money paid to agents, and, still more, in just legal fees due them. The commission, however, unanimously recommend that all claim agents who have been detected in fraud shall be prohibited from further practice, not only directly, but also through any other attorney whatever. Let some suitable attorney or officer be designated to complete and perfect all claims put in by them, the government retaining all fees or other money due them until all their claims are settled, and all frauds known, or that may come to light, are fully and satisfactorily adjusted. The commission are of opinion that not a dollar ought to be allowed to go into the hands of any one of these dishonest agents until full time has elapsed for a thorough investigation of all their operations.

The commission would also recommend that at the time the "blue letter" of the Second Auditor, or duplicate thereof, is sent to the claim agent filing the claim, a copy of the same be sent directly to the officer or agent who is to pay the claimant, in order that he may give the claimant correct information as to his claim, and protect him from fraud by the claim agent, who very frequently makes use of the early information gained by such notice to conceive and arrange his plans to fleece the claimant.

It seems, also, that notwithstanding every care, disbursing officers have in some instances paid the wrong parties. The commission, therefore, recommend that, when the disbursing officer satisfies the Commissioner that he has exercised due care and diligence in such cases, the real claimants be paid what is justly due them from the government. They deem it unjust that either the real claimant or the disbursing officer should suffer loss under those circumstances.

It being apparent that in the matter of pension claims, with the payment of which the bureau has nothing to do, these same dishonest agents are now preying upon the widows and heirs of deceased soldiers in a most nefarious manner, the commission feel it their duty to recommend that some protection be thrown about them similar to that contained in the law relating to bounty. It would seem that the officers and agents engaged in payment of bounties can, with very little additional expense, deliver the certificates to claimants and prepare the necessary papers for collection of pensions due upon certificates now issued, or that may be hereafter issued, and thus protect the pensioners, and also by a thorough investigation of each case protect the government until such, or some other, arrangement can be completed, by which the pension shall be paid directly by a government agent.

The commission are of opinion that pensioners would be protected, and frauds detected, by the publication of all payments made to colored pensioners in some newspapers in the vicinity of each pension agent, giving names of pensioners, amount and date of payment and name of attorney or agent through whom paid.

The commission make these recommendations without any intention of interfering with the pension department, but simply because these frauds seem to be obtaining gigantic proportions, and bear heavily upon those whose interest it has been made the duty of the Commissioner to protect.

We respectfully invite your attention to accompanying tables. Table "A," frauds in payment of bounties; Table "B," frauds in pensions; Table "C," frauds in commutation of rations.

All of which is submitted.

Very respectfully, your obedient servants,
BEN. P. RUNKLE,
Brevet Colonel United States Army.
J. R. LEWIS,
Brevet Colonel United States Army.
J. A. SLADEN,
Brevet Captain United States Army, Recorder.

Official copy:

J. A. SLADEN,
Brevet Captain United States Army, Aide-de-Camp.

BOUNTIES TO COLORED SOLDIERS.

TABLE A.—List of bounty frauds.

Names.	Rank.	Co.	Reg'nt.	Present address.	Claim agent.	Attorney of record.	No. of certificate.	Exhibit of Treasury certificates.					Am't of advances acknowledged by claimant.	Am't of alleged advances with-held from clai't.	Amount actually received.	Letter.	Drew's statem't.	No.
								Amount.	Legal fees.	Advances.	Notarial fees.						
Lansden, Thomas	Private	F	117th	Nashville, Tenn	S. H. Ingersoll	S. H. Ingersoll, (suspec'd)	324984	$206 30	(*)	$100 00	$6 50	$50 00	$850 00	$176 70	A	10	
Hargroves, Henry	do	B	130th	Pulaski, Tenn	C. A. Buckhart	Chipman, Hosmer & Co	367706	223 30	$10 00	40 00	6 50	100 00	20 00	70	A	4	
Jenkins, Jerry	do	K	104th	do	do	do	366730	203 20	10 00	100 00	5 00	100 00	20 00	70	A	8	
Reedus, (L.) William	do	I	101st	do	do	do	366667	300 20	10 00	200 00	7 50	100 00	50 00	135 70	A	1	
Baily, Poldo	do	K	110th	do	do	do	366693	203 20	10 00	100 00	6 50	100 00	50 00	133 70	A	56	
Upshar, Thomas	do	K	110th	do	do	do		203 20	10 00	150 00	6 50	25 00	25 00	203 20	A	53	
Vance, (J.) James	do	I	110th	do	do	do	366681	300 20	10 00	80 00	6 00	100 00	100 00		A	33	
Brown, James	do	I	110th	do	do	do	388665	300 20	10 00	188 00	3 00	35 00	45 00	86 70	A	37	
Hines, Henry	do	H	110th	do	do	do	363225	304 30	10 00	100 00	6 00	80 00	108 00		A	5	
Harvey, Albert	do	K	101st	do	do	do	366704	203 20	10 00	20 00	6 00	50 00	50 00	160 00	A	6	
Ashwood, Charles	do	K	110th	do	D. C. Rugg	D. C. Rugg	346678	248 00	10 00		1 00	15 00	5 00	250 00	A	34	
Tynham, Sallie, mother of Tynham, Calvin		A	110th															
Reedus, Burrill	Private	I	110th	do	M. M. Cloon	John O'Neill	363256	316 33	10 00		50	50			A	40	
Holt, Nathan	do	F	104th	do				193 40		140 00				140 00			
Alexander, Robert	Private		101st	Leicester Sta'n, Ten.	J. B. Coons			219 30		20 00				140 00			
Jones, (alias Hunter,) Noah, father of Hunter, Robert				Pulaski, Tenn														
Webster, Dallas	do	F	13th	Nashville, Tenn	James Gregory	McQuithy & Alden, (suspended.)	451270	216 20	(*)	None.	No'e	None.	None.	125 00	A	42	
Sloss, Anderson	do	B	111th	Pulaski, Tenn	Captain Judd	Major W. Fowler	441561	301 00	None.	104 00	2 50	40 00		115 00	A	29	
Crenshaw, Carey	do	H	100th	Huntsville, Ala				194 20	(†)			50 00	14 00				
Polk, Wilson	Corp'l	F	64th	Memphis, Tenn	Moyers & Dedrick	Moyers & Dedrick						90 00	5 00				
Cartman, Junius	do	G	3d H. A.	do	do	do	191091	221 91	(†)			89 00		210 00	A	43	
Cartman, Madison	Serg't	H	3d H. A.	do	do	do		240 56	10 00			100 00	23 00	231 91			
Small, John	Private	D	64th	do	do	do						77 00		124 06			
McKinney, John	Corp'l	P	3d H. A.	do	do	do	509429	206 79	10 00	89 00	2 50	15 00		105 99	A	46	
Cannon, William	Private	B	11th	do	do	do	484896	205 95	10 00	100 00	2 50	82 50		93 45	A	1	
Thompson, Henderson	Corp'l	P	11th	Independence, (Mo.)	do	do	345370	244 63	10 00			190 00		232 13	A	47	
Fogg, Alfred	Private	I	558th	Co., Miss.	do	do	504542	300 00	10 00	80 00	2 50			206 50	A	44	
Wiggins, John				Memphis, Tenn			294430	221 50		190 00				253 57			
Smith, Albert	do	F	55th	do	do	Moyers & Dedrick	393174	247 87	10 00	200 00	3 50	None.	200 00	Noth'g.	B	13	
Dandridge, William	Q. M. S.	B	3d H. A.	do	do	do	345353	272 09	10 00	50 00	3 50	20 00	30 00	208 59	B	12	
Moody, William	Private	E	11th	do	do	do	391156	296 80	10 00	50 00	2 50	20 00	30 00	143 10	B	11	
Kimball, Cyrus	Serg't	F	11th	do	do	do	391187	300 00	10 00	25 00	3 00	10 00	15 00	261 50	B	13	
Johnson, Green	Art	B	3d H. A.	do	do	do	345361	244 63	10 00	172 50	3 00		72 50	58 63	B	14	
Dillworth, John	Private	H	55th	do	do	do	372813	244 85	10 00	60 00	3 00		30 00	171 35	B	15	
Brown, Warren	Q. M. S.	G	3d H. A.	do	do	do	345312	262 53	10 00	125 00	3 00		50 00	124 03	B	19	

BOUNTIES TO COLORED SOLDIERS. 41

Name	Rank	Co.	Reg't	Where paid	By whom paid								
Buchannen, John	Private	G	11th	do		396280	300 00	10 00	25 00	3 50	10 00	15 00	261 50 B 20
Persauss, Daniel	do	F	11th	do		396269	300 00	10 00	110 00	3 50	60 00	50 00	176 50 B 24
Canaday, Peter	Corp'l	H	11th	do		396329	300 00	10 00	50 00	3 50	30 00	30 00	236 50 B 27
Jupee, W. C.		E	59th	John Ingalls			142 67						E 50
Tucker, Julia, widow of Tucker, Conger.		A or E	59th	M. Coombs, jr., & Co.	B. D. Hyam	263917	287 70	10 00		6 50	None.	Noth'g	271 00 A 38
Booker, Hannah, widow of Booker, Archibald.		I or D	53d	M. Coombs, jr.	do	191178							Noth'g E 21
Harris, Orrin	Corp'l	C	61st	M. Coombs, jr., & Co.	do	265264	300 00	10 00			100 00		Noth'g E 8
Gregor, Dick	Private	O	55th	do	do	293709	252 00						Noth'g E 13
Fussell, Johnson	do	L	55th	Moyers & Dedrick		294436	265 00	10 00		2 50	26 25	26 25	246 20 E 15
Grier, Henry	Corp'l	I	61st	M. Coombs, jr. & Co.	B. D. Hyam	293704	248 31		100 00	8 50	None.	100 00	26 25 E 45
Bellamy, Henry, (dec'd)	Private	G	55th	do	do	338045	225 56	10 00	38 81	4 50	38 81	38 81	107 06 A 18
Key, Frank	do	B	55th	do	do	380518	48 31	5 00	100 00	6 00	42 00		132 31 B 18
Alston, Alexander	do	B	55th	do	do	361737	327 51	10 00	150 00	4 00	58 00	100 00	63 51 B 21
Mesas, Humphrey	Corp'l	M	61st	do	do	337903	304 76	10 00	50 00	50	70 00		169 26 B 22
Marsh, Abraham	Private	L	3d H.A.	do	do	345356	204 00	10 00	80 00	5 50	30 00	70 00	183 50 B 23
Polk, Abraham	do	G	11th	do	do	396311	76 00	10 00	100 00	4 50	40 00	25 00	200 60 B 16
Hilton, Martha, widow of Hilton, Mathew.		B	11th	Moyers & Dedrick.	Tucker & Sells	402941	279 60	10 00	65 00	4 00			
Warren, Mary, widow of Warren, Joseph.	do	B	11th	do		402963	279 60	10 00	60 00	6 00	40 00	20 00	203 60 B 17
Tansel, Vice Anne, widow of Tansel, Moses.	Serg't	B	11th	do		402956	312 06	10 00	150 00	4 50	100 00	50 00	147 56 B 25
Robinson, Samuel	Private	C	55th	Frank Bras	Frank Bras	364369	252 00	10 00	150 00	3 00	50 00	100 00	89 00 B 26
Conley, Washington	do	K	63d	do	do	366427	106 00	10 00	40 00	3 00	25 00	15 00	53 00 B 28
Thomas, William	do	B	17th	Nashville, Tenn.	S. H. Ingersoll, (susp'd)	324934	208 20	(*)			None.		190 00 A 30

*Fees retained by Bureau. †Fees already deducted.

BOUNTIES TO COLORED SOLDIERS.

TABLE A.—*List of bounty frauds*—Continued.

Names.	Taken from claimant exclusive of advances.		Refers to commission records—		Palmer's papers.		Remarks.
	Am't.	By whom.	No.	Place.	Letter.	No.	
Lansden, Thomas	$39 50	Unknown	55	Nashville, Tenn			Witness states that he was paid by J. B. Coons, disbursing officer, Nashville, Tennessee, and by check which called for $176 70 only.
Hargroves, Henry			1	Pulaski, Tenn			Not yet paid. Funds in General Balloch's office.
Jenkins, Jerry			5	do			Voucher sent to Nashville, Tennessee, January 11, 1870. Not yet returned.
Roedus, (1,) William			6	do			The balance of $84 70 the claimant refuses to receive, alleging that $100 more was due him. No receipt of claimant on file.
Baily, Poldo	Total.	Unknown	7	do			The $50 advance is every cent this man ever received on account of bounty and back pay. A. Drew, A. M. states he was paid July 27, 1868, by J. H. W. Mills.
Upshur, Thomas	15 00	M. M. Cloon	10	do			Cloon charged $15 for cashing check.
Vance, (1,) James			13	do			Substantiated by statement of Squire Baugh, (see 12th day's proceedings,) who witnessed the receipts.
Brown, James	63 20	M. M. Cloon	14	do			Cloon cashed his bounty check, and retained the amount of $63 20 from the claimant.
Hines, Henry			31	do			It will be seen that the alleged advances and fees absorb the whole amount due the soldier from the government.
Harvey, Albert			33	do			
Ashwood, Charles	72 00	D. C. Ragg	9	do			Advances were collected twice, and then claimant paid by D. C. Rugg less than was due him.
Tynham, Sallie, mother of Tynham, Calvin	10 00	M. M. Cloon	20	do			M. M. Cloon took this amount from claimant for cashing check.
Roedus, Burrill	51 03	do	32	do			Cloon took up his check and paid him $254 80, cheating the claimant out of the balance and forging his name on the check.
Holt, Nathan	53 40	do	P. 12	11th day's proceedings.			Cloon cashed claimant's check, withholding from him the amount of $53 40.
Alexander, Robert	79 30	do	P. 12	do			Cloon cashed claimant's check, withholding from him the amount of $79 30.
Jones, (alias Hunter,) Noah, father of Hunter, Robert	10 00	do	24	Pulaski, Tenn			Cloon made him pay $10 for alleged services.
Webster, Dallas	93 20	H. E. Eastman	79	Nashville, Tenn			Claimant swears Eastman only paid him $150, and took $25 of that for paying him.
Sloss, Anderson	98 00	M. M. Cloon	25	Pulaski, Tenn			Cloon forged Sloss's name on the check and collected it.
Crenshaw, Carey	65 00		1	Huntsville, Ala			This $65 was either taken by the disbursing officer who paid him, or at Freedmen's Bank, Huntsville, Alabama, according to his affidavit.
Polk, Wilson	100 00	Moyers & Dedrick	1	Memphis, Tenn			Moyers & Dedrick made him pay $160 for $60 in money and clothing he rec'd from them.
Cartman, Junius	154 16	S. J. Quimly and Moyers & Dedrick	3	do			The money was taken by Quimby ostensibly to keep it from Moyers & Dedrick, but was garnisheed out of his hands by the latter firm.
Cartman, Madison	25 00	Moyers & Dedrick	4	do			After claimt got his money, Moyers & Dedrick made him pay $25 as interest on his advances.
Small, John	10 00	do	5	do			Claimant was met as soon as paid by Mr. Moyers, who demanded $24. Claimant refused to pay it, but finally paid $10.
McKinney, John	38 00	do	6	do			This amount of $24 was worried out of claimant after he was paid $10.
Cannon, William	28 00	do	7	do			Moyers & Dedrick garnisheed Freedmen's Bank for the $30, claiming it as int'st on advances.
Thompson, Henderson	50 60	do	12	do			Obtained from claimant by means of threats by Moyers & Dedrick's agents after claimant was paid bounty.
Fogg, Alfred	17 50	do	16	do			This $17 50 was obtained from claimant after he was paid.

BOUNTIES TO COLORED SOLDIERS. 43

Name	Amount	Paid by	Place			Remarks
Wiggins, John	5 43	do			A	5
Smith, Albert	Not'g				D	3	Man found to be a deserter. Nothing paid to him; therefore a fraud on government.
Dandridge, William					F	6
Moody, William					F	6
Kimball, Cyrus					F	6
Johnson, Green					F	6
Dillworth, John					F	6
Brown, Warren					F	7
Buchannen, John					F	7
Persons, Daniel					F	7
Canaday, Peter					F	8
Jupee, W. C.	25 00	John Ingalls	Memphis, Tenn	11	A	1	M. Coombs, jr., collected by forged check.
Tucker, Julia, widow of Tucker, Conger.	142 67	M. Coombs, jr., & Co.	do	15			M. Coombs, jr., charged her $15 as interest for loan, and borrowed $75 of her bounty.
Booker, Hannah, widow of Booker, Archibald.	90 00	do	do	17		
Harris, Orrin	200 00	do			A	2
Gregor, Dick	252 00	do			A	3
Fussoll, Johnson	6 30	do			A	4
Grier, Henry	222 06	do			B	1	The $26 25 is every cent claimant ever received. Probably forgery resorted to.
Bellamy, Henry, (dece'd)					D	5	Widow claims the amount wrongfully withheld.
Key, Frank					F	1	Claimant defrauded out of entire bounty.
Alston, Alexander					F	7
Moans, Humphrey					F	7
Marsh, Abraham					F	7
Polk, Abraham					F	7
Hilton, Martha, widow of Hilton, Mathew.					F	6
Warren, Mary, widow of Warren, Joseph.					F	6
Tansel, Vice Anne, widow of Tansel, Moses.					F	7
Robinson, Samuel					F	8
Conley, Washington					F	8
Thomas, William	30 00	D. W. Glassie	Nashville, Tenn	64			Claimant paid by check, which Glassie cashed, charging therefor $30.

TABLE B.—*List of pension frauds.*

Names.	Rank.	Company.	Regiment.	Present address.	Claim agent.	Attorney of record.	No. of claim.	Amount.	Amount actually received.
Tucker, America, mother of Tucker, Isaac			11th.	Memphis, Tenn.	M. Coombs, jr., & Co	B. D. Hyam	88139	$446 92	About $200
Buford, Mary, widow of Buford, Solomon		G		do	do	do	103678	480 00	Nothing.
Wright, Mary Ann, widow			53d.	do	M. Coombs, jr., & Co.		112220	468 47	About 200
Booker, Hannah, widow of Booker, Archibald	Private	I	111th.	Pulaski, Tenn.	M. M. Cloon.	O'Neill & Dufour.	119091	421 33	Nothing.
Roberts, Winnie, widow of Roberts, Henry	Private	A	12th.	do	do	do	115913	357 47	do
Parkeson, Sophia, widow of Parkeson, Berry	Private	C	59th.	Memphis, Tenn.	John Ingalls		108796	499 59	do
Stanley, Emily, alias Elliott, Emily, widow of Stanley, Jacob.	do	D							do

TABLE B.—*List of pension frauds*—Continued.

Names.	Pension office report.		Amount taken from claimant.	Refers to commission records.		Palmer's papers.		Remarks.
	Letter.	No.		Place.	No.	Letter.	No.	
Tucker, America, mother of Tucker, Isaac	A	5	About $246 22	Memphis, Tenn.	8			Pension paid to M. Coombs, jr.
Buford, Mary, widow of Buford, Solomon			480 00	do	13			Do.
Wright, Mary Ann, widow	A	8	About 268 47	do	13			Do.
Booker, Hannah, widow of Booker, Archibald	A	7	421 33	Pulaski, Tenn.	17			Defrauded out of the amount by M. M. Cloon and W. W. Ingersoll.
Roberts, Winnie, widow of Roberts, Henry			357 47		38			Defrauded out of the amount by M. M. Cloon and W. W. Ingersoll.
Parkeson, Sophia, widow of Parkeson, Berry	A	6	499 59	do	39			Paid to John Ingalls to September 4, 1868.
Stanley, Emily, alias Elliott, Emily, widow of Stanley, Jacob.			Entire amount.	Memphis, Tenn.	2	G	4	

BOUNTIES TO COLORED SOLDIERS. 45

TABLE C.—*List of frauds in payment of commutation of rations.*

Name.	Rank.	Co.	Reg.	Present address.	Claim agent.
Carden, Alexander	Private	F	110th	Pulaski, Tenn	M. M. Cloon
Sloss, Anderson	...do	B	111th	...do	...do
Green, Geo. W., or Jos. W.	...do	K	110th	...do	...do
Harney, Albert	...do	K	110th	...do	...do
Reedus, Burrill	...do	I	110th	...do	...do
Reedus, William	...do	I	110th	...do	...do
Holt, Nathan	...do	F	110th	...do	...do
Braden, or Brady, Horace	...do	E	110th	...do	...do
Harville, Turner	...do	K	110th	...do	...do
Upshur, Thomas	...do	K	110th	...do	...do
Vance, James, (1)	...do	H or I	110th	...do	...do
Brown, James	...do	I	110th	...do	...do
Hines, Henry	...do	H	110th	...do	C. A. Beckert
Hargrove, Henry	...do	K	110th	...do	...do
Jenkins, Jerry	...do	K	110th	...do	...do
Baily, Poldo	...do	K	110th	...do	...do

Name.	Attorney of record.	No. of check.	Amount.	Am't actually rec'd.	Am't taken from claim't.
Carden, Alexander	O'Neill & Dufour	4156	$58 00	$25 00	$33 00
Sloss, Anderson	...do	5749	78 25	Nothing.	78 25
Green, Geo. W., or Jos. W.	...do	3522	50 00	$15 00	35 00
Harney, Albert	...do	4313	57 50	20 00	37 50
Reedus, Burrill	...do	3524	50 00	Nothing.	50 00
Reedus, William	...do	5555	45 25	$20 00	25 25
Holt, Nathan	...do	4684	50 00		50 00
Braden, or Brady, Horace	...do	4310	54 75	$20 00	34 75
Harville, Turner	...do	4878	57 50	25 00	32 50
Upshur, Thomas	...do	5556	54 25	37 30	17 05
Vance, James, (1)	...do	5750	54 75	25 00	29 75
Brown, James	...do	4612	54 75	Nothing.	54 75
Hines, Henry	Chipman, Hosmer & Co.		50 00	$31 00	19 00
Hargrove, Henry	...do		About 57 00	40 00	About 17 00
Jenkins, Jerry	...do		About 57 00	40 00	About 17 00
Baily, Poldo	...do		About 57 00	40 00	About 17 00

Name.	Dufour's evidence.		Refers to commission record.		Remarks.
	List.	No.	No.	Place.	
Carden, Alexander	A	136	22	Pulaski, Tenn	Taken by M. M. Cloon.
Sloss, Anderson	A	97	25	...do	Do.
Green, Geo. W., or Jos. W.	A	112	26	...do	Do.
Harney, Albert	A	24	33	...do	Do.
Reedus, Burrill	A	114	32	...do	Do.
Reedus, William	A	92	6	...do	Do.
Holt, Nathan	A	55	P'ge 12	11th day's proceedings	Do.
Braden, or Brady, Horace	A	22	P'ge 12	...do	Do.
Harville, Turner	A	60	P'ge 12	...do	Do.
Upshur, Thomas	A	93	10	Pulaski, Tenn	Do.
Vance, James, (1)	A	98	13	...do	Do.
Brown, James	A	46	14	...do	Do.
Hines, Henry			31	...do	Taken by C. A. Beckert.
Hargrove, Henry			1	...do	Do.
Jenkins, Jerry			5	...do	Do.
Baily, Poldo			7	...do	Do.

PROCEEDINGS OF COMMISSION APPOINTED BY SPECIAL ORDERS No. 189, DECEMBER 17, 1869, BUREAU OF REFUGEES, FREEDMEN AND ABANDONED LANDS.

In accordance with the following special order, dated War Department, Bureau of Refugees, Freedmen and Abandoned Lands, December 17, 1869, viz:

[Special Orders No. 189.]

A commission of three officers of the army is hereby appointed and ordered to assemble at Nashville, Tennessee, on Wednesday, the 29th instant, for the purpose of a careful hearing of complaints of claimants for government bounty, made against officers or agents of this bureau, or other persons concerned in the payment of bounties to colored soldiers, sailors, or marines. They will sit at Nashville and Columbia, Tennessee, Huntsville, Alabama, or at any other points in the State of Tennessee or Alabama where they shall deem it necessary for a full and careful investigation. They will make a report and recommendations to the Commissioner, to enable him to correct any abuses that may be found to exist, and to do justice to all parties concerned.

Detail for the commission: Brevet Colonel Ben. P. Runkle, superintendent of education for Kentucky; Brevet Colonel J. R. Lewis, superintendent of education for Georgia; Brevet Captain J. A. Sladen, aide-de-camp, Washington, D. C.

By order of Brevet Major General O. O. Howard, Commissioner.

HENRY M. WHITTLESEY,
Acting Assistant Adjutant General.

the commission met at Nashville, Tennessee, on Wednesday, December 29, 1869, and went through a careful examination of all papers referred to it from the Bureau of Refugees, Freedmen and Abandoned Lands, War Department. The commission then adjourned until next day, at nine o'clock a. m.

BEN. P. RUNKLE,
Brevet Colonel United States Army.
J. R. LEWIS,
Brevet Colonel United States Army.
J. A. SLADEN,
Brevet Captain United States Army, Recorder.

SECOND DAY'S PROCEEDINGS AT NASHVILLE, TENNESSEE.

On Thursday, December 30, 1869, the commission met at nine o'clock a. m., and proceeded to the office of the United States district attorney, J. McP. Smith, esq., and obtained all the information in his possession regarding the indictment of Major James L. Wilson, agent of Bureau of Refugees, Freedmen and Abandoned Lands, at Columbia, Tennessee.

Mr. Smith stated to the commission that Mr. Wilson was the only bureau agent who had been brought before the grand jury in his district, to the best of his knowledge and belief, and that all the charges against Mr. Wilson had been brought before the United States commissioner, supported by sufficient evidence to warrant their presentation to the grand jury. The grand jury had nevertheless thrown them out, on the ground that the evidence was not sufficient to warrant an indictment. Mr. Smith also stated to the commission that Mr. M. M. Cloon seemed to be a principal in getting up these charges against Mr. Wilson, and that he (said Mr. Cloon) was an illiterate man, of doubtful reputation. The commission then requested the presence of United States Commissioner L. J. Noah, esq., before whom the charges were originally brought. Mr. Noah reiterated the statement of Mr. Smith, with the exception of that portion relating to Mr. Cloon, with the additional testimony, first, that Mr. Cloon did not appear as a principal; second, that he was a very unimportant witness; and third, that although the evidence brought before him was sufficient to warrant him in presenting the case to the grand jury, yet the original witnesses, with one exception, could not be found when called upon to testify before the grand jury. Mr. Noah very kindly furnished the commission with the following list of witnesses, viz: Minna Carter, colored; Susan Carter, colored; Green Turner, colored; G. T. Fisher, colored, Pulaski; Stephen Sloss, colored; Nino Stevenson, colored.

The commission then decided to invite all the colored clergymen and prominent colored men of Nashville to a conference on Friday morning, at ten o'clock, and the recorder was directed to notify all such to that effect. The recorder making formal application to the Commissioner for the services of a clerk, and it being impracticable to procure an enlisted man, he was directed to employ a civilian at a reasonable compensation. The commission then adjourned till Friday, December 31, at nine a. m.

BEN. P. RUNKLE,
Brevet Colonel United States Army.
J. R. LEWIS,
Brevet Colonel United States Army.
J. A. SLADEN,
Brevet Captain United States Army, Recorder.

THIRD DAY'S PROCEEDINGS AT NASHVILLE, TENNESSEE.

The commission met Friday, December 31, 1869, at nine a. m., and took the following statements of the colored clergymen of Nashville, who had been invited to be present:

Butler Parish, pastor of the Second Christian church, states that he has been living here for three years; that he heard many complaints made against claim agents from soldiers who got only a part of the bounty due them, but cannot name a single case.

Edmund Horn, special pastor of the Methodist Episcopal church, states that he knows a Mrs. Winchester, widow of Sandy Winchester, who lives on Cherry street, south of Broad street, who had tried to collect the bounty due her, and often went to Colonel Thompson for that purpose, but all without success. He has not heard of any more complaints regarding payments of bounties.

W. R. Ravells states that he lives in the State of Indiana; that he was surgeon of a colored regiment during the war, and that he heard many complaints being made against claim agents, but none against bureau agents in the city of Memphis.

Moses R. Johnston, of the First Presbyterian church, states that he has lived here for five months only. Has heard complaints made against claim agents, but none against bureau agents.

Page Tyler, of the St. John's chapel, states that he knows that papers for the collection of bounties were sent back from Washington, on account of not having been correctly made out, but that he never heard of a single case of swindling.

Alexander Buchanon, pastor Second Baptist church, states that he has lived here for twenty-five years, and don't know of a single case of complaint being made, either against claim agents or bureau agents.

C. R. Dickerson, of the Capers chapel, Methodist Episcopal church

South, states that he has been here only three months, and that he never heard any complaint of any kind.

Matt. Hays states that he lived here for thirty-five years, and never heard any complaints.

Jordan Bransford, of the Mount Zion Baptist church, states that he has lived here since 1836, and that he never heard any complaints of any kind.

N. S. Merry, of the First Colored Baptist church, states that he has heard hundreds of complaints made, but cannot give the name of a complainant. He thinks that John Shelton, who was engaged in the Freedmen's Bureau for years, can give much information.

Rev. Nelson McGavocks, of Smeedsville, states that he heard many complaints made by colored soldiers in his county, but could not say anything definite. He never heard any complaint that they had been swindled by bureau agents.

After the foregoing evidence had been taken, the gentlemen present were requested to notify, through their pulpits and otherwise, all those whom they could reach, who had or supposed they had any grounds of complaint against claim agents or agents of the bureau, to present themselves before the commission on Monday morning, at ten o'clock.

The next day being New Year's day, the commission adjourned until January 3, 1870, at nine a. m.

BEN. P. RUNKLE,
Brevet Colonel United States Army.
J. R. LEWIS,
Brevet Colonel United States Army.
J. A. SLADEN,
Brevet Captain United States Army, Recorder.

FOURTH DAY'S PROCEEDINGS, NASHVILLE, TENNESSEE.

The commission met January 3, 1870, at 9 a. m., pursuant to adjournment, when the following evidence was taken, viz :

No. 1.—Alfred Ware, Company A Forty-fourth colored infantry; claim entered by Ingersoll, but not settled; put in 1866.

No. 2.—Benjamin Philipps, Company B Sixth United States colored cavalry, has never had his claim entered.

No. 3.—Silas Cook, Company D One hundred and first colored infantry; claim given to Buck McMellan, Clarksville; claim put in July 31, 1866, and was received by Cobbs, agent Bureau Refugees, Freedmen and Abandoned Lands.

No. 4.—Parker Frey, corporal Company I Sixth United States Artillery; claim entered February 4, 1867, by McQuithy & Alden.

No. 5.—Joseph Lupen, Company D Third heavy artillery, (colored,) swears and testifies that he has never placed his claim in the hands of a bureau agent—this, on account of the statements made to the effect that the bureau agents had nothing to do with it. Complaints are very general against claim agents; nothing against bureau agents.

No. 6.—Martha Taylor, widow of Eureka Taylor, colored cook, Company C Tenth Illinois infantry, who died in the service of the United States; claim was forwarded by McQuithy & Alden, on November 13, 1866. She never was able to get any satisfaction from them.

No. 7.—Elizabeth Jones, sister of William Jones, 2d, private of

BOUNTIES TO COLORED SOLDIERS. 49

Company I One hundredth United States colored troops; claim entered at Nelson & Howard's over two years ago. Copy of letter annexed:

WASHINGTON, *May* 28, 1868.

GENTLEMEN: I am in receipt of your favor of the 25th instant. Owing to the impeachment trial, the departments have done but little for three months past, and are consequently behindhand with their work. It is impossible to hurry the claim of Elizabeth Jones. It must await its turn for settlement. There are about six hundred thousand claims on file, and each claimant wants his or her claim pushed through at once, the same as Mrs. Jones.

Yours truly,

S. J. McCARTY,
Attorney and Counsellor at Law.

Messrs. A. NELSON & Co.,
Nashville, Tennessee.

No. 8.—Ann McClellan, sister of Joseph M. Martin, Company D Fourteenth United States colored infantry. Also, claim of her husband, Elias McClellan, Company D Twelfth United States colored; both entered with Tompkins & Co. Major D. Lloyd advanced her some money; never got any satisfaction, and never saw her papers again. She went to the agent; he sent her to Mr. Glassie. claim agent at Nashville; Glassie sent her to Mr. Coons; Mr. Coons told her to get out, or he would kill her. The first claim she put in June 18, 1867; the last one she don't remember the time.

No. 9.—Robert Conner, sergeant Company F Fifty-sixth United States colored infantry, was put on the roll as a slave, and was paid the amount due for back pay, $52.

No. 10.—Joseph Hazelwood, corporal Company K Seventeenth United States Infantry; claim was settled and paid.

No. 11.—Edas Brown, widow of Philip Brown, One hundred and tenth colored infantry, put in her claim with Mr. Coons. Mr. Coons told her that she must bring two persons who could write their names, and had known her husband, and who knew how long they had lived together, and that her pension papers had been lost in the Pension Office.

No. 12.—Mrs. Lydia Hunter, mother of Mack Galligher, late private Company C Twelfth heavy artillery, went to Mr. Coons; Coons sent her to Mr. Glassie; the latter said, "Go to hell." She never sold her claim or received anything on it. Mr. Coons said Glassie was the man; that he was a claim agent, and was the first one notified. She never heard anything against the bureau.

No. 13.—Malvina Roberts, wife of William Roberts, Company C Fifteenth United States, has got Mr. Coons's receipt, dated April 17, 1869.

No. 14.—Tillman Sherrold, corporal Company G Twelfth heavy artillery, put in his claim with Mr. Glassie; afterward he paid Glassie $2 for his discharge; he went to Mr. Coons; Coons said he could not do anything; to keep his discharge and not lose it. This occurred less than one year ago. (Papers retained.) He never got anything on his discharge; he never heard any complaints against bureau agents.

No. 15.—William Blackburn, Company G Seventeenth United States, received $196 20 from Mr. Coons. He put in his papers with S. B. Brown. (Papers retained.)

No. 16.—Isaac Maxwell, Company H Fifteenth United States colored infantry, put in his papers with McQuithy & Alden, November 30, 1866. He has been to the bureau, (Coons,) and was informed that his claim was not allowed yet. He was there three months ago for the last time. Mr. Coons told him in September that he must see McQuithy; never heard any complaints against bureau agents; Mr. Coons always sent him to Mr. McQuithy.

H. Ex. Doc. 241——4

BOUNTIES TO COLORED SOLDIERS.

No. 17.—Jackson Ewing Company I One hundred and eleventh United States colored infantry, put in his claim with Mr. Coons for commutation of rations, but Mr. Coons informed him that he could not get it. Also put in his claim for bounty on the 12th November, 1869.

No. 18.—Joshua Hall, Company E One hundred and thirty-fifth colored infantry, served eight months. No bounty due.

No. 19.—Eliza Silkins, widow of Michael Silkins, Company E One hundred and first United States; her claim was disallowed.

No. 20.—Ann Barrow was washerwoman in Hospital No. 13, corner of Spruce and Broad; she washed there for eighteen months, but never received any pay; she went to Mr. Coons, who treated her so spitefully that she would not go there again. A great many others got nothing. Signed rolls by mark for two months, but never got any money.

No. 21.—Charlotte Reese, widow of Joseph Reese; claim for work done. She put in her claim with Thompkins & Co. (Papers retained.) Reese paid $15 in advance and never received any money.

No. 22.—Mary Chambers, widow of Martin Chambers, Company G Thirteenth United States. Mr. Coons put in her claim two years ago. She went to Mr. Coons a few days ago, and he said he could not do anything unless she brought two witnesses who could write, and who saw her husband die. She could not get the witnesses.

No. 23.—Cato Hines, (colored,) claim for work on fortification, $10 50. He paid Thompkins $1 60. (His papers were retained.) Never has been to Mr. Coons. Have heard much complaint that government would not pay. I worked fourteen months laying stone and was working for Captain Stewart. I never got but $40 government money when the work was done. The roll was called every morning.

No. 24.—Daniel Jordan, Company F Forty-fourth United States colored infantry. January 8, 1867, with C. H. & Co. Has been to see Mr. Coons three or four times; never got any money. Has written E. B. French several times. Four weeks ago he said his claim was out for settlement.

No. 25.—William Steel, private Company C Fourteenth. Certificate 528847, in favor of mother, June 5, 1867. O'Neil and Dufour, agents. W. H. Morse, sub-agent.

No. 26.—Tyler Freeman, widow of Sandy Freeman, Company I Twelfth infantry. Claim for pension. Put in claim for back pay to Lawyer Bunks, but Mrs. Linsle paid her $70 and would not give her any information as to the amount due.

No. 27.—Maria Work, mother of Ralph Jones, who belonged to a cavalry regiment, put in papers with Judge Lawrence and Judge Coons about three years ago. Went to Mr. Wilkerson, a magistrate, who told her that his office was the only place, and she must pay him $5 and he would get her money. Has not been to L. or C. for two months.

No. 28.—Sarron Goff, private Company C One Hundred and first regiment. Bounty claim put in with W. W. Ingersoll April 30, 1866. Never has heard a word about it. Has been to Coons; Coons sent him to Ingersoll; Ingersoll sent him to Coons; went to Mr. Ingersoll January, 1869; received a letter or paper in March. Mr. Ingersoll told him to come back in ten days; went from time to time there and was put off.

No. 29.—Willis Douglass, Company I Seventeenth United States colored infantry, complains that he only got $193 out of $209; all right.

No. 30.—Atty Prierson, Company B Seventeenth United States colored infantry, mother of Columbus Prierson, put in a claim in March, 1867;

has not seen Judge Coons for nine or ten months. Judge Coons told her that three other women claimed to be Columbus's mother; that Judge Coons told her to get more evidence, but she had been too sick to attend to it.

No. 31.—Robert Smith, corporal Company F Seventeenth United States colored infantry, paid bounty account July, 1861...... $100 00
Paid bounty account July, 1866............................ 100 00
Difference of pay 6 20

Total 206 20
Over-pay in hospital........................ 72 00

Balance paid 134 20

Acknowledges the above, and thought there might be more; has heard reports about Judge Coon to the effect that he did not pay all he should have done.

No. 32.—Franklin King, Company F Seventeenth United States colored infantry, got all the pay and bounty entitled to.

No. 33.—Prince Suggs, Company D Twelfth United States colored infantry, sworn, testifies as follows: That he was mustered out at Nashville something over four years ago. Soon after his discharge, about December, 1865, he sent his discharge by his father, Prince Griffith, to Tompkins & Camp, at Nashville, who gave a receipt for it; he gave this receipt to M. M. Cloon, at Pulaski, in the presence of his father, about Christmas, 1865, taking Cloon's receipt therefor. He went to Cloon three or four times during the next three years. About three months ago he went to Jones, claim agent at Pulaski, and gave up Cloon's receipt and got a receipt from Jones. When he saw Cloon last he said he would get his claim, but he did not know how soon. Has lost Jones's receipt. Swears positively that he has never signed any paper whatsoever, not even when he put in his claim, and that he has never paid any one a cent to prosecute the same.

No. 33½.—Benjamin Ashworth, Company G Fourteenth United States colored troops, paid in full.

No. 34.—Henry McKay, Company A Twelfth United States colored troops, put in his discharge papers with Chipman, Hosmer & Co., Nashville, on the 14th of January, 1867, and never heard of them since. He called on Mr. Coon a year ago. Mr. Coon sent him to Mr. Phillips; never saw Mr. Phillips until he was sent there by M. Coon. Mr. Phillips wrote a letter for him.

After the examination of several unimportant witnesses, the commission adjourned until the next day, January 4, 1870, at 9 a m.

BEN. P. RUNKLE,
Brevet Colonel United States Army.
J. R. LEWIS,
Brevet Colonel United States Army.
J. A. SLADEN,
Brevet Captain United States Army, Recorder.

BOUNTIES TO COLORED SOLDIERS.

FIFTH DAY'S PROCEEDINGS—NASHVILLE, TENNESSEE.

Pursuant to adjournment the commission met January 4, 1870, at 9 o'clock a. m., when a large number of witnesses were examined and the following evidence taken, viz:

No. 35.—John Brown, Company H Twelfth United States colored troops. He received his full amount as per certificate of the Treasury Department, but thinks he might have more.

No. 36.—Harrison Hall, Company I Twelfth United States colored troops. This is the same case as above.

No. 37.—William Butler, hospital steward Twelfth United States colored troops. This is the same case as Nos. 35 and 36.

No. 38.—Wilson Hardison, commissary sergeant Fifteenth United States colored troops, put his claim in about two years ago, but has not heard from it yet.

No. 39.—Simon Harney, Company D Twelfth United States colored troops, put in his claim with M. M. Cloon about two months ago.

No. 40.—Lark Allen, Company F Twelfth United States colored troops, got all the pay due him.

No. 41.—Booker Bowers, sergeant Company D Twelfth United States colored troops, got all the pay due him.

No. 42.—Joseph Harney, sergeant Company D Twelfth United States colored troops, got all his pay.

No. 43.—Maria Williams, widow of Charles Williams, supposed to have belonged to Seventeenth regiment United States colored troops, died at Huntsville, Alabama, about April, 1863. There are no discharge papers in the hands of the widow.

No. 44.—Henry Stevenson, Company K Eleventh United States colored troops, put in his claim with A. Worley Paterson, of Decatur, Tennessee, about sixteen months ago. He transferred his claim to Lawyer Phillips, and never heard of it since. It appears to be all right.

No. 45.—Meredith Woodfolk, cook of Company C Fifth Ohio cavalry, put in his claim with John Newton, Nashville, Tennessee, on the 2d of January, 1868.

No. 46.—John Granderson, private Company A One hundred and tenth United States colored troops, got all the pay due him.

No. 47.—Elois Key, private Company F Fourteenth United States colored troops. His allowance is $176. Says he has received only $120 50. Discharge retained.

No. 48.—Thomas Kimber, Company A Fourteenth United States colored troops, put in his claim without his discharge papers, having lost the same with Mr. Ingersoll two years ago. Also had Mr. Morris to write for him. He has been to Judge Coons, who said that he never heard anything of his claim. He never borrowed anything of anybody.

No. 49.—Joseph Luper, Company C Third United States colored troops. Money was deducted from his pay for destruction done by his regiment; probably all right.

No. 50.—Charles Kelley, Company D One hundred and first United States colored troops, complains that Mr. Ingersoll did not return his discharge.

No. 51.—Sallie Dickerson, widow of Ed. Dickerson, Company A Thirteenth United States colored troops, put his discharge in the hands of Mr. Ingersoll. Claimant was sent to Mr. Ingersoll for information.

No. 52.—Nickerson Ellis, Company H One hundred and first United States colored troops, put his discharge in the hands of Mr. Ingersoll.

No. 53.—Grandison Puryear. Claim of $270 for services rendered in quartermaster's department digging graves. Thomkins & Co., agents. Claim was never entered by Thomkins & Co.

No. 54.—Abraham Price, Company B One hundred and first United States colored troops. Claim for laboring in the Engineer Department. He has received all his bounty due him. Never put in his claim.

No. 55.—Thomas Lansden, Company F Seventeenth United States colored troops, got check of $176 70 of Judge Coons. Paid nothing to any one. No payment indorsed on discharge. His brother says he got one hundred per cent. for lending his money.

No. 56.—Morris Sells, Company I Seventeenth United States colored troops, received all his bounty, but says he cannot get back his discharge.

No. 57.—George Washington Tweedy, Company K Seventeenth United States colored troops, got all the bounty entitled to.

No. 58.—Matt. King. Claim for work in the Engineer Department; put in his claim, but his name could not be found on the rolls.

No. 59.—Edmond Bowers, Company H Twelfth United States colored troops, bounty been paid. Discharge retained.

No. 60.—Harriet Ensley, worked in government hospital No. 16 at Nashville for two years and six months. She has eleven months' pay due her.

No. 61.—Sampson Smithers, Company D Twelfth United States colored troops, was paid in full.

No. 62.—Edmond McGavock, father of Lazarus and Sampson McGavock. Claim for services of sons who died while at work on fortifications.

At 11.30 a. m. the commission proceeded to the office of Mr. Coons, bureau agent, where a thorough examination was made of the manner of paying bounties, &c., and the books and records were examined with reference to certain specific cases in the hands of the commission.

Mr. Coons was also examined as to the frauds practiced by claim agents, and their manner of conducting the same. Mr. Coons complained that claim agents are informed, long before he is, when a claim is allowed. He also stated that letters written to Washington by claimants, asking for information with regard to their claims, are returned to him with the information, but that he is unable to find the writers. He thinks a letter should be written to the claimant from Washington, instructing said claimant to call on him (Coons) for information, at the same time that original is sent from Washington.

Mr. Coons also informed the commission that there are about fifteen hundred claims for labor in and about the hospitals of Nashville, mostly women, have been made out by various parties. The Surgeon General, in reply to a letter concerning these cases, stated that there was no fund out of which these claims could be paid.

The commission then returned to the examination of witnesses, as per the foregoing evidence, and at 3.30 p. m. adjourned until the next day, January 5, 1870, at 9 a. m.

BEN. P. RUNKLE,
Brevet Colonel United States Army.
J. R. LEWIS,
Brevet Colonel United States Army.
J. A. SLADEN,
Brevet Captain United States Army, Recorder.

BOUNTIES TO COLORED SOLDIERS.

SIXTH DAY'S PROCEEDINGS—NASHVILLE, TENNESSEE.

Pursuant to adjournment the committee met January 5, 1870, at 9 a. m., and proceeded to the examination of witnesses.

D. W. Glassie, having been summoned, appeared, and having been interrogated, stated to the commission that he would put his testimony in writing and place it in the hands of the commission the next day.

The following evidence was then taken, viz:

No. 63.—Daniel Watkins, Company F Thirteenth United States colored troops; discharge retained in order to ascertain the fact in regard to his bounty. He has received $100 additional bounty.

No. 64.—William Thomas, private Company B Seventeenth United States colored troops, received his bounty about Christmas, 1868. Total amount of bounty, &c., including fees, $208 20. Received a check from Mr. Coons for $190 40. Took the check to Mr. Glassie, who took up the check and gave him one of his own for $170. He went to Glassie because he was sent there by Mr. Coons, who first told him to go to Mr. Ingersoll. Mr. Ingersoll refused to have anything to do with him; and when he reported about this to Mr. Coons, Coons then sent him to Mr. Glassie. He asked Mr. Glassie what he would go to the bank and identify him for. Mr. Glassie said $10. He told him that $10 was too much, but would give $5, but finally gave him $10. Mr. Coons did not send any one with him.

No. 65.—Moses and Lucy Brannan worked a year in hospital No. 14, Nashville, and got only three months' pay.

No. 66.—Robert Hopkins worked two years on fortifications as a teamster. Got only $20 pay from Captain Irvin, quartermaster.

No. 67.—Boyd Ellison, same case. Got only $90.

No. 68.—Charles Kelley was sent off by Mr. Coons to obtain personal identity, and did not return.

No. 69.—James Kissick, Company B Fifteenth United States colored troops, was obliged to pay $5 to obtain witnesses to go with him to the bank.

No. 70.—Archie Eldridge, private Company G One hundred and first United States colored troops, appears to be all right. Was paid the full amount.

No. 71.—William Stevens, private Company F Forty-fourth United States colored troops, put in his claim with H. Thomkins & Co. on February 21, 1867. After the failure of Thomkins & Co. he went to Mr. Glassie, who said he would collect the claim for $20, and when he refused to pay him that sum, Mr. Glassie told him to leave his office or else he would put him out.

No. 72.—Thomas Thomkins, Company K Thirteenth United States colored troops, put in his claim for collection with Chipman, Hosmer & Co., on March 6, 1867, and never heard from it since.

No. 73.—Silas Elliott, Company K One hundred and first United States colored troops, put in his claim with Thomkins & Co., Nashville, March 14, 1867. Was sent to Mr. Coons for information.

No. 74.—Israel Townsend, Company B One hundred and first United States colored troops, put in his claim and discharge with Mr. Ingersoll, June 8, 1866. Has received no satisfaction. He states that Mr. Ingersoll said that there was no money due him, and would not return his discharge. Case was turned over to Mr. Coons.

No. 75.—Emma Smith makes inquiry regarding claim of her son, Jacob Smith, Company A Fortieth United States colored troops. Was sent to Mr. Coons.

No. 76.—Charley Hart, Company D Fifteenth United States colored troops, deceased. Claim was entered by brothers and sisters. He enlisted under the act of July 4, 1864, consequently there was nothing due him at the time of his death.

No. 77.—Lem. McKissie, private Company G One hundred and tenth United States colored troops, has received his bounty, but his discharge was never returned. He wants commutation of rations while a prisoner, but has never made application for it.

No. 78.—Peter Jackson, Company D Thirteenth United States colored troops, filed his claim about three years ago with Mr. Crunk, claim agent at Nashville. It appears by an indorsement of the Second Auditor's office, dated June 29, 1869, is in a fair way for settlement.

No. 79.—Dallas Webster, late corporal Company F Thirteenth United States colored troops, being sworn, testifies as follows: That in 1867 he made his application, &c., through Mr. James Gregory, claim agent at Columbia, and that he was paid his bounty by Mr. Eastman, bounty agent at Columbia, in June, 1868, and that he only received $150; that his discharge was not returned to him; that he was paid by check, which he cashed at a bank in Nashville, being identified by a colored soldier; that he enlisted in 1863, and that he was discharged in 1866. He states that Mr. Eastman told him he would charge him $25. That after he got his money he went back to Columbia and paid Mr. Eastman $25. He states, further, that Mr. Eastman charged everybody $25. This they have told him. Among these are Alexander Webster, Company E One hundred and eleventh United States colored troops, who is living with Mr. Dobbin, six miles from Columbia; also, Richard Brown, Company B Fortieth United States colored troops, who is living on Knob Creek, about four miles from Columbia; also, Felix Battle, Company F Thirteenth United States colored troops, who is living at the same place as Richard Brown; also, Martin Webster,* Company B Thirteenth United States colored troops, who lives with George Kinsey, about seven miles from Columbia. He further states that Felix Battle sold his claim to Mr. Eastman for $140. He further states that he is living with Mr. Hamilton, who lives on Cherry street, in Nashville, beyond the Decatur depot, and that Mr. Hamilton keeps a shoe store on the corner of College and Church streets, in Nashville. The statement from the bank is to the effect that the amount of the check was $150, payable to Dallas Webster for bounty, signed by Bullock, (Balloch.)

No. 80.—Abraham Summers, Company I Forty-sixth United States colored troops, filed his claim with Mr. Ingersoll about 1866. He states that he received his discharge about four months ago; that he had previously borrowed money from Mr. Ingersoll, about four or five times, in the following amounts: $20, $25, $10, $20, $20, $20, making in all $115; that the last $20 was paid him by Mr. Ingersoll, with the statement that this completed the full sum to which he was entitled; that he has never received a check for the amount of his bounty, but that the last time he called at Mr. Ingersoll's office to obtain the cash installment aforesaid, he was called upon to make his mark on the back of a check, which he did. He was then told to call again for his discharge. He further states that he has never been to Mr. Coon's office; that he never received a check for the amount of his bounty, and that the aforesaid $115 is every cent that he has received, notwithstanding that his discharge shows the amount of his certificate to be $200. He further states that he lives on the corner of Spruce and Cedar streets, in the basement of a frame building.

---

*Paid by Major Wilson, June 26, 1868.

No. 81.—James R. Diggs, private Company M Ninth Tennessee cavalry; Richard White, private Company I Ninth Tennessee cavalry; Willliam H. Goodman, private Company G Ninth Tennessee cavalry; John Harness, private Company L Ninth Tennessee cavalry; William Huckaby, private Company I Ninth Tennessee cavalry; James Parks, private Company L Ninth Tennessee cavalry.

Statement made that William Ross, in connection with C. H. Flourndy, of Knoxville, forged indorsements of soldiers on checks issued by Paymaster —— in payment of bounty.

A. I. Johnson, cases of Wolf, Hart & Co., settled and paid through bureau.

Jackson McClure, Company E First heavy artillery; Frank Malcolm, Company C First heavy artillery; Frank Fine, Company E First heavy artillery; Alexander McSwain, Company E First heavy artillery, certificates issued direct to claimant after the passage of the bureau bounty act, and collected by Wolf, Hart & Co., on forged papers; finally settled by Balloch's check. The claimants had been located at Lafayette, Indiana.

No. 82.—Squire Baker, private Company I Seventeenth United States colored troops, put in his claim with Thomkins & Co., November 7, 1866. He has not received his pay yet; probably no difficulty about it.

No. 83.—Charles Embrey; claim for work on fortifications.

No. 84.—George Easton, Company C Twelfth United States colored troops, states that he lost his discharge a short time after he was mustered out. He further states that he went to Mr. Coons about three months ago, and had his claim made out and filed.

No. 85.—Frances Warren makes inquiries as to the claim of her late husband, London Warren, Company F Fortieth United States colored troops. Her claim was put in by Mr. Miller, of Burnsville, Mississippi. She has never applied to any bureau agent. She was directed to go to Judge Coons.

The commission then adjourned to meet the next day, January 6, 1870, at 9 a. m.

BEN. P. RUNKLE,
Brevet Colonel United States Army.
J. R. LEWIS,
Brevet Colonel United States Army.
J. A. SLADEN,
Brevet Captain United States Army, Recorder.

SEVENTH DAY'S PROCEEDINGS—NASHVILLE, TENNESSEE.

Pursuant to adjournment the commission met at 9 p. m., January 6, 1870, and the following testimony was taken:

Mr. Glassie, having previously written out his testimony, appeared and swore to it.

No. 86.—Dennis Winstead, Company F Thirteenth United States colored troops. He was in the service of the United States two years and a half. He received $211 80, and filed his claim with Mr. Glassie. He received his bounty about fifteen months ago. Appears to be all right.

No. 87.—Mary Edwards, widow of John Edwards, Company H One hundred and first United States colored troops, put in her claim for pension with R. J. Gaines, October 5, 1867. Her husband died while in the service at Clarksville, Tennessee, of small pox. Mr. Coons was called upon by the Washington office to ascertain all the facts in this case, and to return the same, with the original papers, to that office. This appears not to have been done. The case was referred to Mr. Coons.

Statement of Mr. Glassie.

NASHVILLE, TENNESSEE,
January 5, 1870.

GENTLEMEN: In reply to your several questions pertaining to my mode, &c., of loaning money to colored soldiers; the mode adopted by the disbursing officers of the Bureau Refugees, Freedmen, &c., in this city, for paying colored soldiers' bounties, &c.; why there are so many rumors of frauds, &c., on the colored soldiers by the bureau and other agents; why laborers on the fortifications and employés in hospitals, &c., have not been paid, &c., I have the honor to submit the following:

First. I have loaned money to colored soldiers under the following circumstances: When they desired to rent a farm, and required teams, seed, &c.; when they wished to buy a house, a wagon and team, a cow, or anything of that sort that would assist them in making a living; when they had come here from a long distance to look after their claims and had no money to take them home again, and have appealed to me, I have loaned them money. I have also loaned them money to buy necessaries for sick families; to pay doctor's bills; pay funeral expenses; pay fines in court, that they might be free to support their families, and money to employ lawyers to keep them from going to the penitentiary; though I have loaned them but little money since the bureau has instructed Judge Coons to take no more acknowledgments of such advances; this some time in October or November, 1868.

My plan has been this: The soldier and myself would agree upon the amount of money he needed, and what he was willing to pay for it, I to take the chances of his claim coming; I would then draw a check payable to his order for the full amount, hand it to him, make up the papers, send him to the bureau where he could make the acknowledgment, if needs be, show the check; when he returned with the papers properly acknowledged, &c., I would send some one to the bank to identify him and collect the premium on the loan. This was the general mode adopted in the cases in which I was the attorney of record. This money was usually paid at Washington, D. C. Where I loaned parties money whose claims were in the hands of third persons, it was my custom to take two notes, one for the principal and one for the interest. These cases were risky and indulged in but little. I would take up the soldier's receipt for his claim and give him mine; see his attorney of record and agree with him that he would let me know when the claim was allowed and sent to General Howard; hunt up the claimant, send him to the bureau, and in about seven days place a look out over him, and be at the bank or in the neighborhood through a trusty man, who would immediately present his note and collect the money. I have been compelled to rely upon my own vigilance in these cases. I will to-day pay back all the interest, &c., that I have ever collected from colored soldiers, and one thousand dollars in cash, to any one who will secure me in my loans to them.

On several occasions when I had large sums of money loaned to parties, and I had learned that the parties were a little shaky, I have called upon Judge J. B. Coons, stated the facts to him, and asked him to assist me, or to advise the soldier to pay me my money. He would assure me that he could not, or I would get no satisfaction out of him. Subsequently I would meet these parties, and learn from them that they had been paid, and ask them why they had not called and settled with me, and learn from them that Judge Coons had told them that the government had paid all attorneys fees, &c., and not to pay any more, an advice they were very willing to adopt.

Second. The only information I have of the mode of paying these bounties, as adopted by the bureau agent here, is what has come under my own observation in my own business—and that is as follows: I have two forms of printed letters, copies of which are herewith submitted as Exhibits A and B. A is addressed to the bureau agent, and inclosed in B to the claimant; in B I inform the claimant that his claim has been allowed, and that he must call upon the nearest bureau agent and present the inclosed letter, (A.) When the claimant lives a long distance from the bureau agency, I send a copy of A to the agent; inform him that I have notified the claimant to call upon him at a certain time; that he lives a long distance from there, and suggest to him the propriety of writing for the vouchers and check, that the claimant may be saved more than one trip and considerable expense.

Prior to a certain date, about a year ago, when the claimant would call upon Judge Coons for the purpose of indorsing his check or signing their vouchers, the judge would require them to be identified, in addition to their two witnesses, by some one known to him, before he would deliver to them the check, and leave it to the claimant to be identified at the bank, &c. About a year ago this was changed in this way: After the identification, &c., the judge would send his messenger out with the claimant to find some one to identify him at the bank and to see that the claimant received the money himself. This continued several months. During this as well as the preceding period, the claim agents were necessarily compelled to indorse the checks and identify the claimants at the bank. This continued until there was some difficulty between the bureau and the bank; after which time, as I learn, Judge Coons identifies all claimants to the banks. I here assert, as a part of the foregoing statement, that these identifications were all made in the presence of the messenger from the bureau, who inspected everything, and would not let the soldier pay out anything in his presence. I know on one occasion I identified a soldier against whom I had a small note; the soldier was willing to pay it, but the messenger would not permit the payment while he was present. So far as I have been able to see, and I have taken considerable pains to learn, Judge J. B. Coons is one of the most careful disbursing officers I have ever seen. One would believe from his manner of paying that he had reversed the old law maxim, "that every man is deemed to be honest until he is proven to be a rogue." I do not believe he would take a bribe. In my opinion it would not be safe to offer him one. I think if your honors will refer to his treatment of an offer in that direction several months ago, I speak of the Colonel Stevenson or Stevens case, you will bear me out in my assertion. In that case, I am satisfied a direct offer was made him, and he assured of thousands of dollars in a few months if he would adopt the plans then ready to be presented. There his action would have had the appearance of being sanctioned by General Howard, &c., and though there are things or matters in that case not brought out, it not being necessary to checking the swindle in this state, yet there is enough in it to bear me out in my assertion. If he would not take such a good chance I cannot see how he could be induced to take the petty offers that could be made him by any parties here. If a colored man has been swindled by any aid or assistance from Judge

Coons, it is my honest opinion that he, Coons, has been swindled too, for I cannot believe he would allow anything of the kind, knowing it. I think I am fully sustained by the case above referred to, and that said case will show fully the character of the man.

Third. "Why there are so many rumors of frauds on colored soldiers" is a hard question to answer; though I suppose the causes are hydra-headed. Though I have never heard of them in connection with this part of the country, rumor locates a great many in Kentucky, and south of here—some in Memphis; but this latter appear to be by, and not on, the colored men in a majority of cases. The Eastman and Mullen cases, near Clarksville, or Columbia, are the only two that I can recollect of where bureau agents in this section of the State had done anything that could be reflected upon. I have heard that at Memphis the bureau disbursing officers were operating under General Howard's letter. I know nothing of it myself.

I am free to confess that there are a great many claim agents who are not strictly honest—any more so at least than other classes of men; and these no doubt bring out this rumor to a greater or lesser extent—at least it furnished a handle for Madame Rumor to use. But these men are so tied down by the laws, &c., that I cannot see how they can take any advantage of colored soldiers in this part of the State.

I suspect the real causes of the rumor will come under the following heads:

1. The Bureau of Refugees, Freedmen, &c., is not a favorite with the rebels; it is, in fact, obnoxious to a great portion of them, simply because, as they say, it is a "Yankee trick," and is a relic of the war; and the officers and agents in it are, in the classic language of the day, "*Damned nigger-loving Yankees.*" In the minds of the masses the agent is responsible for the existence and continuance of the institution, and of course anything that can be said or done against them is so much done toward breaking down the institution. The newspapers, too, are owned and controlled by this class of people, and are in full sympathy with the people in their hatred of the bureau, and are always open and ready to publish anything against it or its agents, or both, but will never contradict anything.

2. There is here, as there is everywhere else, a lot of leeches that get their living by creating trouble, &c.; who, to get a dollar, would bring a suit in favor of a colored man or anybody else against your honors, if the client could be made to believe there was anything to be gained and the leech could get his dollar. General Fish came near kicking a couple of them out of his court for trying these tricks upon the colored men and keeping up petty excitements to fleece the negroes.

3. The government has been so slow in settling these claims that it is hardly to be wondered at that these men, ignorant as they are, should think that somebody, bureau agents, claim agents, government, General Howard and all, had entered into a conspiracy to cheat them out of their bounty, &c.

4. When these colored men enlisted a larger portion of them were offered and promised $300 bounty by the officers who enlisted them. A enlisted November 20, 1863; the word slave appears on his muster-roll; he receives $108. B enlisted the same day; the word slave does not appear on his muster-roll; he receives $208. C enlisted December 27, 1863, more than a month later; the word slave does not appear on his muster-roll; he receives $300. Now these men serve in the same company, do the same service, and are discharged at the same time.

Is it strange that they should think some one had swindled two of them at least? They cannot understand it.

5. Rebels cannot prosecute claims; the consequence is, those who do must to the people and press be Yankees. This in itself is enough to damn the claim agent; and he and the Yankee bureau and bureau agent are the fellows to perpetrate these frauds set forth in sub-section 4 above.

Fourth. The laborers on the fortifications are not paid, for this reason, as I understand it. When they were first employed on these works there were no provisions made for compensating them. They were taken by general orders as one would take a horse in war times, by confiscation or discovery, consequently no record was kept of this service for many months. After provisions were made for employing them and paying them, their time was kept and the service paid for by Colonel Burrows, who was sent here for that purpose. There are, I suppose, about ten thousand laborers in this country who were employed as first stated, who have not been paid for their service, &c.

Fifth. The persons claiming for services in hospital come under several heads, viz: Those who were employed to assist in and about the hospitals and who were borne properly on the rolls—they signed the rolls every two months and some one got the money. Those who were pressed for a day or two, as on the fortifications, when a large number of hands were required; of these no record was kept. And a third class who, like flies about a kitchen, swarmed about hospitals to find something to eat without working for it. This class are most numerous and loudmouthed. They were always in the way and would steal everything they could lay their hands on, carry it off and sell it to citizens and buy whisky, and smuggle it in to the soldiers, &c.; and now claim pay for having been supported by the government.

There is a large class of claims seldom heard of. I refer to the thousands of colored men who were pressed in as teamsters and who, if ever borne on the rolls, were never paid; here was actual service performed and not paid for.

James H. Holmes, attorney-at-law, &c., room No. 11 Washington Building, Washington, D. C., was through Coffee, Murry, and other counties in that section, a few months ago; got up a large number of these claims, carried them on to Washington, and now reports them disallowed. I am impressed that money was furnished by the government to pay this service at some period, and am satisfied these poor fellows have never been paid.

D. W. GLASSIE.

D. W. Glassie, being sworn, says the statement given above on his own information is true, and that as to what he has heard he believes to be true, this 6th day of January, 1870.

Sworn to before me and subscribed in my presence, this 6th day of January, 1870.

BEN. P. RUNKLE,
Brevet Colonel United States Army.

A.

D. W. GLASSIE'S LAW AND CLAIM OFFICE,
No. 78¼ North Cherry Street, Nashville, Tenn., January 5, 1870.

SIR: The claim of ———— ————, late ———— Company ————, ———— regiment United States colored troops, has been awarded in Treasury certificate No. 999999, and now

BOUNTIES TO COLORED SOLDIERS. 61

awaits your orders at the office of Major General O. O. Howard, Commissioner Bureau Refugees, Freedmen, and Abandoned Lands, Washington, D. C.
It is believed the claimant is within your jurisdiction.
Very respectfully, your obedient servant,

D. W. GLASSIE.

WALTER WIGGINS,
Agent Bureau Freedmen, Buffalo, New York.

B.

D. W. GLASSIE'S LAW AND CLAIM OFFICE,
No. 78½ North Cherry Street, Nashville, Tenn., January 5, 1870.

SIR: Your claim for bounty against the government as ———, Company ———, ——— regiment United States colored troops, has been settled. You will call upon the nearest Freedmen's Bureau agent and hand him the inclosed letter.
Very respectfully, yours,

D. W. GLASSIE.

To ——— ———,

At 1 p. m. the commission adjourned to meet at Columbia, Tennessee, the next day, January 7, 1870, at 9 o'clock a. m.

BEN. P. RUNKLE,
Brevet Colonel United States Army.
J. R. LEWIS,
Brevet Colonel United States Army.
J. A. SLADEN,
Brevet Captain United States Army, Recorder.

EIGHTH DAY'S PROCEEDINGS—COLUMBIA, TENNESSEE.

Pursuant to adjournment, the commission met at Columbia, Tennessee, January 7, 1870, at 9 a. m., in the office of Major J. L. Wilson.

The colored clergymen of the town were sent for and instructed by the commission to bring before it all colored persons who had reason to think that they had been cheated out of their bounty, or any portion thereof.

A very large number of witnesses were examined, but the written evidence of but few was taken.

A number of prominent citizens were examined as to the character and standing of Major Wilson, the bureau agent; and as the Messrs. Hickey (J. M. and A. C.) had been charged with extorting exorbitant fees for prosecuting claims for colored soldiers and their heirs, their sworn statements were taken on these points.

The following is the record of evidence and affidavits, viz:

No. 1.—MARSHALL DOBYNS, Company E Fourteenth United States colored troops, states that Noah & Fuller started a store in Columbia, Tennessee, and gave notice that they would sell on credit to all soldiers having claims against the United States. I purchased $60 worth of goods. The last time I made a purchase Mr. Fuller told me to go up to the bureau, that my money was there. I went up and found Henry Eastman and Mr. Noah. Mr. Eastman paid me $172 less $60, which I owed Noah & Fuller. Received $112. He gave me my discharge, and I afterward gave it to Dr. Cloon, who told me that more was due me. I got the worth of my money, and was satisfied with my bargain. My brother was paid in the same way.

No. 2.—LUCAS GOODMAN, Company I Fifteenth United States colored troops. He first filed his claim with Mr. Eastman, and afterward went to Mr. Cloon, who said he was employed and paid by the government, and then he went to Mr. J. M. Hickey, who said he would collect the claim for him.

No. 3.—BROWN LEFTWICK, Company C Forty-fourth United States colored troops. Filed claim for commutations of rations, while a prisoner of war, with Mr. M. M. Cloon; that he gave the said Cloon his discharge; this about November, 1868.

No. 4.—JAMES WORKMAN, Company D Fifteenth United States colored troops, is precisely the same case as preceding.

Testimony taken at Columbia, Tennessee, on the 7th day of January, 1870.

No. 5.—Mr. L. FRIERSON, being first duly sworn, deposes and says:

Question. What is your name and business ?—Answer. My name is L. Frierson; am assistant cashier of the Bank of Columbia.

Q. How long have you known Mr. Wilson ?—A. I have known Mr. Wilson ever since latter has resided here, viz, about seven months.

Q. Have you transacted business with Mr. Wilson ?—A. Yes, sir.

Q. Please to state the manner of conducting business with Mr. Wilson ?—A. All department checks came to Mr. Wilson, payable to order of claimant. He then came to the bank and stated that he would like the bank to cash those checks, and that he would identify the parties. Sometimes he came with the parties and sometimes without.

Q. Did he pay the money to men in your bank ?—A. Sometimes he paid money to claimants in bank, but usually outside.

Q. Did he bring the claimants to the bank with him ?—A. Sometimes brought the checks himself, but usually paid the parties outside the bank.

Q. Did any white men come with him to the bank when he cashed the checks ?—A. I don't recollect him bringing a white man at any time except this morning.

Q. Who was this white man ?—A. Don't know.

Q. State the manner of making discount on bureau checks ?—A. A register is kept in the bank of discounts, but Mr. Wilson made arrangements to pay discount by the month. This was but a temporary arrangement. Usually the amount is taken when the check is cashed, and is seldom ever above ninety cents.

Q. Are you acquainted with the Messrs. Hickey ?—A. I am acquainted with both the Hickeys.

Q. When he came to the bank, did you ever see any one of the Messrs. Hickey accompany him ?—A. I never saw them accompany Mr. Wilson to the bank, or return to Major Wilson's office with him at such times.

Q. Did you ever hear anybody complain about Major Wilson ?—A. I never heard any complaints of colored people regarding Major Wilson.

Q. Were you acquainted with any of the claimants whose checks you paid ?—A. In many instances I knew the claimants, and would have been likely to have heard such rumors, if any existed.

Q. Are you acquainted with Mr. M. M. Cloon ?—A. I know Mr. Cloon by sight, but am not personally acquainted with him.

Q. Did you ever know of any other Cloon than this one ?—A. I never knew of any other Cloon but this.

Q. Did you ever see the handwriting of Mr. Cloon, enough to identify his signature?—A. I have seen Mr. Cloon's signature often enough to identify it.

Q. Is this his signature?
(Here witness was shown a letter from James Cloon, dated Huntsville, Alabama, November 29, 1869.)
A. It is very much like that of M. M. Cloon, (the Cloon part I have reference to.)

Q. Or is this his writing and signature?
(Was then shown a letter of M. M. Cloon, dated August 2, 1869, from Pulaski.)
A. This signature is not that of M. M. Cloon.

Q. Have you ever cashed checks for Mr. Cloon?—A. I have cashed two or three personal checks for him.

Q. Have you been long engaged in the banking business?—A. I have been engaged in bank business for several years.

Q. What are your opportunities for knowing the character of Mr. Cloon?—A. I have as good an opportunity of knowing Mr. Cloon's character as that of any other man of this community who has not had personal contact with me.

Q. What is Mr. Cloon's general character, and how did he bring himself into notoriety?—A. Mr. Cloon's character is anything but good. I first knew him as a patent medicine vender, and then knew him at the time of personal difficulty with Judge Hughes, the present circuit judge, then State agent at Washington, reflecting on his honesty. This was in a speech on the public square.

Q. Do you think that Mr. Cloon has any interest in the welfare of colored people?—A. I think he has no interest in the colored people, only so far as he can make money out of them.

Q. Have you cashed any of General Balloch's checks for any claim agent?—A. I have never cashed any of General Balloch's checks for any attorneys, except Judge Hughes & Son, L. J. and J. J. Noah.

By Major WILSON:

Q. Was not my business with the bank done in the same manner as my predecessor's, and was it not done in a fair manner?—A. Yes, sir.

LUCIUS FRIERSON.

Sworn to before me and subscribed in my presence this 8th day of January, 1870.

BEN. P. RUNKEL,
Brevet Colonel United States Army.

No. 6.—J. L. BULLOCK sworn:

Question. What is your name and occupation?—Answer. J. L. Bullock, attorney-at-law.

Q. Are you acquainted with Mr. Wilson, bureau agent, &c.?—A. I am.

Q. What is his general reputation?—A. The best of any agent who has been stationed here. He could get more indorsements as to personal honor and integrity than any other one.

Q. Are you acquainted with Major Wilson's manner of transacting business; and if so, how has he conducted himself in that behalf?—A. I am. I have always known him to do right. I have had such confidence in him that I have directed colored men, former servants and clients, to call on him, for the reason that he would do them justice. I have transacted claim business with him.

64   BOUNTIES TO COLORED SOLDIERS.

Q. Do you know anything against Mr. Eastman of your own knowledge?—A. I cannot say without referring to my papers.
Q. Were you acquainted with Colonel Reeves, formerly agent, &c.; and if so, what was his general reputation for honesty and integrity?—A. I had but little acquaintance with him. As far as I heard, he stood well.
                                               J. L. BULLOCK.

Sworn to before me and subscribed in my presence this 7th day of January, 1870.
                                               BEN. P. RUNKLE,
                                      Brevet Colonel United States Army.

No. 7.—Mr. A. C. HICKEY, being first duly sworn, deposes and says:
Question. What is your name and occupation?—Answer. A. C. Hickey, attorney-at-law. I had a claim agent's commission in 1865 and 1866.
Q. Are you acquainted with Mr. Wilson?—A. Yes, sir; ever since he has been stationed here.
Q. I now read to you the following statement. Will you please state whether it is, in whole or part, true or false? "Again, four correspondents of the said firm, namely, J. M. Hickey and A. M. Hickey, of Columbia, Tennessee, and Calvin and Charles A. Jones, of Pulaski, Tennessee, are associated with the aforesaid John L. Wilson, the bureau agent, (for several counties of middle Tennessee,) previously named, in his swindling scheme, which is carried on as follows: The claimant goes to the office of the said Wilson, and asks if his claim is ready for settlement. Wilson says 'No.' The claimant tells him that his claim agent told him that it was settled. Wilson says, 'If you depend upon your claim agent you will never get it;' in the mean time telling claimant to go and see the Hickeys or Joneses, assuring him that they will promptly receive his money. The claimant complies, and goes forthwith to said parties, who tell him that they must get fifteen per cent. for getting his bounty. Of course the poor, illiterate negro would give twenty-five or fifty per cent. as quick as he would fifteen, and complies at once to their proposition, when he is ordered to report at their office in about ten days, at which time he will get his money. Claimant accordingly appears back at the appointed time, and is taken to Wilson's office, after which Wilson goes to the bank with claimant's check for bounty, it having been previously indorsed by the claimant, and draws the amount of said check, returns and pays to the claimant the amount of the same in the presence of the Hickeys, who takes the money out of their claimant's hands, and deducts his fifteen per cent., and the balance he returns to the claimant." (Read from M. M. Cloons's letter to Second Auditor, November 29, 1869.)—A. All this statement is false, except the following: Can't say what claimant does in Wilson's office. If Wilson ever told a claimant any such thing, I never heard it or heard of it, and neither I nor my brother (so far as I know) ever charged any man fifteen per cent. for services rendered concerning his claim. We charged a fee for services rendered as attorneys to colored men, but positively say that I never had any understanding with Major Wilson where, when, or how any claimant or claimants were to be paid. The fees we have received I received at my own office, but never received one at Major Wilson's office in Columbia, but have at Thomas M. Jones's office at Pulaski, where Major Wilson was paying; but never had any arrangement or understanding with Major Wilson in the premises. I have asked him when he would pay at Pulaski, but do not know that

Major Wilson knew that I collected any fees there. The fee that I charged was ten per cent. on the amount collected. Major Wilson paid in Major Jones's back office. Major Wilson occupied the back office. I collected in the front office.

Q. Did you ever, directly or indirectly, pay any money to Major Wilson for any services rendered, directly or indirectly, in connection with the claim business?—A. I never did.

A. C. HICKEY.

Sworn to before me and subscribed in my presence this 7th day of January, 1870.

J. A. SLADEN,
Brevet Captain United States Army, Recorder of Commission.

A recess of one hour was taken from 1 to 2 o'clock p. m. for dinner. The commission, at 5.30 p. m., adjourned until the next day, January 8, 1870, at 9 a. m.

BEN. P. RUNKLE,
Brevet Colonel United States Army.
J. R. LEWIS,
Brevet Colonel United States Army.
J. A. SLADEN,
Brevet Captain United States Army, Recorder.

NINTH DAY'S PROCEEDINGS—COLUMBIA, TENNESSEE.

The commission met at nine o'clock a. m., January 8, 1870. A large number of witnesses were examined, but very little testimony of an important character was elicited.

Very many of the witnesses stated that although they had received the full amount of their bounty and back pay, Doctor Cloon had taken their discharges, telling them that they were going to have more allowed them.

The following is the record of evidence, viz:

No. 8.—THOMAS GORDON, Company A Thirteenth United States colored troops, entered his discharge with Mr. Ingersoll, over three years ago, who gave him a receipt therefor; this receipt he gave to Mr. Eastman, who gave him his receipt therefor. He received $116 30 bounty in July last, and served about two years and six months in the United States service.

Statement of W. Vance Thompson.

No. 9.—W. VANCE THOMPSON, a citizen of Columbia, Tennessee, states, in regard to J. L. Wilson, disbursing agent at that place, as follows: When Major Wilson was arrested by warrant from United States Commissioner L. J. Noah, on a charge of defrauding colored soldiers out of their bounty, or a part thereof, I went on his bond for his appearance, and accompanied him to Nashville, and acted as his attorney in the investigation of the charge before said Noah. I heard all the testimony in said case, and was very much surprised when he was bound over to answer the charge before the United States circuit court. It was clearly proven that Major Wilson invariably, and particularly in the cases specified in the charge on which he was then arraigned, paid the full amount of the bounty, less the small amount charged by the bank for cashing the checks, over to the parties entitled to the same. That he always refused to pay any part thereof to any one else, even when the claimant was indebted to those parties, and had deposited the claim agent's receipt as collateral, and authorized them to draw the money. It was in proof that Major Wilson, having no regular office in Pulaski, and visiting that town only once a week for the purpose of paying off claims due parties living in Giles County, transacted his business in the back room of the Messrs. Jones, attorneys-at-law. The only color of propriety, in the judgment of the commissioner, was the fact that, after Major Wilson had paid the claimants their money, the Messrs. Jones collected from them certain fees, which they claimed were due them for services rendered in corresponding with the department at Washington in regard to their claims for bounty. On one occasion, perhaps, a claimant asked Major Wilson if the Messrs. Jones had any right to charge such fees, and his reply was that his duty was to pay over the entire amount of the check; that there were no charges, so far as he knew, except the small amount charged by the bank for cashing the same; that he had nothing to do with their contract with the Messrs. Jones, and knew nothing about it. It was proven by the Messrs. Hickey, attorneys at this place, that they had done a great deal of business for discharged colored soldiers in the way of corresponding with the department in regard to their bounty and back pay, &c.; that for this they usually contracted with said parties to charge them ten per cent., to be paid when the money was collected; that many claims had been paid to their clients by Major Wilson, but that Major Wilson had in no instance retained any fee for them, nor had any of their clients ever paid them their fee in the presence of Major Wilson, and in many instances, indeed, Major Wilson knew nothing about the fact that they had had any connection with the claims whatever. One M. M. Cloon, at whose instance the warrant had issued, testified that he was claim agent, and had had many claims for collection in Giles County. His chief complaint seemed to be that Major Wilson did not give the check of General Balloch to the claimants themselves, but instead thereof had the check cashed, and paid the proceeds to the claimant. Major Wilson produced his books, &c., which were proven by Major Coons, chief disbursing officer at Nashville, to be properly kept, &c.; he also produced the order of General Balloch, directing all disbursing officers to have the checks cashed, and pay the money over to the claimants, in order to protect them from sharpers, &c. The commissioner, however, bound Major Wilson over to the United States circuit court, and I went on his bond.

Before the session of the said court, I met Commissioner Noah in Nashville, and he told me that he was satisfied Major Wilson would never be convicted before a jury, but still an indictment would certainly be found against him, and he would be put to much trouble and expense; he, therefore, would advise him to pay all costs, so far as they had accrued, and he thought he could induce the Attorney General to drop the matter. I advised the major to this course on the score of economy. But he stated he could not accede to or even entertain the proposition, because the charges preferred were a reflection upon his honor as an officer and a man, and if he should pay the costs it would look like he feared an investigation, and thereby compromise his standing as a government officer; he, therefore, declined the proposition. Subsequently, as I have been informed by a member of the grand jury, the grand jury refused to find a true bill against Major Wilson, but did find several against Cloon, his prosecutor, for defrauding discharged colored soldiers. I have known Major Wilson ever since he came here; have seen him frequently settle with claimants; he is always particular to pay into their own hands the proceeds of the department check;

have never heard any of the colored people complain of him; think he is the most efficient disbursing officer that has ever been on duty at this place. I know the reputation of M. M. Cloon in this community. He first came here as a vender of patent medicine; afterward he went into the claim agency business. Though I know nothing of my own knowledge, as I never had any dealings with him, still I have heard many grave charges against him, and the general opinion here is that he has swindled the colored people of this county and Giles out of many thousand dollars. I never heard any charges against Colonel Reeves, former disbursing officer at this place. Shortly after, Mr. Eastman, who preceded Colonel Reeves, left here, there were many rumors prejudicial to his good standing; it was asserted that he had swindled the colored people out of large amounts, but I know nothing as to the truth or falsity of these charges.

W. VANCE THOMPSON.

Sworn to before me and subscribed in my presence this 8th day of January, 1870.

BEN. P. RUNKLE,
Brevet Colonel United States Army.

Testimony of J. M. Hickey, taken at Columbia, Tennessee, on the 9th day of January, 1870.

No. 10.—Mr. J. M. HICKEY, being first duly sworn, deposes and says:

Question. You have heard the affidavit of your brother, A. C. Hickey; and if so, is it true?—Answer. Yes, as far as I know.

Q. Please make any further statement in the premises within your knowledge.—A. I did the principal part of the business in the name of myself and my brother at Columbia. We were slightly in the business before I met Hon. Samuel Arnell. He called me on the street in Columbia and told me he was glad I had been getting up claims, and if I wanted his assistance he would cheerfully give it to me. He said he was glad I had taken them, and insisted I should get up all I could find in the county. I did so, and made out a complete list of all I had, and mailed them at his request to him at Washington. He said the negroes had been swindled or deceived by claim agents such as Cloon, and he desired the business to be put in the hands of an honest man. I told him I wished to explain the manner in which I had done all this business, and be advised and aided by him. He told me he would cheerfully aid me and give me advice at all times I might call on him. I told him I charged the negroes a fee of about ten per cent. He said he approved of my action; to make out a list, send it to him, and he would put them through as soon as possible; he further said that the colored men supported him; he felt a deep interest in them, and wanted to see them paid off as soon as possible, and did not want to see Cloon and these other fellows have anything to do with the colored people. I then, thinking it all right, went into the business. I had no license as a claim agent, and did not file any claims in my own name, and only a few through Chipman, Hosmer & Co., Washington, D. C. These I acted in were all old claims that I was looking into and inquiring about at the request of claimants.

Q. Do you know M. M. Cloon; and if so, what is his reputation for honesty and integrity?—A. I know him by sight only. He has rather a bad reputation in this county.

Q. Do you know of any other Cloon than the said M. M. Cloon?—A. I do not, nor ever heard of one.

Q. Please state the action of M. M. Cloon in the cases of certain claimants for pension who should have visited the pension commissioner.—A. By correspondence with the department I have official information that pensions have been granted in about nine cases in my possession. I visited the pension commission while they were in Nashville, to obtain information in reference to these cases. They instructed me to come home, get up claimants, and meet the commission in Pulaski on a certain day. The evening before that day I was arrested, sent to Nashville on a warrant obtained by one M. M. Cloon. During my absence from Columbia some person, whom I had reason to believe was an agent of Cloon, read an order at the depot to all the claimants whom I had sent there to go home, and that the commission would be in Columbia in three weeks and pay them off. In nine or ten cases in my hands pension certificates had been sent to O'Neil & Dufour, and in some cases they notified me that the same had been sent to their agent, M. M. Cloon. Cloon has never answered my communications, with one exception, Mary Roundtree's case, and then answered that it was not necessary for her to have her certificate; and the following-named parties of the aforesaid cases have never received their certificates: Mary Roundtree, of Columbia, Tennessee, wife of Henry Roundtree, Company C Seventeenth United States colored troops; Bidder English, of Columbia, Tennessee; Amanda Grimes, of Columbia, Tennessee; Rachel Crawford, of Columbia, Tennessee—Company K Twelfth United States colored troops; Ruthie Fox, Columbia, Tennessee; Rhoda Jones, of Columbia, Tennessee. Most of these parties are well known to me as the identical parties named in their applications.

J. M. HICKEY.

Sworn to before me and subscribed in my presence this 8th day of January, 1870.

BEN. P. RUNKLE,
Brevet Colonel United States Army.

At 4 p. m. the commission decided to return to Nashville, Tennessee, on the night train, and on the next day (Sunday) visit the pension agent, and obtain from his records the statements in the cases of pension claimants mentioned in preceding records, and accordingly adjourned.

BEN. P. RUNKLE,
Brevet Colonel United States Army.
J. R. LEWIS,
Brevet Colonel United States Army.
J. A. SLADEN,
Brevet Captain U. S. Army, Recorder.

TENTH DAY'S PROCEEDINGS—NASHVILLE, TENNESSEE.

The commission met at Nashville, Tennessee, January 9, 1870; but the pension agent being absent from the city, the commission was unable to examine the records, and accordingly adjourned to meet at Pulaski, Tennessee, the next day, January 10, 1870.

BEN. P. RUNKLE,
Brevet Colonel United States Army.
J. R. LEWIS,
Brevet Colonel United States Army.
J. A. SLADEN,
Brevet Captain U. S. A., Recorder.

ELEVENTH DAY'S PROCEEDINGS—PULASKI, TENNESSEE.

The commission met at Pulaski January 10, 1870, at 9 a. m.

In view of the fact that serious charges of swindling the freed people had been preferred against the law firm of Jones & Sons, at this place, they were invited to be present, as well as Major Wilson, bureau agent, and M. M. Cloon, who had preferred the charges against the Joneses and Major Wilson.

Mr. C. P. Jones, of the above-mentioned firm, was present most of the time during the sitting of the commission.

The following is the evidence taken, viz:

No. 1.—HENRY HARGROVE, Company K One hundred and tenth United States colored troops, filed his claim with Captain Beckert about three years ago last Christmas. About two years ago he went with Captain Beckert to Squire Baugh's office, where the captain loaned him $50. He there signed in Squire Baugh's presence a paper purporting to be a note for the amount of money he loaned him, which Squire Baugh witnessed. About last July he received by the hand of a comrade his discharge, inclosing $40, in a sealed envelope; this came from Captain Beckert. This is all the money he has ever received on account of his claims against the government. He was a prisoner of war about eight months, and was entitled to commutation of rations as such. (Mr. M. M. Cloon's receipt for his discharge exhibits as follows: Treasury certificate 366,706, for $203 20.)

HENRY + HARGROVE.
his mark.

Sworn to before me and subscribed in my presence this 11th day of January, 1870.

J. A. SLADEN,
Brevet Captain United States Army, Recorder.

No. 2.—STEPHEN SLOSS, Company B One hundred and eleventh United States colored troops, filed his claim, but did not know who with; went to Captain Judd, at Pulaski, and he told him to go to Mr. Cloon; that he would get his bounty better and quicker than he (Judd) could. Then Dr. Cloon took his claim and put it in for him, and Major Wilson paid him about five or six months ago. Received of Mr. Wilson $301; out of this came legal fees, $11 50. Mr. Jones took him aside and said that he was to pay him something. He replied that it was hard for him if he should pay out anything out of what the government had given him. He asked Major Wilson if it was right that he should pay Mr. Jones $15, and he said that he had got all he was entitled to, and that the legal fees were taken out. He then paid Mr. Jones the $15. He went to Nashville at the request of Mr. Cloon, to testify before Commissioner Noah. He had no notice from any one but Mr. Cloon. He paid his own fare to Nashville, but Fisher paid it back, although he holds him accountable for it. The second time he went to Nashville, he was summoned in writing. He never employed Mr. Jones. A letter came to the post office last Saturday addressed to him, but they would not let him have it till he was identified. He went to Mr. Cloon and he got it for him, and said it was from General Howard, and read it to him, and it purported to be about his pension; that his money was coming soon. Mr. Cloon has told him that Major Wilson ought not to pay in money, but ought to pay in checks. He saw the pension agents at Nashville last summer, and they told him that his case was all right, and that he would get his pension.

                his
           STEPHEN + SLOSS.
                mark.

Sworn to at Pulaski, Tennessee, January 10, 1870.
              J. A. SLADEN,
        Brevet Captain United States Army, Recorder.

No. 3.—NANCY DAILEY, widow of Louis Vance, Company I One hundred and tenth United States colored troops, put in her claim with Mr. Cloon. Mr. Cloon came down to Veto Station, and got several of our claims. I never knew there was any bureau here. I put in my claim about March, 1867. Mr. Cloon told me to come to him and bring money, and he would get my money for me in three months. Jones got the claim from me, when Cloon left. I received from J. M. Hickey, per C. P. Jones, as follows:

Received of Nancy Dailey her paper or receipt of M. M. Cloon, for the purpose of presenting her claim for bounty, &c., for which I am to return or account for as an attorney-at-law.

               J. M. HICKEY,
             Per C. P. JONES.
MAY 22, 1867.

No. 4.—ADELINE WILLIAMS, mother of Isaac Williams, corporal Company K One hundred and tenth United States colored troops. Has got a claim for pension; put it in the hands of Mr. Cloon, February 7, 1868. Her son did not support her. She paid Mr. Cloon one dollar.

No. 5.—JERRY JENKINS, of Company K One hundred and tenth United States colored troops, being duly sworn, deposes and says that he gave his discharge to Captain Beckert, about three years ago last Christmas; that about two years ago Captain Beckert called upon him, and loaned him $20; that he signed his name to some papers, but that no other person was present; that last fall a year ago he received his discharge, inclosing $40 from Captain Beckert; that the $40 inclosed was for commutation of rations while a prisoner of war, and that the foregoing amounts are all that he has received in payment for his bounty and commutation of rations; that his discharge and the $40 aforesaid were brought to him in a sealed envelope by a former regimental comrade.

The exhibit of his discharge shows that the certificate was No. 366,730, for $100 bounty, $100 additional bounty, and $3 20 difference of pay; dated December 10, 1867. He says that more of the colored people think well of Dr. Cloon than think ill of him, although a great many of them think that he has cheated them. Many think that Major Wilson has cheated them by retaining $10 on a hundred.

               his
           JERRY + JENKINS.
              mark.

Sworn to and signed at Pulaski, Tennessee, in the presence of—
             J. A. SLADEN,
       Brevet Captain United States Army, Recorder.

No. 6.—WILLIAM REEDIS, being first duly sworn, deposes and says: I was a private of Company I One hundred and tenth United States colored troops. I filed my claim with Captain Beckert. (Discharge shows that he should have received $300 20, less legal fees, but witness states that he only received $100 advanced on it.) I sold my claims for commutations of rations as a prisoner of war to Dr. M. M. Cloon for

BOUNTIES TO COLORED SOLDIERS. 71

$20. I signed papers in Dr. Cloon's office at the time. I received my discharge at the same time. This happened some time last summer. He, Mr. Cloon, stated to me that he had received it from Captain Beckert. I was a prisoner of war for five months. Captain Beckert stated that he would receive $200 more of his bounty. I know it was Captain Beckert, because he was an officer in my regiment. Major Mann was with Captain Beckert, but seemed to have nothing whatever to do with the latter.

WILLIAM + REEDIS.
his mark.

Sworn to and signed at Pulaski, Tennessee, January 10, 1870, in the presence of—

J. A SLADEN,
Brevet Captain United States Army, Recorder.

P. S.—The certificate on his discharge shows certificate No. 366,667, dated December 7, 1867, $300 bounty, twenty cents difference of pay.

Mr. RICHARD HARRIS, being first duly sworn, deposes and says:

My name is Richard Harris. I am a grocer. I have lived here four years. I know the colored people pretty generally of this town and vicinity. I knew Captain Judd and the officers succeeding him. I know Mr. M. M. Cloon, and never heard of any other Cloon. I know that colored soldiers, or their relatives, have been swindled out of their bounty or a portion thereof. I have a memorandum of their names, but do not remember them. I saw checks from the bureau agents, Captains Judd and Harlan, (? Carlin) which were afterward cashed by Mr. Cloon. Some of these checks I saw before they were taken to Mr. Cloon. On one or two occasions I was present when the claimants received their checks. I saw Green Trotter, a relative of some soldier, go with his check from the bureau agent to Mr. Cloon. I saw this check before it was taken to Cloon, and I afterward counted the money which the man said he had received from Mr. Cloon; this discrepancy amounted to between $100 and $200. This man stated that he had received some advances from Mr. Cloon, but nothing near the amount deducted. It was a common custom that Mr. Cloon, for about six months or more, kept a colored man, Anderson Joyce, as a runner, whose business it was to conduct claimants who had just been paid from the bureau agent's office to Cloon's. I have no positive evidence that the bureau agent was implicated, although while he stated that it was an outrage, he nevertheless seemed loth to break it up. Then I wrote to General Carlin in reference to the same thing, which letter was returned to the agent at this place. During the time that Simpson, agent, and Carlin, his clerk, were here, the same thing was done. I then visited General Carlin in person, and made the same complaints again, when the thing was broken up. An arrangement was then made with Messrs. Cox and L. Roseneau & Co. to cash the checks of claimants; but it seemed not to remedy the matter, as they all commenced to go to Mr. Roseneau. I once made Mr. Roseneau refund fifty dollars from a man from whom he had retained it. This did not occur much during Captain Judd's administration; but mostly during Mr. Simpson's. I have recollection of some ten or fifteen, maybe more, individual cases, but there was a general complaint. It went on all the time while checks were paid, and the complaint is still general. The complaints are now, that charges of ten or fifteen per cent. discount are made by Mr. Jones and Mr. Wilson, and that the same is done at Mr. Jones's office. All complain more or less. The cases that came under my observation when Mr. Cloon cashed the checks, show that he deducted generally about fifty dollars. Mr. Cloon does not stand well with the colored people. Captain Judd stood well among them, but Major Wilson does not. The only reason seems to be that he discounts the amount to be paid.

Memorandum from my records:

May 15, 1868.—Nathaniel Holt Prospect, lives with George Westmoreland; his check calls for $193 40; Cloon only gives him $140 for it. (See testimony of Dufour and list.)

Horace Braidy, lives near Lynnville Station; Cloon bought his commutation check for $20.

Robert Alexander, lives at Lester Station; his check calls for $219 30; Cloon got it for $140.

July 21, 1868.—Turner Harville, Bradshaw Creek; Cloon gets his commutation for $25.

May 18, 1868.—William Alexander, near Lynnville; Cloon sent for him and wanted to buy his claim for $140.

R. HARRIS.

Sworn to at Pulaski, Tennessee, and signed in the presence of—
J. A. SLADEN,
Brevet Captain United States Army, Recorder.

PULASKI, TENNESSEE, *January* 11, 1870.

The undersigned desires to file this paper as an addition to the testimony given by him yesterday relative to frauds which came to his knowledge that have been practiced upon colored bounty claimants by claim agents and others. I stated yesterday that the number of cases that had come to my knowledge in which claimants were swindled was about fifteen; upon reflection I now state that the cases of the above nature were many more than the above number, and that they were numerous. But I cannot now give the precise nature or number of said cases, but will state that ever since bounty claimants have been receiving their bounty or back pay, excepting the brief period during which their bounty was disbursed by Officer Reeves, said claimants have been more or less swindled, or exorbitant prices charged for the collection of bounty. The amount lost in this way depended upon the intelligence or the ignorance of the claimant. I stated yesterday that but few cases of said frauds were practiced during Captain Judd's administration. I now state that some few of these cases were brought to Captain Judd's notice, and he seemed to wink at them. I will further state in regard to the percentage charged by Mr. Jones, during Disbursing Officer Wilson's administration here, that it is generally understood among the colored people that he, Jones, and Wilson, understood each other. If it is asked why I have made myself so officious in regard to wanting these frauds brought to light, I answer from the fact that the parties so swindled are of my own race, ignorant and less fortunate than myself, and that I felt it to be the duty of the good citizen to do all in my power to have these evil-doers exposed, and, if possible, brought to justice.

I was born and raised in Nashville, Tennessee, and have been living here about four years.

RICHARD HARRIS.

Sworn to at Pulaski, Tennessee, January 11, 1870, in the presence of—
J. A. SLADEN,
Brevet Captain United States Army, Recorder.

J. F. FISHER, colored, of Pulaski, being first duly sworn, deposes and says:

My name is J. F. Fisher; I am a grocer, and have lived here four years. I am generally acquainted with the colored people, and have known all the bureau agents. I was cognizant of the Green Trotter case. He acknowledged that Mr. Cloon loaned him $150 to buy a horse with. I found that Mr. Cloon retained about $70, over and above advances, and when I went to Cloon he returned to Trotter about $50, and said to him, " Damn you, I bought the claim for $150, but rather than have any more trouble, take the money." Cloon stated that he had bought the claim for $150, which he had advanced to Trotter. The money which he finally retained was only about principal advanced and ten per cent. interest on the same. George Fogg was paid by Mr. Wilson in the back room of Jones's office, and when he had received his money, Mr. Jones presented his bill for services. Fogg demurred to the amount, but finally paid $10. There were two other cases where sums were paid to Mr. Jones for services, in my presence; these two being after claimants had left Major Wilson's presence. Several claimants came to me; complained that Dr. Cloon had cheated them out of large sums; but in all these cases I found that Dr. Cloon had advanced amounts equal to the amounts retained. In the case of Aleck Everly, Mr. Cloon advanced $100 or $150, every cent of which Dr. Cloon lost. Dr. Cloon has left charges for advances with me for collection; but I have never collected one cent. The colored people regard Mr. Cloon as their friend, and think he has labored hard for their welfare.

Question by Major Wilson: Where are the discharges that Mr. Cloon left in your charge?—Answer. He never left a discharge in my hands, to my knowledge; but he has left, for safe-keeping, in my possession a valise, which I locked in my safe. I saw him take discharges from this valise and return them to colored soldiers. I did not see them pay Dr. Cloon any sum whatever. I have on some occasions acted as Mr. Cloon's agent. I have never received one cent, either directly or indirectly, from Mr. Cloon, nor has Doctor Cloon ever collected one cent for me, on any bills of mine against my customers. Major Wilson came to me and demanded of me the papers Mr. Cloon had left in my possession, but I positively affirm that Major Wilson did not ask for discharges, but for Mr. Cloon's papers. I have never had any difficulty with Mr. Wilson, except since the trial before Commissioner Noah there has been some hard feeling. I never went to Major Wilson to collect my bills, except in the case of one Clay, who owed me $105, and I never asked for permission to collect at the pay table. When I asked Major Wilson about the Clay case, he said he would probably pay him some time here at Pulaski. I have never been summoned in the Major Wilson case, except when I was summoned to appear before Commissioner Noah. The witnesses that appeared before the commissioner, at Nashville, are Green Turner, Stephen Sloss, Mina Carter, and Susan Carter. I swear positively that I have never collected one cent in the Joneses' office; this is to the best of my recollection. I have never received one cent from John Young, or any other person, in the Joneses' office. I wish to add that John Young had paid me some money, but I do not remember whether it was in Jones's office or where, nor the amount.

J. F. FISHER.

Sworn and subscribed to at Pulaski, January 10, 1870, in the presence of—

J. A. SLADEN,
Brevet Captain United States Army, Recorder.

No. 7.—PALDO BAILEY, Company K One hundred and tenth United States infantry. I put in my claim with Captain Beckert, December 19, 1866. Captain Beckert was my captain. Captain B. came to Squire Baugh's office about one year thereafter, and loaned me $50. I signed a note for the money; there was another low, chunky, black-whiskered man present; he did not say anything or sign any papers. No other white man was present. He did not tell me what he would charge me for the money. Said there was $300 coming to me beside my commutation money, in all $350. He said I would have to pay him back when I got my money; that he just lent it to me out of his pocket to accommodate me. Signed only one paper. Thomas Upshaw, Company K One hundred and tenth colored troops, was present. Last year I received from Captain Beckert, through my brother, Doc. Bailey, $40 and my discharge. I was a prisoner eight months. I never have received any further sum of money from any person whomsoever. Discharge shows an allowance per certificate 366693, December 10, 1867, $100 bounty, $100 additional bounty, $3 20 difference of pay; in all $203 20. Commutation of rations settled. Squire Baugh was not at home at the time I received this loan.

his
PALDO + BAILEY,
mark.

Sworn and subscribed to at Pulaski, Tennessee, January 10, 1870, in the presence of—

J. A. SLADEN,
Brevet Captain United States Army, Recorder.

ATHENS, ALA., *December* 19, 1866.

This day received the discharge papers of Paldo Bailey, for the purpose of prosecuting his claims for bounty, &c., due him by the United States government, through Chipman, Hosmer & Co., in Washington, D. C.

BECKERT & ATKIN.

No. 8.—CHARLES ASHWOOD, Company A One hundred and tenth United States colored troops, being first duly sworn, deposes and says: I put in my claim with Colonel Rugg, at Huntsville, in 1866; got no receipt. In 1867 Colonel Rugg lent me $15. Shortly after I received my bounty from Colonel Rugg. At the time I borrowed the money I signed one paper. When I was paid I went to Colonel Rugg, who went to the bureau office, got the money, brought it to his own office, and paid me $160. Can count money. (Tested.) The $160 includes the $15 loaned me. I went to the bureau office, but did not say anything to the officer; Colonel Rugg did all the talking. The discharge shows certificate 346678, November 17, 1867, $100 bounty; $100 additional bounty; $48 difference of pay; in all $248. Colonel Rugg said $160 was all that was coming. I knew more than $160 was coming to me, for my discharge had been previously returned to me by Colonel Rugg. He said I must be careful and not tell any one how much he paid me.

his
CHARLES + ASHWOOD.
mark.

Sworn and subscribed to at Pulaski, Tennessee, January 10, 1870, in the presence of—

J. A. SLADEN,
Brevet Captain United States Army, Recorder.

BOUNTIES TO COLORED SOLDIERS. 75

No. 9.—THOMAS UPSHUR, Company K One hundred and tenth regiment, being sworn, deposes and says: That he put in his discharge with Captain Beckert the 19th day of December, 1866; that Captain Beckert paid him $25, two years ago Christmas, at Squire Baugh's, before whom he signed some papers; that the next spring he got a check from the bureau agent at Pulaski, Mr. Simpson, for $135 70, which he carried to Dr. Cloon, who took it up and paid him $120 70. He (Cloon) told him he (Upshur) owed to the government the amount which he (Cloon) took out; that last summer he got a check from Dr. Cloon for $37 20, which Mr. Fisher took up and paid him $37. That he gave Captain Beckert his note, or supposed it to be a note, for $25; that nothing was said as to what they would charge him for it. When he first gave his discharge to Captain Beckert he told him he would get $100 or $150. The last check of $37 20, which Cloon gave him, was for commutation of rations, which Cloon had collected; Captain Beckert put in the claim for commutation. This is all he has ever received on his claims. Never signed any papers in Mr. Cloon's office until he gave him the check. He saw Mr. Cloon some two weeks before he got the check for commutation, and Cloon said he would collect it. He told me to come in two weeks. In two weeks he went, and was told to come in the afternoon. He went in the afternoon, and was paid; his discharge is at home. He enlisted the 15th of December, 1863, and was mustered out the 6th day of February, 1866, the same as Jerry Jenkins of his company and regiment.

THOMAS + UPSHUR.
his mark.

Sworn and subscribed to at Pulaski, Tennessee, January 10, 1870, in the presence of—

J. A. SLADEN,
Brevet Captain United States Army, Recorder.

No. 10.—JOHN YOUNG, Company F One hundred and eleventh United States colored troops, being first duly sworn, deposes and says: I filed my claim with Captain Judd some three years ago, and was paid by Major Wilson about last month. I have only received $100, and think I ought to have received more. I took my discharge immediately to Mr. Cloon, who gave me a receipt for it, and told me that I would have $200 more. At the time I received my money in the back room Fisher was standing close by me, and told me to come into the front room. When we had come into the front room Fisher showed me a note for $100, which I had given to Adam Garrett, about four months before, and demanded that I should pay the full amount of the note. This I would not do, but finally paid him $55, and promised to pay the balance when I got the rest of my bounty.

JOHN + YOUNG.
his mark.

Sworn and subscribed to this the 10th of January, 1870, in the presence of—

J. A. SLADEN,
Brevet Captain United States Army, Recorder.

No. 11.—GREEN TURNER, Company A First United States colored heavy artillery, being first duly sworn, deposes and says: I put in my claim with M. M. Cloon, at Pulaski; received my bounty, $302, last June, from Major Wilson, in Jones & Son's back office. He paid me money. He did not say anything except that the bank charged a small amount for discount. I then came into the front room, and Lawyer Jones being there I asked him how much I owed him; he said $20, and I paid it without any words. Some time previous, about three weeks, I brought Mr. Cloon's receipt for discharge to Mr. Jones, and asked him to hurry up the money. He said he could do so, and said that he would charge me $20, which I agreed to pay. Never went to any bureau agent, but went to Mr. Jones, because so many were getting their money, and could hear nothing from mine. I never heard a word against Captain Judd, who was bureau agent at the time I filed my claim, but went to Mr. Cloon because all seemed to think he was the man. I thought Mr. Cloon was a government agent, for he told me so in his office. The last time I saw Mr. Cloon, previous to going to Mr. Jones, he told me the claim was payable. I don't know whether he said he was a claim agent or a government agent. I thought he was sent out by the government, and so did all the colored people. Mr. Jones told me he was not a claim agent, but acted as my attorney, but would not have anything to do with the claim agency business, because there was so much swindling. When I paid Mr. Jones $20 Major Wilson was not present, the door between the two rooms being closed. I was first notified that I must go to Nashville, by Mr. Cloon. I got no summons. The second time I was summoned, and went before a large court, at least a dozen men. Paid my own expenses on the first trip, and have not been paid. The second time I was paid.

GREEN $\overset{\text{his}}{+}$ TURNER.
mark.

Sworn and subscribed to at Pulaski, Tennessee, January 10, 1870, in the presence of—

J. A. SLADEN,
Brevet Captain United States Army, Recorder.

No. 12.—JAMES VANCE, 1st, Company I One hundred and tenth United States colored troops, being first duly sworn, deposes and says: I gave my claim to Captain Beckert in December, 1866. In about one year Captain Beckert came to me and loaned me $50. Colonel Reeves only paid me about $130. My discharge shows the amount of my bounty, &c., to $300 20. Colonel Reeves told me that this was all that was coming to me. I sold my claim of commutations of rations to Dr. Cloon for $25—it was worth probably about $50—as I was in prison for eight or nine months. I got my discharge before I got my bounty. Captain Beckert sent it to me. Colonel Reeves told me to bring my discharge, but when I brought it the colonel did not look at it.

Question to both witnesses, *i. e.*, this witness and James Brown following, by M. M. Cloon: Did you receive the money advanced from Captain Beckert or from Major Mann?

Answer by James Vance and James Brown: From Captain Beckert. He was a captain in my own regiment, and his name was Beckert.

Question by Mr. M. M. Cloon to both witnesses, *i. e.*, this witness and James Brown: Did you give your notes for the money received, or were they by you acknowledged before a justice of the peace or any other officer?

Answered by James Vance: I did give my note before Squire Baugh.
Answered by James Brown: I did give my note before Squire Baugh.

Question by Mr. M. M. Cloon to both witnesses as above: Did they tell you what interest, if any, they would charge you?

Answered by James Vance: They said nothing about interest.
Answered by James Brown: They said nothing about interest.

JAMES + VANCE.
his mark.

Sworn and subscribed to at Pulaski, Tennessee, January 10, 1870, in presence of—

J. A. SLADEN,
Brevet Captain United States Army, Recorder.

No. 13.—JAMES BROWN, Company I One hundred and tenth United States colored troops, being first duly sworn, deposes and says: My bounty check was first given to me by Mr. Simpson. Then took my check, by Simpson's direction, to Dr. Cloon, and he paid me $140. (Here the witness showed his discharge, which shows the amount to have been $300 bounty, and difference of pay twenty cents.) In December, 1866, I gave my discharge to Captain Beckert, and about one year later, Captain Beckert came to me and loaned me $35. When Dr. Cloon paid me the amount of my check, he told me he would settle with Captain Beckert for the amount I was owing him. I received my discharge from Dr. Cloon several months after I had received my bounty. I saw James Vance borrow $25 of Captain Beckert at the same time that I got my money from him.

JAMES + BROWN.
his mark.

Sworn to and subscribed on the 10th of January, 1870, in presence of—

J. A. SLADEN,
Brevet Captain United States Army, Recorder.

No. 14.—REUBEN P. CLARK, private Company K Forty-fourth United States colored troops, being first duly sworn, deposes and says: When Simpson was bureau agent here, claimants complained that when they were paid they first received their checks from Simpson, and then they went to Cloon to have it cashed. Cloon seemed always to know when a check came, and hunted up the claimant, and advised him to come back to him with check, and on claimant's returning he would pay him less than the face of the check—this without rendering any service under contract with claimant. Harris and I complained to General Carlin, and the cashing of checks was taken out of Cloon's hands, but the same business went on as before.

I have been here four years, teaching school; I am well acquainted with the colored people, and I know Cloon well; his character is generally bad, from his conduct in defrauding colored people; I could scarcely believe him under oath. I believe he would cheat any man he could; he was in the habit of loaning money and charging what he pleased; he would, when he found a man hard up, offer to loan him money and then charge him outrageously for it; he came here as a magic oil man, and it is said would advance bottles of his oil to soldiers and call it an advance in money.

I am well acquainted with James F. Fisher, colored grocer in this place; I judge from his conduct that he is in league with Cloon; he tries to make them believe Cloon is doing right; I hold him at least as guilty as Cloon, if not more so, for he is a colored man and ought to try to protect his own people. When the pension commission was here,

Cloon and Fisher tried to induce the witnesses to go away and not appear; I heard them say so in Harris's store.

REUBEN P. CLARK.

Sworn and subscribed at Pulaski, Tennessee, January 10, 1870, in presence of—

J. A. SLADEN,
Brevet Captain United States Army, Recorder.

No. 15.—CHARLES A. HALL, photographer, (white,) being first duly sworn, deposes and says: I have a slight recollection that as I was passing through the office of Jones & Son, I heard Stephen Sloss ask about his fees. I understood Captain Jones was charging a fee of $15; Sloss said he was willing to pay a fee, and think he did pay it; this was in the other or back room. I know Mr. Jones well, and never heard of his charging a fee where he had not rendered professional service. Major Wilson seemed to be busy; did not notice what he was doing; I paid little attention to it.

CHAS. A. HALL.

Sworn and subscribed to at Pulaski, Tennessee, January 10, 1870, in presence of—

J. A. SLADEN,
Brevet Captain United States Army, Recorder.

The commission adjourned at 9 p. m., having been in session all day with the exception of a short recess for dinner and for tea.

BEN. P. RUNKLE,
Brevet Colonel United States Army.
J. R. LEWIS,
Brevet Colonel United States Army.
J. A. SLADEN,
Brevet Captain United States Army, Recorder.

TWELFTH DAY'S PROCEEDINGS—PULASKI, TENNESSEE.

Pursuant to adjournment, the commission met at 9 a. m., January 11, 1870, when the following testimony was taken, viz:

No. 16.—LOUIS REED, Company D One hundred and tenth United States colored troops—thought he was defrauded, but an examination of his discharge, and his own statements, show that he got all that was due him.

No. 17.—MOSES CARROLL, Company D One hundred and tenth United States colored troops, is a similar case to the above.

No. 18.—DAVID RHODES, Company G One hundred and tenth United States colored troops—same case as above.

No. 19.—WASHINGTON GILLMORE, Company D Fourteenth United States colored troops, put in a claim May 29, 1868, with Mr. M. M. Cloon; he never got any money; he paid Cloon only fifty cents. Being captured and absent sick from his regiment, he never got his discharge. (He was advised to go to Major Wilson.)

No. 20.—SALLIE TYNHAM, mother of Calvin Tynham, Company ——— One hundred and tenth, was paid check by Captain Judd for $250, which Mr. M. M. Cloon cashed, giving her only $240.

No. 21.—THEODORE M. GREED, Company I One hundred and tenth

United States colored troops, filed his claim originally with Doctor Cloon. He was paid about last summer by Major Wilson. He went to the Joneses, and the Joneses promised to hurry it up, and when Major Wilson paid him in the back room, Mr. Jones spoke to him in the front room, and asked him for the $15, which he paid. He told him he thought it was too much, but he thought he should charge him something.

No. 22.—ALEXANDER CAEDEN, Company F One hundred and tenth United States colored troops, filed his claim for bounty, and it was paid; but Cloon paid him $25 for his claim for commutation of rations, and he was prisoner of war for eight months.

No. 24.—NOAH JONES, alias HUNTER, (colored,) being duly sworn, deposes and says: In 1866, just before the One hundred and first regiment United States colored troops was mustered out, my son, Robert Hunter, died in hospital at Nashville, Tennessee. I immediately put in a claim at the bureau office in Nashville for his back pay and bounty, and paid $2 at the court-house, witnessed by two corporals of Roberts's company, (H, One hundred and first regiment;) a year after, I went to Captain Coons, at Nashville, who sent me to Captain Judd, at Pulaski, giving me some papers to bring to Captain Judd. Captain Coons told me I ought to have attended to it, and I would have got it long ago. Captain Judd got a return from it, and then I had to go to the court-house and make oath, and pay fifty cents. Then Captain Judd went away. I did not go to any one about it, until last Christmas I carried it to Mr. Cloon; Cloon said he would try to get the money, and charged me $10, which amount I paid Mr. Cloon.

NOAH + JONES.
his mark.

Sworn and subscribed to at Pulaski, Tennessee, January 11, 1870, in the presence of—

J. A. SLADEN,
Brevet Captain United States Army, Recorder.

No. 25.—ANDERSON SLOSS, being first duly sworn, deposes and says: That my name is Anderson Sloss, Company B One hundred and eleventh United States colored troops. I filed my claim with Captain Judd, bureau agent at Pulaski, Tennessee, about three years ago. Mr. Cloon met me on the street, about two months after, and asked me if I had been a soldier, and when I told him I had, he requested me to go with him to his office. He there told me that he was the only one in the place that could collect these claims, and that he was a government agent for the collection of these claims. He then took the receipt, which I had received from Captain Judd, and gave one of his own. This was during the summer. About September, Doctor Cloon sent for me, and offered me $40, which I took, and he offered to buy my whole claim for $60, but I refused to sell it. I then signed a paper which Doctor Cloon told me was to show that I had received the $40. About a year later, Doctor Cloon sent for me and told me to go to the bureau office and get my pay, but he sent a man with me to see that I came straight back to his office. I then went to Captain Simpson's office, and received a paper like the one you now show me, (here witness was shown the check of G. W. Balloch, payable to Anderson Sloss, or order, for $301, which was his own check,) and this paper I took back to Cloon's office. Cloon then took that paper and counted out to me a sum of money, which he said, with the $40 he had paid me before, made $100; about one year afterward I met him on the street and he told me to go to his office again. I did so, and he then paid me $15, which he said was for my pension. I am perfectly sure that these three sums named before are all that I have ever received, and that I have never put my mark or my name on the paper you show me, (here witness was shown his own check again,) or any paper like it, but I did sign two papers in Captain Simpson's office at the time he gave me my check. About three or four months ago I heard a talk among the colored people that some gentlemen were here to see about our pensions. I started to see them, but while standing in front of the door waiting to be called in, Doctor Cloon came up to me and told me that there was no use for me to go in and see them, and that I had better go home. I took him at his word and went home. I was a prisoner of war over a year. (Exhibition of discharge shows certificate No. 441561, April 27, 1868, $300 bounty; $1 difference of pay. Discharge also exhibits that his claim for commutation of rations while prisoner of war has been settled.) Was prisoner of war over twelve months.

              ANDERSON + SLOSS.
                   his
                     mark.

Sworn to and subscribed at Pulaski, on the 10th of January, 1870, in the presence of—

                 J. A. SLADEN,
          Brevet Captain United States Army, Recorder.

Further states that when he refused to sell his claim to Doctor Cloon, Doctor Cloon said, "If you don't get out of my office, I'll knock you down with a stick."

              ANDERSON + SLOSS.
                  his
                   mark.

No. 26.—JOSEPH W. GREEN, Company K One hundred and tenth United States colored troops, being sworn, deposes and says: That he first put in his discharge for collection of his bounty claim with Mr. Shelton, a colored man in Pulaski, in 1866; that in 1867 he put Shelton's receipt into Mr. Cloon's hands, and Mr. Cloon paid him the bounty in 1868. The check called for $180. He carried the check to the bureau agent, who sent him to Mr. Roseneau, who paid him $180. Dr. Cloon has the discharge now, or at least told him so this evening; that he sold his claim for commutation of rations while a prisoner, to Dr. Cloon, for $15; was a prisoner about six months; was captured at Athens, Alabama, and returned to his regiment while it was at White's Bluff on the Northwestern railroad; that Cloon offered to buy his claim for bounty for $80; have heard parties say that they had sold their claims to Dr. Cloon.

             JOSEPH W. + GREEN.
                  his
                   mark.

Sworn and subscribed to at Pulaski, Tennessee, January 11, 1870, in the presence of—

                 J. A. SLADEN,
         Brevet Captain United States Army, Recorder.

No. 27.—JAMES H. JACKSON, being first duly sworn, deposes and says: My name is James H. Jackson; I am a livery-stable keeper; I do not know much about this business; I attended to the claim of Katie

Gardner, who had a claim against government, on account of her son; I think Mr. Jones collected her claim; at least he was prosecuting it; I am not certain who paid it, Captain Jones or Major Wilson; it was in Mr. Jones's office, and Major Wilson was present; I do not remember whether she signed any paper or not; about $300 was due her; I received, I think, $285; the woman was here just before, and left me to get her money; I am positive Mr. Jones paid me, and that Major Wilson did not first count and then hand the money to me; after I received the money I paid Jones $15, and had $285 or thereabout left; I paid Jones $15; I cannot say whether or not the woman received the money in the back room and handed it to Jones; I don't think the woman had the money in her hands.

Question asked by Mr. Wilson. Do you know of a transaction that occurred wherein a claim was transferred to you by M. M. Cloon without your knowledge, and the claim was collected by M. M. Cloon, the aforesaid claim being fraudulent?—Answer. I do not. I believe I spoke to Major Wilson about the per cent. He said it was customary to charge something for collections made. The woman is in town.

Question asked by Mr. Wilson. Was money placed in your hands to pay a note to a colored man in Cloon's absence?—Answer. No, sir; not that I recollect.

Question asked by Major Wilson. Did not Cloon place money in your possession, and did you not pay it to a negro?—Answer. I think I did.

Question asked by the commission. Was any note taken?—Answer. I never took any note.

Q. Was not a note given for that money, prosecuted in a civil court?—A. I have heard that it was.

Q. How long did you hold money before it was paid to negroes?—A. It may have been ten days. My memory is bad. I had no interest in the transaction. If I had known a note was taken in my name I would not have sanctioned the transaction. I have never indorsed any such note, and cannot recollect what Cloon told me when he gave me the money. I don't think Cloon explained the transaction when he gave me the money.

J. H. JACKSON.

Sworn to and subscribed on the 11th of January, 1870, in presence of—

BEN. P. RUNKLE,
Brevet Colonel United States Army.

No. 28.—AMOS R. RICHARSON, of Pulaski, being first duly sworn, deposes and says: My name is Amos R. Richarson; I am an attorney-at-law, and have resided here for twenty-five years; I know that I was employed by a colored man, Gabe Higdon, to defend him in a suit brought upon a note given to James Jackson, and payable to him. The suit was prosecuted by Cloon. The negro was summoned, but the suit was continued, (on the day set for trial,) as we both understood, until some future day at 2 o'clock, but the indorsement on the paper was 10 o'clock. I appeared for the negro about 12 o'clock, but the justice had rendered judgment against him by default. I failed to induce the justice to reopen the case and hear the evidence—spoke of taking an appeal, but the negro could not give security. I then told the negro that when the execution issued I would supersede it and have the case tried *de novo* in the circuit court. The negro has never called on me. Jackson

BOUNTIES TO COLORED SOLDIERS.

repudiated the whole transaction when it was mentioned to him, and disclaimed any interest in it.

AMOS R. RICHARSON.

Signed and sworn to this 11th day of June, 1870, Pulaski, Tennessee, in the presence of—

J. A. SLADEN,
Brevet Captain United States Army, Recorder.

No. 29.—W. A. BAUGH, of Elkton, Giles County, Tennessee, being first duly sworn, deposes and says, that Captain D. S. Mann and Major C. A. Beckert came to my house, by appointment, with some negro soldiers, and were at my house one day and two nights. This was in January or February, 1868. I was then a justice of the peace. They were getting claims for back pay, bounty and pensions. They advanced money; they gave men who had been soldiers money, taking their receipts therefor. I do not know what amount was shown in the body of the receipt, whether it corresponded with the amount advanced or not. My brother, Lewis Baugh, witnessed some of the receipts, but I do not believe he knew anything about the amounts. In my official capacity I took evidence in connection with claims being made out. I did not take any acknowledgments from the men to the amount they received. No such acknowledgments were taken at the time by any one. I don't believe they took the men to any other justice of the peace to have any acknowledgment taken to the amount they received at my house. They mostly got their money and went home. They, Mann and Beckert, took some kind of a paper in each case, but no official acknowledgment. William Reddus got what purported to be $100; one Jim Vance got $50; then another Jim Vance got $25 there, and $25 sent me for him; Paul Harvey got $50 there at the time. Some fifteen or twenty got money at that time, and most of them got $50. Dick Brown, at Elkton, got $50. They paid me my legal fees, and gave me, one evening as we were going in to bed, twenty one-dollar bills, saying it was for my trouble. I never received anything else.

W. A. BAUGH.

Sworn to before me and subscribed in my presence, this 11th day of January, 1870.

BEN. P. RUNKLE,
Brevet Colonel United States Army.

No. 30.—D. A. WELBORN, being first duly sworn, deposes and says: I am clerk of the county court of Giles County, Tennessee. I served in the national army during the war.

Question. Do you know James Cloon, and if so, please state any transaction that may have taken place between you.—Answer. I know a man by the name of Cloon; what his right name is I can't say, he goes by several names; sometimes he signs James Cloon, again he signs M. M. Cloon. I once asked him why he signed his name both ways; his answer was, that his name was James M. M. Cloon.

Q. Please state the circumstances under which you asked him why he signed his name in different ways.—A. I discovered that his name was signed James Cloon when it had been signed before M. M. Cloon.

Q. What is your opinion of James *alias* M. M. Cloon, based on your general knowledge of the man ?—A. I know but little about the man. His reputation is, as a general thing, bad.

Q. Have you qualified Cloon to various papers signed James Cloon ?—

A. I have, but never to any signed M. M. Cloon, that I remember, but have seen his name signed M. M. Cloon, and knew him as M. M. Cloon.

Q. Do you know the Messrs. Jones, and if so, what is their general character as to honesty and fair dealing with colored men?—A. I know them, but never heard anything about it one way or the other. The firm is one of the leading firms in the county as a law firm. Their character is good.

Q. Would or would not a claimant, whose claim M. M. Cloon was prosecuting, do well to employ the Messrs. Jones to attend to their business?—A. That depends on Cloon's facilities for cheating.

Q. Do you know Major John S. Wilson, and if so, what is his reputation as a disbursing officer?—A. I know him; I never heard anything for or against him except what Cloon says.

D. A. WELBORN.

Sworn to before me and subscribed in my presence this 11th day of January, 1870.

BEN. P. RUNKLE,
Brevet Colonel United States Army.

No. 31.—HENRY HINES, private Company H One hundred and tenth regiment United States colored troops, being first duly sworn, deposes and says: I put in my claim with Captain Beckert, in 1866. Mr. Goldsmith advanced me $80, and no more—$40 in money and $40 in trade. Mr. Thorlow was in the store, but no one was standing by. I signed a paper then, and no one saw me sign it except Mr. Goldsmith. I never was paid any money since. This happened about one year ago. I was a prisoner seven or eight months. I put in claim for commutation of rations with Captain C. A. Beckert. Before the time I got the money advanced me by Goldsmith, Beckert sent for me and showed me a check which he said was for prison money, and called for $50. He gave me two $10s, two $5s, and one $1 bill. He said he charged $15 for collecting the money. I never received any other money than mentioned above. (Discharge shows $100 bounty, $100 additional bounty, and $4 20 difference of pay.)

HENRY + HINES.
his mark.

Sworn to before me and subscribed in my presence this 11th day of January, 1870.

BEN. P. RUNKLE,
Brevet Colonel United States Army.

No. 32.—BURT REEDUS, Company I One hundred and tenth United States colored troops, being first duly sworn, deposes and says: That he first filed claim in 1866 with a colored claim agent named Sheldon. About a year after I filed my claim again with Dr. Cloon, say September, 1867. About the 19th of the following December, Dr. Cloon sent for me, and offered to buy my claim for $125; when I refused, he offered me $60, and said it was part of my bounty. I did not sign any papers when I got the $60, but Cloon has indorsed it on the receipt of his, which I had. On the 16th of January, 1868, I went to Captain Judd and he gave me a check, which he told me called for $305 84. He then told me to take my check to Dr. Cloon and he would tell me what to do. I then went to Cloon's office and he took my check and asked me why I did not come and take the $125, which he had offered me. He finally offered me $194 80, and told me if I did not take that I would not get any. So, for fear I should not get any, I took the $194 80. I was a prisoner of war eight months, and Cloon offered to buy my claim for commutation of rations for $25. When I refused to sell it, he cursed me out of his office, and told me he would take a stick to me. I am positively sure that I never put my name on any check, or made my mark on the same. I have never got my discharge from Dr. Cloon, and he tells me that he has lost it, but will try to find it.

BURT + REEDUS.
his mark.

Signed and sworn to this 11th day of January, 1870, at Pulaski, Tennessee, in the presence of—

J. A. SLADEN,
Brevet Captain United States Army, Recorder.

No. 33.—ALBERT HARNEY, Company K One hundredth United States colored troops, being duly sworn, deposes and says: That he filed his claim about four years ago with Captain Beckert. Some months after he came to me and offered me $50, which I took. I then signed my name to some papers in Squire Baugh's presence. About last July, Major Wilson paid me $87, and told me that was all I had coming to me. I had previously filed a claim with Dr. Cloon for commutation of rations, and he gave me $20 for it. This is all I have ever received.

ALBERT + HARNEY.
his mark.

Signed in the presence of—

J. A. SLADEN,
Brevet Captain United States Army, Recorder.

No. 34.—NANCY JOHNSON, (colored,) being first duly sworn, deposes and says: I put in my claim with Mr. M. M. Cloon more than three years ago; it was for bounty, back pay, &c., due my late husband, Ben. Johnson, Company D One hundred and tenth United States colored troops, who died at hospital at Pulaski, Tennessee, before his regiment was mustered out. I have been to Mr. Cloon a great many times, and he always tells me that I will get it in a short time. I have signed papers twice in Mr. Cloon's office. I never paid only $1 to Mr. Cloon, and never got any money from him, and I have never been paid any money on my claim. Mr. Cloon has never put in a claim for pension for me, that I know of. I heard the people say that Mr. Cloon cheated them, and did not pay them, so I came to Mr. Jones some time last summer to have him collect my claim. I have never paid him anything, and made no bargain with him.

NANCY + JOHNSON.
her mark.

Sworn and subscribed to at Pulaski, Tennessee, January 11, 1870.

J. A. SLADEN,
Brevet Captain United States Army, Recorder.

No. 36.—KATIE GARDNER, colored, prosecuted a claim for pay and bounty due her son, Alexander Gardner, Company D One hundred and eleventh United States colored troops, who died in the service. She put her claim in the hands of M. M. Cloon three years ago. The first of last year Mr. Cloon sent her, by Mr. James Jackson, $160. Cloon sent for her. She was sick, and could not go. Mr. Jackson went and got the

BOUNTIES TO COLORED SOLDIERS. 85

money. She signed no paper at that time. Last fall she went to Mr. Jones; was told by Mr. Cloon to go. She went three times to Mr. Jones. The first time she went to Mr. Jones he told her he would charge her $15 to get her money. Mr. Cloon cursed her away, and she told Mr. Jones she would pay him well if he would get her money. Mr. Wilson went out and got the money the third time she went; brought it and handed it to Mr. Jones, who handed it to her. She swears positively that Mr. Jones handed the money to her, and she handed it to Mr. Jackson, and asked him to count it. She told Mr. Jackson to pay Mr. Jones what was right out of it. She then went home, leaving Mr. Jackson to bring her the money. Mr. Jackson brought the money home to her, and said he had paid Mr. Jones, and there was the rest of the money, every dollar of it. He said he paid Mr. Jones $15; don't know how much money he brought to her; that about three months ago she heard there were men here looking after pension claims. She went to Mr. Cloon and asked him what she should do. Mr. Cloon told her to go home, that they did not want her. This was at Mr. Cloon's office. She knows that Mr. Jackson brought her less than $200 the last time she was paid; is not aware that she ever put in a claim for pension money. At the time she got her first money, Mr. Cloon sent word it was bounty money. Mr. Jackson brought her the message that Cloon wanted to see her.

KATIE + GARDNER.
her
mark.

Sworn and subscribed to at Pulaski, Tennessee, January 11, 1870, in the presence of—

J. R. LEWIS,
Brevet Colonel United States Army.

No. 38.—WINNIE ROBERTS, being duly sworn, deposes and says: That she is the widow of Henry Roberts, Company A One hundred and eleventh United States colored troops; filed claim first with a Mr. Sheldon, four years ago; filed claim again about three years ago with Dr. Cloon; has received the bounty, but not the pension. About four months ago I heard some gentlemen were here to see about my pension. I went to see them, and while standing in front of the door to be called in, Dr. Cloon came up to me and told me not to go in, as it was no use, and that I ought to go home; that those men would fool us out of all of our money; that that was what they were here for, and he cursed us for wanting to go in. He stood round the door all the time, and kept telling other people the same thing, in my presence. I have never received one cent of pension money from any source whatever. I also heard Fisher tell other people the same thing. I thought that Fisher was working for Cloon, from the way in which he talked.

WINNIE + ROBERTS.
her
mark.

Lives with Stephen Williams, five miles south of Pulaski, Tennessee.

Sworn to and signed, this 11th day of January, 1870, in the presence of—

J. A. SLADEN,
Brevet Captain United States Army, Recorder.

No. 39.—SOPHIA PARKSON, widow of Berry Parkson, Company C Twelfth United States colored troops, being first duly sworn, deposes and says:

I put in my pension claim with M. M. Cloon. I have never received any money. I was before the pension commission, but Cloon tried to keep me from going. He offered me $50 if I would go away and not appear before the commission. He told me if I went I would not get any money; that it would be flung out. I told him I would go; I had not received any money, and wanted to see any way. He then said I was a d——d fool, and pushed me off the sidewalk, and I went around and went in the other gate. He said he had a check of mine, but he could not pay it to me. When I would go to him he would say so.

SOPHIA + PARKSON.
her
mark.

Sworn to and subscribed in the presence of—
J. A. SLADEN,
Brevet Captain United States Army, Recorder.

PULASKI, January 11, 1870.

WILLIAM ROPE, colored teacher and minister of the Methodist Episcopal Church South, being first duly sworn, deposes and says: I know Mr. Cloon. He is accused of cheating and swindling. The colored people generally think him a bad man. I don't know any act of Cloon's, of my own knowledge.

WILLIAM ROPE.

Sworn to before me and subscribed in my presence, this 11th day of January, 1870.
BEN. P. RUNKLE,
Brevet Colonel United States Army.

WILLIAM J. PARKES, being duly sworn, deposes and says: That he is the cashier of the Richland Savings Bank of Pulaski, Tennessee; states Major Wilson is in the habit of bringing the checks of General Balloch, for amounts due colored claimants, to his bank, and there having them cashed; that most of the claimants are paid by Major Wilson in the bank; that sometimes Major Wilson brings the checks and has them cashed, and takes the money to Mr. Jones's office to pay the claimants—not very often; thinks that in two or three instances the checks have been brought to the bank by Mr. Jones; that he charges usually one-fourth of one per cent. for cashing the checks; that no other parties have brought General Balloch's checks to the bank since Major Wilson has been here; does not know of any checks having been cashed by other parties since Major Wilson came here. Major Wilson bears a good character among all parties for transacting his business fairly and honestly.

W. J. PARKES.

Sworn to and subscribed this 11th day of January, 1870, at Pulaski, Tennessee, in my presence.
J. R. LEWIS,
Brevet Colonel United States Army.

JAMES T. MCKISSACK, being first duly sworn, deposes and says: That he is an old resident of Pulaski, and has known M. M. Cloon ever since the latter has been here. His general reputation among both white and black is very bad. The blacks say that he has swindled them; have had no transactions with Cloon whatever. I have advised the colored people to go to Messrs. Jones and Mr. Hickey, to have their claims settled, because I believed that they would do them justice.

JAS. T. McKISSACK.

Signed and sworn to this 11th day of January, 1870, at Pulaski, Tennessee, in the presence of—

J. A. SLADEN,
Brevet Captain United States Army, Recorder.

No. 40.—GEORGE BARLOW, Company I Thirteenth United States colored troops, being duly sworn, deposes and says:

That he filed his claim for bounty, &c., with M. M. Cloon two years ago last November; that he paid only fifty cents for stamps; had lost his discharge; that he borrowed $2 two years ago this month of Cloon, who offered to advance half the claim, but he (Barlow) would not take it; Cloon wished to buy the claim, and offered to give $100, but he would not do it; has never heard from the claim, only Cloon said it would come. The last time he went to him, last week, Cloon said that he thought the claim had been disallowed, but when he looked on his books he said no, he had never heard from it. In June he came to Mr. Jones, because he had got uneasy and he could hear nothing from it. Mr. Jones did not say what he would charge; Mr. Jones has heard nothing from it, or if he has, he has never told me anything about it; has never received anything from anybody except the $2 from Cloon.

GEORGE + BARLOW.
his mark.

Sworn to before me and subscribed in my presence this 11th day of January, 1870.

BEN. P. RUNKLE,
Brevet Colonel United States Army.

No. 41.—DANIEL G. ANDERSON, being duly sworn, deposes and says:

That he is an old resident of Pulaski, and knows Mr. M. M. Cloon, and knows his general reputation; it is bad. He is generally believed to be a swindler. He bears a very bad reputation among the people, both white and colored. In one instance where Cloon sued a colored man for a balance claimed to be due on a note, the case was tried before him, (Anderson,) and from the evidence adduced on the trial, he rendered a decision against Cloon, and required him to pay the costs.

DANIEL G. ANDERSON.

Sworn to before me and subscribed in my presence this 11th day of January, 1870.

BEN. P. RUNKLE,
Brevet Colonel United States Army.

Transcript from docket.

June 26, 1868.—James H. Jackson *vs.* Gabriel Higdon.—For plaintiff and against defendant for $95 30.

Cost: Warrant, 50 cents; inspection, 75 cents.

For value received I assign this judgment to M. M. Cloon this 26th day of June, 1868.

J. H. JACKSON.

Execution issued to M. M. Cloon November 14, 1868.

W. H. ABERNATHY,
Justice Peace.

BOUNTIES TO COLORED SOLDIERS.

Copy of note or evidence of debt.

PULASKI, TENNESSEE, *June* 2, 1868.

I, Gabriel Higdon, owe J. H. Jackson the sum of ninety-five dollars ($95) of borrowed money.

GABRIEL +his mark HIGDON.

Witnessed by M. M. CLOON.

The above is a true copy of an instrument in my office of J. H. Jackson against Gabriel Higdon. That the above judgment of $95 30 was based upon this. January 11, 1870.

W. H. ABERNATHY,
Justice of the Peace for Giles County, Tennessee.

Mr. JAMES MICHAEL MCGINNIS CLOON, being first duly sworn, deposes and says: My name is James Michael McGinnis Cloon.

Question. How do you usually sign your name?—Answer. I sometimes sign my name M. M., sometimes James M. M., and sometimes James Cloon.

Q. Have you ever said in writing over the signature of J. M. M. Cloons that you had no connection with a person named M. M. Cloon?—A. I have never said in writing over the signature of James M. M. Cloon that I had no connection with a person named M. M. Cloon.

Q. Have you ever over the signature of M. M. Cloon said, or intimated in writing, that you have no connection with a person named James Cloon?—A. I do not propose to answer any question tending to criminate myself.

Q. Have you any friend or acquaintance in this vicinity named James Cloon?—A. I do not propose to answer any such question.

Q. Are you a citizen of the United States?—A. I am not a citizen of the United States.

Q. Are you a claim agent, and have you license as such?—A. I am a claim agent and have a license as such.

Q. Have you ever practiced as a claim agent before the departments at Washington?—A. I have been practising as a claim agent before the departments at Washington.

Q. Have you ever been debarred from practicing as a claim agent in any of the departments at Washington?—A. I have not been debarred from practicing in any of the departments that I am aware of.

Q. Who is the high official referred to as guilty of the grossest fraud in your communication of the 29th November, 1869, to the Second Auditor?—A. The highest official referred to in my communication of November 29, to Second Auditor, is General Balloch.

Q. Please state to the commission what you know tending to criminate General Balloch.—A. About eighteen months ago I was approached by Captain Charles A. Beckert, who informed me that Chipman, Hosmer & Co., for whom he was acting as sub-agent, had sent out a man named Major Mann, whose object it was to loan money to colored claimants, and who did so loan to colored claimants, certificates for whose bounty the said Chipman, Hosmer & Co. were possessed of at that time. The money was to be advanced in proportion to the amount of each party's certificate; that is to say, if the certificate called for $300 or upward, the sum of $75 or $100 was advanced to said claimant, whose note was to be taken for double the amount advanced; on the other hand, if the certificate called for $200, more or less, the sum of $25 was

BOUNTIES TO COLORED SOLDIERS. 89

to be advanced, and notes to be taken for double the amount of advances; said notes were to be acknowledged before a justice of the peace paid for that purpose. Those notes were to be presented with each party's certificate to General Balloch, who was to deduct the amount of each note from each certificate to which it applied, to be paid over to Chipman, Hosmer & Co., and he, General Balloch, was to receive twenty-five per cent. of the net profits.

Q. Do you know anything further tending to criminate General Balloch?—A. I know nothing further criminating General Balloch; but I know that General Balloch has been informed of this matter. I wish to make a further statement criminating this man Mr. Wilson with the grossest fraud.

Mr. Cloon here called for the reading of his testimony which the recorder had taken down; and when the sentence inclosed in parenthesis had been read, he objected to it, and wanted it entirely stricken out. This the commission refused to do, but gave him the privilege of making any statement regarding it he might choose; he declined, however, to proceed unless the whole was stricken out; but the commission again declining to comply with his request, he left the room.

Sworn to and given at Pulaski, Tennessee, January 11, 1870, in the presence of—

BEN. R. RUNKLE,
Brevet Colonel United States Army.
J. R. LEWIS,
Brevet Colonel United States Army.
J. A. SLADEN,
Brevet Captain United States Army, Recorder.

STATE OF TENNESSEE, *County of Giles, ss:*

On this 11th day of June, 1870, I, M. M. Cloon, of Pulaski, Giles County, Tennessee, do enter this my protest against the partial proceedings of a military commission now in session in said town, county, and State, composed of the following named officers, to wit, Generals Lewis and Runkle, and Captain Sladen, said commission being convened for the purpose of investigating frauds committed on colored people in the payment of their bounties, &c.

I charge that said commission ignores everything tending to show that all the frauds committed as above referred to were committed by and with the advice and consent of bureau agents, by asking the witnesses leading questions and permitting them to be answered only as they (commission) direct, thereby compelling the witnesses to ignore all testimony tending to implicate bureau agents.

I further charge that said commission failed to investigate any of the frauds committed in the county of Maury and State of Tennessee, which frauds amounted to about twenty-five thousand dollars, and which had been exclusively committed by bureau agents in person.

I further charge that if a witness perchance implicate a bureau agent in any of the said swindling alluded to, he is afterwards cross-examined and so annoyed, until he so mixes his statements that he knows not of what he deposes. And if he is intelligent enough as not to contradict his statement implicating a bureau agent, he then is taken into a separate apartment and there questioned in relation to his statements until he finally has to succumb to their farce.

I further charge that no witnesses are sent for by the commission, only those who by their testimony implicate, indirectly or directly, claim agents exclusively in frauds; that all the names of the bureau victims are ignored and nothing said of them.

I further charge that the said commission hold their councils and investigations in the office of Charles P. Jones, who is a party to the frauds committed by John L. Wilson, the present incumbent of the bureau for this section, and wherein all the frauds complained of have been committed, and that in view of said fact claimants are intimidated in giving testimony in the presence of the Joneses in their own house, tending to show that they have been fleeced and robbed out of their legitimate dues by the said Joneses.

I further charge that persons other than bureau agents are not allowed to contradict or rebut testimony detrimental to their honor and character. Against the above and other transactions of the commission I do hereby most solemnly protest, in the name of justice, honor, and decency.

M. M. CLOON.

C. P. JONES, being duly sworn, deposeth as follows: He is a lawyer in the town of Pulaski, and has been practicing law in said town for over two years; that some time during the year 1869, he does not recollect what month, he had a conversation with Captains A. C. and J. M. Hickey, brothers, practicing law in the town of Columbia, Tennessee, in regard to collecting or prosecuting claims for colored soldiers in the federal army. Captain J. M. Hickey stated during the conversation that he had consulted the Hon. Connelly F. Trigg, judge of the federal court, then at Nashville, in regard to charging a fee for inquiring into and investigating said claims, and stating at the time and in said conversation with Judge Trigg, that there was general complaint among the negroes that M. M. Cloon was swindling and cheating them out of their bounty and pension money; that Judge Trigg told him he had a perfect and legal right to inquire into and investigate said claims when solicited by claimants, as lawyers, and to charge a reasonable fee for services. Shortly after this, we, my brother and myself, were solicited by the Messrs. Hickey to act as their agents in inquiring into said claims. At first we refused to have anything to do with the claim, it being a notorious fact that the negroes were being defrauded by the various claim agents throughout the country; we were, however, so often and earnestly entreated by the negroes to investigate and inquire into their claims, and also solicited by a great number of the citizens of Giles County to take charge of their claims for bounty and pension, or that they (the colored claimants) would be cheated out of everything by Cloon and his associates, that we finally consented to inquire into and investigate their claims in connection with the Hickeys above alluded to as attorneys-at-law, we at all times making a contract with them in regard to a fee being paid for services rendered, before we touched their claims or receipts.

When the receipts or claims were given to us we gave them a receipt, agreeing to prosecute their claims as lawyers, said receipt being signed, A. C. & J. M. Hickey, per C. or C. P. Jones, or A. C., or J. M. Hickey. For reference, said receipt, marked Exhibit A, is here filed and made a part of this statement.

The claims were sometimes paid off in the office of T. M. Jones & Sons by Major J. L. Wilson, who, in every instance while I was present, paid them the full amount due them in the presence of two white and two colored witnesses, or they were taken by him to the bank, and there paid off. The negroes who contracted with us would sometimes pay us a fee, and sometimes they would not; but never at any time did Major Wilson pay one cent of money into my or my brother's hands, and whenever we obtained a fee, it was only through the negro, and only from those with whom we had previously contracted, and rendered with the assistance of the Hickeys' valuable services.

In regard to the claim of Stephen Sloss, deponent states that he recollects distinctly contracting with said Sloss, who agreed in the presence of three witnesses to pay us $15 when said claim was collected; that he had possession of the same over four months before the same was paid, and when paid by Major Wilson, that Sloss came out of the back room of the office of T. M. Jones & Sons, where Major Wilson was paying claimants, into the front room, and came up and asked what we charged him; we told him $15, which he paid us, and went out. About two weeks after this he came back and said he had been sent by Cloon for the money he had paid us; that Cloon said he owed him $15, and he could not afford to pay both.

As previously stated, most of the claimants paid off were carried to the bank by Major Wilson, and paid in the presence of the cashier.

C. P. JONES.

A. C. & J. M. HICKEY'S LAW AND COLLECTING OFFICE,
Pulaski, Tennessee, June 30, 1869.

Received of Richard Peters, late a private of Company G Fourteenth regiment, United States colored infantry, his claim for bounty against M. M. Cloon, agent, or against any other party or firm that may have possession of the claim, check, or certificate, which claims we promise to prosecute and collect, or account for as attorneys at law.

A. C. & J. M. HICKEY,
Per A. C. HICKEY.

Sworn and subscribed to this 11th day of January, 1870, at Pulaski, Tennessee, in the presence of—

J. A. SLADEN,
Brevet Captain United States Army, Recorder.

JOHN L. WILSON, being duly sworn, deposes and says: That he is bounty agent and disbursing officer of the Bureau Refugees, Freedmen and Abandoned Lands; that it is his universal custom to have the checks sent him for payment of claims cashed at the banks in Columbia and Pulaski, and pays the amount, less the bank discount, usually one-fourth of one per cent., to the claimants in money; that he usually pays the money to the claimants in the bank; sometimes, when he has a number to pay at one time, he takes the checks to the banks, gets them cashed, and pays the money to the claimants at his office, always in the presence of witnesses; that when in Pulaski, his office is with Messrs. Jones, and he sometimes pays claimants in the back room of said office; that he always takes pains to explain to the claimants that all the attorneys' and notarial fees have been paid by the government, and the money paid is all their own; that he knew that Messrs. Hickey, at Columbia, and Messrs. Jones, at Pulaski, were doing writing for and assisting claimants, but never knew they were charging a percentage on the claim, or a regular fee; that these and many other attorneys in the country were writing constantly for the freedmen to the Second Auditor and others in Washington, to ascertain the condition of claims; that many of them came to him to inquire as to the condition of claims; that they many times brought letters from the Second Auditor to him, which stated that certain claims had been allowed, or that certain additional evidence was required; that he sometimes furnished such additional evidence himself, sending it to Washington; that sometimes, when requested, he furnished the attorneys with blanks on which to make up such evidence; that he has sent blanks to attorneys at a distance on which to make up necessary additional evidence; that he supposed such attorneys were paid at the time, or subsequently, for their services, but that no fees for such services were ever paid by him, or in his presence; that the first time he came to Pulaski, J. T. Fisher, colored, came to him with a long list of accounts against claimants, and requested to be paid at the pay-table; that he refused to do it, or allow him to be paid at the time of payment made by him, and that he was obliged to drive him from the room; that soon after he came to Columbia, Mr. M. M. Cloon came to him and requested that the claimants might be paid in checks; that he refused to do it or to recognize Mr. Cloon as a claim agent, or to have anything to do with him; that said Cloon made advances to Messrs. Hickey to enter into an arrangement with him (Cloon) to defraud the colored claimants, and that Messrs. Hickey gave the letter to him immediately, which is hereby presented, and dated Athens, Alabama, May 31, 1869; says that Cloon and Fisher have constantly traduced and abused him to the colored people, and through these means have doubtless made him more or less unpopular with the freedmen.

JOHN L. WILSON.

Sworn and subscribed to at Pulaski, Tennessee, this 11th day of January, 1870, in the presence of—

J. A. SLADEN,
Brevet Captain United States Army, Recorder.

ATHENS, ALABAMA, May 31, 1869.

DEAR SIR: While in conversation a few days since with Mr. Calvin Jones, of Pulaski, he suggested the propriety of associating myself with him in matters pertaining to the disbursement of claims to colored soldiers and their heirs, and remarked that you were the party through which this thing can be accomplished successfully and profitably to all parties interested; or, in other words, if I work into your (including Jones's) hands, that you will work into mine. In reply, I said that I had no objections to him or you making money out of the disbursement of said claims, providing it was done to my satisfaction, and with and by my consent; and whereas nearly all the claims in the counties of Maury, Marshall, Lewis, Lincoln, Franklin, Giles, Rutherford, and Limestone County, Alabama, have been in my hands for collection, and which are now ready for payment, and I guess are being daily paid off, hence I could not consent that "outsiders" would step in and make money out of the parties directly interested in said claims without my consent. I would here remark that all the claims in the aforesaid counties have been completed and nearly all collected by me, except what was filed by bureau agents. Other men who filed claims having transferred their interests therein to me for a certain sum, (with a few exceptions,) I have advanced a large sum of money to some of those claimants; and whereas I am now extremely busy operating in North Alabama with a large force of clerks, hence time don't permit me to be present personally for the collection of such advancements, and therefore I would feel glad to procure your services in the premises. We are comparatively strangers to each other—knowing each other only by character and personal appearance—hence, on this occasion, a more intimate acquaintance, reciprocated on both sides, would, I doubt not, prove equally profitable to us jointly. Nothing gives me greater pleasure than an association with worthy and reliable gentlemen on all occasions; and I can flatter myself that when such an acquaintance is once formed it is always highly appreciated by the opposite party as well as by myself. You, I dare say, are well acquainted with the prejudices which I had to overcome for the past three years by a community which knew nothing of my antecedents or relations. And in view of the fact that they were not only prejudiced against me, but also against my business, therefore I did not attempt to court the acquaintance of anybody, as my stay among you is not perpetual. And in conclusion, I must say, that inasmuch as I am not a citizen of the United States, and have no party feelings to be gratified, it therefore behooves me to treat everybody with due respect, whether he be a northern or southern man, as the one is as much to me as the other. Hence, anybody who is gentlemanly, confidential, and trustworthy, has in me a friend, and one on whom he may depend. I stopped over at Columbia on Friday evening for the purpose of seeing a friend, and in the meantime at the solicitation of hundreds of my claimants I wanted to have an interview with Mr. Wilson, the present disbursing agent, who prevented the same by his abruptness and partial insolence. I wish to have no trouble with Wilson nor any other disbursing agent who may take his place, but I can assure them that when they begin to interfere with my business, that their pleasantest time is not then at hand, as his predecessors Carlin, Simpson, and Reeves can testify to that fact.

I hope that a reply may be received at your earliest convenience in regard to the matter herein referred to; or it may be perhaps better to have a personal interview in the premises. You will please be the judge.

Respectfully, &c.,

M. M. CLOON.

J. C. HICKEY, Esq.,
   Attorney at Law, Columbia, Tennessee.

At the close of the examination of Mr. A. R. Richardson, the witness stated to the court that if Mr. M. M. Cloon would like to ask any questions he would be glad to answer them.

Permission having been given, Mr. Cloon turned to the commission and said, "I can show by evidence that the statements made by Mr. Richardson are incorrect," (or words to that effect.) Mr. Richardson said to him, "Do you mean to say that the statements I have just made are incorrect?" (or words to that effect.) Mr. Cloon replied, "I do, sir."

Mr. Richardson then said, "Do you mean to say that I lie?" (or words to that effect.) Mr. Cloon replied, "I do, sir." Here Mr. Richardson reached to the floor and laid hold of the tongs, when Mr. Cloon drew from his pocket a pistol, with motions as if he intended to point it at Mr. Richardson, when the commission interfered, and Mr. Cloon was ordered to leave the room, and told that when he was wanted by the commission he would be sent for. He did so, but protested against the whole manner of procedure on the part of the commission, and was told to reduce his protest to writing.

He again returned without having been sent for by the commission. He was then informed that he must leave the room or apologize to the commission for his conduct. He then said he had nothing to apologize for, and would not apologize; that he was armed at all times, and would use them if necessary. He was informed that he had drawn arms in the presence of the commission, which was contemptuous and insulting. He was again ordered to leave the room, when he laid his protest in writing before the commission, and asked if the commission desired to examine him as a witness. The commission then decided to examine him at once, Colonel Runkle voting against his examination on the ground that he had insulted the commission, and that he was, from evidence already before the commission, not entitled to credit under oath.

Mr. Richardson left the room at the time of the difficulty, but returned and apologized to the commission for his part in the affair, stating that it was his intention when he picked up the tongs to request the commission to protect him from insult, or he should feel obliged to protect himself.

At 5.30 p. m. the commission adjourned to meet at Huntsville, Alabama, the next day, January 12, 1870.

BEN. P. RUNKLE,
Brevet Colonel United States Army.
J. R. LEWIS,
Brevet Colonel United States Army.
J. A. SLADEN,
Brevet Captain United States Army, Recorder.

THIRTEENTH DAY'S PROCEEDINGS—HUNTSVILLE, ALABAMA.

Pursuant to adjournment the commission met at 4 o'clock p. m. January 12, 1870, at the office of Captain Wager, bureau agent at Huntsville, Alabama, and the recorder was instructed to write notices, to be read in all the colored churches this evening, inviting all claimants who had reason to suppose that they had not received their just dues to present themselves to the commission the following day at 9 o'clock a. m.

Request was made by the commission to the post commander, Brevet Major General S. W. Crawford, for the services of a soldier as orderly, which request was complied with, as per annexed Special Order No. 7, headquarters post of Huntsville, Alabama.

The commission then examined Captain Wager relative to frauds in and about Huntsville, Alabama, and then adjourned to meet the next day at 9 a. m.

BEN. P. RUNKLE,
Brevet Colonel United States Army.
J. R. LEWIS,
Brevet Colonel United States Army.
J. A. SLADEN,
Brevet Captain United States Army, Recorder.

[Special Order No. 7.]

HEADQUARTERS POST OF HUNTSVILLE,
Huntsville, Alabama, January 13, 1870.

I. Private George Reynolds, Company G Second Infantry, is hereby detailed on daily duty as orderly for the military commission now in session in this city, and he will report at once to Brevet Colonel B. P. Runkle, president of the commission, for duty.

By order of General Crawford:

JAS. M. INGALLS,
Lieutenant Second Infantry, Post Adjutant.

BOUNTIES TO COLORED SOLDIERS. 95

FOURTEENTH DAY'S PROCEEDINGS—HUNTSVILLE, ALABAMA.

The commission met at 9 o'clock a. m. January 13, 1870. A large number of witnesses were examined, but as most of the complaints were imaginary ones, but little testimony was recorded.

The commission, however, decided to summon a very important witness, Captain Charles A. Beckert, who was supposed to be in Winston County, Alabama, and ordered Captain Wager, the bureau agent, to proceed to Decatur, Alabama, and after ascertaining the whereabouts of this witness, to find him and bring him before the commission.

The following is the evidence taken, viz:

No. 1.—CAREY CRENSHAW, Company H One hundred and tenth United States colored troops, being first duly sworn, deposes and says: That I was paid in the office of General John B. Callis. There were present General Callis, Colonel Rugg, and another gentleman across the counter, who, from his appearance, I judge to be John W. Raines, (I am not positive as to that.) Some man, I don't remember who, gave me a check. I handed this over to a gentleman behind the counter, and he handed me over the money; that is to say, they asked me how much money I wanted; I said I wanted $50. This amount he handed me, and gave me a check-book for the balance. (Witness examined and found competent to count money.) This is the check-book I received: (Check-book No. 83 shows, January 15, 1868, a credit of $79 20 deposited in Freedmen's Savings and Trust Company, Huntsville Alabama.) I further state that I never had a dollar advanced or loaned me by any one on account of my bounty. The gentleman behind the counter was the same person referred to in the first part of this affidavit as John W. Raines.

his
CAREY + CRENSHAW.
mark.

Sworn to before me and subscribed in my presence this 13th day of January, 1870.

BEN. P. RUNKLE,
Brevet Colonel United States Army.

No. 2.—HARRY ROBINSON, father of George Robinson, late Company E One hundred and first United States colored troops, being first duly sworn, deposes and says: I put in my claim for bounty with M. M. Cloon, at Huntsville, Alabama, August 14, 1869. I had but one witness present, named George Granger, and no acknowledgment was taken before any justice of the peace or other civil officer. I signed some papers.

his
HARRY + ROBINSON.
mark.

Sworn to before me and subscribed in my presence, this 13th day of January, 1870.

No. 3.—MARTHA DRAKE, mother of Lafayette Drake, Company G One hundred and first regiment United States infantry, says: That on the 23d of August, 1869, she put in her claim with M. M. Cloon, at Huntsville, Alabama, and that she took but one witness before said Cloon, to wit, Tom Moore, as he is known at home, but he said he was called Philpot in the army. There were no other parties present, and no acknowledgment taken before a justice or any other civil officer; nor did I sign (by mark) any papers.

MARTHA + DRAKE.
her mark.

Sworn to before me and subscribed in my presence, this 13th day of January, 1869.

BEN. P. RUNKLE,
Brevet Colonel United States Army.

No. 4.—WILLIAM LOVE, Company B One hundred and first regiment United States colored troops, being first duly sworn, deposes and says: That he put in his claim for bounty with M. M. Cloon, at Huntsville, Alabama, on September 14, 1869, as shown by his receipt. That he had no witnesses to prove his identity, though he signed papers.

WM. + LOVE.
his mark.

Sworn to before me and subscribed in my presence, this 14th of January, 1870.

J. A. SLADEN,
Brevet Captain U. S. A., Recorder Mil. Com.

No. 5.—JOHN W. RAINES, being first duly sworn, deposes and says: My name is John W. Raines; I am a clerk in the internal revenue office at Huntsville, Alabama; was formerly clerk for Colonel Callis, and sometimes acting cashier of the Freedmen's Savings Bank; I recognized the entry of a deposit of $79 20 in the bank-book of Cary Crenshaw, colored, as being in my own handwriting; I recognized my signature as a witness to the signature of, and payment of $194 20 to Cary Crenshaw, in outside claim-book, page 45, now in the hands of Captain Wager, disbursing officer. If Crenshaw's check was drawn on the Freedmen's Bank, at Huntsville, Alabama, I paid him the full amount, $194 20, less the amount deposited.

JOHN W. RAINES.

Sworn to and subscribed to, at Huntsville, Alabama, January 13, 1870, in presence of—

J. A. SLADEN,
Brevet Captain United States Army, Recorder.

At 5 p. m. the commission adjourned until the next day.

BEN. P. RUNKLE,
Brevet Colonel United States Army.
J. R. LEWIS,
Brevet Colonel United States Army.
J. A. SLADEN,
Brevet Captain United States Army, Recorder.

FIFTEENTH DAY'S PROCEEDINGS—HUNTSVILLE, ALABAMA.

The commission met at 9 a. m., January 14, 1870, when the following evidence was taken, viz:

No. 6.—LEWIS M. DOUGLASS, of the city of Huntsville, being first duly

sworn, deposes and says: I am probate judge of Madison County. M. M. Cloon sent me from time to time during the past year three or four sets of papers (affidavits) by the hands of the affiants, that I might qualify them thereto, and affix my official signature to the papers. On one occasion I found on examining an affiant (a colored man) that he was about to perjure himself, as he stated he did not authorize Cloon to write in the affidavit a statement that he saw a certain colored soldier die or knew he was dead, and that he knew nothing about said soldier alleged to be dead. I returned the papers, sending Cloon word not to send me any more papers, as I would not have anything more to do with his papers.
LEWIS M. DOUGLASS.

Sworn to before me and subscribed in my presence, this 14th day of January, 1870.
BEN. P. RUNKLE,
Brevet Colonel United States Army.

No. 7.—LOUISA FENNELL, widow of Shedrick Fennell, Company ——— regiment ———, being first duly sworn, deposes and says: I put in my claim for bounty, August 9, 1869, through M. M. Cloon, at Huntsville, Alabama. I had two witnesses, William Acklin and Frank Horton; Acklin saw my husband die; the other did not know it of his own knowledge. We all touched the pen, but did not swear to it there or anywhere else. There was no other white man present. He also put in a claim for pension, I suppose, because he asked me about my children— how old they were, &c.

LOUISA + FENNELL.
her
mark.

Sworn to before me and subscribed in my presence, this 14th day of January, 1870.
BEN. P. RUNKLE,
Brevet Colonel United States Army.

No. 8.—ELIZABETH FANELL, widow of Egbert Fanell, alias Heywood, being first duly sworn, deposes and says: I filed my claim on the 28th of August, 1869, with M. M. Cloon. I had one witness, and no more, that saw my husband die, and there was no one else present who knew anything, of their own knowledge, concerning my husband's death, and no acknowledgment was taken before any public officer, and Mr. Cloon was the only white man present in the office. I do not know whether he took up my claim for pension for me or not, but he asked me how many children I had. I replied that I had but one.

ELIZABETH + FANELL.
her
mark.

Signed and sworn to, at Huntsville, Alabama, January 14, 1870.
J. A. SLADEN,
Brevet Captain United States Army, Recorder.

No. 9.—WILLIAM FINLEY, brother of Alexander Finley, Company D Fifteenth regiment United States colored troops, being first duly sworn, deposes and says: I went to M. M. Cloon's office, August 18, 1869, and filed a claim on account of my deceased brother. I took one witness to prove that my brother died while in the service. I had no other witness. We touched the pen, but did not go outside of Cloon's office.

[It appears from discharge (in hands of Captain Wager) of Alexander

Finley, that he was allowed bounty and arrears of pay $300 20, by certificate 437,754, April 17, 1868.]

WILLIAM + FINLEY.
his mark.

Sworn to and signed, at Huntsville, Alabama, January 14, 1870, in the presence of—

J. A. SLADEN,
Brevet Captain United States Army, Recorder.

NOTE.—This claim was put in by Colonel Rugg while he was bureau agent at this town.

No. 9.—MARY GARRISON, widow of Coleman Garrison, regiment and company unknown, being first duly sworn, deposes and says: That I filed my claim with M. M. Cloon, and took with me one witness who belonged to the same company and regiment, and who was with my husband when he died, at Fort Donelson, and John Martin who belonged to the same regiment, but who was in Nashville when my husband died. We went nowhere else with Mr. Cloon or by his direction, and no other white man was present. I did touch the pen to some papers, but we did not have to take oath to anything.

MARY + GARRISON.
her mark.

Sworn and subscribed to at Huntsville, Alabama, January 14, 1870, in the presence of—

J. A. SLADEN,
Brevet Captain United States Army, Recorder.

The commission learning by the following telegram that Captain Wager could not get back to Huntsville until Monday following, it was decided to adjourn to Memphis, Tennessee, thence to return to Decatur Alabama.

[Telegram dated Decatur, Alabama, January 14, 1870; received January 14.]

To CAPTAIN SEATON, *Military Commission:*

Beckert is forty-five miles. Cannot get here until Monday.

J. H. WAGER.

The commission accordingly, at 4.30, adjourned.

BEN. P. RUNKLE,
Brevet Colonel United States Army.
J. R. LEWIS,
Brevet Colonel United States Army.
J. A. SLADEN,
Brevet Captain United States Army, Recorder.

SIXTEENTH DAY'S PROCEEDINGS—MEMPHIS, TENNESSEE.

The commission met at the office of Colonel Palmer, agent Bureau Refugees, Freedmen and Abandoned Lands, January 15, 1870, at 3 p. m., and made examination of papers in cases of fraud in that office.

At 5 p. m. the commission adjourned to meet Monday, January 17, 1870.

BEN. P. RUNKLE,
Brevet Colonel United States Army.
J. R. LEWIS,
Brevet Colonel United States Army.
J. A. SLADEN,
Brevet Captain United States Army, Recorder.

SEVENTEENTH DAY'S PROCEEDINGS—MEMPHIS, TENNESSEE.

The commission met at 9 a. m., January 17, 1870, and proceeded to the examination of witnesses.

The following is the evidence taken in writing, viz:

No. 1.—WILSON POLK, corporal Company F Sixty-fourth United States colored troops, being first duly sworn, deposes and says: I put in my claim with Moyers & Dedrick, and borrowed money of them twice, to wit: the first time $20; the second time a coat, for which I was to pay $25, a pair of boots, for which I was to pay $15—in all, $60. I bought the coat of Moyers's brother; also the boots. Colonel Palmer paid me about $210. I took the money and stepped out of the door of Colonel Palmer's office, and Moyers & Dedrick's clerk met me and demanded $160. This man's name was, as he said, Captain Dean. Dean said if I did not pay $160 he would have me put in the station-house. I paid him because I did not know any better.

I can count money.

WILSON + POLK.
his mark.

Sworn to before me and subscribed in my presence this 17th day of January, 1870.

BEN. P. RUNKLE,
Brevet Colonel United States Army.

No. 2.—EMILY ELLIOTT, widow of Granville Elliott, Company A Fifty-ninth United States colored troops, being first duly sworn, deposes and says: I put in a claim for bounty on account of services of Granville Elliott, with Parnell and McAllister, in Memphis, Tennessee. Afterward I put in a claim for bounty on account of services of Jacob Stanley, private Company D Fifty-ninth colored troops, to whom I was married, and whose widow I was previous to marriage to Granville Elliott; I was paid bounty for Jacob Stanley, but not for Granville Elliott. I put in a claim for pension on account of the services of Jacob Stanley with Dr. John Ingalls, of Memphis, the same man who put in and prosecuted my claim for bounty on account of said Jacob Stanley, my first husband. I was Dr. Ingalls's washerwoman for some months, when he was in the regiment, the Fifty-ninth United States colored troops, and he knows, having been in my house, that I was married to Elliott after the death of Stanley. He was our family physician, and he knew all about me.

EMILY + ELLIOTT.
her mark.

Sworn to before me and subscribed in my presence, January 17, 1870.
BEN. P. RUNKLE.

No. 3.—JUNIUS CARTMAN, corporal Company G Third United States colored heavy artillery, being first duly sworn, deposes and says: I first put my claim in with Lieutenant Garrett, agent of the bureau, but it was afterward turned over to Moyers & Dedrick. I received in advances of M. & D. $40, and not one cent more. I received of Colonel Palmer $231 91. As soon as I received this money I put it in the hands of Dr. S. J. Quinby, who was to take care of it for me. The whole amount was garnisheed in the hands of Quinby by Moyers & Dedrick, for the amount of $66, which they claimed to be due them for advances. Dr. Quinby gave me back $25 the day I was paid, and after the case was tried, Dr. Q. gave me back $12 75 more. This is every cent I have received on account of my bounty. About a week after I was paid I called at the office of Moyers & Dedrick, and they told me all the conversation that I had with Dr. Quinby, as well as I could have told it myself. When I left Colonel Palmer's office I was met at the door by Moyers's brother, who asked me if I was going to the office. I replied that I would go up in a little while. Then Dr. Quinby, who had been waiting outside the door for me, came up to me, and told me that I had better give him all of my money, in order to keep it out of the hands of M. & D. About eight days before this I met Dr. Quinby on the street and he told me that he would make out a bill for medical services against me, for the full amount of my bounty, so that I could keep it out of the hands of M. & D., who had been locking up the colored men, because they would not pay them large amounts for their advances. When I met Dr. Q. at the door of Colonel Palmer's office, I took him at his word, and gave him all of my money, and he gave me in return a bill, which I supposed was for the full amount of my bounty, but which I afterward ascertained to be for only $50. As soon as Dr. Q. had received my money, he started for his office, and when I ran to overtake him, he ran so fast that I could not reach him. I then observed that the sheriff was running after the doctor, and when I saw Dr. Quinby again, he told me that the sheriff got to his office before he did, and immediately garnisheed the money. I thought at first that the sheriff was following me, but when I turned off on a by street, I noticed that the sheriff did not follow me at all, but kept on after Dr. Quinby. The only person who saw me hand this money to the doctor, to the best of my knowledge and belief, was Jesse Bigee, my brother-in-law. Captain Thomson, who was collecting for Pettit & Siddons, also garnisheed my money for $93, which they claimed I owed them for clothing; but I only owed them $52. They did not claim the difference as interest, but the whole as the full amount of the bill.

JUNIUS + CARTMAN.
his
mark.

Sworn and subscribed to at Memphis, Tennessee, January 17, 1870, in the presence of—

J. A. SLADEN,
Brevet Captain United States Army, Recorder.

No. 4.—MADISON CARTMAN, sergeant Company G Third United States colored heavy artillery, being first duly sworn, deposes and says: First filed claim with Lieutenant Garrett in the bureau, and afterward it was turned over to Moyers & Dedrick. Received as advances from M. & D. $50 in money, and $40 worth of clothing; but I made oath before Colonel Palmer that I had received the worth of $104. This $104 was taken from my pay and bounty at Washington, and when I was paid the balance by Colonel Palmer, I paid them $25, and promised to pay them $20 more. I have not yet paid that $20, nor do I ever intend to do so. I have never been able to obtain my discharge. Moyers & Dedrick claimed this $59 as interest on the $90 that I owed them. My brother was with me when I paid Dedrick $95. His name is Junius Cartman. I paid it because I did not want to go to jail, as some had to for refusing to pay. I received from Colonel Palmer $124.

MADISON + CARTMAN.
his mark.

Signed and sworn to at Memphis, Tennessee, this January 17, 1870, in the presence of—

J. A. SLADEN,
Brevet Captain United States Army, Recorder.

No. 5.—JOHN SMALL, private Company H Third United States colored heavy artillery, being first duly sworn, deposes and says: I first filed my claim with Moyers & Dedrick. I have received in advances of Moyers & Dedrick, in all, the sum of $75, in three sums, viz: $40; $31 of which I paid immediately to Moyers's brother down stairs for goods I had purchased—$10 in cash, for which I gave a receipt for $15, and $20 which they gave me to pay for goods I had purchased of Moyers's brother down stairs. When I was paid I was met at Colonel Palmer's door by Moyers's brother, who demanded of me $24, which he said I owed them as interest. I refused to do this, but went to Moyers & Dedrick's office, where they insisted that I should pay them the $24. I reckoned up with them all I had received, and showed them that I did not owe them any such amount. Mr. Dedrick then said they had made a mistake, and that I only owed them $10. This I paid, and I left the office.

JOHN + SMALL.
his mark.

Sworn and subscribed to at Memphis, Tennessee, January 17, 1870, in the presence of—

J. A. SLADEN,
Brevet Captain United States Army, Recorder.

No. 6.—JOHN MCKINNEY, corporal Company D Sixty-fourth regiment United States colored troops, being first duly sworn, deposes and says: That I first filed my claim with Moyers & Dedrick. I have received in money of Moyers & Dedrick the sum of $89, all of which I paid to G. C. Moyers, down stairs, for goods, with the exception of $15 which I carried away in money. Besides these advances, I borrowed, a few days before I was paid, $7, for which I promised to pay them $10. When I was paid by Colonel Palmer, Mr. G. C. Moyers met me at the door and told me to go to Moyers & Dedrick's office and settle with them. I did not go till the next day, when they told me that I was owing them about $80. I did not have so much money left, but I paid them $10 then in payment for the seven I had received a short time before. They worried me so that I went again in a few days and paid them $25, which was all the money I could raise. I paid this money very reluctantly, for Colonel Palmer told me when I was paid that this money I had borrowed had been taken out of my pay in Washington.

JOHN + MCKINNEY.
his mark.

Sworn and subscribed to at Memphis, Tennessee, January 17, 1870, in the presence of—

J. A. SLADEN,
Brevet Captain U. S. A., Recorder Mil. Com.

BOUNTIES TO COLORED SOLDIERS.

No. 7.—WILLIAM CANNON, private Company F Third heavy artillery, colored, being first duly sworn, deposes and says: I put in my claim with Moyers & Dedrick. On September 9, 1868, I received from Moyers & Dedrick $10, and certified before Colonel Palmer that I had received $15. On October 14, 1868, I received $42 in clothing and ten-in money, and acknowledged before Colonel Palmer that I had received $60. On October 29, 1868, I received $15, and certified that I had received $25. In all, I received $77, but made oath before Colonel Palmer, at Moyers & Dedrick's direction, that I had received $100, which was deducted from my bounty, and I received from Colonel Palmer $89 45. I paid some debts and left the rest in the Freedmen's Bank. Moyers & Dedrick garnisheed it, and took the balance, about $30. They claimed this for interest on advances.

WILLIAM + CANNON.
mark.

Sworn to before me and subscribed in my presence, this 17th day of January, 1870.

BEN. P. RUNKLE.

No. 8.—A. M. SPERRY, being duly sworn, deposes and says: That he is a cashier of the Freedmen's Savings and Trust Company, in charge of the Branch at Memphis, Tennessee, and that in accordance with an arrangement made with the Pension Office, at Washington, D. C., he is an agent for the payment of such pensions as are payable at Nashville, Tennessee. That as such agent, he collected and paid the pension of America Tucker, mother of Isaac Tucker, claim No. 88,137, some time in the month of November, 1869, due her September 4, 1869; that the amount thus collected was $96, less the legal fees of collection, for preparing vouchers and oaths required—this being in full satisfaction of her claim for pension to September 4, 1869; that this pensioner is totally blind, and has always been accompanied, when attending to her pension claim, by her former mistress, Mrs. E. Oakley, residing at No. 55 Exchange street extended—such being Mrs. Oakley's statement made to affiant; that it appears from Mrs. Oakley's statement made to affiant, that M. Coombs, jr., or M. Coombs, jr., & Co., was the attorney in the case, and that from him, the said M. Coombs, the pensioner, America Tucker, has received some $200 or thereabouts—Mrs. Oakley having the exact amount thus paid on record; that the records of the pension office at Nashville show this pension has been regularly paid, and that the aggregate payments thus made amount to $446 22; that it thus appears the pensioner has been defrauded of a large part of the pension due her; and further, affiant states that all the facts herein set forth can be fully substantiated by the different parties herein referred to.

A. M. SPERRY,
Cashier.

Sworn to before me and subscribed in my presence, this 17th day of January, 1870.

BEN. P. RUNKLE,
Brevet Colonel United States Army.

No. 9.—HENRY MILLER, Company F Third United States colored heavy artillery, being first duly sworn, deposes and says: I put in my claim with Moyers & Dedrick. I borrowed money of Moyers & Dedrick, as follows: The first time, $10, and the second time $10, and that was all. I was paid by Colonel Palmer about $196, January 9, 1869; paid what I owed, but did not pay Moyers & Dedrick. They arrested me and put me in jail; they wanted $50; they did not give me any time to pay the $20, but arrested me when I went out of the bank just as I had been paid; I was in jail one night and one day, and was released, but I never paid the $20 to Moyers & Dedrick; only paid $10 to a lawyer.

HENRY MILLER.

Sworn to before me and subscribed in my presence, this 17th day of January, 1870.

BEN. P. RUNKLE,
Brevet Colonel United States Army.

No. 10.—THOMAS BRANCH, Company F Third United States colored heavy artillery, being first duly sworn, deposes and says: I first filed my claim with Lieutenant Garrett, bureau agent, and it was afterward turned over to Moyers & Dedrick. Before I got my bounty, I received from Moyers & Dedrick the sum of $45; thirty-eight of this was to pay for clothing bought of Moyers's brother down stairs; this is every cent I have ever received from Moyers & Dedrick. When I was paid last month by Colonel Palmer, I was met at the door by Mr. Moyers, brother of Moyers of the firm, who claimed $7 as interest on the money they had lent me. I owed Dr. Quinby $53 for medical services, which I paid him just as soon as I came out of Colonel Palmer's office.

THOMAS BRANCH.

Sworn and subscribed to at Memphis, Tennessee, January 17, 1870, in the presence of—

J. A. SLADEN,
Brevet Captain United States Army, Recorder.

No. 11.—WILLIAM C. JUPEE, Company E Fifty-ninth United States colored troops, being first duly sworn, deposes and says: I put in my claim with Dr. John Ingalls; Ingalls loaned me $10 at one time, and at another, $15; he said he would charge me half a dollar on every dollar. I was paid by Colonel Palmer, and he, Ingalls, caught me right outside of the door of the colonel's office and made me pay him $50. He said all those who did not pay would be put in jail. Lieutenant Maxwell, formerly of the Fifty-ninth, was with him; Lieutenant Maxwell took the money out of my own hands.

his
WILLIAM C. + JUPEE.
mark.

Sworn to before me and subscribed in my presence, this 17th day of January, 1870.

BEN. P. RUNKLE,
Brevet Colonel United States Army.

No. 12.—HENDERSON THOMPSON, private Company B Third regiment United States colored troops, being first duly sworn, deposes and says: I put in my claim with Moyers & Dedrick, of Memphis, Tennessee. Moyers & Dedrick loaned me $15, and that was all. Colonel Palmer paid me, and Mr. Ryan caught me just out on the steps, and I paid him $25, and Captain Dean $25 for Moyers & Dedrick. Dean said I had that money to pay or go to the station-house, and I paid rather than have any trouble. I had the money about three months.

HENDERSON $\overset{\text{his}}{+}$ THOMPSON.
mark.

Sworn to before me and subscribed in my presence, this 17th day of January, 1870.

BEN. P. RUNKLE,
Brevet Colonel United States Army.

No. 13.—MARY BUFORD, widow of Solomon Buford, Company G Eleventh United States colored troops, being duly sworn, deposes and says: That she filed her claim for bounty and pension with Mr. M. Coombs, jr., three or four years ago, and that her bounty was paid her by Colonel Palmer, a year ago last August—he, Colonel Palmer, paying her $311; that shortly before she got her bounty, she borrowed $5 of Mr. Coombs, which is all the money that was ever advanced to her by Mr. Coombs; that when she got her bounty, she went to Mr. Coombs and offered to pay him, but he said he would take it out of her pension; that she never got any money from Mr. Coombs in any way whatever, except the $5 borrowed before she got her bounty; that just before last Christmas, she received from Mr. A. M. Sperry, cashier of Freedmen's Bank at Memphis, about $120 pension money, and that this is all the pension money she has ever received; that last week she learned that Mr. Coombs was looking for her, and she went to him and inquired what he wanted, when he demanded $10 of her, which she paid him at the time.

MARY $\overset{\text{her}}{+}$ BUFORD.
mark.

Sworn to before me and subscribed in my presence, this 17th day of January, 1870.

BEN. P. RUNKLE,
Brevet Colonel United States Army.

Pension certificate 103,678, November 26, 1867.
Mary Buford was first paid to September 4, 1867, again to March 4, 1868, and again to September 4, 1868. Paid to her agent M. Coombs, jr., & Co., in each case. Paid in all, $480 20.
Mary Ann Wright has been paid three times: first, to September 4, 1867; March 4, 1868; and September 4, 1868. Paid to M. Coombs, jr., & Co., in each case. Paid in all, $468 47.
These women assert that they have been paid but about $200 each.

SPERRY.

The above is an original memorandum furnished by Mr. Stokes, pension agent, at Nashville.

No. 15.—JULIA TUCKER, being first duly sworn, deposes and says: That I am the widow of Conger Tucker, of Company E Fifty-ninth United States colored troops, who died at Corinth while in the United States service. I went to M. Coombs, jr., to file my claims; he made out some papers, and I made my mark. He then told me that I must pay him $10 before he would send off the papers. I tried to raise the money but failed. He then said that he would put in the papers for $2 50, but I could not even raise that amount, and I never went to him again. One reason why I did not return to him again was, because he used my witness, a young girl named Lucy Reeves, in a very outrageous manner, throwing her down on a sofa, and then thrusting me out of the room. I supposed that he had not put in my claim, and so about two years, more or less, afterward, I went to Dr. John Ingalls, and filed my claim with him. I never saw Coombs from that day until the 23d day of August, 1869, when I was sent to him by Colonel Palmer. I never gave him any authority to sign my name, and never knew that my claim was settled till informed of the fact by Colonel Palmer, and I have never received one cent of bounty from any source whatever.

JULIA ^{her}+_{mark.} TUCKER.

Sworn and subscribed to at Memphis, Tennessee, January 17, 1870, in presence of—

J. A. SLADEN,
Brevet Captain U. S. A., Recorder Mil. Com.

No. 16.—ALFRED FOGG, late corporal Company F Eleventh regiment United States colored troops, being duly sworn, deposes and says: That he put in a claim for bounty, &c., with Messrs. Moyers & Dedrick about *three years* ago; that about a year since he went to Mr. Moyers's house and got a pair of pants, a shirt, four pair socks, and a hat, for which Moyers said he would charge $22; that about two months afterward he went to Moyers's office and borrowed $5, for which Moyers said he would charge him $10; that, about two weeks after, he borrowed $10 of Moyers, who said he would charge him $20; that about a year ago he got a pistol for $15, a gun for $15, and a pair of pants for $15, which Mr. Moyers gave him $45 to pay for, and he paid it all for the three articles mentioned; that this is all the money or advances of any kind he ever received from Moyers & Dedrick; that on the 30th of December, 1869, Colonel Palmer paid him $206 50, having given him a slip of paper showing that $93 50 had been deducted at Washington from his bounty for fees and advances due Moyers & Dedrick, and that Colonel Palmer told him that all he owed them had been paid; that after he left Colonel Palmer's office, Mr. S. C. Davis came to him and said he must pay what he owed Moyers & Dedrick, and made him pay $17 50, which he claimed was due them, and for which he gave me the receipt herewith presented.

ALFRED ^{his}+_{mark.} FOGG.

MEMPHIS, *December 27,* 1869.

Received of Alfred Fogg seventeen dollars and fifty cents, in full of all demands up to date.

MOYERS & DEDRICK.
Per S. C. DAVIS.

Sworn to before me and subscribed in my presence, this 11th day of January, 1870.

BEN. P. RUNKLE,
Brevet Colonel United States Army.

No. 17.—HANNAH BOOKER, widow of Archibald Booker, late private of Company I Fifty-third regiment United States colored troops, being duly sworn, deposes and says: That on the twenty-fourth day of January, 1867, she put in a claim for bounty, additional bounty, and arrears ~v with Mr. M. Coombs, jr., and that she did not know that he put in ιm for pension; that he never told her she had put in a claim for pension; that in the summer of 1868 she borrowed $55 of Mr. M. Coombs, without any bargain as to how much she was to pay him for it; that on March 30, 1869, Colonel Palmer paid her $271 20 bounty, &c.; that the next week she went to Mr. Coombs to pay him, and Mr. Coombs demanded $70, which she paid him in the presence of a witness who is known to her as Charlie Crook, (colored;) that in a week or two Mr. Coombs came to her house and wanted to borrow $75, which she loaned him, he agreeing to pay her $100 for it in three weeks, giving her his note for $75, payable in thirty days, which note he has not paid, but has renewed two or three times, the last note being dated October 26, 1869; that she has never received any money for her claims from any one, except the $271 20 paid her by Colonel Palmer, and the $55 which she received from Mr. Coombs, and for which she paid him $70; that she put in a claim for pension with Colonel Palmer on July 29, 1869, after which it was found that a claim had been already put in and allowed—No. 112220, payable at Nashville agency, at rate of $8 per month, commencing 11th April, 1864, certificate dated 25th April, 1868, and sent to B. D. Hyam, Washington, D. C., (act 14th June, 1862, Book 6, vol. 14, page 97, House Clerk.)

HANNAH + BOOKER.
her
mark.

Sworn to before me and subscribed in my presence, this 17th day of January, 1870.

BEN. P. RUNKLE,
Brevet Colonel United States Army.

[Two-cent postage stamp.]
$75]

MEMPHIS, TENNESSEE, *October* 26, 1869.

Thirty days after date we promise to pay to the order of Mrs. H. Bucher seventy-five dollars, at our office, Memphis, Tennessee, value received.

M. COOMBS, JR., & CO.

No. 2. Due November 26, 1869.

True copy:

J. R. LEWIS,
Brevet Colonel U. S. A.

EIGHTEENTH DAY'S PROCEEDINGS—DECATUR, ALABAMA.

The commission met at Decatur, Alabama, at 1 o'clock p. m., January 18, 1870.

Captain Wager reported that he had been to Winston County, and found Captain Charles A. Beckert, and had presented the summons to him, but that he refused to return with him, but promised to report to him at Huntsville, Alabama, on Tuesday evening, January 18, 1870.

It was then decided that one of the members of the commission should proceed to Huntsville, Alabama, to take the deposition of Charles A. Beckert.

The commission then adjourned to meet in Nashville, Tennessee, for the purpose of examining the records of the pension office, and procuring copies of the indictments against M. M. Cloon.

BEN. P. RUNKLE,
Brevet Colonel United States Army.
J. R. LEWIS,
Bvevet Colonel United States Army.
J. A. SLADEN,
Brevet Captain United States Army, Recorder.

NINETEENTH DAY'S PROCEEDINGS—NASHVILLE, TENNESSEE.

The commission met at Nashville, January 19, and at once proceeded to the examination of the records of the pension office. The result of this examination is shown by the notes made in red ink on the pension cases. After examination of the records of circuit court for copies of indictments against M. M. Cloon, (copies herewith attached,) the commission adjourned to meet at Washington, D. C., in accordance with the following telegram, viz:

WASHINGTON, D. C., *January 13, 1870.*

To Captain J. A. SLADEN:

Special Orders No. 189 is hereby extended, to direct the board to meet at Washington, D. C., after concluding investigation in Tennessee and Alabama.
By order, &c.

HENRY M. WHITTLESEY,
Assistant Adjutant General.

Colonel J. R. Lewis, being designated by the commission at Decatur, Alabama, to proceed to Huntsville, Alabama, to receive the testimony of Captain Charles A. Beckert, proceeded to that place and remained till 11 o'clock p. m. Tuesday evening, Mr. Beckert not having reported up to that time. Letter of John D. Wager, January 21, 1870, herewith appended, showing that Captain Beckert did not report during the two days following.

BEN. P. RUNKLE,
Brevet Colonel United States Army.
J. R. LEWIS,
Brevet Colonel United States Army.
J. A. SLADEN,
Brevet Captain United States Army, Recorder.

Circuit court of the United States for the middle district of Tennessee— October term, 1869.

The grand inquest of the United States for the middle district of Tennessee, upon their oaths present that, on or about June 24, 1868, within said district, M. M. Cloon caused and procured to be falsely made, forged, and counterfeited a paper writing purporting to be a power of attorney to receive a pension due from the United States, in this—one Lucy Chambers, as the widow of Philip Chambers, a soldier in the army of the United States, to wit, in the One hundred and eleventh regiment of United States colored volunteers, was entitled to a pension from the United States from March 6, 1865, to March 4, 1868, and said Cloon caused to be falsely executed a paper writing purporting to be a power of attorney from said pensioner to one W. W. Ingersoll, authorizing him, as the true and lawful attorney of said pensioner, for her and in her name, to receive from the agent of the United States for paying pensions, in Nashville, in the State of Tennessee, the said pension; said false and counterfeit power of attorney being so caused to be made in order that the said Ingersoll might receive the said pension.

And further, that at said time and in said district said Cloon did willingly aid and assist in falsely making, forging, and counterfeiting the paper writing aforesaid to receive the said pension, with the intent thereby to aid and assist said Ingersoll to receive the same from the said agent of the United States.

And further, that at said time and in said district said Cloon did cause and procure to be forged and counterfeited the name of said Lucy Chambers to said paper writing purporting to be such power of attorney, with the intent that thereby said Ingersoll might receive from said agent said pension.

And further, that at said time and at said district said Cloon did willingly assist and aid in forging and counterfeiting the name of said pensioner to said paper writing purporting to be such power of attorney, with the intent thereby to aid said Ingersoll in receiving said pension from said agent. And further, that at said time and in said district said Cloon did knowingly and fraudulently endeavor to have said pension to be received by said Ingersoll, by virtue of such false, forged, and counterfeited power of attorney, contrary to the form of the statute in such case made and provided, and against the peace and dignity of the United States.

R. McP. SMITH,
United States District Attorney.

A true copy:

E. R. CAMPBELL,
Clerk United States District and Circuit Court.

First indictment.—W. W. Ingersoll, for wrongfully withholding pension money due Lucy Chambers, widow of Philip Chambers, private Company F One hundred and eleventh regiment United States colored volunteers.

Second indictment.—For his agency in manufacture of spurious power of attorney to himself, in order to obtain said pension.

Against Cloon for aiding in the forgery of said power of attorney.

Theory of the prosecution.—That Ingersoll, in Nashville, and Cloon, in Pulaski, combined for the purpose of manufacturing a fictitious power of attorney, purporting to be made by Lucy Chambers, at Pulaski, authorizing said Ingersoll to draw her pension, at Nashville; that, accordingly, said Cloon procured a negro woman, at Pulaski, to personate said Lucy Chambers in executing said power, which was thereupon prepared and acknowledged and witnessed in due form, the genuine Lucy Chambers being all the while at Nashville; their object being to enable said Ingersoll to get into his hands said pension, which the pension agent would have insisted on paying to the pensioner in person had he known that she was at Nashville. The matter succeeded, and Ingersoll got the money, and kept it.

OFFICE OF AGENT BUREAU REFUGEES,
FREEDMEN AND ABANDONED LANDS,
Huntsville, Alabama, January 21, 1870.

COLONEL: I have the honor to return, as per your instructions, the letter left by the commission for Captain C. A. Beckert, who has not up to this time made his appearance.

I am, colonel, very respectfully, your obedient servant,

JOHN H. WAGER, *Agent.*

Brevet Colonel J. R. LEWIS,
Superintendent of Education, Atlanta, Georgia.

TWENTIETH DAY'S PROCEEDINGS.

Pursuant to adjournment at Nashville, the commission met at Washington, D. C., January 28, 1870, and proceeded to the examination of the evidence, with a view to investigating in the departments each case of alleged fraud, both of bounty and pensions.

At 3.30 p. m. the commission adjourned.

BEN. P. RUNKLE,
Brevet Colonel United States Army.
J. R. LEWIS,
Brevet Colonel United States Army,
J. A. SLADEN,
Brevet Captain United States Army, Recorder.

TWENTY-FIRST DAY'S PROCEEDINGS.

The commission met at 9.30 a. m., January 29, (Saturday,) 1870, and continued the examination and collation of the cases of frauds, and commenced to make out their report upon the evidence in their possession.

A communication was received from John H. Wager, bureau agent at Huntsville, Alabama, inclosing the affidavit of Charles A. Beckert, made in answer to certain written questions propounded to him by the commission. The letter and inclosure is herewith attached.

At 3.30 the commission adjourned.

BEN. P. RUNKLE,
Brevet Colonel United States Army.
J. R. LEWIS,
Brevet Colonel United States Army.
J. A. SLADEN,
Brevet Captain United States Army, Recorder.

HUNTSVILLE, ALABAMA, *January 25, 1870.*

SIR: On the 16th instant I received your summons to appear before the military commission then in session at Huntsville, Alabama, to investigate "certain alleged frauds committed upon colored soldiers and their heirs in the payment of bounties, pensions, &c." According to the summons, I left for Huntsville on the 17th instant in the morning, intending to be at that place on Tuesday night, but was delayed on the road by the accidental injuring and falling of my horse, and the drawing off of myself; in consequence of this accident I did not arrive here until to-day, and I hasten to make the following statement relative to the charges and accusations made by a certain M. M. Cloon:

1. In regard to the advances to colored soldiers on their bounties I would state that, to the best of my knowledge and belief, Messrs. Chipman, Hosmer & Co., of Washington, D. C., (whose correspondent I am,) had no knowledge of the same, and are not concerned in the same; Major D. S. Mann, of New York, came to this neighborhood about the 20th day of December, 1867, and made several advances to soldiers on their bounty claims, taking their notes, but in all instances, as far as I have seen, the amounts stipulated with the soldiers were paid, interest for the advance was charged according to agreement, and to the satisfaction of the soldier. About the same time I formed the acquaintance of this M. M.

Cloon, who kept an office as correspondent for General O'Neil at Pulaski, Tennessee, and solicited the bounty claims for said O'Neil, claim agent at Washington, D. C. In conversation with him on business concerning claims, &c., he proposed to me to act with him in partnership; to advance money on claims, as we could as well make the percentage as others; he could raise the money; he could furnish $6,000 for this purpose. I refused to do anything with him in that line, as I presumed, from all his conversations, that he was working out a scheme which would have been to no advantage to me, but would have ruined me. He came to see me at Decatur, Alabama, my home, about the middle of September of the same year, and renewed the proposition, telling me, that he had made already over $6,000, and wished me to assist him and share the profits. I again declined. After this he took up the receipts I had given claimants for, their claims, discharges, &c., in the name of Chipman, Hosmer & Co., of Washington, D. C., and attempted to prosecute the claims, always assuring me that he would not interfere with our business. In the month of November, 1869, I visited him, the said M. M. Cloon, in his office, at Huntsville, Alabama, where he exhibited to me a large lot of pension certificates, which he had received from colored pensioners, for the purpose, as he told me, to hold them until the decision was made concerning their payment.

2. In regard to the charges preferred by said M. M. Cloon against Mr. J. H. Wager, agent Refugees, Freedmen and Abandoned Lands, at Huntsville, Alabama, I would state that, to the best of my knowledge and belief, the same are untrue and without any foundation, as I have known the said J. H. Wager, esq., as an efficient and strict officer, (as disbursing officer,) and know of no instance of complaint against him in the exercise of his duties. And I further believe that the charges against the other officers, preferred by the said M. M. Cloon, are of the same character, as the bureau officers were in his way to execute his plans.

I am, sir, very respectfully, your most obedient servant,

CHAS. A. BECKERT.

J. A. SLADEN,
  Brevet Captain United States Army,
    Recorder of Military Commission, Washington, D. C.

P. S.—As to the remarks I should have made to the said M. M. Cloon, that General Balloch was implicated in the advancing of money to colored soldiers on their claims; that I had said to the said Cloon General Balloch *did* receive twenty-five per cent. of the profit on said advances, is untrue and false, and without any foundation, as I only knew that the advances were made by said D. S. Mann on his own responsibility, and in accordance with a circular issued by General O. O. Howard regulating advances on said colored claims. In the conversation with said Cloon at Pulaski, Tennessee, he remarked to me that advances could be made without conflicting with the laws regulating the payments of said claims.

CHAS. A. BECKERT.

Sworn to and subscribed before me this the 25th day of January, A. D. 1870.

JAMES H. BONE,
  Clerk Circuit Court.

OFFICE AGENT BUREAU REFUGEES,
FREEDMEN AND ABANDONED LANDS,
Huntsville, Alabama, January 25, 1870.

CAPTAIN: I have the honor to herewith transmit the inclosed statement of Captain C. A. Beckert.

He said he just reached town. Was detained by his horse falling, hurting the horse and himself.

I stated to him, as far as I could remember, the contents of a letter left for him by Colonel Lewis.

After which he handed me the statement.

I am, respectfully,

JOHN H. WAGER, *Agent.*

Captain SLADEN,
Recorder of Military Commission, Washington, D. C.

TWENTY-SECOND DAY'S PROCEEDINGS.

The commission met January 31, 1870, (Monday,) at 9.30 a. m., and adjourned at 3.30 p. m., the day being spent in examining the records and making out and forwarding lists of names to Mr. W. P. Drew, of those names concerning which the commission desired further information.

BEN. P. RUNKLE,
Brevet Colonel United States Army.
J. R. LEWIS,
Brevet Colonel United States Army.
J. A. SLADEN,
Brevet Captain United States Army, Recorder.

TWENTY-THIRD DAY'S PROCEEDINGS.

The commission met February 1, 1870, (Thursday,) at 9.30 a. m., and continued the examination of the records and the collation and arranging of cases.

Adjourned at 3.30 p. m.

BEN. P. RUNKLE,
Brevet Colonel United States Army.
J. R. LEWIS,
Brevet Colonel United States Army.
J. A. SLADEN,
Brevet Captain United States Army, Recorder.

TWENTY-FOURTH DAY'S PROCEEDINGS.

The commission met at 9.30 a. m., February 2, (Wednesday,) 1870, and continued the examination of the records and the collation and arranging of cases.

Adjourned at 3.30 p. m.

BEN. P. RUNKLE,
Brevet Colonel United States Army.
J. R. LEWIS,
Brevet Colonel United States Army.
J. A. SLADEN,
Brevet Captain United States Army, Recorder.

TWENTY-FIFTH DAY'S PROCEEDINGS.

The commission met at 9.30 a. m., February 3, (Thursday,) 1870, and proceeded to the office of the Commissioner of Pensions for the purpose of examining the records of that office in cases of alleged frauds on pension claimants.

After this examination the commission continued the examination of their own records.

Communications were sent to the Commissioner of the Bureau Refugees, Freedmen and Abandoned Lands, asking that certain information be obtained from the Surgeon General and the Chief Engineer of the army concerning the claims of employés of those departments.

BEN. P. RUNKLE,
Brevet Colonel United States Army.
J. R. LEWIS,
Brevet Colonel United States Army.
J. A. SLADEN,
Brevet Captain United States Army, Recorder.

TWENTY-SIXTH DAY'S PROCEEDINGS.

The commission met at 10 a. m. Friday, February 4, 1870, and continued the examination of the evidence and the work upon the report.

The commission adjourned at 4 p. m.

BEN. P. RUNKLE,
Brevet Colonel United States Army.
J. R. LEWIS,
Brevet Colonel United States Army.
J. A. SLADEN,
Brevet Captain United States Army, Recorder.

TWENTY-SEVENTH DAY'S PROCEEDINGS.

The commission met at 10 o'clock a. m. Saturday, February 5, 1870, and continued the examination of the evidence, and the work upon the report.

Communication was sent to Mr. Wm. P. Drew, chief of claim division, Bureau of Refugees, Freedmen and Abandoned Lands, asking for statements in cases of certain bounty claimants.

At 4 p. m. the commission adjourned.

BEN. P. RUNKLE,
Brevet Colonel United States Army.
J. R. LEWIS,
Brevet Colonel United States Army.
J. A. SLADEN,
Brevet Captain United States Army, Recorder.

TWENTY-EIGHTH DAY'S PROCEEDINGS.

The commission met at 10 a. m. Monday, February 7, 1870, and continued the examination of the records and the collection of cases, and the work upon the report.

A communication was received from General G. W. Balloch, (hereto attached,) containing evidence of forgery on the part of M. M. Cloon, in making up the applications of a widow for bounty.

At 4 p. m. the commission adjourned.

BEN. P. RUNKLE,
Brevet Colonel United States Army.
J. R. LEWIS,
Brevet Colonel United States Army.
J. A. SLADEN,
Brevet Captain United States Army, Recorder.

DISBURSING OFFICE OF CLAIMS—BUREAU, &C.,
Columbia, Tennessee, January 21, 1870.

DEAR SIR: Inclosed please find an application purporting to be from Lina Ballentine, widow of Sullivan. The paper was got up by M. M. Cloon. When first sent me, I did not notice the writing particularly, but upon its return I noticed it, and took it to Pulaski, when I saw a colored man who was present in the clerk's office, and who said there was no such men as B. J. Sheridan and Jim Morgan there, and as to John Green and Matthew Lipscomb, there are no such men in the country. It is evidently a forgery of Cloon's getting up. The woman's old master told me Cloon wanted him to go her security for $15, and he would get her the money. Since the commission was here he has been charging the colored people in advance. This paper inclosed should become part of others the commission have. The name of Sheridan no doubt was signed by his clerk, J. Morris; while in Jim Morgan his (Cloon's) writing sticks out in every feature. I have not read the late circular in regard to witnesses who write their names, and you have one set of papers in the case of Eliza Leonard.

Very respectfully yours,

JOHN L. WILSON,
Disbursing Officer of Claims—Bureau, &c.

General GEO. W. BALLOCH,
Chief Disbursing Officer, Bureau, &c., Washington City, D. C.

PULASKI, TENNESSEE, *December* 17, 1869.

DEAR SIR: I inclose herewith my application for the bounty and other allowances of my deceased husband, Sullivan Ballentine, late of Company G Twelfth United States colored infantry, who died since making application for the bounty, &c., due him; which I understand has been settled by certificate No. 484,521, and turned over to the bureau, and probably has been received by you. If so, you will please return, if necessary, the vouchers in your hands issued in favor of my husband, with the inclosed application, and have them replaced by ones in my favor. And if not yet received by you, you will be kind enough to forward the inclosed application, and request my vouchers to be forwarded to you.

My destitution compels me to request your early action in the premises.

Very respectfully, &c.,

LINA BALLENTINE.
Per J. M., *Clerk.*

Major J. L. WILSON,
Agent of Bureau, &c.

H. Ex. Doc. 241——8

BOUNTIES TO COLORED SOLDIERS,

Widow's application for bounty.

STATE OF TENNESSEE, *County of Giles, ss:*

On this 16th day of December, 1869, personally appeared before me, a clerk of the county court in and for the county and State aforesaid, Lina Ballentine, who, being duly sworn, deposes and says that she is the widow of Sullivan Ballentine, deceased, late a resident of the county of Giles, and State of Tennessee, who was a private in Company G, of the Twelfth regiment of United States colored infantry volunteers, who enlisted at Elk River Bridge, in the State of Tennessee, on or about the 1st day of August, 1863, and who died out of the service aforesaid, at Elkton, in the State of Tennessee, on or about the 16th day of July, 1869, leaving her as widow. She further says, that she was married to the said Sullivan Ballentine on 13th day of October, 1868, at Elkton, county of Giles, and State of Tennessee, by John Bonner, a colored minister of the gospel, whose affidavit is hereto annexed. Deponent further says that the best proof of her said marriage is hereto annexed, as may be seen thereby; that her name before her said marriage was Lina Butler; that she makes this application for the purpose of recovering the amount of treasury certificate No. 484521, which certificate had been issued in favor of her said deceased husband from the United States government, and which yet remains in the possession of the Bureau of Refugees, Freedmen and Abandoned Lands, and desires that the certificate of pay, when issued in satisfaction hereof, may be sent to her at Pulaski post office, county of Giles, and State of Tennessee, and I hereby constitute and appoint John L. Wilson, Bureau Agent at Columbia, Tennessee, attorney to present and prosecute this claim, and authorize him to receive and receipt for any certificate, check, or draft that may be issued for the same, or to do any other act or thing necessary, or that I might do if personally present at the doing thereof, with full power of substitution and revocation, hereby countermanding all former authority given for the above specified purpose.

            her
         LINA + BALLENTINE
            mark.

Signed in presence of—
 JIM MORGAN.
 B. J. SHERIDAN.

Subscribed and sworn to before me. And also personally appeared John Green and Mathew Libscomb, of the county of Giles, and State of Tennessee, who being duly sworn according to law, depose and say, that they are well acquainted with the above-named claimant, and know that she is the widow of Sullivan Ballentine, deceased, who was a private in Company G, of the Twelfth regiment of United States colored infantry volunteers, and who died out of the service of the United States, as above stated, leaving the above-named widow. Deponents further say that they were well acquainted with the said Sullivan Ballentine before his death, and know that he and the said Lina Ballentine lived and cohabited as man and wife, and were so reputed in the community in which they lived; and that she is the widow of the identical Sullivan Ballentine named above, and who made application for the bounty and other allowances due him prior to his death through Messrs. O'Neill and Dufour, of Washington, D. C., and which claim said firm reports as having been settled by certificate No. 484521. Deponents further say that they were personally present at the death and inhumation of the said Sullivan Ballentine, and depose from their personal knowledge of all the facts in the case.

Deponents further say, that their knowledge of these statements of facts is derived from a personal and very intimate acquaintance with the whole of said family, having lived near neighbors for twenty years. They further say that they have no interest whatever, neither directly nor indirectly, in this matter.

JOHN + GREEN.
_{his   mark.}

MATHEW + LIBSCOMB.
_{his   mark.}

Signed in presence of—
JIM MORGAN.
B. J. SHERIDAN.

Subscribed and sworn to before me, this 16th day of December, 1869 and I certify that claimant and witnesses are credible and worthy, and that they understood fully the foregoing declaration and joint affidavit before signing their names thereto, and I am not interested in this matter.

[SEAL.] D. A. WILBURN,
Clerk Giles County Court.

STATE OF TENNESSEE, *Giles County* :

Personally appeared before me, D. A. Wilburn, clerk of the county court of said county, John Bonner, colored, a minister of the Gospel, with whom I am personally acquainted, and made oath in due form of law that about the last of October, 1868, he solemnized the rites of matrimony between Solomon Ballentine, colored, and Lina Butler, colored, and that he returned the license authorizing such marriage, with the proper indorsement of their execution on the same, to the clerk of the county court of said county. This December 16, 1869.

JOHN + BONNER.
_{his   mark.}

Attest:
J. T. ROSE.
W. P. GRIGSBY.

Sworn to and subscribed before me 16th December, 1869.

D. A. WILBURN,
Clerk.

STATE OF TENNESSEE, *Giles County* :

I, D. A. Wilburn, clerk of the county court of said county, do hereby certify that I have made diligent search in my office for the marriage license of Solomon Ballentine to Lina Butler, and am unable to find the same.

Witness my hand and official seal this December 16, 1869.
[SEAL.] D. A. WILBURN,
Clerk Giles County Court.

TWENTY-NINTH DAY'S PROCEEDINGS.

The commission met at 10 a. m., Tuesday, February 8, 1870, and continued the examination of the record and the work upon the report. Communications were sent to the Bureau of Refugees, Freedmen and Abandoned Lands, asking for certain information.
At 4 p. m. the commission adjourned.

BEN. P. RUNKLE,
Brevet Colonel United States Army.
J. R. LEWIS,
Brevet Colonel United States Army.
J. A. SLADEN,
Brevet Captain United States Army, Recorder.

THIRTIETH DAY'S PROCEEDINGS.

The commission met at 10 a. m., Wednesday, February 9, 1870, and continued the examination of the records and the labor upon the report. A communication was received from W. P. Drew, chief of claim division, Bureau of Refugees, Freedmen and Abandoned Lands, containing information in cases of certain claimants for bounty, called for by the commission, which document is appended to the proceedings of the commission, marked Drew's Statement A.
At 4 p. m. the commission adjourned.

BEN. P. RUNKLE,
Brevet Colonel United States Army.
J. R. LEWIS,
Brevet Colonel United States Army.
J. A. SLADEN,
Brevet Captain United States Army, Recorder.

THIRTY-FIRST DAY'S PROCEEDINGS.

The commission met at 10 a. m., Thursday, February 10, 1870, and continued its labor in examining the evidence and arranging specific cases and in making up the report. A communication was received from W. P. Drew, chief of claim division, Bureau of Refugees, Freedmen and Abandoned Lands, in answer to requests from the commission, containing information in certain bounty cases, which document is appended to proceedings of commission, and marked Drew's Statement B.
At 4 p. m. the commission adjourned.

BEN. P. RUNKLE,
Brevet Colonel United States Army.
J. R. LEWIS,
Brevet Colonel United States Army.
J. A. SLADEN,
Brevet Captain United States Army, Recorder.

BOUNTIES TO COLORED SOLDIERS.

THIRTY-SECOND DAY'S PROCEEDINGS.

The commission met at 10 a. m., Friday, February 11, 1870, and continued to examine the record and the work upon the report.

Communications were sent to Bureau of Refugees, Freedmen and Abandoned Lands, asking for certain information.

At 4 p. m. the commission adjourned.

      BEN. P. RUNKLE,
    Brevet Colonel United States Army.
      J. R. LEWIS,
    Brevet Colonel United States Army.
      J. A. SLADEN,
  Brevet Captain United States Army, Recorder.

THIRTY-THIRD DAY'S PROCEEDINGS.

The commission met at 11 a. m., Saturday, February 12, 1870, and continued the examination of the proceedings and the labor upon the report.

A communication (hereto attached) was received from Wm. P. Drew, chief of claims division, Bureau Refugees, Freedmen and Abandoned Lands, inclosing copy of his letter of June 25, 1869, to M. M. Cloon.

Communications were written to the Commissioner Bureau Refugees, Freedmen and Abandoned Lands, calling for certain information.

At 4 p. m. the commission adjourned.

      BEN. P. RUNKLE,
    Brevet Colonel United States Army.
      J. R. LEWIS,
    Brevet Colonel United States Army.
      J. A. SLADEN,
  Brevet Captain United States Army, Recorder.

  War Department, Bureau of Refugees,
Freedmen and Abandoned Lands, Claim Division,
    Washington, D. C., February 11, 1870.

Colonel: In accordance with your request of the 10th instant, I am directed to inclose herewith copy of letter from this office addressed to M. M. Cloon, under date of June 25, 1869.

The letter was intended to be sarcastic, but it would seem from subsequent developments that Mr. Cloon interpreted it literally, and as in some measure justifying his conduct.

In this connection your attention is respectfully invited to copy of letter from this office dated July 26, 1869, addressed to J. B. Coons, esq., agent and disbursing officer of this bureau at Nashville, Tennessee.

Very respectfully, your obedient servant,
      WILLIAM P. DREW,
   *Agent Bureau Refugees, Freedmen
  and Abandoned Lands, Chief of Claim Division.*

Brevet Colonel B. P. Runkle, U. S. A.,
 *President Military Commission Bureau Refugees,
  Freedmen and Abandoned Lands, Washington, D. C.*

WAR DEPARTMENT, BUREAU OF REFUGEES,
FREEDMEN AND ABANDONED LANDS, CLAIM DIVISION,
Washington, D. C., June 25, 1869.

SIR: In acknowledging the receipt of your communication of the 15th instant, I beg to assure you that there has been no intention on the part of this office to accuse you unjustly, and to express the earnest hope that success may attend your laudable exertions to expose and punish dishonesty, whether perpetrated by private persons or by officials.

Very respectfully, your obedient servant,
WILLIAM P. DREW,
*Agent Bureau Refugees, Freedmen
and Abandoned Lands, Chief of Claim Division.*

M. M. CLOON, Esq.,
Pulaski, Tennessee.

THIRTY-FOURTH DAY'S PROCEEDINGS.

The commission met at 10 a. m., Monday, February 14, 1870, and continued the examination of the records, the collection of cases, and the work upon the report.

In reply to communications from the commission, W. P. Drew, chief of claim division Bureau Refugees, Freedmen and Abandoned Lands, sends, first, copy of letter written by M. M. Cloon to Chipman, Hosmer & Co., (hereto attached;) second, statement in case of Elvis Key, late private Company F Fourteenth regiment United States colored troops, (attached to the proceedings of the commission and marked Drew's Statement C;) and third, statement in case of William Reedus, late corporal Company I One Aundred and Tenth regiment United States colored troops, (attached to report of commission and marked Drew's Statement D.)

At 4 p. m. the commissioned adjourned.

BEN. P. RUNKLE,
Brevet Colonel United States Army.
J. R. LEWIS,.
Brevet Colonel United States Army.
J. A. SLADEN,
Brevet Captain United States Army, Recorder.

WAR DEPARTMENT, BUREAU OF REFUGEES,
FREEDMEN AND ABANDONED LANDS, CLAIM DIVISION,
Washington, D. C., February 12, 1870.

CAPTAIN: In answer to your letter of the 11th instant, I am directed to inclose herewith letter of the 15th ultimo, addressed to Messrs. Chipman, Hosmer & Co., attorneys, &c., by M. M. Cloon, of Pulaski, Tennessee, and to request return of the same after examination.

Very respectfully, your obedient servant,
WILLIAM P. DREW,
*Agent Bureau Refugees, Freedmen
and Abandoned Lands, Chief of Claim Division.*

Brevet Captain J. A. SLADEN, U. S. A.,
*Recorder for Military Commission Bureau Refugees,
Freedmen and Abandoned Lands, Washington, D. C.*

(Inclosure returned to W. P. Drew, esq., in accordance with his request, March 4, 1870.)

THIRTY-FIFTH DAY'S PROCEEDINGS.

The commission met at 10 a. m., February 15, 1870, and took the testimony of Thomas Wilson, attorney and claim agent, A. A. Hosmer, attorney and claim agent, of the firm of Chipman, Hosmer & Co., and B. D. Hyam, claim agent, all of Washington, and whose testimony is hereto attached. Statements in cases of certain pension claimants were received, in reply to requests from the commission from the Pension Bureau, which are attached to the proceedings, and marked "Pension Office A." A communication from W. P. Drew, chief of claim division Bureau Refugees, Freedmen and Abandoned Lands, inclosing letter from M. M. Coon to the Second Auditor, hereto attached.

At 4 p. m. the commission adjourned.

BEN. P. RUNKLE,
Brevet Colonel United States Army.
J. B. LEWIS,
Brevet Colonel United States Army.
J. A. SLADEN,
Brevet Captain United States Army, Recorder.

WAR DEPARTMENT, BUREAU OF REFUGEES,
FREEDMEN AND ABANDONED LANDS, CLAIM DIVISION,
Washington, February 14, 1870.

CAPTAIN: In accordance with your letter of the 12th instant, I am directed to inclose herewith communication addressed to the Hon. Second Auditor of the Treasury by Mr. M. M. Cloon, dated Pulaski, Tennessee, January 18, 1870, and to particularly request return of the same to this office, after desired examination by the commission.

Very respectfully, your obedient servant,
WILLIAM P. DREW,
*Agent Bureau Refugees, Freedmen,
and Abandoned Lands, Chief of Claim Division.*

Brevet Captain J. A. SLADEN, U. S. A.,
*Recorder for Military Commission,
Bureau Refugees, Freedmen and Abandoned Lands.*

PULASKI, TENNESSEE, *January* 18, 1870.

DEAR SIR: Pardon me for again taking the liberty of writing to you personally; but circumstances are such as to compel me to beseech your aid in the following case. The military commission sent here to investigate the frauds complained of in my recent letter to you entirely ignored their duty, and failed intentionally to inquire into the official conduct of bureau agents. It is not necessary that I should here give you any of the proceedings of the said commission, but would refer you to a protest that is being gotten up here by the Union element of our citizens, complaining of the proceedings of the same. They would not permit anybody to depose against bureau agents; and if any, perchance, did so, they construed the testimony so as to destroy its original intent and meaning, after which it was by them written. It would be an insult to your intelligence to attempt to inform you that claim agents could cheat colored claimants out of bounty in any of the lately rebellious States without the co-operation of bureau agents. My name having been extensively used in connection with bounty frauds in this part of the country, I therefore deem it my duty to exonerate myself of such charges, and to throw full light on the subject, that the guilty ones may be known.

Now, sir, some time ago I was employed by certain bureau agents to buy such bounty claims as they directed, giving for them such amounts as they directed. This I accordingly did in conformity with our contract, until finally the negroes began to complain of the matter, after which I refused to purchase any more claims, and advised the said bureau agents to immediately stop the same or else I would report the matter. They still operated, and I reported them time after time to General George W. Carlin, then chief commissioner of the Freedmen's Bureau for the State of Tennessee. Some of the agents were afterwards requested to resign, which they accordingly did. Others of them were removed and their places refilled by men who have from time to time robbed the negroes in like manner. Against this I have been fighting for the past twelve months. Week after week have I written to General Howard about the matter, without avail, and finally gave it up and determined not to annoy myself with it any more, and when I wrote to you I did not anticipate that it would cause a commission to be appointed; if I did, I would have complained to you long before then. I am sorry, however, that the commission were not more impartial in their investigation, as I have already said they would not take any testimony into consideration unless it implicated a claim agent and exonerated a bureau agent.

The honorable Commissioner of Pensions has seemingly suspended me from further practice in his office, for what cause I know not, other than he writes to the firm of O'Neill & Dufour, claim agents of your city, saying that my name is one thing to-day and another to-morrow. My name in full is J. M. M. Cloon. I sometimes contract my name by using only the M. M. and sometimes the J; the name being rather copious, I find it often essential to contract the same for which reason. I did not engage in claim business until solicited by the colored people. They having confidence in my integrity, requested me to attend to the collection of their claims, which I accordingly did. I am innocent of any charges brought against me other than that of buying claims, which, as I have already stated, was done in favor of bureau agents. Since I began to file claims for adjustment in my own case I defy anybody to show where, when, or how I have violated the rules of honor and honesty. The charges which I am charged with were committed over two years ago in the manner just prescribed, and I could to-day, to-morrow, or at any other time since I first reported bureau agents, have bought colored bounty claims for twenty-five cents on the dollar if I would do it; but because I would not make any compromise with the bureau ring, but, on the contrary, have continually reported them, therefore I must be abused and censured because I would not comply with their wicked designs. It is well known to you that if I was guilty of the offenses charged to me in connection with colored bounty frauds that I would not have from week to week solicited a board of investigation in the premises. A man don't often cut a twig with which to stripe his own flesh.

Now, my dear sir, this the foregoing is my status as well as I can give it in a small space. I most solemnly declare before God that it is not my intention to neither cheat, swindle, nor rob the government nor claimants out of any portions of that which belongs to them, all reports to the contrary notwithstanding. I further certify that I don't intend filing any more claims other than what is already in my office, which is about two hundred claims for bounty and back pay. Those are already completed, are sworn to, properly witnessed, and are ready for transmission if I receive the assurance from you that they will be favorably received and considered. Each paper has cost me and the claimants about $1 50 for its preparation and notarial advancements. If the claims would have to be destroyed that would be lost, and besides the claimants would incur a good deal of inconvenience and annoyance. I have given you facts as they are, and now if you think that I deserve suspension from further practice in your department then I will in good faith receive and abide your decision, knowing that your honor will be governed by justice and impartiality in the premises. On the other hand, if you permit me to file the claims now in my office, and with the others already on file in my name to prosecute the same to a successful issue, I assure you that I will have nothing more to do with new claims, and will not attempt to solicit nor prosecute new business. This I request in justice to the poor claimants that have intrusted their business to my care, as I am the only person who in this section attends to any business of that class presently. If necessary I will give bond for the faithful discharge of my duties as claim agent toward my said claimants. Hoping to hear from you soon,

I remain your very obedient servant,

JAS. CLOON.

Hon. E. B. FRENCH,
   Second Auditor, War Department, Washington, D. C.

THOMAS WILSON, being first duly sworn, deposes and says: I am an attorney at law, practicing in Washington as such, and as a claim agent. I am doing business for Moyers & Dedrick in two capacities, one for them, as the successors of Lee & Flory. Lee & Flory had about five hundred or seven hundred claims which they employed us, that is, Owen & Wilson, to prosecute before the departments. They were claims for bounty and back pay of colored soldiers. They prepared the claims; we presented and filed them as the attorney of record. Long afterward, when Captain Lee was about to be appointed agent of the bureau for the payment of bounties at Vicksburg, it became necessary for him to dispose of his interest in these as well as all other claims. He presented them to us, but we were unable to make satisfactory arrangements for their purchase. At this time the firm of Lee & Flory had dissolved, and Lee had succeeded to the business. Captain Lee then disposed of his business, or rather his interest in these claims, to Moyers & Dedrick, and authorized us to pay to them what before was due to him. The preparation of none of these claims fell to Moyers & Dedrick, and I believe they have had nothing to do with them whatever, except to receive the money, which was before due to Captain Lee. The other capacity in which I act as their attorney is by authority of circular November 29, 1867, from the War Department, that I suppose you are acquainted with. I am now prosecuting before the bureaus of the Treasury and War Departments all cases entered by Moyers & Dedrick, however, only of colored soldiers and their heirs, under the authority of this circular.

THOMAS WILSON.

Sworn to in the presence of—

J. A. SLADEN,
   Brevet Captain United States Army, Recorder.

FEBRUARY 15, 1870.

ADDISON A. HOSMER, being duly sworn, deposes and says: I am an attorney at law, of the firm of Chipman, Hosmer & Co. I have been in business in Washington since December, 1865. We have done business generally throughout the States where negro troops were enlisted, and throughout all the States and Territories of the Union. Have done business generally through what we term correspondents, not wishing to recognize them as agents. We advertised in our circulars for correspondents who should take up all kinds of claims and divide the fees, we to be the recognized attorneys of record. This is the only plan we have ever adopted with our correspondents. In 1866 we opened branch offices in New York, Louisville, Nashville, and St. Louis. Some colored claims might have been received through these branch offices which were all closed within a year, however, and business subsequently carried on through correspondents. We had no arrangement here with the bureau with regard to advances previous to the time they were given, or at any time. If there was any law or order authorizing these advances to be made, I read it and knew of it at the time, and believe there was such a law or order. To the best of my knowledge there was no understanding with any officer of the government as to how we should collect these advances. We were governed in these cases by the law or authority governing all persons alike. As to the manner of making these advances and securing the proper evidence for their collection, I must refer you to General Gilmore, who had the matter in charge. I know nothing about it of my own knowledge, and never had a private conversation with any bureau official on the subject. We have received one claim of an officer, and, perhaps, half a dozen other claims from M. M. Cloon, but do not know how long he acted as our correspondent. I had charge of the correspondence in our office from the fall of 1867 to November, 1868, and it was during this time that I knew of the one case sent us by M. M. Cloon. Colonel Hill was a correspondent of ours at Pulaski, in sending claims for quartermaster stores. Charles A. Beckert was our correspondent at Decatur. I first met Beckert about one year ago. He was employed as our correspondent in the usual way, by applying to us and sending us cases. I never saw him before he was our correspondent. Major Mann was a correspondent, but neither agent nor partner of ours; he was what might be termed an itinerant correspondent, that is, he was constantly traveling and collecting cases which he forwarded to us. We first employed Major Mann as a clerk, immediately after his muster out of the volunteer service, in 1866, on the strength of previous friendship between him and me. He was at one time our bookkeeper during the absence of our regular bookkeeper. He had been an officer on the staff of General Ullman, and had had considerable experience in the organization of colored troops. He grew restive in our office as clerk, and he arranged to do business as a correspondent. When he left our office and his situation as a clerk he severed all business relations existing between the firm and himself except such as existed between any other correspondents and the firm. I do not know whether he was ever authorized to make advances, and refer you to General Gilmore. Major Mann at any rate was governed by the same arrangements made by us with other correspondents. To my knowledge we have not furnished any money to correspondents previous to the time the advances were made, but it may possibly so have been furnished. It is possible, though I am not aware of it, that checks signed by our firm, or drafts procured by the firm, were furnished Major Mann before he went out, or in his absence, but do not think it probable. I cannot say when advances were made, whether before or after the treasury certificate was issued, but presume it was before. The matter did not pass under my hand or eye. I never collected any advances in my life, only knew the general practice.

As far as my understanding goes it was done in this way. A correspondent would send us the receipt of the person for whom the advance had been made acknowledged before a civil officer, as provided by the regulations, (if there were such regulations, and it is my impression there were,) the claimant (soldier) acknowledging that he had received such advance accompanied with (I suppose) a request to collect the amount. There may have been other papers, I do not know. These papers were, together with a certificate signed by a member of our firm, filed in the Bureau of Refugees, Freedmen and Abandoned Lands. This certificate was acknowledged before a civil magistrate, as required by the regulations of the bureau. The reason I cannot give more definite information is, that our business is very extensive and divided into branches. This branch did not come directly under my personal supervison or even general cognizance. Any statements made by any person that we had any arrangement with any officer of the Bureau of Refugees, Freedmen and Abandoned Lands to make advances, collect the same with certain interest, and to pay to said officers a per cent. of profit, is, to the best of my knowledge and belief, unqualifiedly false. Beckert is still a correspondent of our firm; Major Mann is not to my knowledge, only in the closing up of all old cases. We have no regular correspondent at Memphis, but several parties send us cases occasionally, viz: Moyers & Dedrick, probably no soldiers' claims, but of quartermaster's stores, and Frank Bros. We take up the business of suspended claim agents with the consent of the Second Auditor; in fact, we cannot do it without his consent. We take from them general powers of attorney; we then divide the fees with them. Any new business they bring up we put in on our own blanks, and we furnish our blanks to any one applying. At Nashville we left our branch office in the charge of General A. Dawson. We have received cases from Mr. Glassie. McQuithy and Alden were correspondents of ours, but I believe it was after they were suspended. We still do business with Major Mann in the settlement of old cases. He ceased to be a clerk in our office on his own motion, He ceased to send us cases on his own motion, and the only trouble we ever had with him was with regard to his signing the name of General Gilmore. It was possible for Major Mann to advance to claimants a less amount than he represented to us. If there was ever any regulation of the bureau made as to the certificate required in the case of advances, I think it must have been done with the concurrence of the Second Auditor or Second Comptroller, and it is my impression that the regulation was made with the latter's concurrence. Neither the Hickeys, of Columbia, Tennessee, nor the Joneses, of Pulaski, Tennessee, are correspondents of our firm to my knowledge, although both firms may have written to us for information.

ADDISON A. HOSMER.

Witness to signature: J. DRUMMERT.

Sworn to before me this 15th day of February, 1870.

J. A. SLADEN,
Brevet Captain United States Army, Recorder.

BENJAMIN D. HYAM, being first duly sworn, deposes and says: I am an attorney-at-law and a claim agent. I have been in the claim business since August, 1864. I now have no partner. I collect claims for colored and white soldiers. I receive claims from local agents, but these agents are not regarded as subordinates of mine, but I am looked upon by them as their subordinate. These agents I recognize as correspondents, and not as agents. The departments will not recognize or furnish information to a claim agent in any case, unless he is the attorney of record. I have made no advances individually, directly. M. Coombs, jr., & Co. have at times had large sums of money accumulated in their hands of mine, of fees received by them belonging to me, and which I take for granted he advanced to colored soldiers, sending me up receipts or affidavits; and when the advances so made were collected they were credited by me to him, (M. Coombs, jr.) To collect such advances, I had to make affidavit, based on the receipt or affidavit of the claimant. At first I received only the receipts of the correspondence, but I saw this might get me into trouble, and I required their affidavits, (viz., the soldiers'.) I have collected advances also for B. H. Harrington, Cambridge, Missouri. Some cases sent me by J. W. Bush, Smithland, Kentucky, were rejected by the bureau. Also have collected some cases from H. Tomkins & Co., Nashville, Tennessee. Tompkins & Co. sent me fortification and hospital claims, amounting to about seventy thousand dollars. One case was presented to the department as a test case by me, and was rejected, if my memory serves me correctly, on the ground that the claimant had been paid all he was entitled to, while the claim was made out for a much larger sum. This was a fortification claim. I have never done business to my knowledge for suspended claim agents. I know I might, but I prefer not to do so. I have never had any understanding with the officers of the bureau concerning the payment of advances, previous or since the time I collected the aforesaid advances. About three years ago, the executive committee of the Claim Agents' Association, of which I was a member, met in consultation with the Second Auditor and First and Second Comptroller, General Howard, and Mr. Alvord, at which the subject of advances then outstanding was considered, and the justice of securing the local agent, through the attorney of record, was recognized. Nothing was said as to future advances, and what was said, as above, led me to collect advances made subsequent to that time. The fees charged and collected from the bureau by me were predicated upon the statements sent me by correspondents. Wishes to say that the bill making bounties payable through the bureau was framed and passed by the advice and urgent wish of claim agents in Washington, to prevent frauds being committed upon them and the soldiers and heirs by their correspondents. The following list exhibits some advances collected by me, and kind of evidence submitted by me, so far as I can recollect:

Names.	Co.	Regiment.	Advances paid.	How received from Freedmen's Bureau.
Henry Clay, corporal.	A	61st U. S. C. T...	$100, June 10, 1867	By receipt and my affidavit.
William Young......	A	55th U. S. C. T...	200, Jan. 31, 1868	By soldier's affidavit, receipt, and my affidavit.
Henry Bellamy......	G	61st U. S. C. T...	100, Feb. 24, 1868	By soldier's affidavit, receipt, and my affidavit.
Archer Booker......	I	53d U. S. C. T...	None, Jan. 23, 1869	
Frank Key	B	3d U. S. H. A... 55th U. S. C. T...	$38, Feb. 24, 1868	By soldier's affidavit, receipt, and my affidavit.
David Allen, serg't ..	D	55th U. S. C. T...	40, June 12, 1868	By soldier's affidavit, receipt, and my affidavit.
Reuben Sikes........	K	11th U. S. C. T...	20, July 21, 1868	By soldier's affidavit, receipt, and my affidavit.
John Ingraham	C	55th U. S. C. T...	100, May 12, 1868	By soldier's affidavit, receipt, and my affidavit.
Moses Pedan.........	A	55th U. S. C. T...	60, July 21, 1868	By soldier's affidavit, receipt, and my affidavit.
Isam Strong	K	11th U. S. C. T...	40, Mar. 10, 1868	By soldier's affidavit, receipt, and my affidavit.
Alexander Alston....	B	55th U. S. C. T...	100, Feb. 24, 1868	By soldier's affidavit, receipt, and my affidavit.
Humphrey Means....	E	61st U. S. C. T...	150, Dec. 17, 1867	By soldier's affidavit, receipt, and my affidavit.
Abraham Polk.......	G	11th U. S. C. T...	100, Mar. 12, 1868	By soldier's affidavit, I believe, receipt, and my affidavit.

BOUNTIES TO COLORED SOLDIERS. 125

Joseph Manley, of Davidson County, Tennessee, for work on fortifications: $620 20. (To chief engineer, November 13, 1865. Returned by him January 25, 1867. Sent to Secretary of War the same day, and submitted by him to claim commission. No action thereon yet.)

Jo. Watson, of Davidson County, Tennessee, for work on fortifications: $161. (To chief engineer Delafield, November 28, 1865, and there the papers appear to be.)

Lewis Wilson, of Davidson County, Tennessee, for work on fortifications: $622. (To General Delafield, November 28, 1865. Rejected, and claim retained by him April 25, 1866.

These three cases are docketed to H. Tomkins & Co, Nashville, Tennessee.

Without some clue being given, by name or otherwise, I am unable to discover, through the large mass of business on my dockets, any cases filed for hospital services.

B. D. HYAM.

THIRTY-SIXTH DAY'S PROCEEDINGS.

The commission met at 10 a. m., Wednesday, February 16, 1870, and continued the examination of the records of the commission and the collation of specific cases.

The evidence of Charles Gilmore, of the firm of Chipman, Hosmer & Co., was taken and is hereto attached.

Communication was forwarded to General Balloch, calling for certified copies of checks on which Dallas Webster and Elvis Key had been paid.

At 4 p. m. the commission adjourned.

BENJ. P. RUNKLE,
Brevet Colonel United States Army.
J. R. LEWIS.
Brevet Colonel United States Army.
J. A. SLADEN,
Brevet Captain United States Army, Recorder.

CHARLES GILMORE, of the firm of Chipman, Hosmer & Co., attorneys-at-law and claim agents, of Washington, D. C., being first duly sworn, deposes and says:

Question. How long have you been in the claim business?—Answer. Since January, 1866.

Q. Have you had charge of the colored bounty claims division of Chipman, Hosmer & Co.'s business?—A. I have had more charge of it than any other member of our firm. We have a chief clerk of that division of the work who has exclusive charge thereof, that is to say, of the records and mechanical work.

Q. Did you ever make any arrangement, verbal or written, with any officer of the Bureau of Refugees, Freedmen and Abandoned Lands, to the effect that the firm of Chipman, Hosmer & Co., or any member or agent thereof, should make advances to colored soldiers, and same to be audited and paid by said bureau? If so, please state the terms of such arrangment.—A. We never made any arrangement whatever with any bureau officer or any one, before making or collecting advances. Whatever we did we so did under the laws and regulations.

Q. Did you ever have any conversation with Mr. Drew or other officer or agent of the bureau on the subject of advances, and if so, please state its terms?—A. I advised Mr. Drew to have an order issued that no advances should be paid through the bureau without its being acknowledged before some bureau officer; and before that order was issued we had several cases that were not acknowledged in that way, which we returned to our correspondents to be so acknowledged before we would collect the advances. Subsequently this order was issued by the bureau. I went to see Mr. Drew often on this subject. I had conversation with Mr. Alvord on this subject, also with General Balloch. In some cases I desired General Balloch to send the whole amount to his local disbursing officer, and let him decide whether the soldier had received the advances charged against him, and pay it or not as he saw fit. This is the case of advances sent us to collect where we refused to collect the advances.

Q. Did the firm of Chipman, Hosmer & Co. ever, directly or through agents or correspondents, make such advances to colored soldiers?—A. Yes, in a very few cases, directly in three or four cases. Indirectly in, I think, not over fifty or sixty cases.

Q. Through what correspondents or agents did you make these advances?—A. The indirect advances were made in this way: Correspondents had in their possession money belonging to us, the same being fees due white cases accumulated in their hands, asked permission to make advances, which we granted, and these advances were collected. Upshur, of Norfolk, drew on us once for money; we honored his draft, and the only remuneration we received for the use of the money was his business. We had advanced money through D. S. Mann, Charles A. Beckert, and a man named Goldsmith, and C. C. Brown. I think these were all.

Q. Did the firm of Chipman, Hosmer & Co., or any member of the said firm, ever furnish D. S. Mann or Charles A. Beckert with checks or drafts, or money in any way, directly or indirectly, to advance to colored soldiers?—A. In no way except as stated as above.

Q. Has M. M. Cloon ever been a correspondent of your firm?—A. Never to my knowledge.

Q. Are the Hickeys, (J. M. and A. C.,) of Columbia, or the Joneses, (Calvin and C. A.,) of Pulaski, Tennessee, regular correspondents of your firm at the present time, or have they ever been so?—A. Not to my knowledge.

Q. Will you please state what kind of evidence you were required to produce at the bureau in order to collect the advances made by you or your correspondents?—A. At first, my impression is, in all cases the acknowledgment of the soldier before some magistrate of the receipt of the money from our correspondent was required, and the receipt of the correspondent for the money from our firm, together with our affidavit that we had paid the money. Afterward they required that the soldier should certify before a bureau officer that he had received the amount.

Q. Do you recollect the nature of the papers certified by Justice Baugh, near Pulaski, Tennessee?—A. I do not remember his name.

Q. What are the names of your Memphis correspondents?—A. Frank Brass, Green, and Workman, but think they filed all their claims for colored soldiers direct.

Q. Is M. Coombs, jr., & Co., of your correspondents?—A. No, sir; never was.

Q. Are Moyers & Dedrick?—A. No, sir; never were.

Q. Did you ever make any advances through any correspondents in Nashville or Memphis?—A. Not any in either place.

Q. What per cent, if any, of the profits on the advances made by Mann, or Beckert, or any other correspondent, did your firm receive?— A. Not anything. We simply collected these advances in order to retain the business of these men, who were doing business through us, and being responsible for these advances, we were anxious that such safeguards should be thrown around the advances by the bureau as would secure us.

Q. Who are your correspondents at Nashville?—A. We have had the business of McQuitley & Alden, suspended claim agents, at their request, but have not collected any advances for them. We took this business with the consent of the Second Auditor of the Treasury. We had a general power-of-attorney from McQuitley & Alden.

Q. How many suspended claim agents are you doing business for and dividing fees with?—A. Not any, for we cannot do business for them without a power-of-attorney from them stating that they will do no more new business. We are really put in their stead. I don't remember any but McQuitley & Alden. If there is anything very bad against the claim agent, we cannot take the business. Take the case of Ingersoll, of Nashville, who is charged with retaining bounty of white soldiers. He sent us a general power-of-attorney. We wrote him that if he would allow us to pay up the money he had retained, the Auditor would permit us to take up his business, otherwise not. He demurred, and we did not take his business.

Q. How many colored soldiers claims have you prosecuted?—A. I suppose about ten thousand.

Q. On what evidence do you make up your bill of fees?—A. From lists sent from our correspondents, on which we rely when they are not apparently exorbitant.

Q. How can notarial fees amount to $5, $6, or $6 50 per case?—A. Cases were made out in 1866, on blanks for pay department. These afterward (being turned over to Auditor) had to be made out anew. So making two applications. Two dollars and fifty cents is about the average of notarial fees in ordinary cases. We put in an extra affidavit here that we have no interest in the case. We send a fee bill with such case stating each affidavit. The following is a specimen thereof; we send every dollar notarial fees, except fee for our affidavits, to the correspondents.

Q. Do you admit your responsibily in cases of advances made by Mann, Beckert, and other correspondents?—A. Yes, if they were not properly made, we hold ourselves ready to pay the amounts ourselves.

Q. From your knowledge of the claim business, your acquaintance with claim agents through the country, what, in your opinion, would have been the result of the payment of the bounties, had not the law approved ——— ———, made the same payable through government officials?—A. I don't think they would have got fifty per cent. of it in many places. This is my opinion from our knowledge of the manner in which many white soldiers were swindled by unprincipled men.

Name of soldier.	Co.	Regiment.	Correspondent who made advances.	Amount advanced collected.
William H. Palmer, quartermaster s'g't.	....	36th U. S. colored troops.	J. B. Upshur & Co	$75 00
John Tallier	A	......do	D. S. Mann	138 00
Joseph Fuller	A	1st U. S. colored cavalry	J. B. Upshur & Co	100 00
Joseph H. Scratchings	G	38th U. S. colored troops	D. S. Mann	86 00
Isaac King	A	1st U. S. colored cavalry	J. B. Upshur & Co	160 00
Jerry Jinkins	K	110th U. S. colored troops	D. S. Mann	40 00
Bazil Holt	I	......do	......do	70 00
Wesley Redus	I	......do	......do	100 00
Samuel A. Kinson	I	......do	Captain C. A. Beckert	100 00
George Reed	I	......do	D. S. Mann	100 00
J. Hardgrove	I	......do	......do	100 00
Ruffen Brown	I	......do	......do	100 00
Thomas Upshur	K	......do	......do	50 00

BOUNTIES TO COLORED SOLDIERS.

Name of soldier.	Co.	Regiment.	Correspondent who made advances.	Amount advanced collected.
James Brown	I	110th U. S. colored troops	D. S. Mann	$80 00
Turner Lader	K	......do	C. A. Beckert	187 02
Henry Hines	H	......do	......do	188 00
Wash. Woodward	G	......do	......do	100 00
Robert Brown	I	......do	......do	250 00
Samuel Smith	H	1st U. S. colored troops	Chipman, Hosmer & Co	20 00
Frank P. Reed	F	110th U. S. colored troops	D. S. Mann	40 00
John Jackson	I	......do	M. Goldsmith	225 00
Samuel Anderson	D	23d U. S. colored troops	Chipman, Hosmer & Co	50 00
Henry McRea	B	1st U. S. colored cavalry	D. S. Mann	60 00
Purket Harris	C	75th U. S. colored troops	D. H. Reese	150 00
Charles Kemp	E	44th U. S. colored troops	C. A. Beckert	150 00
James Harney	G	38th U. S. colored troops	D. S. Mann	100 00
George M. Arnold, hospital steward.		4th U. S. colored troops	C. H. & Co. advanced $75	44 00
William Williams	H	80th U. S. colored troops	D. S. Mann	90 00
George Adams	C	38th U. S. colored troops	A. Moise	60 00
John Adams	F	......do	......do	60 00
William Murden	F	......do	J. B. Upshur & Co	175 00
James Watson	E	2d U. S. colored cavalry	......do	153 00
Jasper Smith	E	......do	......do	280 00
Andrew Eason	I	......do	......do	170 00
Peter Jones	C	......do	......do	100 00
Clarkson Billops	C	......do	Upshur, $21; C. C. Brown, $50	71 00
Richard Jones	C	......do	C. C. Brown	20 00
Peter Loach	C	......do	C. C Brown, $15, $35	50 00
Axom Moone	C	......do	Brown, $20; Upshur, $150	170 00
William T. Fuller	C	......do	Brown, $80; Upshur, $175	255 00
Richard E. Johnson	C	......do	J. B. Upshur & Co	162 25
Thomas Britton	D	......do	......do	130 00
Albert Harney	K	110th U. S. colored troops	D. S. Mann	100 00
William Redus	I	......do	......do	200 00
Paldo Bailey	K	......do	......do	100 00
James Vance	I	......do	......do	150 00
Henry Haregrove	K	......do	......do	100 00
Henry Thorn	B	......do	......do	236 00
Charles Wright	H	......do	......do	190 00
Benjamin Webb	K	......do	Captain C. A. Beckert	189 20
Green Stanley	B	......do	......do	236 00
Charles Bailey	K	......do	D. S. Mann	188 00
Spenson Benson	F	......do	......do	100 00
Adam Simpson	B	......do	......do	192 00
Turner Luder	K	......do	M. Goldsmith	187 00
Samuel Atkinson	I	......do	D. S. Mann	100 00
George Reed	I	......do	......do	100 00
Squire Camba, musician		......do	......do	233 00
Paul Harney	K	......do	Captain C. A. Beckert	140 00
Isaac Hardgrow	I	......do	D. S. Mann	100 00
Ruffin Broon	I	......do	......do	100 00
Bazil Holt	I	......do	......do	70 00
Godfrey Maples	I	......do	Captain Charles A. Beckert	90 00
Clinton Malone	H	......do	D. S. Mann	190 00
Dock Bailey	K	......do	......do	185 00
Jim Morrill	K	......do	......do	100 00
George Harney	K	......do	......do	100 00
Henry Bingleton	K	......do	Captain C. A. Beckert	188 20
Dick Brown	K	......do	D. S. Mann	100 00
Archy Isabel	C	......do	......do	223 00
Claybourn Harris	A	......do	......do	211 00
Coleman Murry	H	......do	......do	180 00
Hubbard Bradyford	I	......do	......do	150 00
Total				9,527 85

I have examined our records from 1867 to 1870, and believe that the seventy-three cases named above are all the colored soldiers' cases upon which we have collected any advances made by ourselves direct, and by our correspondents, as named above.

CHARLES D. GILMORE.

Sworn to before me and subscribed in my presence, 23d day of February, 1870.

BEN. P. RUNKLE,
Brevet Colonel U. S. A.

BOUNTIES TO COLORED SOLDIERS.

LAW OFFICES OF CHIPMAN, HOSMER & CO.,
Washington, D. C., March 4, 1870.

COLONEL: Upon further examination of the records of colored soldiers' claims in our house, I find that some advances were collected in 1867, for Captain T. F. Lee, of Raleigh, North Carolina, from twenty-eight cases of soldiers of the Thirty-sixth and Thirty-seventh United States colored troops, a schedule I have the honor to transmit herewith.

When I went through the former examination and made a schedule of claims in which Chipman, Hosmer & Co. had received advances from the bureau, I thought I had found all such cases.

The clerk who kept our records of this class of business, from the commencement of filing claims, has been absent sick for more than a month, and as it would require more time to make further examination than it would to get a full schedule from the bureau, I respectfully ask that you call on Mr. Drew, chief of the claims division, Bureau Refugees, Freedmen and Abandoned Lands, to furnish such other information as you desire.

Very respectfully,

C. D. GILMORE.

Colonel B. P. RUNKLE,
*President Military Commission
Bureau Refugees, Freedmen and Abandoned Lands.*

Name of soldier.	Co.	Regiment.	Correspondent who made advances.	Amount advanced collected.
Alfred Comesal	K	36th U. S. colored troops	T. F. Lee, Raleigh, N. C	$18 50
Daniel Cooper	K	do	do	25 93
Charles Campbell	K	do	do	2 43
Benjamin Franklin	K	do	do	3 46
W. Whitish	K	do	do	1 25
John A. Freeman	F	37th U. S. colored troops	do	79 26
Sammy Herton	F	do	do	1 71
Joseph Jones	F	do	do	1 68
Harry Christea	F	do	do	34 24
Jordan Brooks	F	do	do	82 53
Robert Gill	F	do	do	20 51
John Ellis	F	do	do	62 98
George Cooper	F	do	do	98 68
Peter Barker	F	do	do	1 68
Henry Patterson	F	do	do	1 71
William Christian	F	do	do	1 71
Jerry Jones	F	do	do	1 74
David Butts	F	do	do	68 74
John Bowman	F	do	do	127 96
Major Cole	F	do	do	1 71
Ranson Boss	F	do	do	57 16
Peter Jones	F	do	do	35 29
Daniel Robinson	F	do	do	82 54
James Hull	F	do	do	155 09
Robert Coleman	F	do	do	67 38
Edward W. Tucker	F	do	do	26 86
Thomas Barnett	F	do	do	44 14
Major E. Harrison	F	do	do	70 90

THIRTY-SEVENTH DAY'S PROCEEDINGS.

The commission met at 10 a. m., Thursday, February 17, 1870, and continued the labor upon the report and examination of the records.

A communication was received from the Pension Office in answer to one from the commission, giving information in certain cases of pension claimants, which document is appended to the proceedings of the commission, and is marked, "Pension Office B."

BOUNTIES TO COLORED SOLDIERS.

Several communications were written to the Commissioner Bureau Refugees, Freedmen and Abandoned Lands, and his officers, asking for information.

At 4 p. m. the commission adjourned.

BEN. P. RUNKLE,
Brevet Colonel United States Army.
J. R. LEWIS,
Brevet Colonel United States Army.
J. A. SLADEN,
Brevet Captain United States Army, Recorder.

THIRTY-EIGHTH DAY'S PROCEEDINGS.

The commission met at 10 a. m. Friday, February 18, 1870, and continued the examination of the records. The evidence of C. C. Tucker, claim agent, J. J. McCarthy, attorney and claim agent, and J. M. Dufour, of the firm of O'Neill & Dufour, claimants, was taken, and is hereto attached. A communication was received (hereto attached) from General G. W. Balloch inclosing certified copies of checks on which Dallas Webster, late private Company F Fourteenth United States colored troops, was paid. Also, a communication from W. P. Drew, inclosing a memorial, alleged to be from loyal citizens of Tennessee, protesting against the action taken by this commission, which the commission at once answered, and returned both memorial and answer to General O. O. Howard, Commissioner Bureau Refugees, Freedmen and Abandoned Lands.

At 4 p. m. the commission adjourned.

BEN. P. RUNKLE,
Brevet Colonel United States Army.
J. R. LEWIS,
Brevet Colonel United States Army.
J. A. SLADEN,
Brevet Captain United States Army, Recorder.

WAR DEPARTMENT, BUREAU OF REFUGEES,
FREEDMEN AND ABANDONED LANDS, CLAIM DIVISION,
Washington, D. C., February 17, 1870.

COLONEL: I am directed by the commission to inclose herewith for your examination and report a "memorial" received at this bureau from the honorable Secretary of War, purporting to be signed by citizens of Pulaski, Tennessee, remonstrating against the action of your commission during its recent session at that place, and reflecting upon the methods pursued by the commission in investigating cases of suspected frauds.

Please return the "memorial" to this office with report.

Very respectfully, your obedient servant,
WILLIAM P. DREW,
Agent Bureau Refugees, Freedmen and Abandoned Lands,
Chief of Claim Division.

Bvt. Col. B. P. RUNKLE, U. S. A.,
President Military Commission Bureau Refugees,
Freedmen and Abandoned Lands, Washington, D. C.

BOUNTIES TO COLORED SOLDIERS.

ROOMS OF THE MILITARY COMMISSION FOR
THE INVESTIGATION OF FRAUDS AGAINST
COLORED SOLDIERS AND SAILORS,
Washington, D. C., February 16, 1870.

GENERAL: I have the honor, respectfully, to request that you furnish this commission with copies of checks, (with the indorsements thereon,) by which the bounty of the following named soldiers were paid, viz: Dallas Webster, late Company F Thirteenth United States colored troops; Elvis Key, late Company F Fourteenth United States colored troops; it appearing, by evidence, that Webster was paid by Eastman and not by Wilson. Key was paid by check No. 1381.

Very respectfully, your obedient servant,
BEN. P. RUNKLE,
Brevet Colonel U. S. A., President of Commission.

General GEORGE W. BALLOCH,
*Chief Disbursing Officer Bureau Refugees,
Freedmen and Abandoned Lands.*

[Indorsement.]

WAR DEPARTMENT, BUREAU OF REFUGEES,
FREEDMEN AND ABANDONED LANDS,
Washington, D. C., February 17, 1870.

Respectfully returned to Colonel Ben. P. Runkle, with copies of checks, as requested.

GEO. W. BALLOCH,
Brevet Brigadier General and Chief Disbursing Officer.

CHARLES C. TUCKER, being first duly sworn, deposes and says: That his name is as above; that he is a claim agent; that he has been in the business for about twenty years. I have no correspondents at Nashville, nor at Columbia. No person named M. M. Cloon has ever been a correspondent of our firm at Pulaski or elsewhere. Moyers & Dedrick have not acted as my correspondents, except to close up old business, for about two years. Reuben Daily and J. W. Strycker sent me one thousand one hundred or one thousand two hundred claims, which have been suspended. A Mr. Dougherty, now deceased, has sent me claims, which Colonel Palmer is closing up. I have had correspondents who have made advances. In these cases I have assumed the responsibility of these advances and have made the usual affidavits to that effect, forwarding with said affidavits the receipt from the correspondent that the claimant had received the money.

CHAS. C. TUCKER.

Witness to signature: J. DRUMMERT.

Sworn to in my presence, at Washington, D. C., this 18th day of February, 1870.

J. A. SLADEN,
Brevet Captain United States Army, Recorder.

WASHINGTON, D. C., *February 22, 1870.*

SIR: This morning a copy of my testimony, given before you, was presented to me for my signature and signed. In it is stated that some claims, sent me by F. P. Dougherty, now deceased, were perfected by Colonel F. S. Palmer, of Memphis, Tennessee.

Since your messenger left I have thought that this statement, without explanation, might be doing an act of injustice to Colonel Palmer; that it might induce a belief that he was acting as a claim agent for remuneration. I will be much pleased if you will have added to this paper the statement I made to you that I do not know that Colonel Palmer ever received, either directly or indirectly, any compensation for his services in these claims. I will add that I have never remitted to him, or for him, any portion of the fees received on these claims; and I have never received a word from him, either in writing or verbally, in reference to the fees or any portion of them.

I called at your office this morning to make this request in person, but you were absent, and, at the suggestion of your clerk, I now make it in writing.

Very respectfully, your obedient servant,
CHAS. C. TUCKER.
Captain J. A. SLADEN,
Recorder Military Commission.

JUSTUS I. MCCARTY, attorney-at-law and claim agent of Washington City, being first duly sworn, deposes and says:

Question. Have you any correspondents in the United States through whom you do business for colored claimants for bounty, pension, &c.? If so, please name them.—Answer. Yes; M. M. Cloon has sent me between six and one dozen bounty and pension cases. Have had correspondence with Moyers & Dedrick, of Memphis, who bought out a claim agent firm named Pannell & McCallister, and have corresponded with them concerning the business of this firm.

Never had any business with M. Coombs, jr., at Memphis; did not want to have anything to do with him. Had no correspondents in Nashville; have had nothing to do with Messrs. Jones of Pulaski, or Hickey of Columbia, Tennessee.

Q. Have you advanced any money to colored claimants in Tennessee or Alabama?—A. No, sir.

Q. Can you state what was done with the pension certificate of Rhoda Jones, widow of Nelson Jones, No. 131,748, sent to you July 14, 1869?—A. See appended list.

Q. Is the attached list a full and complete account of all pension certificates issued in cases prosecuted by you and sent by you to M. M. Cloon?—A. It is.

J. I. MCCARTY.

Signed and sworn to in my presence, this 26th day of February, 1870, at Washington, D. C.

J. A. SLADEN,
Brevet Captain United States Army, Recorder.

Memoranda of pension cases in which the certificates were sent to M. M. Cloon by J. I. McCarty.

1. Rhoda Jones, widow of Nelson Jones, Company D Thirteenth United States colored troops. Certificate No. 131,748, sent M. M. Cloon August 20, 1869.

2. Hannah Young, widow of Wm. Young, Company F One hundredth United States colored troops. Certificate No. 129,275, sent M. M. Cloon May 29, 1869.

3. Mary Wilson, widow of General Wilson, Company D Forty-fourth United States colored troops. Certificate No. 128,031, sent M. M. Cloon May 7, 1869.

J. M. Dufour's evidence.

J. M. DUFOUR, being first duly sworn, deposes and says: That his name is as above; that he is a claim agent of the firm of O'Neill & Dufour. That M. M. Cloon is a correspondent of our firm. He does not write to us over any other initials than those of M. M. to the best of my knowledge. I have been a member of the firm since March, 1868, and Mr. Cloon has been a correspondent of our firm ever since and before that time. We received notice from the Pension Office about last November, instructing us to drop Mr. Cloon as a correspondent, and to obtain and return to that office all pension certificates we had forwarded to him. We did not receive back from him one of these certificates, but he stated to us that he had given out the most of them, and had still but few in his possession. The Second Auditor and Mr. Drew, chief of the claim division of the Freedmen's Bureau, have never communicated with us in writing concerning Mr. Cloon, although both of these gentlemen have said to me that he was impudent or insolent. Since the notice from the Pension Office above alluded to, we have not retained Mr. Cloon as a correspondent, and we have notified him that we could not correspond with him until he was set right before the departments. I am under the impression that Mr. Moulton, in the Second Auditor's office, informed my clerk, Mr. Miller, that he did not care if we retained Mr. Cloon as a correspondent, inasmuch as the Freedmen's Bureau had thrown around the fees such safeguards as to prevent fraud in that direction. Inasmuch, too, as Mr. Cloon had informed us that he was innocent of these charges, and could prove it to the satisfaction of the departments, we notified him that, of course, he could not expect us to settle with him until he had exonerated himself of the charges before the departments. He has also forwarded to us claims for the collection of commutation of rations of prisoners of war.

We have sometimes complained to him of discrepancies in his evidence gotten up in cases of claims, but attributed it to his loose way of doing business; and we have filed some of these claims in order to show him the effect of these discrepancies when brought to the notice of the departments. Neither the Hickeys of Columbia, nor the Joneses of Pulaski, Tennessee, are correspondents of ours. We have no correspondents at Memphis, Tennessee. At Nashville, Tennessee, our correspondents are Mr. Glassie, Mr. John Newton, one or two other white men, and two colored men, whose names I do not remember.

J. M. DUFOUR.

134 BOUNTIES TO COLORED SOLDIERS.

A.—*List of names for whom checks for commutation of rations have been forwarded from the office of O'Neill & Dufour to M. M. Cloon, Pulaski, Tennessee.*

Name.	Co.	Regiment.	When settled.	No. check.	Am't.
Edwin Asser	A	111th U. S. C. T.	Mar. 14, 1868	3517	$58 25
Amis Rasson	B	111th U. S. C. T.	Mar. 14, 1868	3540	58 25
Clayborne Murray	H	110th U. S. C. T.	Mar. 14, 1868	3543	50 00
Donald Hobson	A	111th U. S. C. T.	Mar. 14, 1868	3514	50 00
Harry Henry	B	111th U. S. C. T.	Mar. 14, 1868	3537	57 25
Leman McGrew	F	110th U. S. C. T.	Mar. 14, 1868	3530	54 50
Henry Bass	A	111th U. S. C. T.	Mar. 14, 1868	3528	58 25
Braxton Bass	A	111th U. S. C. T.	Mar. 14, 1868	3527	57 25
Horace Bramlett	D	110th U. S. C. T.	Mar. 14, 1868		54 75
Mark Bruce	F	110th U. S. C. T.	Mar. 30, 1868	3944	54 50
Mack Marks	F	110th U. S. C. T.	Mar. 30, 1868	3941	50 00
Peter Hobson	A	111th U. S. C. T.	Mar. 30, 1868	3938	50 00
John Bell, (sergeant major)		110th U. S. C. T.	Mar. 30, 1868	3942	50 00
Marion Brown	F	110th U. S. C. T.	Mar. 30, 1868	3943	54 50
Rufus Oliver	H	111th U. S. C. T.	Apr. 17, 1868	4150	57 00
Thomas Green	A	111th U. S. C. T.	Apr. 17, 1868	4151	49 75
Jackson Conner	D	110th U. S. C. T.	Apr. 17, 1868	4154	57 50
George Ross	B	111th U. S. C. T.	Apr. 17, 1868	4155	57 25
Horace Carr	F	110th U. S. C. T.	Apr. 17, 1868	4157	58 00
Burrell Reedus, 2d	I	110th U. S. C. T.	Apr. 21, 1868	4226	58 00
Alex. Johnson	D	110th U. S. C. T.	Apr. 21, 1868	4225	58 00
Horace Braden	E	110th U. S. C. T.	Apr. 21, 1868	4310	54 75
Samuel Holt	D	111th U. S. C. T.	Apr. 24, 1868	4312	50 00
Albert Harney	K	110th U. S. C. T.	Apr. 24, 1868	4313	57 50
William Dailey	D	110th U. S. C. T.	Apr. 24, 1868	4319	54 25
Sweeney Howell	I	110th U. S. C. T.	Apr. 24, 1868	4318	54 75
George Harvell	F	111th U. S. C. T.	Apr. 24, 1868	4317	56 25
Samuel Woods	B	111th U. S. C. T.	Apr. 24, 1868	4316	57 75
Obadiah Reynolds	D	110th U. S. C. T.	Apr. 24, 1868	4314	54 75
William Lammiere	K	110th U. S. C. T.	Apr. 30, 1868	4431	58 25
Jarrett Clack	E	110th U. S. C. T.	Apr. 30, 1868	4437	54 75
Myers Stephenson	K	111th U. S. C. T.	Apr. 30, 1868	4434	57 25
Sonney Reed	F	110th U. S. C. T.	Apr. 30, 1868	4435	54 50
Anthoney Harney	K	110th U. S. C. T.	Apr. 30, 1868	4432	50 00
Patrick Webster	B	111th U. S. C. T.	Apr. 30, 1868	4436	57 75
Idol Wright	F	110th U. S. C. T.	May 13, 1868	4506	54 50
William Dobbins	A	111th U. S. C. T.	May 13, 1868	4507	58 75
William Gilbert	F	110th U. S. C. T.	May 13, 1868	4502	54 50
Silas Martin	E	110th U. S. C. T.	May 13, 1868	4503	54 75
Anderson Wheeler	I	110th U. S. C. T.	May 27, 1868	4614	54 75
Nathan Williams	F	110th U. S. C. T.	May 27, 1868	4615	54 50
Bailey Watson	F	110th U. S. C. T.	May 27, 1868	4613	54 50
John Brown	F	110th U. S. C. T.	May 28, 1868	4646	54 50
William Rutledge	E	110th U. S. C. T.	May 28, 1868	4647	54 75
William Sylvester	I	110th U. S. C. T.	May 28, 1868	4645	54 75
James Brown	I	110th U. S. C. T.	May 28, 1868	4612	54 75
William Ordway, (or Odaway)	A	111th U. S. C. T.	May 28, 1868	4644	57 25
Ben. Lowry	B	110th U. S. C. T.	June 12, 1868	4686	49 25
Jackson Hobson	A	111th U. S. C. T.	June 12, 1868	4688	57 75
James Lewis	A	106th U. S. C. T.	June 12, 1868	4690	58 00
John Archie	K	44th U. S. C. T.	June 12, 1868	4689	45 75
Jerry Johnston	K	44th U. S. C. T.	June 12, 1868	4687	57 00
Thomas Butler	F	110th U. S. C. T.	June 12, 1868	4683	54 50
Sol. Short	H	110th U. S. C. T.	June 12, 1868	4685	58 00
Nathan Holt	F	110th U. S. C. T.	June 12, 1868	4684	50 00
Paul Brinkley	A	111th U. S. C. T.	June 25, 1868	4842	57 25
Albert Knight	D	110th U. S. C. T.	June 25, 1868	4843	54 75
Joseph Harrison	D	110th U. S. C. T.	June 25, 1868	4845	54 75
Louis Overton	D	110th U. S. C. T.	June 25, 1868	4844	54 75
Turner Harville	K	110th U. S. C. T.	July 2, 1868	4878	57 50
Nias Watson	E	110th U. S. C. T.	July 15, 1868	4504	54 50
Harry Holloway		110th U. S. C. T.	July 15, 1868	4905	2 00
Jackson Butler	K	110th U. S. C. T.	July 20, 1868	4956	57 25
Thomas Corpier	F	110th U. S. C. T.	Aug. 17, 1868	5070	50 00
John Valentine, (or Ballentine)	B	110th U. S. C. T.	Aug. 17, 1868	5071	57 25
Peter Harwood	D	110th U. S. C. T.	Aug. 17, 1868	5073	28 25
Thomas Abernathy	K	110th U. S. C. T.	Aug. 17, 1868	5072	54 50
William Knight	D	110th U. S. C. T.	Sept. 15, 1868	5282	52 00
Paul Bridgefort	K	110th U. S. C. T.	Sept. 15, 1868	5288	57 25
Tonny Swift	D	111th U. S. C. T.	Sept. 15, 1868	5290	46 50
Hanibal Stacy		110th U. S. C. T.	Sept. 15, 1868	5284	54 75
Hebbard Bridgeford	I	110th U. S. C. T.	Sept. 15, 1868	5281	54 75
Alex. Edmondson	F	110th U. S. C. T.	Sept. 15, 1868	5299	54 50
Gilbert Phillips	E	110th U. S. C. T.	Sept. 15, 1868	5283	54 75
James Odaway	A	111th U. S. C. T.	Sept. 15, 1868	5297	114 50
Gordon Green	D	111th U. S. C. T.	Oct. 30, 1868	5467	59 50
Madison Bledsoe	A	111th U. S. C. T.	Oct. 30, 1868	5466	57 25
Robert McLairin	F	111th U. S. C. T.	Oct. 30, 1868	5464	57 25
George Bledsoe	A	111th U. S. C. T.	Oct. 30, 1868	5461	57 75

BOUNTIES TO COLORED SOLDIERS. 135

A.—*List of names for whom checks for commutation of rations, &c.*—Continued.

Name.	Co.	Regiment.	When settled.	No. check.	Am't.
John Collins	I	111th U. S. C. T.	Oct. 30, 1868	5455	57 75
Jacob English	D	110th U. S. C. T.	Oct. 30, 1868	5458	26 50
Harrison Gilbert	A	111th U. S. C. T.	Oct. 30, 1868	5462	32 25
Joseph Carter	D	110th U. S. C. T.	Oct. 30, 1868	5456	54 75
Samuel Gilbert	F	110th U. S. C. T.	Oct. 30, 1868	5463	54 50
Joshua Warren	C	106th U. S. C. T.	Oct. 30, 1868	5465	50 75
Joseph Troupe	C	106th U. S. C. T.	Oct. 30, 1868	5460	50 75
Austin Ford	C	106th U. S. C. T.	Oct. 30, 1868	5459	50 75
Richard Donnegan	C	106th U. S. C. T.	Oct. 30, 1868	5457	50 75
Samuel Drayton	I	110th U. S. C. T.	Nov. 25, 1868	5554	54 75
Thomas Atkinson	I	110th U. S. C. T.	Nov. 25, 1868	5552	54 75
Koff Marie, (or Maire)	K	110th U. S. C. T.	Nov. 25, 1868	5551	57 50
William Reedus, 1st	I	110th U. S. C. T.	Nov. 25, 1868	5555	45 25
Thomas Upshan	K	110th U. S. C. T.	Nov. 25, 1868	5556	54 25
Spencer Sloss	B	111th U. S. C. T.	Nov. 25, 1868	5553	75 50
Richard Schurles	A	106th U. S. C. T.	Jan. 16, 1869	5748	57 50
John Perkins	D	111th U. S. C. T.	Jan. 16, 1869	5744	41 75
Anderson Sloss	B	111th U. S. C. T.	Jan. 16, 1869	5749	78 25
James Vance	H	110th U. S. C. T.	Jan. 16, 1869	5750	54 75
Anderson Woods	B	111th U. S. C. T.	Jan. 16, 1869	5745	58 00
James Moore	I	111th U. S. C. T.	Feb. 15, 1869	5834	58 25
Jacob Whitfield	D	111th U. S. C. T.	Mar. 30, 1869	5926	59 00
Lafayette Martin	D	110th U. S. C. T.	Apr. 14, 1869	5948	54 75
John Bledsoe	A	111th U. S. C. T.	Apr. 14, 1869	5951	21 75
Pink Leatherman	D	110th U. S. C. T.	May 19, 1869	6084	54 75
Toliver Reedus	I	110th U. S. C. T.	Feb. 19, 1868	3287	50 00
John Butler	I	110th U. S. C. T.	Feb. 19, 1868	3288	50 00
William Shadden	D	110th U. S. C. T.	Mar. 14, 1868	3531	50 00
Benjamin Nelson	I	110th U. S. C. T.	Mar. 14, 1868	3518	50 00
Spencer Taylor	C	110th U. S. C. T.	Mar. 14, 1868	3516	50 00
Graham Mason	D	110th U. S. C. T.	Mar. 14, 1868	3523	50 00
Cager Ezell	D	110th U. S. O. T.	Mar. 14, 1868	3529	50 00
George W. Green	K	110th U. S. C. T.	Mar. 14, 1868	3522	50 00
Henry Fields	I	110th U. S. C. T.	Mar. 14, 1868	3526	50 00
Burrell Reedus, 1st	I	110th U. S. C. T.	Mar. 14, 1868	3524	50 00
Jerry Meals, (or Neals)	I	110th U. S. C. T.	Mar. 14, 1868	3519	50 00
Monroe Abernathy	F	110th U. S. C. T.	Mar. 14, 1868	3540	50 00
Cæsar Reedus	F	110th U. S. C. T.	Mar. 14, 1868	3534	50 00
Joseph Howard	F	110th U. S. C. T.	Mar. 14, 1868	3525	50 00
John Carden	F	110th U. S. C. T.	Mar. 14, 1868	3533	50 00
Abel Benson	F	110th U. S. C. T.	Mar. 14, 1868	3542	50 00
Frank Reed	F	110th U. S. C. T.	Mar. 14, 1868	3515	50 00
Jeff Brunson	F	110th U. S. C. T.	Mar. 14, 1868	3532	50 00
Giles Carden	F	110th U. S. C. T.	Mar. 14, 1868	3538	50 00
Lewis Butler	F	110th U. S. C. T.	Mar. 14, 1868	3536	50 00
Joseph Corper	F	110th U. S. C. T.	Mar. 14, 1868	3535	50 00
John Reed	F	110th U. S. C. T.	Mar. 14, 1868	3538	50 00
Edmond Reed	F.	110th U. S. C. T.	Mar. 14, 1868	3520	50 00
Peter Kimber	F	110th U. S. C. T.	Apr. 17, 1868	4153	50 00
Tyler Abernathy	F	110th U. S. C. T.	Apr. 17, 1868	4152	50 00
Samuel Logan	C	106th U. S. C. T.	Apr. 21, 1868	4232	50 75
Henry English	D	110th U. S. C. T.	Apr. 24, 1868	4311	54 75
Columbus Washington	B	106th U. S. C. T.	Apr. 24, 1868	4315	50 75
Ezekiel Hobson	A	111th U. S. C. T.	Feb. 19, 1868	3289	50 00
Pink Steele	D	110th U. S. C. T.	Feb. 19, 1868	3286	54 75
McGilbert Tucker	C	110th U. S. C. T.	Feb. 19, 1868	3284	50 00
Alex. Carden	F	110th U. S. C. T.	Apr. 17, 1868	4156	58 00

BOUNTIES TO COLORED SOLDIERS.

Amount collected in these and all other claims for commutation of rations, when paid, number, date, and amount of certificate, and to whom sent.

No.	Name.	Co.	Regiment.	Remarks.
....	Henry Hargrove......	K	110th U. S. colored troops	Have no record of thi claim, (Chipman & Hosmer.)
....	Jerry Jenkins	K	......do	Rejected October 2, 1868; was settled through Messrs. Chipman, Hosmer & Co.
92	William Reedus	I	......do	Settled November 25, 1868; check 5555, $45 25.
....	Poldo Baily...........	K	......do	Rejected September 25, 1868. The claim was settled through Messrs. Chipman, Hosmer & Co.
93	Thomas Upshur	K	......do	Settled November 25, 1868; check 5556, $54 25.
98	James Vance, 1st	I	......do	Settled January 16, 1869; check 5750, $54 75.
46	James Brown.........	I	......do	Settled April 28, 1868; check 4612, $54 75.
....	Washington Gilmore..	D	14th U. S. colored troops.	Have no record of this claim.
136	Alexander Caden.....	F	110th U. S. colored troops	Settled April 17, 1868; check 4156, $58.
97	Anderson Sloss	B	111th U. S. colored troops.	Settled January 16, 1869; check 5749, $78 25.
112	Joseph W. Green	K	110th U. S. colored troops.	Have a Geo. W. Green, Company K, 110th U. S. colored troops. Settled March 14, 1868; check 3522, $50.
....	Aleck Gardner........	D	......do	Have not this case.
....	Henry Hines.........	H	......do	Have not this case.
114	Burll Reedus..........	I	......do	Have Reedus, 1st and 2d; see our list. Settled April 21, 1868; check 4226, $58.
24	Albert Harney........	K	......do	Anthony Harney; this seems identical with Albert. Settled April 24, 1868; check 4432, $50.
....	George Barlow........	I	13th U. S. colored troops.	Have claim on file for bounty only.

B.—List of pensions.

The date of settlement as given in cases below, is date of receipt of certificates on the same date they were forwarded to Cloon.

List of pension certificates forwarded from the office of O'Neill & Dufour to M. M. Cloon, Pulaski, Tennessee.

No.	Name.	Co.	Regiment.	Remarks.
....	Peggy Grigsby.........			
137	Widow of Jesse McKinney, Vienna.	G	101st U. S. colored troops.	Settled April 18, 1868, by certificate 111,592, and sent to Cloon same date.
138	Widow of Chas. Taylor, Frank.	A	111th U. S. colored troops.	Settled June 10, 1868, by certificate 114,382, and sent to Cloon same date.
139	Guardian of child of Simon Taylor, Jenkins, Sallie A.	E	12th U. S. colored troops	Settled June 12, 1868, by certificate 114,436, and forwarded to Cloon same date.
140	Widow of Alex. Parkeson, Sophia.	I	17th U. S. colored troops.	Settled July 13, 1868, by certificate 115,860, and forwarded to Cloon same date.
141	Widow of Berry McKinney, Isabelle.	C	12th U. S. colored troops.	Settled July 14, 1868, by certificate 115,913, and sent to Cloon same date.
142	Widow of John Upshaw, Emiline.	....	111th U. S. colored troops.	Settled July 21, 1868, by certificate 116,102, and sent to Cloon same date.
143	Widow of Jasper Henderson, Clicy.	D	......do	Settled July 24, 1868, by certificate 116,281, and sent to Cloon same date.
144	Widow of Harry Roberts, Winey.	I	110th U. S. colored troops.	Settled September 10, 1868, by certificate 118,331, and sent to Cloon same date.
145	Widow of Henry Stevenson, Arabella.	A	111th U. S. colored troops.	Settled September 25, 1868, by certificate 119,091, and sent to Cloon same date.
146	Widow of Frank Howard, Annie.	A	111th U. S. colored troops.	Settled September 25, 1868, by certificate 119,090, and sent to Cloon same date.
147	Widow of Giles Horn, Lucy A.	F	......do	Settled December 23, 1868, by certificate 122,461, and sent to Cloon same date.
148	Widow of Lafayette Rivers, Maria.	D	110th U. S. colored troops.	Settled January 2, 1869, by certificate 122,830, and sent to Cloon same date.
149	Widow of Burrell Fitzpatrick, Judy.	D	111th U. S. colored troops.	Settled January 2, 1869, by certicaate 120,831, and sent to Cloon same date.
150	Widow of Abraham Lewis, Nicy.	G	110th U. S. colored troops.	Settled January 16, 1869, by certificate 123,373, and sent to Cloon same date.
151	Widow of Frederick Hammonds, Viny.	D	......do	Settled January 23, 1869, by certificate 123,632, and sent to Cloon same date.
152	Widow of Cary Loyd, Lucy.	I	13th U. S. colored troops.	Settled February 6, 1869, by certificate 124,190, and sent to Cloon same date.

BOUNTIES TO COLORED SOLDIERS. 137

List of pension certificates, &c.—Continued.

No.	Name.	Co.	Regiment.	Remarks.
153	Widow of Marshall Stone, Parathena.	F	111th U.S. colored troops.	Settled February 6, 1869, by certificate 124,188, and sent to Cloon same date.
154	Widow of Richard Wilkerson, Mary.	B	15th U.S. colored troops	Settled February 12, 1869, by certificate 124,501, and sent to Cloon same date.
155	Widow of Dock Pepper, Sarah.	D	110th U.S. colored troops.	Settled February 12, 1869, by certificate 124,500, and sent to Cloon same date.
156	Widow of James McGrew, Martha.	C	111th U.S. colored troops.	Settled March 13, 1869, by certificate 125,692, and sent to Cloon same date.
157	Widow of Monroe Kimble, Josephine.	D	110th U.S. colored troops	Settled March 17, 1869, by certificate 125,930, and sent to Cloon same date.
158	Widow of Jerry Hadley, Rachel.	F	......do..............	Settled March 17, 1869, by certificate 125,931, and sent to Cloon same date.
159	Mother of Isaiah Riggs, Mylinda.	A	15th U.S. colored troops.	Settled March 24, 1869, by certificate 126,246, and sent to Cloon same date.
160	Widow of Jack Wadkins, Maria.	I	17th U.S. colored troops	Settled April 3, 1869, by certificate 126,902 and sent to Cloon same date.
161	Widow of Alfred Stockard, Mary.	E	111th U.S. colored troops.	Settled April 3, 1869, by certificate 126,904, and sent to Cloon same date.
162	Widow of Ned Driver, Mary E.	A	15th U.S. colored troops	Settled April 16, 1869, by certificate 127,473, and sent to Cloon same date.
163	Widow of Pleasant Fitzpatrick, Elmira.	G	111th U.S. colored troops	Settled April 17, 1869, by certificate 127,519, and sent to Attorney Cloon same date.
164	Widow of Milan Fitzpatrick, Paralle.	E	......do..............	Settled June 12, 1869, by certificate 130,169.
165	Widow of John Butler, Famie.	B	110th U.S. colored troops.	Settled June 12, 1869, by certificate 130,168.
166	Mother of William Crofford, Rachel.	C	12th U.S. colored troops	Settled June 21, 1869, by certificate 130,476.
167	Widow of Henderson Richie, Mary A.	K	......do..............	Settled June 23, 1869, by certificate 130,571.
168	Widow of Moses Kennedy, Mylinda.	A	111th U.S. colored troops	Settled July 10, 1869, by certificate 131,234.
169	Widow of Jacob Rountree, Mary.	E	14th U.S. colored troops	Settled July 15, 1869, by certificate 131,483.
170	Widow of Albert Joyce, Henrietta.	C	17th U.S. colored troops.	Settled July 17, 1869, by certificate 131,535.
171	Widow of John Carden, Margret.	A	13th U.S. colored troops.	Settled August 11, 1869, by certificate 132,930.
172	Widow of Nathan Rutledge, Caroline.	F	110th U.S. colored troops	Settled August 5, 1869, by certificate 132,687.
173	Widow of Freeman Lofton, Gracie.	G	......do..............	Settled August 17, 1869, by certificate 133,143.
174	Mother of Paul Coffey, Jane.	D	17th U.S. colored troops.	Settled September 3, 1869, by certificate 133,779.
175	Widow of James Watkins, Fanny.	D	110th U.S. colored troops	Settled September 11, 1869, by certificate 134,069.
176	Widow of Milton Fox, Ruthie.	G	......do..............	Settled September 14, 1869, by certificate 134,162.
177	Widow of Benjamin McDonald, Francis.	A	13th U.S. colored troops.	Settled September 12, 1869, by certificate 134,437.
178	Widow of Robert Arnell, Sally.	C	111th U.S. colored troops	Settled April 23, 1869, by certificate 127,887.
179	Widow of Marshall Cooper, Louisa.	A	15th U.S. colored troops.	Settled May 14, 1869, by certificate 128,879.
180	Widow of Geo. Gollody, Milly.	A	......do..............	Settled May 12, 1869, by certificate 128,733.
181	Widow of Godfrey Anderson, Harriet.	K	13th U.S. colored troops	Settled May 12, 1869, by certificate 128,732.
182	Widow of Isam McDougle, Rachel.	E	14th U.S. colored troops	Settled May 15, 1869, by certificate 129,012.
183	Widow of George Brown, Agnes.	A	40th U.S. colored troops	Settled May 15, 1869, by certificate 128,964.
184	Widow of Burt Lee; Silla.	D	110th U.S. colored troops.	Settled May 19, 1869, by certificate 129,192.
185	Widow of Sam'l Boyd, Abie.	A	15th U.S. colored troops.	Settled May 19, 1869, by certificate 129,194.
186	Widow of Dandridge Rucker, Maria.	E	110th U.S. colored troops	Settled May 19, 1869, by certificate 129,191.
187	Widow of Willis Garrett, Cornelia.	D	13th U.S. colored troops.	Settled May 19, 1869, by certificate 129,195.
188	Widow of Judge Howard, Paralee.	G	110th U.S. colored troops.	Settled May 21, 1869, by certificate 129,326.
189	Widow of Jefferson Sloss, Anderson.	C	15th U.S. colored troops.	Settled May 21, 1869, by certificate 129,327.
190	Mylinda Fogg........	B	110th U.S. colored troops.	Settled May 24, 1869, by certificate 97,836.
191	Widow of John Green, Emeline.	B	12th U.S. colored troops.	Settled May 28, 1869, by certificate 129,642.
192	Widow of Washington.	F	111th U.S. colored troops.	Settled June 3, 1869, by certificate 129,827.

138   BOUNTIES TO COLORED SOLDIERS.

Pension certificates.

No.	Name.	Co.	Regiment.	Remarks.
167	Rachel Crofford, wid. of Henderson Crofford.	K	12th U. S. colored troops	Settled by certificate 130,571 for $8 per month, and one child, June 23, 1869, sent to Cloon.
193	Bidda I. English, wid. of Franklin English.			Settled May 25, 1869, by certificate 129,441, and sent to Cloon.
194	Amanda Grimes, wid. of Alfred Grimes.			Settled May 25, 1869, by certificate 129,442, for self and two children, and sent to Cloon.
170	Mary Roundtree, wid. of Albert Roundtree.	C	17th U. S. colored troops.	Settled July 17, 1869, by certificate 131,535, at $8 per month, three children, and sent to Cloon.
141	Sophia Parkeson, wid. of Berry Parkeson.	C	12th U. S. colored troops	Settled July 14, 1868, by certificate 115,913, for her three children, to begin April 16, 1868, sent to Cloon, and reissue settled October 9, 1868, to begin January 18, 1865.
	Mother of Wm. Steel..	C	14th U. S. colored troops.	Have no such claim on our books.
145	Winnie Roberts. wid. of Henry Roberts.	A	111th U. S. colored troops	Settled September 25, 1868, by certificate 116,091, for self and two children, and sent to Cloon.
	Hannah Booker, wid. of Archib'd Booker.	I	53d U. S. colored troops ..	No such claim on our books. (M. Coombs, jr., through B. D. Hyam.)
	Mary Edwards, wid. of John Edwards.	H	101st U. S. colored troops.	Have no such claims on books. (R. J. Gaines, attorney, in hands of J. B. Coons.)

THIRTY-NINTH DAY'S PROCEEDINGS.

The commission met at 10 a. m., Saturday, February 19, 1870, and continued the examination of the records and the elimination of special cases. Communications hereto attached, from the Bureau Refugees, Freedmen and Abandoned Lands, giving information called for by the commission, were received.

At 4 p. m. the commission adjourned.

BEN. P. RUNKLE,
Brevet Colonel United States Army.
J. R. LEWIS,
Brevet Colonel United States Army.
J. A. SLADEN,
Brevet Captain United States Army, Recorder.

WAR DEPARTMENT, BUREAU OF REFUGEES,
FREEDMEN AND ABANDONED LANDS, CLAIM DIVISION,
Washington, D. C., February 18, 1870.

CAPTAIN: In answer to your letter of the 17th instant, requesting information whether J. C. McMullin is an agent of this bureau, and a member of the firm of Buck & McMullin, I am directed to inform you that the records of this office show that the firm of Buck & McMullin (J. Jay Buck & J. C McMullin) was dissolved January 1, 1867, the unsettled business of the firm falling to Mr. Buck, and that J. C. McMullin was appointed April 23, 1867, agent and disbursing officer of this bureau at Clarksville, Tennessee, which appointment he has continued to hold up to the present time.

Shortly after the dissolution of the firm, Mr. Buck was appointed register in bankruptcy.

Very respectfully, your obedient servant,
WILLIAM P. DREW,
Agent Bureau Refugees, Freedmen and Abandoned Lands,
Chief of Claim Division.

Brevet Captain J. A. SLADEN, U. S. A.,
Recorder of Military Commission, Bureau Refugees,
Freedmen and Abandoned Lands, Washington, D. C.

WAR DEPARTMENT, BUREAU OF REFUGEES,
FREEDMEN, AND ABANDONED LANDS,
Washington, D. C., February 18, 1870.

CAPTAIN: I am directed by the Commissioner to acknowledge the receipt of your letter of 17th instant asking for information of certain officers, agents, and clerks, late on duty in Tennessee, and, in reply, to state that Henry A. Eastman, agent, resigned, to take effect September 30, 1868; George W. Carlin, clerk, was discharged on account of reduction of force, to take effect October 31, 1868; Charles R. Simpson, agent, was discharged on account of reduction of force, to take effect October 31, 1868; John Mills, agent, was on duty at Athens, Alabama; Colonel T. H. Reeves was a retired officer of the army; he was transferred from Columbia to Cleveland in May, 1869; from Cleveland to Jonesboro in July, 1869. He requested to be relieved from duty in the bureau, to accept the assistant clerkship of the Tennessee legislature, and he was relieved accordingly by Special Orders No. 222, Adjutant General's Office, September, 1869. Captain George E. Judd, United States Army, was transferred from Pulaski to Nashville, March 30, 1868; from Nashville to Murfreesboro in October, 1868, and was transferred from Tennessee to Kentucky by Special Orders No. 81, series 1869, from these headquarters. He was relieved from duty in this bureau at the special request of General Sherman, by Special Orders No. 197, Adjutant General's Office, August, 1867.

Very respectfully, your obedient servant,
HENRY M. WHITTLESEY,
Acting Asst. Adjt. General.

Brevet Captain J. A. SLADEN,
Recorder of Commission to Investigate Frauds, Washington, D. C.

FORTIETH DAY'S PROCEEDINGS.

The commission met at 10 a. m. Monday, February 21, 1870, and continued the work upon the report.

A communication, hereto attached, was received from the Surgeon General, through the Bureau of Refugees, Freedmen and Abandoned Lands, concerning employés in hospitals at Nashville. Communications were sent to the Commissioner of the Bureau of Refugees, Freedmen and Abandoned Lands, asking for certain information.

At 4 p. m. the commission adjourned.
BEN. P. RUNKLE,
Brevet Colonel United States Army.
J. R. LEWIS,
Brevet Colonel United States Army.
J. A. SLADEN,
Brevet Captain United States Army, Recorder.

ROOMS OF THE MILITARY COMMISSION FOR
THE INVESTIGATION OF FRAUDS AGAINST
COLORED SOLDIERS AND SAILORS,
Washington, D. C., February 3, 1870.

GENERAL: We have the honor to state that certain colored persons appeared before the commission while in session at Nashville, Tennessee, and stated that they had been employed in the United States hospital at Nashville during the war, and that although they signed rolls every two months during the time of their service, they never received the amount due them for such services.

We learned also that there were a large number of such claimants, many of whom suppose that they have been defrauded by the bureau or claim agents, and thereby have given rise to many rumors of fraud.

We therefore respectfully request that the Surgeon General United States Army be requested to furnish information whether all employés in hospitals at Nashville, Tennessee, during the war, were taken up on regular hospital rolls, and if so, do the records show that they have all been paid.

Very respectfully, your obedient servants,
BEN. P. RUNKLE,
Brevet Colonel United States Army.
J. R. LEWIS,
Brevet Colonel United States Army.
J. A. SLADEN,
Brevet Captain United States Army, Recorder.

[Indorsements.]

WAR DEPARTMENT, BUREAU OF REFUGEES,
FREEDMEN AND ABANDONED LANDS,
Washington, February 4, 1870.

Respectfully forwarded to Brevet Major General J. K. Barnes, Surgeon General United States Army, with the request that the information be furnished if possible.

O. O. HOWARD,
Brevet Major General, Commissioner.

SURGEON GENERAL'S OFFICE,
February 17, 1870.

Respectfully returned to General O. O. Howard, United States Army, Commissioner Bureau Refugees, Freedmen and Abandoned Lands. It is not possible to furnish the information asked for from the records of this office, but it can probably be obtained from the Adjutant General's, Paymaster General's, and Second Auditor's Offices.

J. K. BARNES,
Surgeon General.

WAR DEPARTMENT, BUREAU OF REFUGEES,
FREEDMEN AND ABANDONED LANDS,
Washington, February 19, 1870.

Respectfully returned to Colonel Ben. P. Runkle, president of commission to investigate frauds, Washington, D. C.; attention invited to the indorsement of Surgeon General United States Army hereon.

By order of Brevet Major General O. O. Howard:
HENRY M. WHITTLESEY,
Acting Asst. Adjt. General.

FORTY-FIRST DAY'S PROCEEDINGS.

The commission met at 10 a. m. Tuesday, February 22, 1870, and continued the examination of the proceedings and the work upon the report.

Communication (hereto attached) was received from William P. Drew, chief of claim division, Bureau Refugees, Freedmen and Abandoned Lands, containing information in the cases of Thomas Branch and William Cannon, of Company F Third United States colored heavy artillery, called for by the commission.

At 4 p. m. the commission adjourned.

BEN. P. RUNKLE,
Brevet Colonel United States Army.
J. R. LEWIS,
Brevet Colonel United States Army.
J. A. SLADEN,
Brevet Captain United States Army, Recorder.

WAR DEPARTMENT, BUREAU OF REFUGEES, FREEDMEN,
AND ABANDONED LANDS, CLAIM DIVISION,
Washington, February 21, 1870.

CAPTAIN: In answer to your letter of the 19th instant, requesting information as to the cases of William Cannon and Thomas Branch, late of Company F Third United States colored heavy artillery, viz: "when paid, by whom, amount of advances, to whom paid, number of certificate, and date of blue letter," I am directed to inform you that the records of this bureau show the case of William Cannon, as above, settled by Second Auditor's certificate No. 484,869, (blue letter dated October 22, 1868,) for $201 95, of which amount $100 advances, and $12 50 fees, were paid October 27, 1869, at Washington, by the chief disbursing officer of this bureau to Messrs. Moyers & Dedrick, attorneys in the claim, and the balance ($89 45) paid to the claimant December 6, 1869, by Lieutenant Colonel F. S. Palmer, disbursing officer, at Memphis, Tennessee.

The claim of Thomas Branch, as above, was settled by Second Auditor's certificate No. 484,863, (blue letter dated October 22, 1868,) for $208 88, of which amount $45 advances, and $12 50 fees, were paid October 27, 1869, at Washington, by the chief disbursing officer of this Bureau, to Messrs. Moyers & Dedrick, and the balance ($151 38) paid to the claimant December 11, 1869, by Colonel Palmer, at Memphis, Tennessee.

These certificates were received at this office from the attorneys November 9, 1868, and payment of the same withheld in consequence of circular dated "War Department, Adjutant General's Office, November 25, 1868," suspending the attorneys.

October 26, 1869, orders were received from the Secretary of War, authorizing this bureau to pay to the attorneys the advances referred to.

It is proper to add that the advances in these cases were duly certified by Colonel Palmer.

Very respectfully, your obedient servant,
WILLIAM P. DREW,
Agent Bureau Refugees, Freedmen and Abandoned Lands,
Chief of Claim Division.

Brevet Captain J. A. SLADEN, U. S. A.,
Recorder for Military Commission, Bureau R. F. and A. L.,
Washington, D. C.

142   BOUNTIES TO COLORED SOLDIERS.

FORTY-SECOND DAY'S PROCEEDINGS.

The commission met at 10 a. m. Wednesday, February 23, 1870, and continued the examination of the record, the writing of the report, and the collation of frauds.

A communication was sent to Mr. Drew, calling for information as to the date of the act of Congress ordering that certificates for bounty be sent to the Bureau of Refugees, Freedmen and Abandoned Lands, instead of to the claim agents.

At 4 p. m. the commission adjourned.

BEN. P. RUNKLE,
Brevet Colonel United States Army.
J. R. LEWIS,
Brevet Colonel United States Army.
J. A. SLADEN,
Brevet Captain United States Army, Recorder.

FORTY-THIRD DAY'S PROCEEDINGS.

The commission met at 10 a. m. Thursday, February 24, 1870, and continued the work upon their report and the examination of the records.

A report of cases made up from information from the Second Auditor's Office, called for by the commission, was received from W. P. Drew, chief of claim division, Bureau of Refugees, Freedmen and Abandoned Lands, and is attached to the proceedings of the commission, and marked "Drew's Statement E."

Commission (hereto attached) also received from General Balloch, containing information concerning the case of Carey Crenshaw.

At 4 p. m. the commission adjourned.

BEN. P. RUNKLE,
Brevet Colonel United States Army.
J. R. LEWIS,
Brevet Colonel United States Army.
J. A. SLADEN,
Brevet Captain United States Army, Recorder.

ROOMS OF THE MILITARY COMM'N FOR INVESTIGATION OF
FRAUDS AGAINST COLORED SOLDIERS AND SAILORS,
Washington, Feb'y 21, 1870, (Room No. 7, Plant's Building.)

GENERAL: I am directed by the commission to request you to furnish this office with a certified copy of the check by which the bounty of Carey Crenshaw, late of Company H One hundred and tenth regiment United States colored troops, was paid. He was paid by Colonel J. B. Callis, at Huntsville, Alabama.

Very respectfully, your obedient servant,
J. A. SLADEN,
Brevet Captain United States Army, Recorder.

General GEORGE W. BALLOCH,
Chief Disbursing Officer Bureau Refugees, Freedmen, &c.

P. S.—Please furnish this information with the least possible delay.

[Indorsement.]

WAR DEPARTMENT,
Bureau of Refugees, Freedmen, &c., February 23, 1870.

Respectfully returned. I am unable to furnish a copy of the draft within referred to, as it was a transfer draft drawn by Freedmen's Savings and Trust Company of this city on the branch at Huntsville. The draft was drawn in favor of Brevet Brigadier General John B. Callis, then agent at Huntsville, and was dated January 11, 1868, for $466 89, to pay—

Carey Crenshaw	$194 20
Abraham Reynold	272 69
	466 89

The present residence of General Callis is not known.

GEO. W. BALLOCH,
Bvt. Brig. Gen. and Chief Disbursing Officer.

FORTY-FOURTH DAY'S PROCEEDINGS.

The commission met at 10 a. m. Friday, February 25, 1870, and continued the examination of the proceedings and the work upon the reports.

Several communications were received from William P. Drew, chief of claim division, Bureau of Refugees, Freedmen and Abandoned Lands, (hereto attached,) containing information called for by the commission.

The commission called in person upon the Second Comptroller of the Treasury Department, and asked for copies of vouchers in cases of advances on file in his office. This request was granted. A clerk was sent by the commission for the purpose of making copies of the same.

At 4 p. m. the commission adjourned.

BEN. P. RUNKLE,
Brevet Colonel United States Army.
J. R. LEWIS,
Brevet Colonel United States Army.
J. A. SLADEN,
Brevet Captain United States Army, Recorder.

WAR DEPARTMENT,
BUREAU OF REFUGEES, FREEDMEN, &C.,
Claim Division, Washington, Feb. 24, 1870.

COLONEL: In accordance with your verbal request of the 10th instant, I have the honor to inclose herewith a schedule showing the number and value of treasury certificates adjusted at the claim division of this bureau, and sent to the chief disbursing officer for payment, from April 23, 1867, to February 1, 1870, and the amounts paid thereon by the chief disbursing officer; also the number of certificates on which advances have been allowed, and the amount of such advances.

The report of advances claimed by attorneys and disallowed by this office will be delayed for a few days, owing to the thorough examination of the records necessary to ascertain the amounts.

It may be of interest to add that there are now in this office about twelve hundred certificates awaiting adjustment.

Very respectfully, your obedient servant,
WILLIAM P. DREW,
Agent Bureau of Refugees, Freedmen, &c., Chief of Claim Div'n.

Brevet Colonel BEN. P. RUNKLE, U. S. A.,
Pres't Military Comm'n, Bureau Refugees, Freedmen, &c.

Schedule showing the number of treasury certificates adjusted at the claim division, Bureau of Refugees, Freedmen and Abandoned Lands, and sent to the chief disbursing officer for payment, the value of the same, and the amount paid thereon by the chief disbursing officer; also the number of certificates on which advances have been allowed, and the amount of such advances.

Total number of certificates sent to chief disbursing officer, from April 23, 1867, to January 31, 1870, inclusive	40,443
Amounting in value to	$7,937,985 37
Amount paid by chief disbursing officer on account of above certificates	6,700,427 76
Balance remaining unpaid	1,237,557 61
Total number of certificates on which advances have been allowed	2,672
Total amount of advances allowed	$125,224 70

WAR DEPARTMENT,
BUREAU OF REFUGEES, FREEDMEN, &C.,
Claim Division, Washington, Feb. 24, 1870.

CAPTAIN: I am directed to return herewith the inclosed three reports, originally forwarded to you from this office on the 8th, 9th, and 12th instants, respectively, in which have been inserted the number of certificates and the date of the Auditor's letter transmitting the same in each case, as requested in your letter of the 17th instant.

Added to the inclosed report, marked A, please find the names of John Young, late of Company F One hundred and eleventh United States colored troops, and Burrell Reedus, 1st, and Burrell Reedus, 2d, both late of Company I One hundred and tenth United States colored troops, the same being settled and paid cases, and previously omitted from the report.

Very respectfully, your obedient servant,
WILLIAM P. DREW,
Agent Bureau of Refugees, Freedmen, &c., Chief of Claim Div'n.

Brevet Captain J. A. SLADEN, U. S. A.,
Recorder of Military Comm'n, Washington, D. C.

BOUNTIES TO COLORED SOLDIERS.

BUREAU REFUGEES, FREEDMEN AND ABANDONED LANDS,
OFFICE DISBURSING AGENT OF CLAIMS,
Nashville, Tennessee, February 21, 1870.

SIR: Joseph Johnson, deceased, late corporal Company C Seventeenth United States colored infantry, left a widow and one child. The widow received the bounty due her husband, and shortly afterward died. A pension claim was filed by the widow, but never settled. The grandmother of the child states she gave the papers in the claim to the late board of officers sent out by General Howard. Can you inform this office if there is any such claim on file; if so, its present condition?

Respectfully, &c.,

J. B. COONS, *Agent, &c.*

WM. P. DREW, Esq.,
Chief Claim Div., Bureau R. F. and A. L., Washington, D. C.

[Indorsement.]

WAR DEPARTMENT, BUREAU OF REFUGEES,
FREEDMEN AND ABANDONED LANDS, CLAIM DIVISION,
Washington, February 24, 1870.

Respectfully referred to Brevet Colonel Ben. P. Runkle, United States Army, president military commission Bureau Refugees, Freedmen and Abandoned Lands, Washington, D. C., with request for the papers mentioned within, if in his possession.

By order of Brevet Major General O. O. Howard, United States Army, Commissioner.

WILLIAM P. DREW,
Agent Bureau R. F. and A. L., Chief of Claim Division.

WAR DEPARTMENT, BUREAU OF REFUGEES,
FREEDMEN AND ABANDONED LANDS, CLAIM DIVISION,
Washington, D. C., February 24, 1870.

COLONEL: In answer to your letter of the 23d instant, requesting information "when the Second Auditor ceased to send certificates for bounty, &c., direct to claim agents, and sent them to the bureau," I am directed to state that such certificates were ordered to be sent to this bureau direct by act of Congress approved April 10, 1869, and that the first certificate forwarded under said act was received at this bureau April 21, 1869, since which date they have been sent regularly to this bureau.

Very respectfully, your obedient servant,

WILLIAM P. DREW,
Agent and Chief of Claim Division.

Brevet Colonel B. P. RUNKLE, U. S. A.,
President Military Commission, Bureau R. F. and A. L.

FORTY-FITH DAY'S PROCEEDINGS.

The commission met at 10 a. m., Saturday, February 26, 1870, and continued the examination of the proceedings and the work upon the report.

At 4 o'clock p. m. the commission adjourned.

BEN. P. RUNKLE,
Brevet Colonel United States Army.
J. R. LEWIS,
Brevet Colonel United States Army.
J. A. SLADEN,
Brevet Captain United States Army, Recorder.

FORTY-SIXTH DAY'S PROCEEDINGS.

The commission met at 10 a. m., Monday, February 28, 1870, and continued work upon the report.

Communication (hereto attached) furnishing information called for by the commission was received from William P. Drew, chief of claim division, Bureau Refugees, Freedmen and Abandoned Lands, copies of vouchers from Second Comptroller, herewith attached. The commission adjourned at four p. m.

BEN. P. RUNKLE,
Brevet Colonel United States Army.
J. R. LEWIS,
Brevet Colonel United States Army.
J. A. SLADEN,
Brevet Captain United States Army, Recorder.

WAR DEPARTMENT BUREAU OF REFUGEES,
FREEDMEN AND ABANDONED LANDS, CLAIM DIVISION,
Washington, February 26, 1870.

COLONEL: In answer to your letter of the 25th instant, requesting information as to the number of treasury certificates on which advances have been collected through this bureau by Messrs. Moyers & Dedrick, attorneys, the total amount of such advances, and the circumstances under which they were allowed and paid, I am directed to inform you that the records of this bureau show that to January 31, 1870, advances amounting to $51,321 80 have been paid to said firm on seven hundred and thirty-nine certificates. Advances were allowed and paid to this firm upon the usual evidence required by bureau circulars until November 25, 1868, at which date the firm was suspended by the War Department, and their further recognition by its bureaus prohibited. At this date there were on file in this office and unadjusted one hundred and fourteen certificates received from them, on which advances amounting to $7,781 were claimed.

Payment of their fees and advances in these cases was finally made by this bureau, under orders of the honorable Secretary of War, dated October 26, 1869.

November 29, 1869, by circular of the War Department, (copy inclosed,) the firm was relieved from suspension so far as the business of their "white clients" was concerned, and were authorized to "settle all business for colored claimants" by their attorney, Thomas Wilson, "in conjunction with the proper officers of the Freedmen's Bureau." This bureau being in doubt whether the circular would authorize payment of fees and advances claimed by them on certificates withheld by the honorable Second Auditor during the year of their suspension, and which were sent by him to this bureau, when circular of November 29, 1869, was issued by the War Department, the question was referred to the honorable Secretary of War, who, under date of December 9, 1869, ordered payment of the same to Mr. Wilson, as attorney for Messrs. Moyers & Dedrick. Of the number (some fifteen hundred) thus withheld and received, advances were allowed and paid on two hundred and ninety-six certificates.

Very respectfully, your obedient servant,
WILLIAM P. DREW,
Agent Bureau of Refugees, Freedmen and Abandoned Lands,
Chief of Claim Division.

Brevet Colonel B. P. RUNKLE, U. S. A.,
President Military Commission, Bureau Refugees,
Freedmen and Abandoned Lands, Washington, D. C.

[Circular.]

WAR DEPARTMENT, ADJUTANT GENERAL'S OFFICE,
Washington, November 29, 1869.

The officers appointed to hear the answers to charges against certain attorneys and claim agents having reported that the complaints against the firm of Moyers & Dedrick "*relate exclusively to their dealings with their colored clients, and that from the nature of the evidence an examination of these cannot for some time be completed,*" it is ordered by the Secretary of War, pending the result of such examination, and with a view to the relief of claimants, that so much of the circular of September 11, 1869, from this office, as relates to the said firm, be revoked, *in so far as it affects their white clients.*

It is ordered, further, by the Secretary of War, that Thomas Wilson, the attorney for the firm of Moyers & Dedrick, be permitted, in conjunction with the proper officers of the Freedmen's Bureau, and subject to the further orders of the War Department, to adjust and settle all business for *colored claimants* in which the firm is concerned.

E. D. TOWNSEND,
Adjutant General.

DISTRICT OF COLUMBIA, *County of Washington, ss :*

On this 29th day of January, 1868, personally appeared before me, the undersigned, a notary public within and for the District aforesaid, C. D. Gilmore, who, being duly sworn, declares and says that he is a member of the firm of Chipman, Hosmer & Co.; that the money cited in the within receipt was paid as therein stated, in good faith, by D. S. Mann, as agent of the firm, and not on his personal account.

C. D. GILMORE.

Sworn to and subscribed before me, the day and year first above written.

T. J. GARDNER,
Justice of the Peace.

A true copy :

BEN. P. RUNKLE,
Brevet Colonel United States Army.

148　BOUNTIES TO COLORED SOLDIERS.

Received of Chipman, Hosmer & Co., attorneys at Washington, D. C., this 20th day of January, 1868, fifty dollars, being for money paid on the 15th day of October, 1867, to Thomas Upshaw, private of K Company One hundred and tenth regiment United States colored troops.

DANIEL S. MANN.

Fees of Chipman Hosmer & Co., attorneys, for settlement in claim of Thomas Upshaw, Company B One hundred and tenth regiment of United States colored troops, volunteers.

No. of treasury certificate, 366,726; amount of treasury certificate, $203 20.

Legal fees, act March 29, 1867	$10 00
Notarial fees	3 00
Advances, per voucher	50 00
Attorney's affidavit as to advances	50
Attorney's affidavit as to itemized bill	50
Attorney's affidavit as to non-interest	50
Attorney's affidavit in second application	3 00
Total	67 50

Approved, and payment ordered.

Major General, Commissioner.

Received at Washington, D. C., this 3d day of February, 1868, from Brevet Brigadier General George W. Balloch, chief disbursing officer, Bureau Refugees, Freedmen and Abandoned Lands, sixty-seven dollars and fifty cents, in full for fees as above cited.

CHIPMAN, HOSMER & CO.

A true copy:

BEN. P. RUNKLE,
Brevet Colonel United States Army.

DISTRICT OF COLUMBIA, *County of Washington, ss:*

On this 30th day of January, 1868, personally appeared before me, the undersigned, a justice of the peace within and for the District and county aforesaid, C. D. Gilmore, who, being duly sworn, declares and says that he is a member of the firm of Chipman, Hosmer & Co., and that the notarial and other expenses cited in within bill are correct and just.

C. D. GILMORE.

Sworn to and subscribed before me, the day and year first above written.

T. J. GARDNER,
Justice of the Peace.

DISTRICT OF COLUMBIA, *County of Washington, ss:*

On this 29th day of January, 1868, personally appeared before me, the undersigned, a notary public within and for the District aforesaid, C. D. Gilmore, who, being duly sworn, declares and says that he is a member of the firm of Chipman, Hosmer & Co.; that the money cited in the

BOUNTIES TO COLORED SOLDIERS. 149

within receipt was paid as therein stated, in good faith, by D. S. Mann, as agent of the firm, and not on his personal account.

C. D. GILMORE.

Sworn to and subscribed before me, the day and year first above written.

T. J. GARDNER,
Justice of the Peace.

A true copy:

BEN. P. RUNKLE,
Brevet Colonel United States Army.

Received of Chipman, Hosmer & Co., attorneys at Washington, D. C., this 30th day of January, 1868, $40, being for money paid on the 17th day of October, 1867, to Jerry Jenkins, of Company K One hundred and tenth regiment United States colored troops.

DANIEL S. MANN.

Fees of Chipman, Hosmer & Co., attorneys, for settlement in claim of James Brown, Company I One hundred and tenth regiment of United States colored troops, volunteers.

No. of treasury certificate, 366,665; amount of treasury certificate, $300 20.

Legal fees, act of March 29, 1867	$10 00
Notarial fees	3 00
Advances, per voucher	80 00
Attorney's affidavit as to advances	50
Attorney's affidavit as to itemized bill	50
Attorney's affidavit as to non-interest	50
Attorney's affidavit on additional evidence	2 50
Total	97 00

Approved and payment ordered.

―――― ――――,
Major General, Commissioner.

Received, at Washington, D. C., this 3d day of February, 1868, from Brevet Brigadier General George W. Balloch, chief disbursing officer Bureau Refugees, Freedmen and Abandoned Lands, $97, in full for fees as above cited.

CHIPMAN, HOSMER & CO.

A true copy:

BEN. P. RUNKLE,
Brevet Colonel United States Army.

DISTRICT OF COLUMBIA, *County of Washington, ss:*

On this 30th day of January, 1868, personally appeared before me, the undersigned, a justice of the peace within and for the District and county aforesaid, C. D. Gilmore, who, being duly sworn, declares and says that

150 BOUNTIES TO COLORED SOLDIERS.

he is a member of the firm of Chipman, Hosmer & Co., and that the notarial and other expenses cited in within bill are correct and just.

C. D. GILMORE.

Sworn to and subscribed before me, the day and year first above written.

T. J. GARDNER,
Justice of the Peace.

DISTRICT OF COLUMBIA, *County of Washington, ss:*

On this 29th day of January, 1868, personally appeared before me, the undersigned, a notary public within and for the District and county aforesaid, C. D. Gilmore, who, being duly sworn, declares and says that he is a member of the firm of Chipman, Hosmer & Co.; that the money cited in the within receipt was paid as therein stated, in good faith, by D. S. Mann, as agent of the firm, and not on his personal account.

C. D. GILMORE.

Sworn and subscribed before me, the day and year first above written.

T. J. GARDNER,
Justice of the Peace.

A true copy:

BEN. P. RUNKLE,
Brevet Colonel United States Army.

Received of Chipman, Hosmer & Co., attorneys at Washington, D. C., this 20th day of January, 1868, $80, being for money paid on the 15th day of October, 1867, to James Brown, private of Company I One hundred and tenth regiment United States colored troops.

DANIEL S. MANN.

Fees of Chipman, Hosmer & Co., attorneys, for settlement in claim of Jerry Jenkins, Company K One hundred and tenth regiment of United States colored troops, volunteers.

No. of treasury certificate, 666,730; amount of treasury certificate $203 20.

Legal fees, act March 29, 1867	$10 00
Notarial fees	3 00
Advances, per voucher	40 00
Attorney's affidavit as to advances	50
Attorney's affidavit as to itemized bill	50
Notarial fees	50
At Elkton, additional evidence	3 00
Total	57 50

Approved and payment ordered.

Major General, Commissioner.

Received at Washington, D. C., this 31st day of January, 1868, from Brevet Brigadier General George W. Balloch, chief disbursing officer

Bureau of Refugees, Freedmen and Abandoned Lands, $57 50, in full for fees as above cited.

CHIPMAN, HOSMER & CO.

A true copy:

BEN. P. RUNKLE,
Brevet Colonel United States Army.

DISTRICT OF COLUMBIA, *County of Washington, ss:*

On this 29th day of January, 1868, personally appeared before me, the undersigned, a justice of the peace within and for the District and county aforesaid, C. D. Gilmore, who, being duly sworn, declares and says that he is a member of the firm of Chipman, Hosmer & Co., and that the notarial and other expenses cited in within bill are correct and just.

C. D. GILMORE.

Sworn to and subscribed before me, the day and year first above written.

T. J. GARDNER,
Justice of the Peace.

DISTRICT OF COLUMBIA, *County of Washington, ss:*

On this 3d day of January, 1868, personally appeared before me, the undersigned, a notary public within and for the District and county aforesaid, C. D. Gilmore, who, being duly sworn, declares and says that he is a member of the firm of Chipman, Hosmer & Co.; that the money cited in the within receipt was paid as therein stated, in good faith, by Daniel S. Mann, as agent of the firm, and not on his personal account.

C. D. GILMORE.

Sworn to and subscribed before me, the day and year first above written.

T. J. GARDNER,
Justice of the Peace.

A true copy:

BEN. P. RUNKLE,
Brevet Colonel United States Army.

Received of Chipman, Hosmer & Co., attorneys at Washington, D. C., this 10th day of December, 1867, $150, being for money paid on the 9th day of October, 1867, to James Vance, 1st, private of Company I One hundred and tenth regiment United States colored troops.

DANIEL S. MANN.

Fees of Chipman, Hosmer & Co., attorneys, for settlement in claim of James Vance, Company I One hundred and tenth regiment of United States colored troops, volunteers.

No. of treasury certificate, 366,681; amount of treasury certificate, $300 20.

Legal fees, act March 29, 1867	$10 00
Notarial fees at Alabama on original application	2 50
Advances, per voucher	150 00
Attorney's affidavit as to advances	50

152   BOUNTIES TO COLORED SOLDIERS.

Attorney's affidavit as to itemized bill	$0 50
Attorney's affidavit as to non-interest	50
Notarial fees on additional evidence	2 50
Total	166 50

Approved and payment ordered.

―――― ――――,
Major General, Commissioner.

Received at Washington, D. C., this 7th day of January, 1868, from Brevet Brigadier General George W. Balloch, chief disbursing officer Bureau of Refugees, Freedmen and Abandoned Lands, $166 50, in full for fees as above cited.

CHIPMAN, HOSMER & CO.

A true copy:

BEN. P. RUNKLE,
Brevet Colonel United States Army.

DISTRICT OF COLUMBIA, *County of Washington, ss:*

On this 3d day of January, 1868, personally appeared before me, the undersigned, a justice of the peace within and for the District and county aforesaid, C. D. Gilmore, who, being duly sworn, declares and says that he is a member of the firm of Chipman, Hosmer & Co., and that the notarial and other expenses cited in within bill are correct and just.

C. D. GILMORE.

Sworn to and subscribed before me, the day and year first above written.

T. J. GARDNER,
Justice of the Peace.

DISTRICT OF COLUMBIA, *County of Washington, ss:*

On this 3d day of January, 1868, personally appeared before me, the undersigned, a notary public within and for the District and county aforesaid, C. D. Gilmore, who, being duly sworn, declares and says that he is a member of the firm of Chipman, Hosmer & Co.; that the money cited in the within receipt was paid as therein stated, in good faith, by Daniel S. Mann, as agent of the firm, and not on his personal account.

C. D. GILMORE.

Sworn and subscribed before me, the day and year first above written.

T. J. GARDNER,
Justice of the Peace.

A true copy:

BEN. P. RUNKLE,
Brevet Colonel United States Army.

Received of Chipman, Hosmer & Co., attorneys at Washington, D. C., this 10th day of December, 1867, $100, being for money paid on the 23d day of October, 1867, to Paldo Baily, private of K Company, One hundred and tenth regiment United States colored troops.

DANIEL S. MANN.

BOUNTIES TO COLORED SOLDIERS. 153

Fees of Chipman, Hosmer & Co., attorneys, for settlement of claim of Paldo Baily, Company K One hundred and tenth regiment of United States colored volunteers.

No. of treasury certificate, 366,693; amount of treasury certificate, $203 20.

Legal fees, act March 29, 1867	$10 00
Notarial fees	2 50
Advances, per voucher	100 00
Attorney's affidavit as to advances	50
Attorney's affidavit as to itemized bill	50
Attorney's affidavit as to non-interest	50
Attorney's affidavit as to additional evidence	2 50
Total	116 50

Approved, and payment ordered.

―――― ――――,
Major General, Commissioner.

Received at Washington, D. C., this 7th day of January, 1868, from Brevet Brigadier General George W. Balloch, chief disbursing officer Bureau Refugees, Freedmen and Abandoned Lands, $116 50, in full for fees as above cited.

CHIPMAN, HOSMER & CO.

A true copy:

BEN. P. RUNKLE,
Brevet Colonel United States Army.

DISTRICT OF COLUMBIA, *County of Washington, ss:*

On this 3d day of January, 1868, personally appeared before me, the undersigned, a justice of the peace within and for the District and county aforesaid, C. D. Gilmore, who, being duly sworn, declares and says that he is a member of the firm of Chipman, Hosmer & Co., and that the notarial and other expenses cited in within bill are correct and just.

C. D. GILMORE.

Sworn to and subscribed before me, the day and year first above written.

T. J. GARDNER,
Justice of the Peace.

DISTRICT OF COLUMBIA, *County of Washington, ss:*

On this 3d day of May, 1868, personally appeared before me, the undersigned, a notary public within and for the District and county aforesaid, C. D. Gilmore, who, being duly sworn, declares and says that he is a member of the firm of Chipman, Hosmer & Co.; that the money cited in the within receipt was paid as therein stated, in good faith, by Daniel S. Mann, as agent of the firm, and not on his personal account.

C. D. GILMORE.

Sworn to and subscribed before me, the day and year first above written.

T. J. GARDNER.
Justice of the Peace.

A true copy:

BEN. P. RUNKLE,
Brevet Colonel United States Army.

BOUNTIES TO COLORED SOLDIERS.

Received of Chipman, Hosmer & Co., attorneys at Washington, D. C., this 10th day of December, 1867, $100, being for money paid on the 17th day of September, 1869, to Albert Harney, of K Company One hundred and tenth regiment United States colored troops.

DANIEL S. MANN.

Fees of Chipman, Hosmer & Co., attorneys for settlement in claim of Albert Harney, Company K One hundred and tenth regiment of United States colored troops, volunteers.

No. of treasury certificate, 366,704; amount of treasury certificate, $203 20.

Legal fees, act March 29, 1867	$10 00
Notarial fees, at Decatur, Alabama, on application	2 50
Advances, per voucher	100 00
Attorney's affidavit as to advances	50
Attorney's affidavit as to itemized bill	50
Notarial fees here, non-interest	50
Notarial fees at Decatur, Alabama, on new application	2 50
Total	116 50

Approved, and payment ordered.

————— —————,
Major General, Commissioner.

Received at Washington, D. C., this 7th day of January, 1868, from Brevet Brigadier General George W. Balloch, chief disbursing officer, Bureau Refugees, Freedmen and Abandoned Lands, $116 50 in full for fees as above cited.

CHIPMAN, HOSMER & CO.

A true copy:

BEN. P. RUNKLE,
Brevet Colonel United States Army.

DISTRICT OF COLUMBIA, *County of Washington, ss:*

On this 3d day of January, 1868, personally appeared before me, the undersigned, a justice of the peace within and for the District and county aforesaid, C. D. Gilmore, who, being duly sworn, declares and says that he is a member of the firm of Chipman, Hosmer & Co.; and that the notarial and other expenses cited in within bill are correct and just.

C. D. GILMORE.

Sworn to and subscribed before me, the day and year first above written.

T. J. GARDNER,
Justice of the Peace.

DISTRICT OF COLUMBIA, *County of Washington, ss:*

On this 3d day of January, 1868, personally appeared before me, the undersigned, a notary public within and for the District and county aforesaid, C. D. Gilmore, who, being duly sworn, declares and says that he is a member of the firm of Chipman, Hosmer & Co.; that the money cited in the within receipt was paid as therein stated, in good faith, by Daniel S. Mann, as agent of the firm, and not on his personal account.

C. D. GILMORE.

Sworn and subscribed before me, the day and year first above written.

T. J. GARDNER,
Justice of the Peace.

A true copy:

BEN. P. RUNKLE,
Brevet Colonel United States Army.

Received of Chipman, Hosmer & Co., attorneys at Washington, D. C., this 10th day of December, 1867, $100, being for money paid on the 9th day of October, 1867, to Henry Hargrove, of Company K One hundred and tenth regiment United States colored troops.

DANIEL S. MANN.

Fees of Chipman, Hosmer & Co., attorneys for settlement in claim of Henry Hargrove, Company K One hundred and tenth regiment of United States colored troops, volunteers.

No. of treasury certificate, 366,706; amount of treasury certificate, $203 20.

Legal fees, act of March 29, 1867	$10 00
Notarial fees at Pulaski, Tennessee, on application	2 50
Advances, per voucher	100 00
Attorney's affidavit as to advances	50
Attorney's affidavit as to itemized bill	50
Attorney's affidavit as to non-interest	50
Notarial fee at Pulaski, Tennessee, on additional application	2 50
Total	116 50

Approved, and payment ordered.

―――― ――――,
Major General, Commissioner.

Received at Washington, D. C., this 7th day of January, 1868, from Brevet Brigadier General George W. Balloch, chief disbursing officer Bureau Refugees, Freedmen and Abandoned Lands, $116 50, in full for fees as above cited.

CHIPMAN, HOSMER & CO.

A true copy:

BEN. P. RUNKLE,
Brevet Colonel United States Army.

DISTRICT OF COLUMBIA, *County of Washington, ss :*

On this 3d day of January, 1868, personally appeared before me, the undersigned, a justice of the peace within and for the District and county aforesaid, C. D. Gilmore, who, being duly sworn, declares and says that he is a member of the firm of Chipman, Hosmer & Co., and that the notarial and other expenses cited in within bill are correct and just.

C. D. GILMORE.

Sworn to and subscribed before me, the day and year first above written.

T. J. GARDNER,
Justice of the Peace.

WAR DEPARTMENT,
BUREAU REFUGEES, FREEDMEN AND ABANDONED LANDS,
Claim Division, Washington, D. C., February 28, 1870.

COLONEL: In answer to your letter of the 25th instant, inclosing a list (herewith returned) of advances furnished your commission by Messrs. Chipman, Hosmer & Co., with request to be informed whether they have collected advances in any cases which do not appear on such list, I am directed to state that the records of this office show that, to February 1, 1870, advances have been collected by the above-named firm on one hundred and fourteen treasury certificates issued in settlement of claims in which they were attorneys of record.

Please observe that six cases of duplicate entry in the list transmitted by you have been noted at this office by green pencil-mark drawn through such cases.

In the case of Godfrey Maples, late of Company I One hundred and tenth United States colored troops, on which an advance of $80 appears in the list, I have the honor to state that the records of this office show that no advances were allowed.

Very respectfully, your obedient servant,
WILLIAM P. DREW,
Agent Bureau Refugees, Freedmen, &c., Chief of Claim Div'n.

Brevet Colonel R. P. RUNKLE, U. S. A.,
*President of Military Commission, Bureau Refugees,
Freedmen, &c., Washington, D. C.*

FORTY-SEVENTH DAY'S PROCEEDINGS.

The commission met at 10 a. m. Tuesday, March 1, 1870, and continued the work of making up the report.

A communication was received from W. P. Drew, chief of claim division Bureau of Refugees, Freedmen and Abandoned Lands, containing information called for by the commission in certain bounty cases, which document is attached to the proceedings of the commission and marked "Drew's Statement F."

At 4 p. m. the commission adjourned.

BEN. P. RUNKLE,
Brevet Colonel United States Army.
J. R. LEWIS,
Brevet Colonel United States Army.
J. A. SLADEN,
Brevet Captain United States Army, Recorder.

FORTY-EIGHTH DAY'S PROCEEDINGS.

The commission met at 10 a. m. Wednesday, March 2, 1870, and continued the work upon the report.

Communication, containing information called for by the commission, was received from W. P. Drew, chief of claim division, (hereto attached.)

The commission adjourned at 4 p. m.

BEN. P. RUNKLE,
Brevet Colonel United States Army.
J. R. LEWIS,
Brevet Colonel United States Army.
J. A. SLADEN,
Brevet Captain United States Army, Recorder.

WAR DEPARTMENT,
BUREAU REFUGEES, FREEDMEN, AND ABANDONED LANDS,
Claim Division, Washington, D. C., March 1, 1870.

COLONEL: In answer to your verbal request to be informed what amount of advances has been disallowed in adjusting for payment of bills of attorneys on treasury certificates payable through this bureau, I am directed to state that, from such examination of the records of this office as it has been practicable to make thus far, it is believed that, to the 1st ultimo, claims for advances, amounting to at least $20,000, have been disallowed.

It is regretted that want of time has prevented the preparation of a detailed statement of disallowed advances for your information. Such a statement will, however, be prepared as soon as practicable.

Very respectfully, your obedient servant,
WILLIAM P. DREW,
Agent Bureau Refugees, Freedmen, &c., Chief of Claim Div'n.
Brevet Colonel B. P. RUNKLE, U. S. A.,
President Military Commission, Bureau Refugees,
Freedmen, &c., Washington, D. C.

FORTY-NINTH DAY'S PROCEEDINGS.

The commission met at 10 o'clock a. m. Thursday, March 3, 1870, and continued the work upon the report and examination of the proceedings.

At 4 p. m. the commission adjourned.
BEN. P. RUNKLE,
Brevet Colonel United States Army.
J. R. LEWIS,
Brevet Colonel United States Army.
J. A. SLADEN,
Brevet Captain United States Army, Recorder.

PALMER, A.

BUREAU REFUGEES, FREEDMEN AND ABANDONED LANDS,
OFFICE DISBURSING OFFICER OF CLAIMS,
Memphis, Tenn., January 24, 1870.

CAPTAIN: I have the honor, in accordance with the request made by the president of your commission, to transmit herewith copies of correspondence in regard to the following cases in which bounty, &c., was allowed previous to the passage of the law making the money payable through the bureau, and in which the claimants claim to have been defrauded of their bounty money by their attorneys, either in whole or in part, to wit:

Julia Tucker, widow of Congo Tucker, private Company A Fifty-ninth United States colored troops, L. B., No. 653, September 9, 1869.

Orrin Harris, corporal Company C Sixty-first United States colored troops, L. B., No. 864, November 22, 1869.

Dick Gregor, private Company C Fifty-fifth United States colored troops, L. B., No. 1024, December 9, 1869.

Johnson Fusill, private Company I Fifty-fifth United States colored troops, E. B., No. 161, December 23, 1869.

John Wiggins, private Company I Fifty-fifth United States colored troops, affidavits dated January 13 and 15, 1870.

The case of Henry Green, corporal Company B Fifty-fifth United States colored troops, transmitted herewith is supposed to be of a similar character with the above; but I have no information that the claim has as yet been allowed.

I also transmit, as directed, the papers relating to frauds upon claimants perpetrated and attempted by William Walker, claim agent. I will endeavor to send the balance of the papers asked for to-morrow.

I am, captain, very respectfully, your obedient servant,
THOS. S. PALMER,
Disbursing Officer of Claims.

Captain J. A. SLADEN,
*Recorder Military Commission, Bureau Refugees,
Freedmen, &c., Washington, D. C.*

PALMER, A—CASE 1, No. 653.

BUREAU REFUGEES, FREEDMEN AND ABANDONED LANDS,
OFFICE DISBURSING OFFICER OF CLAIMS,
Memphis, September 9, 1869.

SIR: I have the honor to submit the following report in the case of Julia Tucker, widow of Congor or Congo Tucker, late private Company A Fifty-ninth United States colored troops:

On the 26th day of August, 1869, I made demand on the first national bank for the money in the above case, as directed. (See Exhibit A.) Mr. F. S. Davis, the president of the bank, informed me that they acknowledged their responsibility, if the signature was forged, and would refund the money on condition that the certificate was turned over to them, so that they could recover from the parties from whom they received it. On the 3d instant I received from you the authority to surrender the certificate on condition that the bank refund the money. I immediately called again on Mr. Davis, the president of the bank, and tendered him the certificate and renewed my demand for the money. Mr. Davis stated that as there might be some impropriety in his paying the money unless there could be no possible doubt as to the signature on the certificate being forged, requested that he be permitted to submit the case with all proof to his attorneys for their advice. I furnished him the papers, as requested, and this day Messrs. Hutchinson and Townsend, attorneys for the bank, informed me that after looking at the inclosed papers, and the receipt and other papers furnished for their inspection by M. Coombs, jr., "it appears to us very clearly that the said Julia Tucker has received her money, and we think it would so be decided by a jury, hence, we are compelled to advise the bank not to pay the money upon your demand." (See their letter of this date inclosed, marked Exhibit B.)

Your attention is invited to inclosed affidavit of Julia Tucker, dated August 23, 1869, explaining how she come to file two separate claims for the same bounty. Also her denial of ever having received any bounty money from Mr. Coombs, or of ever having made her mark to the treasury certificate issued in her favor, &c. (See Exhibit C.)

I also inclose papers relating to the identity of the claimant, Julia

Tucker, being the affidavits of herself, Henderson Harvey, late private Company D Fifty-ninth United States colored troops, and Jesse Jones. Also a letter from Whitfield Boyd, esq., of Somerville, the former owner of the claimant, dated August 28, 1869. (See Exhibits D and E, respectively.)

On the 23d of August, 1869, I wrote M. Coombs, jr., & Co., a letter, requesting information as to the present status of the claim for bounty of said Julia Tucker. He replied that the *cases* of Julia Tucker seems all right so far. I have this day called up the same and will let her know *their* condition in about ten days. (See Exhibit F.)

Mr. Coombs, jr., insists that he paid the money to the proper person, and that he has witnesses to prove it. He may be able to produce parties who will swear that they saw him pay her the money, but I would remain of the same opinion, that Julia Tucker, the party whose affidavit is inclosed, never received the money. In my opinion Coombs has either committed a fraud in this case or been swindled by some person who has passed herself off on him as Julia Tucker. In either case he is legally responsible for the money. Coombs, jr., holds a paper purporting to be a receipt of Julia Tucker for the money, witnessed by two parties, dated January 20, 1867, being one day previous to the date of her assignment of the certificate to Mr. D. H. Evans.

I return herewith the certificate No. 237,917, together with all papers in the case received from your office.

I am, sir, very respectfully, your obedient servant,
FRED. S. PALMER,
Disbursing Officer of Claims.

Hon. E. B. FRENCH,
Second Auditor, Washington, D. C.

Through chief of claim division, Bureau Refugees, Freedmen and Abandoned Lands, Washington, D. C.

I certify that the above is a true copy as taken from the records of the agent and disbursing officer of claims, Bureau Refugees, Freedmen and Abandoned Lands, at Memphis, Tennessee, this day exhibited to me. Given under my hand and seal, at Memphis, Tennessee, this 22d day of January, 1870.

[SEAL.] MARK EDWARDS,
U. S. Commissioner.

PALMER, A—CASE 2, No. 864.

BUREAU REFUGEES, FREEDMEN AND ABANDONED LANDS,
OFFICE DISBURSING OFFICER OF CLAIMS,
Memphis, Tennessee, November 22, 1869.

SIR: I have the honor to return herewith the papers received from you in the case of Orrin Harris, late corporal Company C Sixty-first regiment United States colored troops. I also transmit the following additional papers, to which your attention is respectfully invited, to wit:

1. Affidavit of Orrin Harris, dated November 16, 1869, in which he states that he received in the month of March, 1867, at two different times, the sum of $50 and $40 dollars, from M. Coombs, jr., and in the month of December, 1868, the further sum of $10, making $100, which, he states, is all the money he ever received from said M. Coombs, jr., & Co. That he filed a claim for additional bounty with Coombs, jr.,

160   BOUNTIES TO COLORED SOLDIERS.

January 31, 1867, and that in October, 1869, said Coombs informed him that said claim for additional bounty had not yet been allowed.

2. Affidavit of N. H. Isabell, esq., a merchant at Rossville, Tennessee, dated November 20, 1869, in which he states that Mr. Coombs informed him, some time during the year 1867, that he had paid Harris $100, which was all the bounty he was entitled to.

3. The receipt of M. Coombs, jr., & Co., in Coombs's own hand writing, for the claim of Orrin Harris, for extra bounty, under the act of July 28, 1866, dated January 31, 1867. This receipt bears the impress of M. Coombs, jr., & Co.'s office seal, dated March 15, 1867, which is about the time Harris states in his affidavit that Coombs paid him the $90, and at which time Mr. Coombs must have known how much bounty Harris was entitled to, as the certificate appears from Mr. Hyam's letter to have been assigned by claimant to D. H. Evans February 6, 1869.

From the papers herewith transmitted, I am of the opinion that Harris has received but $100 of his bounty money, as sworn to in his affidavit of November 11, 1869.

I am, sir, very respectfully, your obedient servant,
FRED. S. PALMER,
Disbursing Officer of Claims.

WM. P. DREW, Esq.,
Chief Claim Division, Washington, D. C.

I certify that the above is a true copy as taken from the records of the agent and disbursing officer of claims, Bureau Refugees, Freedmen and Abandoned Lands, at Memphis, Tennessee, this day exhibited to me. Given under my hand and seal at Memphis, Tennessee, this 22d day of January, 1870.

[SEAL.]   MARK EDWARDS,
U. S. Commissioner.

PALMER, A—CASE 3, No. 1024.

BUREAU REFUGEES, FREEDMEN AND ABANDONED LANDS,
OFFICE DISBURSING OFFICER OF CLAIMS,
Memphis, Tennessee, December 9, 1869.

SIR: I have the honor to call your attention to the case of Dick Gregor, private Company C Fifty-fifth United States colored troops, whose claim for bounty, &c., was allowed for $252, as per certificate, No. 293,709. This certificate appears to have been assigned by claimant to D. H. Evans, April 20, 1867. (See inclosed copy of certificate, marked Exhibit A.) M. Coombs, jr., & Co. claim to have paid the money in this case to claimant on the same day that the above assignment was executed. (See copy of receipt first held by them, marked Exhibit B.) Dick Gregor denies ever having received said bounty money, and claims that he was not in the city of Memphis at the time M. Coombs, jr., & Co. claim to have paid the same to him. (See affidavits of Dick Gregor, Dr. L. M. Jelks, John A. Yearwood, esq., and Abram Gregor, marked Exhibit C.) I also inclose two letters from M. Coombs, jr., & Co., to Messrs. E. J. and J. C. Read, attorneys for Gregor, at Brownsville, Tennessee, dated March 23, 1868, and May 26, 1868, respectively, in both of which they state that Gregor's claim had not at those dates been paid. (See Exhibit D.) On the 23d day of April, 1869, I put this case in the hands of T. B. Woodward, esq., attorney at law, with directions to recover from M. Coombs, jr., the amount due Gregor, if possible. Mr. Woodward informed me that Coombs, jr., acknowledged his liability, claiming, however, that he had paid (?) some other person the money, and that he, Coombs, jr., agreed to settle the case by paying him, for Gregor, $184 50. The balance, $67 50, Coombs claimed to have been consumed in fees, discounts, &c. (See statement in the handwriting of Coombs, jr.,marked Exhibit E.) This payment Coombs promised to make as soon as he could obtain money from Washington on his claims. After having waited for over five months for Mr. Coombs to receive his money, Mr. Woodward returned the papers to me with the information that he was unable to make the money out of Coombs. I would state that suit was not brought in the courts to recover the money for the reason that we did not know where we could find any property belonging to Coombs with which to satisfy an execution in case we obtained a judgment. I submitted the papers in the case to the United States district attorney for his opinion as to whether a criminal action could be maintained against Coombs in this case. He replied that he thought not, as, upon Mr. Coombs showing that he had paid the money to some party the charge of fraud would drop to the ground. I am satisfied that Gregor never was paid the money, and it would appear from Coombs's letter to Messrs. E. J. and J. C. Reed that he intended to keep Gregor in ignorance of the fact of his claim ever having been allowed. I would therefore recommend that the money be collected by the department at Washington, D. C., from Mr. Coombs or his Washington attorney, as it is impossible to make the collection here.

I am, sir, very respectfully, your obedient servant,
FRED. S. PALMER,
Disbursing Officer of Claims.
WILLIAM P. DREW, Esq.,
Chief of Claim Division, Washington, D. C.

I certify that the above is a true copy as taken from the records of the agent and disbursing officer of claims Bureau Refugees, Freedmen and Abandoned Lands, at Memphis, Tennessee, this day exhibited to me.

Given under my hand and seal, at Memphis, Tennessee, this 22d day of January, 1870.

[SEAL.] MARK EDWARDS,
U. S. Commissioner.

PALMER, A—CASE 4.

Copy of indorsement on communication of E. B. French, Auditor.

WASHINGTON, D. C., *October* 25, 1869.

Incloses copy of treasury certificate in the case of Johnson Fusill, showing that Moyers & Dedrick obtained the money in April, 1867. Requests that the case be investigated and facts reported to him. Also send him letter in which the agents say that the claim has not been paid and certificate returned to bureau.

BUREAU REFUGEES, FREEDMEN AND ABANDONED LANDS,
Memphis, Tennessee, December 23, 1869.

Respectfully returned to E. B. French, Second Auditor, Washington, D. C., (through office chief claim division.) On the 8th instant John-

162   BOUNTIES TO COLORED SOLDIERS.

son Fusill, late private Company I Fifty-fifth United States colored troops, called at this office and established his identity. He stated that he was at Moyers & Dedrick's office in August, 1869, and received from Mr. Moyers $30 in groceries and $10 in cash on this claim. That Mr. Moyers told him that his money had been collected, but had been sent back to Washington because they had heard that he was dead, and that they would send for it, and forward it to him by express. I sent for Mr. Dedrick, and he called at the office and stated that their books showed that the money had been paid to a man claiming to be Johnson Fusill, April 19, 1867; that they were now satisfied that they had paid the wrong man, and upon Fusill establishing his identity they would pay him the balance his due. On the 10th instant Mr. Dedrick called again at my office and gave Fusill the sum of $206 20, which he stated was the balance due him, as per the following statement:

Amount of certificate.................................... $265 00

Amount paid him in August, 1869... .... $41 00
Discount on certificate............................ 5 30
Legal fees.. 10 00
Notarial fees...... .... 2 50
Balance paid claimant December 10, 1869 .... 206 20
                                                   ────── 265 00

FRED. S. PALMER,
Disbursing Officer of Claims.

I certify that the above is a true copy as taken from the records of the agent and disbursing officer of claims, Bureau Refugees, Freedmen and Abandoned Lands, at Memphis, Tennessee, this day exhibited to me.
Given under my hand and seal at Memphis, Tennessee, this 22d day of January, 1870.
[SEAL.]   MARK EDWARDS,
                                 U. S. Commissioner.

PALMER, A—CASE 5.

STATE OF TENNESSEE, *County of Shelby, ss:*
On this 13th day of January, 1870, before me, a United States commissioner for the district of West Tennessee, in the county and State above named, personally appeared John Wiggins, of the county of De Soto, State of Mississippi, who, being duly sworn according to law, deposes and says: That he is the same John Wiggins who was a private in Company I of the Fifty-fifth regiment United States colored troops; that on or about the 27th day of August, 1866, he filed his claim for bounty, &c., for collection with Moyers & Dedrick, claim agents at Memphis, Tennessee; that about the first of February, 1868, he was informed by Colonel Moyers, of the aforesaid firm, that his (Wiggins's) claim had been allowed, but the money had never been received. He would, however, advance him $20 on his claim, and he (Wiggins) should allow him $15 interest on the $20 when he received the money due him on his claim. Colonel Moyers then gave him $20, and told him to come back in about three weeks and he thought his money would then be there. At the

BOUNTIES TO COLORED SOLDIERS. 163

end of three weeks, about the latter part of February, 1868, he (Wiggins) went back again for his money, but was again informed by Colonel Moyers that his money had not yet come, but that he would advance him $20 more on his claim on the same conditions that he let him have the other $20, which he (Wiggins) accepted, and that Colonel Moyers then told him (Wiggins) that he owed him (Moyers) $70 for the $40 in money that he had advanced him. About four weeks from that time, in the month of March, 1868, he went back again to the office of the aforesaid firm, and was again informed by Colonel Moyers that his money had not yet come, but that he would advance him $150 on his claim, and told him that if he took that, his bounty money, when received, would all belong to Moyers & Dedrick, the aforesaid firm; that he (Wiggins) agreed to that, not knowing how much was coming to him or when he would get it, and also at the time being greatly in need of money. Colonel Moyers then gave him a check on the City Bank for $150; that Colonel Moyers told him to call in his office some time when he was in town, and he would give him (Wiggins) his discharge; that some three or four months after that he called at the office as directed, and was informed by one of the clerks that his discharge was not there. Some two or three months after that he called again for his discharge, and was told by Colonel Moyers that it had not been received from Washington; that he would send there for it, and when received would forward it to him, Wiggins; that he never received the discharge, and has never been to their office since that time; that about the first part of the month of December, 1867, he called at the office of the aforesaid firm, Moyers & Dedrick, and was informed by Colonel Moyers that his claim had not yet been allowed, but that he would advance him (Wiggins) some money on his claim, which he (Wiggins) refused to accept; that the $40 in money and a check on the bank for $150, as stated above, making in all the sum of $190, is all he ever received in any shape or manner whatever on his claim for bounty; that he was then living in De Soto County, Mississippi, where he now lives.

JOHN WIGGINS.

Signed in presence of—
 FRED. S. PALMER.
 ISAAC PORTER.

Sworn to and subscribed before me, this 14th day of January, 1870.
[SEAL.]   MARK EDWARDS,
                     U. S. Commissioner.

STATE OF TENNESSEE, *County of Shelby, ss:*

On the 15th day of January, 1870, before me, a United States commissioner for the district of West Tennessee, in the county and State aforesaid, personally appeared John Wiggins, late a private in Company I Fifty-fifth regiment United States colored troops, who, being duly sworn according to law, deposes and says: That on the 14th day of January, 1870, he went to the office of Moyers & Dedrick and demanded of them the balance of his bounty money remaining in their hands; that Mr. Moyers, of said firm, told him that he had paid him his bounty money in full and did not propose to pay him the second time; that Mr. Moyers stated that he had paid affiant at one time $10 and at another time $25 more than affiant is willing to admit he ever received; that Moyers said he had affiant's receipts for said $35, both receipts signed by + mark; that affiant can write his own name, and is positive that he has never signed his name by + mark since he was mustered out of service. He afterward stated that if the money had not been received by affiant it had been paid by them to some other party. Mr. Moyers then told him to come up to his office and he would settle with him in the morning; that if he had to pay him the money he thought they would have to divide the loss, as he had already paid out the money once; that affiant went to his office this morning and was told by Mr. Moyers that if he would get his discharge paper from Colonel Palmer's office and bring it to him, and then convince him that he had received but $190 claimed by affiant, then he, Mr. Moyers, would settle with him; that he would settle if affiant would bring witness to prove that he had not received but the $190 as claimed; that finally Mr. Moyers informed him that he would not settle with affiant unless he brought his discharge paper to his office.

JOHN WIGGINS.

Subscribed and sworn to before me this 15th day of January, 1870, at Memphis, Tennessee.

[SEAL.] MARK EDWARDS,
U. S. Commissioner.

BUREAU REFUGEES, FREEDMEN AND ABANDONED LANDS,
OFFICE DISBURSING OFFICER OF CLAIMS,
Memphis, Tennessee, January 24, 1870.

The claim of John Wiggins, as shown by the indorsement on his discharge, was allowed March 27, 1867. The indorsement is as follows: "Bounty, additional bounty, and arrears pay, $271 50, paid by certificate 294,430, March 27, 1867."

On the 19th instant, Mr. Dedrick, of the firm of Moyers & Dedrick, claim agents of this city, called at my office and paid me, for said John Wiggins, late private of Company I Fifty-fifth United States colored troops, the sum of $63 57. This settlement was made in accordance with the following statement:

Amount of certificate No. 294,430 .... $271 50

Discount on certificate, two per cent................ $5 43
Fees for collection............................... 12 50
Paid Wiggins as per his affidavit................... 190 00
Paid me for Wiggins, January 19, 1870.............. 63 57
——————— $271 50

FRED. S. PALMER,
Disbursing Officer of Claims.

PALMER, B—CASE 1, No. 881.

BUREAU REFUGEES, FREEDMEN AND ABANDONED LANDS,
OFFICE DISBURSING OFFICER OF CLAIMS,
Memphis, Tennessee, November 26, 1869.

SIR: I have the honor to state that Henry Grier, late a corporal in Company B Fifty-fifth United States colored troops, called at this office yesterday, and stated that in 1866 he filed his claim for bounty through M. Coombs, jr., & Co., of this city; that in the spring of 1868 Coombs advanced him $26 25 on his claim, as follows: One shot-gun and trimmings, $21 25, and cash $5, which is all of his bontuy money that he has ever received; that June 1, 1869, Coombs gave him a note for $200, payable thirty days after date; that Coombs has never paid said note or any part thereof, but puts him off from time to time whenever payment is demanded. Inclosed you will find Grier's affidavit to the facts as set forth above. Also, attached thereto, a copy of the $200 note given him by Coombs. The note is drawn up in Coombs's own handwriting, and is stamped with two two-cent internal revenue stamps. I am of the opinion that Coombs has collected and appropriated this man's bounty to his own use, as I can see no other reason why he should give the note referred to above. Will you please have the case looked up at the Auditor's office. If the certificate in this case was ever sent to Coombs, cannot the bureau at Washington compel him to refund the amount, as it would be useless, so I am informed by attorneys, to attempt to recover on the note in our courts here, for if we obtained a judgment we could not find any property of Coombs with which to satisfy an execution. Grier states that he can produce no other evidence than Coombs's note referred to above, and which he will forward to you if desired.

Very respectfully, your obedient servant,
FRED. S. PALMER,
Disbursing Officer of Claims.

WM. P. DREW. Esq.,
Chief Claim Division, Washington, D. C.

I certify that the above is a true copy as taken from the records of the agent and disbursing officer of claims, Bureau Refugees, Freedmen and Abandoned Lands, at Memphis, Tennessee, exhibited to me this 24th day of January, 1870.

Given under my hand and seal at Memphis, Tennessee, this 24th day of January, 1870.

[SEAL.] MARK EDWARDS,
U. S. Commissioner.

PALMER, C—CASE 1, No. 478.

BUREAU REFUGEES, FREEDMEN AND
ABANDONED LANDS, SUB-DISTRICT OF MEMPHIS,
Memphis, Tennessee, April 9, 1868.

GENERAL: I have the honor to return herewith the receipted vouchers of William Black, late sergeant Company E Fifty-fifth regiment United States colored troops. There has been stopped for advances the sum of $46 75. Black states that he has never received any advances whatsoever from his attorney, William Walker; and that instead of owing Walker, Walker owes him some $90 32 for services rendered in 1866. I have no doubt but that Black's statement is correct. I have myself seen a memorandum due-bill in Black's possession for the amount he says Walker owes him. I have known this man William Walker since December, 1866. He that year ran a plantation in the State of Mississippi. He failed to settle with any of his hands. I made an attempt to force a settlement out of him at that time, but the case was so covered up that no property could be found. I have always thought that Walker had swindled his employés, but never could see any way in which I could obtain redress for them.

I believe Walker intends further to defraud these parties by making fraudulent charges of advances against them, and no advances should in my opinion be allowed him until each case had been thoroughly investigated.

Very respectfully, your obedient servant,
FRED. S. PALMER,
Lieutenant Colonel and Sub-Assistant Commissioner.

Brevet Brigadier General GEO. W. BALLOCH,
Chief Disbursing Officer, Washington, D. C.

PALMER, C—CASE 2, No. 506.

Colonel Palmer to General Balloch.

BUREAU REFUGEES, FREEDMEN AND
ABANDONED LANDS, SUB-DISTRICT OF MEMPHIS,
Memphis, Tennessee, April 15, 1868.

GENERAL: I have the honor to state that on the 11th instant I paid Edmund Barnett, late private Company C Fifty-fifth United States colored troops, his bounty money, amounting to $195 25. There had been stopped for fees and advances made by his attorney the sum of $56 75. Barnett states that this is not correct; that he never received any advance from his attorney, William Walker, but that the said William Walker owes him the sum of $92 82, balance due for services rendered on Walker's plantation in the year 1866. Inclosed you will please find Barnett's affidavit setting forth the facts in the case as stated above. This is another one of those cases referred to in my communication of the 9th instant, and to which your attention is respectfully invited.

Very respectfully, your obedient servant,
FRED. S. PALMER,
Lieutenant Colonel and Sub-Assistant Commissioner.

Brevet Brigadier General GEO. W. BALLOCH,
Chief Disbursing Officer, Washington, D. C.

PALMER, C—No. 649.

Colonel Palmer to General Balloch.

BUREAU REFUGEES, FREEDMEN AND
ABANDONED LANDS, SUB-DISTRICT OF MEMPHIS,
Memphis, Tennessee, May 19, 1868.

GENERAL: I have the honor to state that, in accordance with your instructions of the 8th instant, in the case of Edmund Barnett, late private Company C Fifty-fifth United States colored troops, *vs.* his attorney, William Walker, for moneys fraudulently charged against him as advances, amounting to $46 75, I demanded of said William Walker the return of said money to Barnett. Walker refused to return the money, and stated that the amount stopped as advances was for the following items, to wit:

Trip to Washington, D. C., to see about claim, March, 1867.... $10 00
Trip to Vicksburg, Mississippi, to see about claim, January, 1868.   20 00

BOUNTIES TO COLORED SOLDIERS. 167

Paid sheriff of Tunica County for State and county tax levied
 on said Barnett in 1866.................................... $9 75
Paid lawyers' fees for said Barnett in 1867.................... 5 00
Notarial fees... 2 00

  Total... 16 75

 Walker stated that he had never advanced to said Barnett any cash other than in the manner stated above. He admitted being indebted to Barnett for services rendered in 1866, as stated in Barnett's affidavit.
 Very respectfully, your obedient servant,
          FRED. S. PALMER,
    Lieutenant Colonel and Sub-Assistant Commissioner.
Brevet Brigadier General GEO. W. BALLOCH,
   Chief Disbursing Officer, Washington, D. C.

PALMER, C—CASE 3.

Fred. S. Palmer, Esq., Disbursing Officer of Claims, to William P. Drew, Esq., Chief of Claim Division, &c.

BUREAU REFUGEES, FREEDMEN AND ABANDONED LANDS,
  OFFICE DISBURSING OFFICER OF CLAIMS,
   Memphis, Tennessee, March 6, 1869.

SIR: I have the honor, in accordance with your indorsements of September 28 and October 27, 1869, in reference to the removal of the suspension in the case of William Walker, to submit the following report. I have conversed with Mr. Walker and ten of the bounty claimants, and from their statements and the records of the courts, I have obtained the following information upon the subject, and which I believe to be correct. It appears that William Walker, in 1866, cultivated what is known as the Driver Plantation, near Austin, Tunica County, Mississippi; that he hired his hands by the month; that at the end of the year T. T. Green & Co., merchants of this city, who had furnished Walker supplies to run the plantation, levied on the crop, and taking it to Memphis, applied the proceeds to liquidating their claim against Walker. Walker alleges that Green & Co. agreed to pay the hands the balance of the wages due from Walker. Green & Co. refusing to do so, Walker had the following-named freedmen, with others, bring suit against Green & Co. for the various amounts set opposite their respective names, the same being the balance due from Walker for services rendered as laborers on the Driver Plantation in the year 1866, to wit:

Peter Conner............	$25 20	Samuel Allen............	$8 30
Meldon Miller...........	23 63	Caro Williams...........	18 59
Duncan Benton..........	19 08	Charles Kirkpatrick.....	34 69
Philip Clark............	81 99	Osband Jones...........	26 63
James Dixon............	30 76	Clayburn Thompson.....	66 35
George Washington......	32 42	Shepard Wells..........	92 62
Wm. Polk...............	26 38	Granderson Lewis.......	45 75
Aaron Williams.........	50 24	Charles Brown..........	107 64
Willis Brown............	45 58	James Campbell........	12 29
Richard Woodruff.......	18 46	Haynes Sharkey........	46 18
Wesley Burk............	44 29	Providence Barris.......	94 60
Perry Linsley...........	13 04	Moses Douglas.........	85 79

168   BOUNTIES TO COLORED SOLDIERS.

The above amounts were taken from the original papers in the various suits now on file in the law court of Memphis. There appears to have been seven other suits brought at the same time, but the papers were missing from the file. These suits were all brought before H. S. Lee, esq., a justice of the peace, in the month of December, 1866, and judgments were given in each case for the defendants, T. T. Green & Co. Walker then had the freedmen take an appeal to the law court of Memphis. The case came on for trial at the February term, 1869, and on the 2d day of April, 1869, on motion of Green, P. Fonte, attorney for Walker and the freedmen, the cases were dismissed and judgment rendered against the freedmen and their security for costs; and thus fell through Walker's attempt to hold Green & Co. liable for the amount owed by Walker to his hands for services rendered in 1866. If there are any suits now pending against Green & Co., for wages due the freedmen, I was unable to find the record, and cannot but believe that Walker's statement in his letter of October 22, 1869, that "these cases have not come up yet," is false. Mr. Walker still claims that Green & Co. are liable for the amount due the hands employed by Walker in 1866; but with the decisions in two courts against him, in the last of which the cases are dismissed on motion of plaintiffs' counsel, it is but reasonable to suppose that the liability really rests on Walker and not on Green & Co.

Now, with the records of the State courts against him, as shown above, let us look at the record of the United States court for the district of West Tennessee. I find there recorded that this man Walker filed, on the 13th day of November, 1867, his petition in bankruptcy in said court praying that he may be discharged as a bankrupt. With his petition he filed a schedule of his liabilities, regularly sworn to.

Among other creditors I find the names of the following laborers whom Walker states under oath he is indebted to for labor done in Mississippi, in the year 1866, in the various amounts set opposite their respective names, viz:

Silas Driver	$188 18	E. Ramett	$90 08
Charles Brown	107 64	A. Washington	84 00
P. Barris	94 60	M. Douglas	85 79
S. Wells	92 67	P. Hunt	67 86
W. Black	90 30	G. Hunt	65 00
Philip Clark	82 00	W. Burk	44 29
G. Lewis	45 75	H. Sharkey	46 18
D. Booker	44 40	D. Washington	43 04
C. Kirkpatrick	34 69	R. Driver	34 13
C. Thompson	66 35	G. Washington	32 42
Willis Brown	45 48	O. Jones	26 63
Nathan Driver	91 07	Peter Conner	25 20
A. Williams	50 24	Jack Driver	23 81
Jim Dickson	30 76		

Now if Green & Co., and not Walker, were really liable for the amounts due the above parties as Walker claims, why did Walker go into the bankrupt court and swear that he (Walker) owed them as set forth above?

Mr. Walker, in his letter of October 22, states that he does not owe any of these parties one cent, and that he would not take one cent from them; that he would rather give them something. How does that agree with his oath in the bankrupt court? Is the $1,732 56 of which he has robbed his hands, as set forth above, nothing? Is that what he terms giving them something? The only thing that he has given them, that I

BOUNTIES TO COLORED SOLDIERS. 169

can discover, is the privilege of going to the law court and paying the costs in the cases he persuaded them to bring against Green & Co.—actions which he should have known could not be successfully sustained on trial.

Mr. Walker furnished me with a statement of his accounts against the claimants for bounty, which is indorsed and marked Exhibit A. I notified him that I must have a bill of items in each particular case, showing in detail what they received from him, and when; and, also requested a statement showing how much he owed the parties for labor performed in 1866. He agreed to furnish both; but instead, presented himself at my office, accompanied by his brother, son, and a gentleman by the name of Casey, whom he informed me would testify to the correctness of the accounts as set forth in Exhibit A. I refused to allow them to certify to the correctness of the accounts unless he furnished the desired bill of items in each case, believing that if they did certify to the correctness of the accounts in the shape rendered from memory, their statements might contain errors; and if from books in which the entries had been originally made, it would not prejudice Mr. Walker's case to produce them, if his accounts were correct. Mr. Walker stated that he could not produce the books, although he admitted that they were in the hands of his attorney in this city. So much for Mr. Walker's statement that I refused to hear the testimony of his witnesses. Mr. Walker, in his letter of August 13, 1869, states that he has made advances on all the claims filed by him. I indorsed the affidavits of the following-named parties, (all of the claimants whom I have seen since called upon for this report,) each of whom swear that they have never received any advances whatsoever on their claims for bounty from Mr. Walker, to wit: Peter Conner, Philip Clark, Samuel Fairchild, Providence Barris, Moses Douglas, Perry Linsey, Austin Peterson, Samuel Allen, Lewis James, and Duncan Benton. These affidavits were all sworn to before me, and not before a clerk of a court, in order to avoid expense. Attention is especially invited to the affidavit of Providence Barris, in which he states that Walker kept out of his wages in the year 1868 the sum of $25 for extra service in prosecuting his claim for bounty. As an example of what Mr. Walker considers as legitimate advances, I would state that April 11, 1868, I paid the bounty due Edmund Barnett, late private Company C Fifty-fifth United States colored troops. There was stopped out of said bounty as advances made by Walker the sum of $46 75. Under direction of General Balloch, I demanded of Walker that he refund said money. Walker refused, and stated that the advances had been made as follows:

Trip to Washington, D. C., to see about claim, March, 1867....	$10 00
Trip to Vicksburg, Mississippi, January, 1868, to see about claim.	20 00
Paid sheriff, Tunica County, Mississippi, for State and county tax levied on Barnett in 1866	9 75
Paid lawyer's fees for Barnett in 1867	5 00
Notarial fees	2 00
Total	46 75

Walker stated in explanation that he went to Washington and Vicksburg to see about the claims he had filed, and charged the expenses of said trips to claimants, and that Barnett's share amounted to $30, as set forth above. Attention is invited to the fact that Walker swore in the bankrupt court, November 13, 1867, that he owed this same Barnett the sum of $90 08, for services rendered as a laborer in Mississippi in the year 1866.

Mr. Walker states in his letter of October 22, 1869, that he could collect these claims against the freedmen in any court of law. I would suggest that he be allowed the privilege of making the attempt. If he really thinks so, why is he calling so piteously upon the bureau for assistance? Mr. Walker's protestations of friendship, sympathy, and pity for the "poor, ignorant beings," as he terms these claimants, are altogether uncalled for. They are too transparent. The records show them to be hypocritical. I do not desire to do any injustice to Mr. Walker; but from what I know of his transactions the conviction forces itself upon my mind that he is a great rascal. I was satisfied when I wrote the inclosed letter to General Balloch on the 9th day of April, 1868, that Mr. Walker had swindled his employés in 1866, and that he intended to further defraud these parties by making fraudulent charges of advances against them; and recent investigation only confirms the opinion then entertained. I do not believe that any of his advances should be allowed by the bureau, or that he should be recognized as an attorney by the department; and if it can be lawfully done, I would recommend that the legal fees allowed Mr. Walker be transmitted to those claimants to whom he is indebted for labor performed in 1866, and who can give him credit on account for the same.

I return herewith all papers received from you in this case.

I am, sir, very respectfully, your obedient servant,

FRED. S. PALMER,
Disbursing Officer of Claims.

WM. P. DREW, Esq.,
Chief of Claim Division, Washington, D. C.

BOUNTIES TO COLORED SOLDIERS. 171

Statement showing the amount of advances and fees claimed by William Walker as attorney, &c., in the following cases.

No.	Names of claimants.	Date of advance.	Am't of advance.	Legal fees.	Notarial fees.	Total.
1	Austin Peterson	Dec. 8, 1866	$13 00	$10 00	$2 00	$25 00
2	George Allen	Dec. 8, 1866	24 00	10 00	2 00	36 00
3	Aaron Glass	Dec. 8, 1866	26 25	10 00	2 00	38 25
4	Peter Connor	Dec. 8, 1866	10 45	10 00	2 00	22 45
5	Henry Gaines	Dec. 12, 1866	68 30	10 00	2 00	80 30
6	Nelson Burk	Mar. 28, 1868	37 60	10 00		47 60
7	Meldon Miller	Apr. 3, 1868	36 47	10 00		46 47
8	Green Hoffman	Mar. 22, 1869	25 00	10 00		35 00
9	Ransom Wiebank	Mar. 3, 1869	31 37	10 00		41 37
10	Lewis James	Aug. 28, 1869	118 17	10 00		128 17
11	Duncan Benton	Aug. 28, 1869	12 00	10 00		22 00
12	Philip Clark	Aug. 27, 1869	12 00	10 00		22 00
13	James Dickson	Mar. 4, 1868	17 00	10 00		27 00
14	Samuel Allen	Dec. 8, 1866 / Mar. 20, 1866	67 95 / 14 00	10 00		91 95
15	Caro Williams	Mar. 6, 1869	29 00	10 00		39 00
16	Charles Kirkpatrick	Dec. 14, 1866 / Jan. 11, 1868	14 00 / 18 30	10 00		42 30
17	Osband Jones	June 13, 1868	3 80	10 00		13 80
18	Clayborne Thompson	Feb. 22, 1869	24 00	10 00		34 00
19	George Washington	July 11, 1868	24 30	10 00		34 30
20	Lewis Spite			10 00	2 00	12 00
21	Leander Dickinson			10 00	2 00	12 00
22	Shepard Wells			10 00	2 00	12 00
23	William Polk			10 00	2 00	12 00
24	Samuel Fairchilds			10 00	2 00	12 00
25	Grandison Lewis			10 00	2,00	12 00
26	Baalam Arnold			10 00	2 00	12 00
27	Alfred Chambers			10 00	2 00	12 00
28	Aaron Williams			10 00	2 00	12 00
29	Charles Brown			10 00	2 00	12 00
30	Willis Brown			10 00	2 00	12 00
31	James Campbell			10 00	2 00	12 00
32	Richard Woodruff			10 00		10 00
33	William Carpenter			10 00		10 00
34	Haynes Sharkey			10 00		10 00
35	Wesley Burk			10 00		10 00
36	Providence Barris			10 00		10 00
37	Peter Austin			10 00		10 00
38	Perry Linsley	Dec. 4, 1866	5 36	10 00		15 36
39	Moses Douglas	Dec. 25, 1868	6 15	10 00		16

The above is a true copy of the statement furnished me by William Walker.

FRED. S. PALMER,
Disbursing Officer of Claims.

NOVEMBER 4, 1869.

I certify that the above is a true copy as taken from the records of the agent and disbursing officer of claims, Bureau Refugees, Freedmen and Abandoned Lands, at Memphis, Tennessee, this day exhibited to me. Given under my hand and seal at Memphis, Tennessee, this 24th day of January, 1870.

MARK EDWARDS,
U. S. Commissioner.

PALMER, D—CASE 1.

BUREAU REFUGEES, FREEDMEN AND ABANDONED LANDS,
OFFICE DISBURSING OFFICER OF CLAIMS,
Memphis, Tennessee, January 25, 1870.

CAPTAIN: I have the honor, in accordance with the request made by the president of your commission, to transmit herewith copies of papers relating to the following cases, in which claim agents had stopped, or attempted to have stopped, as advances made by them to claimants for bounty, sums of money, amounting to one and two hundred dollars. In some of these cases, the claimants denied ever having received any advances whatsoever from their attorneys, and in the others that fact is admitted by the claim agents themselves, viz:

Henry Clay, Company A Sixty-first United States colored troops.
Wm. Young, Company A Fifty-fifth United States colored troops.
Albert Smith, Company F Fifty-fifth United States colored troops.
Edward Robinson, Company B Third United States colored heavy artillery.
Henry Bellamy, Company G Sixty-first United States colored troops.

FRED. S. PALMER,
Disbursing Officer of Claims.

Captain J. A. SLADEN,
Recorder Military Commission, Bureau Refugees,
Freedmen and Abandoned Lands, Washington, D. C.

STATE OF ARKANSAS, *County of Cross,* ss :

I, Henry Clay, corporal of Company A Sixty-first regiment colored infantry, do solemnly swear that I have not received any advance whatever (due me on my bounty due from the United States) from Coombs, of Memphis, Tennessee, or any other party or parties whatsoever.

In witness whereof, I have hereunto subscribed my name, August the 23d, A. D. 1867.

[SEAL.]   HENRY + CLAY.
              his mark.

I, James M. Levesque, clerk of the circuit court, and *ex-officio* recorder, within and for the county of Cross and State of Arkansas, do hereby certify that the above-named Henry Clay voluntarily appeared before me and made oath to the above affidavit after hearing the contents read and fully explained.

In testimony whereof, I have hereunto set my hand and affixed my official seal at office, in Cleburne, this August the 23d, A. D. 1867.

[SEAL.]   JAMES M. LEVESQUE, *Clerk.*

BUREAU REFUGEES, FREEDMEN AND ABANDONED LANDS,
Memphis, Tennessee, January 25, 1870.

In the above case of Henry Clay, Company A Sixty-first United States colored troops, M. Coombs, jr., & Co., Memphis, Tennessee, the claimant's attorneys, refunded to this office on the 15th day of August, 1867, the sum of $100, which had been deducted out of the bounty due said Clay as advances made to him by his attorneys. M. Coombs, jr., admitted that he had not advanced to said Clay any sum of money whatever.

FRED. S. PALMER,
Disbursing Officer of Claims.

PALMER, D—CASE 2.

BUREAU REFUGEES, FREEDMEN AND
ABANDONED LANDS, SUB-DISTRICT OF MEMPHIS,
Memphis, Tennessee, May 25, 1868.

GENERAL : I have the honor to inclose the vouchers in case of William Young, late a private in Company A Fifty-fifth United States colored troops. Your attention is called to the fact that $200 have been stopped as advances. I have the proof in my office that said Young died on or about September 27, 1866. I called upon M. Coombs, jr., & Co., the claim agents, in regard to these advances, and Mr. Coombs, after careful scrutiny of his books, informed me that he had never made any advances whatever to the said William Young, deceased. It is evidently fraud on the part of the claim agent to obtain his money, knowing that the man is dead. Young has left five children, who will, as soon as they can obtain the necessary evidence, apply for their father's bounty money.

Very respectfully, your obedient servant,
FRED. S. PALMER,
Lieutenant Colonel and Sub-Assistant Commissioner.
Brevet Brigadier General GEO. W. BALLOCH,
Chief Disbursing Officer, Washington, D. C.

I certify that the above is a true copy, as taken from the records of the agent and disbursing officer of claims, Bureau of Refugees, Freedmen and Abandoned Lands, at Memphis, Tennessee, this day exhibited to me.

Given under my hand and seal, at Memphis, Tennessee, this 24th day of January, 1870.

[SEAL.] MARK EDWARDS,
U. S. Commissioner.

BUREAU REFUGEES, FREEDMEN AND ABANDONED LANDS,
Memphis, Tennessee, January 25, 1870.

In the case of the above-mentioned William Young, Company A Fifty-fifth United States colored troops, I received from General Balloch, chief disbursing officer, July 18, 1868, the sum of $200, refunded by D. B. Hyam, of Washington, on account of M. Coombs, jr., & Co., of this city.

FRED. S. PALMER,
Disbursing Officer of Claims.

PALMER, D—CASE 3.

BUREAU REFUGEES, FREEDMEN AND
ABANDONED LANDS, SUB-DISTRICT OF MEMPHIS,
Memphis, Tennessee, August 21, 1868.

SIR: I have the honor, in obedience to Brevet Brigadier General Balloch's indorsement of April 16, 1868, on General Howe's communication to him of the same date, in reference to advances made by claim agents to their clients, to transmit herewith the affidavit of Albert Smith, late private Company F Fifty-fifth United States colored troops; and to call your attention to the fact that the vouchers received here for his signature show that the sum of $200 has been stopped out of said bounty as advances made by his attorneys. This Smith claims is not correct, and in his affidavit declares that he never received from his attorneys, Moyers & Dedrick, any advance whatsoever on his claim.

Smith is, in my opinion, a deserter from the Tenth United States Cavalry, and I have turned him over as such to the post commander at this station. He claims to have been forwarded with a detachment of recruits from this city to Leavenworth, Kansas, in the spring of 1867 by Cap-

174   BOUNTIES TO COLORED SOLDIERS.

tain Davis, who was recruiting for the regiment, and to have since been discharged for disability.
Very respectfully, your obedient servant,
FRED. S. PALMER,
Lieutenant Colonel and Sub-Assistant Commissioner.
WM. P. DREW,
Agent in charge of Claim Division, Washington, D. C.

I certify that the above is a true copy as taken from the records of the agent and disbursing officer of claims, Bureau Refugees, Freedmen and Abandoned Lands, at Memphis, Tennessee, this day exhibited to me.
Given under my hand and seal, at Memphis, Tennessee, this 24th day of January, 1870.
[SEAL.]   MARK EDWARDS,
                                      U. S. Commissioner.

PALMER, D—CASE 4.

Copy of indorsement on communication from William P. Drew, chief of claim division.

WASHINGTON, D. C., *October* 26, 1868.
Incloses what purports to be vouchers to "an advance of $200 by Messrs. Moyers & Dedrick to Edward Robinson, late private Company B Third United States colored heavy artillery, since deceased; and requests you satisfy yourself whether the claimant did or did not receive the amount as alleged; desires that the investigation be made as far as possible without reference to Moyers & Dedrick. These papers to be returned."

BUREAU REFUGEES, FREEDMEN AND ABANDONED LANDS,
Memphis, Tennessee, November 30, 1868.
Respectfully returned to Wm. P. Drew, esq., chief of claim division, Washington, D. C., (through office assistant commissioner, Nashville, Tennessee,) with the information that I have investigated the within case, and am of the opinion that Moyers & Dedrick did not make the advance of $200 to the within named Edward Robinson, late private Company B Third United States colored heavy artillery, on or about the 13th day of April, 1868, as sworn to by them in their affidavit of the 29th day of September, 1868; and that they never did advance to said Robinson, at any time, any sum of money whatever on his claim for bounty. The facts in the case appear to be as follows:

The said Robinson had been living with a half-breed woman for some time before his death, and Dr. S. J. Quimby, whose affidavit of September 30, 1868, as to Robinson's acknowledgment of the advance before a civil magistrate is inclosed, had been rendering said Robinson and his family medical attendance, for which he charged him $150; that on the 13th day of April, 1868, shortly before Robinson's death, Quimby had Mr. T. L. Dean, who is a clerk in Moyers & Dedrick's office, go with him to Robinson's house and take Robinson's affidavit, acknowledging that he (Robinson) had received from Moyers & Dedrick the sum of $200 in cash, as an advance on his claim for bounty. This affidavit was not taken in person before M. D. L. Stewart, circuit court clerk, by whom it is certified to, but was taken before the said T. L. Dean, clerk of Moyers & Dedrick, who holds an appointment from said M. D. L. Stewart, clerk of circuit court of Shelby County, Tennessee, as a "special deputy clerk to administer oaths to applicants and witnesses to claims against the government of the United States, and all other oaths necessary in and about the collection of the same," a copy of which appointment is herewith inclosed. The understanding at the time, as explained by Dr. Quimby and the half-breed woman who was living with Robinson, appears to have been that when Moyers & Dedrick had received from the government the $200 from said Robinson's bounty, they were to pay $150 to said Quimby for his bills or medical services rendered said Robinson, and give the remaining $50 to half-breed woman. Dr. Quimby also informed me that he had received from Moyers & Dedrick, in the month of August, 1868, the sum of $75 on said claim, which, in my opinion, is the only money that has changed hands in the whole transaction.

FRED. S. PALMER,
Disbursing Officer of Claims.

I certify that the above is a true copy as taken from the records of the agent and disbursing officer of claims, Bureau Refugees, Freedmen and Abandoned Lands, at Memphis, Tennessee, this day exhibited to me.

Given under my hand and seal at Memphis, Tennessee, this 22d day of January, 1870.

[SEAL.] MARK EDWARDS,
U. S. Commissioner.

PALMER, D—CASE 5, No. 882.

BUREAU REFUGEES, FREEDMEN AND ABANDONED LANDS,
OFFICE DISBURSING OFFICER OF CLAIMS,
Memphis, Tennessee, November 26, 1869.

SIR: I have the honor to state that on the 12th day of December, 1868, I paid the bounty due in the case of Henry Bellamy, late private Company G Sixty-first United States colored troops, amounting to $107 06. There was stopped out of said bounty, for advances made by the claim agents, the sum of $100. When Bellamy signed his vouchers in November, 1868, he denied ever having received the money, and stated that he had not only not received any advance whatever from his attorney, but that he had not been in the city of Memphis from some time in the month of March, 1867, until the 18th day of November, 1868. On the 25th day of November, 1868, I forwarded his vouchers for payment to General Balloch, accompanied by Bellamy's affidavit to statement of the facts as set forth above, and to which your attention is invited.

Bellamy is reported to have died August 20, 1869, and his widow now asks that the hundred dollars in dispute be collected of M. Coombs, jr., & Co., and paid over to her.

Mr. Coombs, on the 24th day of August, 1869, informs me that the advance was made to Bellamy on the 1st day of October, 1867. (See his letter of that date, inclosed.)

Manda Bellamy, the widow, and Sol Bellamy, a fellow servant, on the 3d day of September, 1869, swear that Henry Bellamay did not go to Memphis from March, 1867, until November 18, 1868. (See their affidavits, inclosed.)

Mr. A. C. Craig, by H. B. Craig, from Harrison's Station, Mississippi, under date of November 26, 1869, states that Henry Bellamy lived with him from March to December, 1867, and that he does not believe he visited Memphis during that time, and that he was confident that he was not in Memphis October 1, 1867, as claimed by Coombs. (See his letter, inclosed.)

Very respectfully, your obedient servant,
FRED. S. PALMER,
Disbursing Officer of Claims.

WILLIAM P. DREW, Esq.,
Chief Claim Division, Washington, D. C.

I certify that the above is a true copy as taken from the records of the agent and disbursing officer of claims, Bureau Refugees, Freedmen and Abandoned Lands, at Memphis, Tennessee, this day exhibited to me.

Given under my hand and seal at Memphis, Tennessee, this 24th day of January, 1870.

[SEAL.]
MARK EDWARDS,
U. S. Commissioner.

PALMER, E.

BUREAU REFUGEES, FREEDMEN AND ABANDONED LANDS,
OFFICE DISBURSING OFFICER OF CLAIMS,
Memphis, Tennessee, January 25, 1870.

CAPTAIN: I have the honor, in accordance with the request made by the president of your commission, to transmit herewith copies of papers relative to the following cases, in which perjury has been resorted to by claimants and their witness in perfecting their claim for bounty, &c., viz:

1. Felix Mooney, father of Alfred Mooney, Company F Second regiment United States colored light artillery.
2. Emily Scales, widow of John Scales, Company F Second regiment United States colored light artillery.
3. Jane Lundy, widow of Joseph Lundy, Company E, Third United States colored heavy artillery.
4. Hattie Davis, sister of James Lewis, Company C Eleventh United States colored troops.
5. Marshall Johnson, brother of Richard Kellick, Company A Fifty-fifth United States colored troops.
5. Marshall Johnson, brother of Logan Kellick, Company A Fifty-fifth United States colored troops.
6. John Horton, brother of Robert Horton, Company B sixty-first United States colored troops.
7. Queen Garner, widow of Albert Garner, Company F Third United States colored heavy artillery.
8. Martha Martin, widow of Lee Martin, Company E Sixty-first United States colored troops.
9. Emily J. McCauley, widow of Burges McCauley, Company G Eleventh United States colored troops.
9. Phillis Jeems, sister of Babe Smith, Company F Sixty-first United States colored troops.
9. Virginia Taylor, sister of Richard Taylor, Company C Eleventh United States colored troops.
•10. Albert Benson, brother of Henry Benson, Company E Forty-sixth United States colored troops.

BOUNTIES TO COLORED SOLDIERS. 177

11. Adeline Maren and Aggie Parish, sisters of Pope Body, Company F Third United States colored heavy artillery.
12. Hannah Ross, sister of Philip Dickson, Company A Third United States colored heavy artillery.
13. Rebecca Harvey, sister of William Goode, Company F Sixty-first United States colored troops.
13. Rebecca Harvey, sister of Washington Goode, Company F Sixty-first United States colored troops.

I have sent you more of these cases than you possibly desire, but I have done so for the reason that you may form some idea of the kind of evidence used in perfecting claims of this class.

I am, captain, very respectfully, your obedient servant,
FRED. S. PALMER,
Disbursing Officer of Claims.
Captain J. A. SLADEN,
Recorder Military Commission, Bureau of Refugees,
Freedmen and Abandoned Lands, Washington, D. C.

PALMER, E—CASE 1.

BUREAU REFUGEES, FREEDMEN AND ABANDONED LANDS,
SUB-DISTRICT OF MEMPHIS,
Memphis, Tennessee, September 4, 1868.

GENERAL: I have the honor to call your attention to the claims for bounty of Felix and Annie Mooney, parents of Alfred Mooney, late Company F Second United States colored light artillery, certificate No. 446,506. The money to pay these claims, amounting to $85 50 and $119 36, respectively, was received from you August 28, 1868. From the inclosed affidavit it will be seen that Felix Mooney is not entitled to any of this money, as he is only step-father to said Alfred Mooney. Shall I pay Felix Mooney his share of this money, as per the vouchers signed by him, or shall I pay the money in both claims to Annie Mooney, the mother of Alfred Mooney?

Very respectfully, your obedient servant,
FRED. S. PALMER,
Sub-Assistant Commissioner.
Brevet Brigadier General GEO. W. BALLOCH,
Chief Disbursing Officer, Washington, D. C.

PALMER, E—CASE 2.

BUREAU REFUGEES, FREEDMEN AND ABANDONED LANDS,
SUB-DISTRICT OF MEMPHIS,
Memphis, Tennessee, September 23, 1868.

GENERAL: I have the honor to return herewith the papers forwarded to you September 9th, 1868, by Moyers & Dedrick, claim agents in this city, in the claim of Emily Scales, widow of John Scales, late a corporal in Company F Second United States colored light artillery, and which were referred to me by your indorsement of the 14th instant. I desire to make the following statement in regard to this case, and

H. Ex. Doc. 241——12

respectfully request instructions which may govern my action in similar cases in the future:

This woman, Emily Scales, called at this office for the purpose of obtaining the bounty which had been allowed her. She brought the following named parties as her witnesses to prove her identity, stating to me that they were all present and eye-witnesses of her marriage to said John Scales, to wit: John Hall, John Graham, Katie Martin and Samuel Martin. I separated these parties and took their statements in regard to what they said they knew about her marriage. The following is a synopsis of the statements of the various parties: Emily Scales states that she was married in the month of January, 1863, in the Methodist church at Holly Springs, Mississippi, one Sunday afternoon, by a preacher by the name of Scruggs; that there was but one room to the church, and that it was furnished with the customary benches and desks; that the four persons mentioned above were all present, and that one of them, Katie Martin, is her sister.

John Hall stated that he was present and saw Emily married; that the services took place in a small room of a dwelling-house in the edge of the town; that there was a family living in the house at the time; that the only furniture in the room was a table and a few chairs. John Graham corroborates this statement, and both he and Hall are positive that she was not married at the church. Katie Martin, her sister, states that she did not see her married, but that Emily had told her that she was married to Scales in a church building used by the colored people, located about fifteen miles from Holly Springs. Samuel Martin states that he was present and saw Emily married; that the service took place in the basement of a two-story brick church in the town of Holly Springs.

I questioned these witnesses thoroughly, and am of opinion that the woman Emily was not married to John Scales at the time and place she claimed, or at least, the persons she brought up as eye-witnesses of the ceremony were not present; I therefore refused to pay her the money unless she produced other and more satisfactory witnesses as to her identity, as the widow of the said Scales. There is no doubt in my mind but that she is the person who put in and perfected the claim.

I have heretofore required the widows of deceased soldiers to produce proof of their marriage before I would pay them their bounty which had been allowed. I was not satisfied with the simple proof that they had been living together as man and wife, unless they had so lived in slavery times. My reason for this is that I am satisfied that a great many of these widows' claims are fraudulent; that is, that they are being prosecuted by parties who were never married to the person whose bounty they lay claim to. They simply "took up" with the soldiers and lived with them for a short time. This class of widows' claims now being forwarded from this city is undoubtedly on the increase, and I have reason to believe that there are many claims now being forwarded in which the so-called widow never even "took up" or lived with the soldier at all.

During the war, many of the companies, after they had been in the service a year or two, got up and had printed what were called company records, showing, among other things, the name and date of death of all members of the organization who had died up to that time. These records are now in the hands of persons who go around town and hunt up women who file their claims as widows of these deceased soldiers. I have been informed by the clerk of a court of record that he has had several cases where the assumed widow and her witnesses have appeared before him for the purpose of swearing to the declaration for bounty, in which the woman had forgotten the name of the soldier for whose bounty she was applying as his widow. I have also been told by a United States commissioner that he had also had several similar cases in which the widow could not give her husband's name. Information has also been received at this office from parties who have been importuned by these persons in possession of these company records to put in their claim as the widow of some soldier whose death was set forth on said record, but of whom they had never before heard.

In view of these facts I have felt it was my duty to go back of the simple fact that the claim for bounty was put in and perfected by claimant, and required them to bring proof of marriage, or cohabitation as man and wife while in a state of slavery. Please inform me if I shall continue to do so, or shall I pay to the claimant upon being satisfied that she is the party who put in and perfected the claim?

Very respectfully, your obedient servant,
FRED. S. PALMER,
Sub-Assistant Commissioner.
Brevet Brigadier General GEO. W. BALLOCH,
Chief Disbursing Officer, Washington, D. C.

PALMER, E—CASE 3.

BUREAU REFUGEES, FREEDMEN AND ABANDONED LANDS,
Memphis, Tennessee, November 9, 1868.

GENERAL: I have the honor to invite your attention to the case of Jane Lundy, widow of Joseph Lundy, late private Company E Third United States colored heavy artillery, whose claim has been allowed as per United States Treasury certificate No. 484,833. I have investigated the case and find the facts to be as follows: A woman by the name of Jane Lundy lived with said Joseph Lundy as his wife for eight years while in slavery, and afterward up to the month of July, 1864, when he parted from her and was married on the 31st of that month by the chaplain of his regiment to another woman by the name of Catharine Lundy, with whom he lived up to the day of his death, which occurred in the month of May, 1866. Neither of these women have any children now living who are the offspring of said Joseph Lundy. Please inform me to whom, under the circumstances, the bounty rightfully belongs.

Very respectfully, your obedient servant,
FRED. S. PALMER,
Disbursing Officer of Claims.
Brevet Brigadier General GEO. W. BALLOCH,
Chief Disbursing Officer, Bureau of Refugees, Freedmen and Abandoned Lands, Washington, D. C.

PALMER, E—CASE 4.

BUREAU REFUGEES, FREEDMEN AND ABANDONED LANDS,
Memphis, Tennessee, November 9, 1868.

GENERAL: I have the honor to return herewith the vouchers in the case of Hattie Davis, sister of James Lewis, late private Company C

Eleventh United States colored troops, whose claim has been allowed, as per United States treasury certificate No. 406,029. Your attention is respectfully invited to her affidavit of the 12th ultimo, which is inclosed. From which it will be seen that she is not the only next of kin to said James Lewis, but that she has six brothers and sisters still living, as follows: Mary, Eliza, Susan, Sandy, Surgeon, and Thomas. These parties are represented as now living with William Darnall, their former owner, between Spring Creek and Cotton Grove, in Madison County, Tennessee. The slip attached to her affidavit Hattie brought to the office, stating that she had visited Mr. Darnall's place, and that he had written it at the request of her brothers and sisters. The woman Hattie voluntarily informed me that her brothers and sisters were alive, and stated that she had been told by the claim agent that it would be all right for her to draw the money and divide it with her brothers and sisters.

I have written to Mr. Darnall upon the subject, but received no answer. Please inform me what action will be necessary for those heirs to take to obtain the bounty.

I am, general, very respectfully, your obedient servant,
FRED S. PALMER,
Disbursing Officer of Claims.

Brevet Brigadier General GEO. W. BALLOCH,
Chief Disbursing Officer, Bureau Refugees, Freedmen and Abandoned Lands, Washington, D. C.

PALMER, E—CASE 5.

BUREAU REFUGEES FREEDMEN, AND ABANDONED LANDS,
Memphis, Tennessee, December 14, 1868.

COLONEL: I have the honor to state that a colored man by the name of Marshall Johnson is prosecuting two claims for bounty through the office of Moyers & Dedrick, claim agents of this city, as follows: first, as the brother of Richard Killick, late corporal Company A Fifty-fifth United States colored troops; and second, as the brother of Logan Killick, late sergeant Company A Fifty-fifth United States colored troops. This man Johnson called at my office for the purpose of having me certify, under the provision of circular No. 1, current series, from the Commissioner's office, to the acknowledgment of the receipt of advances from his claim agent. Believing from the appearance and conduct of the man that there was something wrong, I proceeded to investigate the case, and am fully of the opinion that both claims are fraudulent. Johnson represented to me that the names of his parents were Charles and Leathe, and that his brothers were named Richard and Logan, and that he was known as John. That they all belonged at one time to James Hill, of Bibb County, Alabama, who lived five miles from Scottsville; that his father and mother died some sixteen or seventeen years ago. I immediately wrote a letter to Mr. James Hill for such information as he could give me on the subject, and, in reply, I received on the 10th instant a communication from Lorenzo Oldham, dated Mars Post Office, Bibb County, Alabama, November 15, 1868, which is inclosed. The Charles and Leathe referred to in this letter are evidently the Charles and Leathe whom Johnson claims as his parents, and are still living in that vicinity. Johnson is, in my opinion, no kin to Richard or Logan Killick, for whose bounties he has applied. This man, Marshall Johnson, is a noted horse thief, and is now confined in the county jail, in this city, awaiting trial. He was arrested in my office on the 19th ultimo. I would respectfully suggest that this communication be forwarded to Washington for the information of the Second Auditor.

I am, colonel, very respectfully, your obedient servant,
FRED. S. PALMER,
Disbursing Officer of Claims.

Brevet Lieutenant Colonel JAMES THOMPSON,
Assistant Commissioner, Nashville, Tennessee.

PALMER, E—CASE 6, No. 12.

BUREAU REFUGEES, FREEDMEN, AND ABANDONED LANDS,
OFFICE DISBURSING OFFICER OF CLAIMS,
Memphis, Tennessee, January 7, 1869.

GENERAL: I have the honor to call your attention to the claims for bounty of John Horton, brother of Robert Horton, late private Company B Sixty-first United States colored troops, the money to pay which, amounting to $384 83, was forwarded by you on the 9th of December, 1868, being included in your check No. 357 on the First National Bank of this city. John Horton presented himself at this office for the purpose of receiving said money, and brought with him two of his former fellow servants, or slaves, William Horton and Allen Horton, to establish his identity. John Horton states that he and his family were at one time the slaves of Brook Harris, who lives one mile from the Gulf, in Chatham County, North Carolina. That about fifteen years ago he was taken by Harris's son-in-law, Edward Horton, to a plantation two miles from Okolona, Mississippi. That his father and mother both died in Chatham County, North Carolina, while he was the slave of Brook Harris, and before he was taken to Missisippi, and that he never had any other brother than Robert.

William Horton stated that in the second year of the war Edward Horton took himself, John Horton, Robert Horton, Allen Horton, and his other slaves, back to Brook Harris's, in Chatham County, North Carolina, to prevent them from being freed by the federal army. That while he was in Chatham County he saw the reputed father and mother of John and Robert Horton on the Brook Harris plantation; that John and Robert acknowledged them to be their father and mother. That Edward Horton kept his slaves one year in Chatham County, and then brought them back to Mississippi. That at the time they all returned to Mississippi John and Robert Horton's father and mother were alive and the slaves of Brook Harris.

Allen Horton stated that he was taken to Chatham County, North Carolina, with Edward Horton's other slaves in the second year of the war; that he remembered seeing a colored man there by the name of Ned, whom John and Robert Horton acknowledge to be their brother. That Ned was alive and living on the Brook Harris place when Horton took his slaves back to Mississippi.

Will you please inform me if, under the circumstances, I shall pay the money to the said John Horton?

Very respectfully, your obedient servant,
FRED S. PALMER,
Disbursing Officer of Claims.

Brevet Brigadier General GEO. W. BALLOCH,
Chief Disbursing Officer, Washington, D. C.

I certify that the foregoing, as entered on pages numbered from one to sixteen, inclusive, are true copies as taken from the records of the agent and disbursing officer of claims, Bureau Refugees, Freedmen and Abandoned Lands, at Memphis, Tennessee, this day exhibited to me.

Given under my hand and seal at Memphis, Tennessee, this 25th day of January, 1870.

[SEAL.]   MARK EDWARDS,
U. S. Commisssoner.

PALMER, E—CASE 7, No. 105.

BUREAU OF REFUGEES, FREEDMEN AND ABANDONED LANDS,
OFFICE OF DISBURSING OFFICER OF CLAIMS,
Memphis, Tennessee, February 19, 1869.

GENERAL: I have the honor to call your attention to the claim of the bounty, &c., of Queen Gainer, widow of Albert Gainer, deceased, late artificer of Company F Third regiment United States colored heavy artillery, whose vouchers were forwarded to you November 24, 1868. This woman, when she called at this office to identify herself, stated that she was married to said Albert Gainer, at Memphis, Tennessee, in the month of May, 1865, by a colored preacher by the name of Woodfall. From the inclosed affidavit of Isaac Gainer it would appear that Albert and a woman by the name of Lotta, a slave of a Mr. Murray, lived together as man and wife, while in a state of slavery, during three or four years, and afterwards during part of the time while Albert was a soldier in the army.

I have in my possession a record book of marriages kept by the Rev. C. P. Taylor, late chaplain of the Third regiment United States colored heavy artillery. From said record I find that on the 27th day of January, 1865, he united in marriage Albert Gainer, Company F, and Lettie Gainer. Lettie is evidently the same woman who is called Lotta by Isaac Gainer. There is no doubt in my mind as to the claim of Queen Gainer's being a fraudulent one.

Please inform me what disposition shall be made of the vouchers in this case.

Very respectfully, your obedient servant,
FRED S. PALMER,
Disbursing Officer of Claims.

Brevet Brigadier General GEO. W. BALLOCH,
*Chief Disbursing Officer, Bureau Refugees, Freedmen
and Abandoned Lands, Washington, D. C.*

PALMER, E—CASE 8, No. 106.

BUREAU REFUGEES, FREEDMEN AND ABANDONED LANDS,
OFFICE OF DISBURSING OFFICER OF CLAIMS,
Memphis, Tennessee, February 19, 1869.

GENERAL: I have the honor to call your attention to the claim for bounty, &c., of Martha Martin, widow of Lee Martin, late private Company E Sixty-first regiment United States colored troops, which has been allowed, as per treasury certificate No. 489,758.

When this woman attempted to prove her identity at this office, she brought the following named witnesses: Nelson Maddix, Shedrick Kirkman, James Falls, and Reddick Whitchell, whom she stated were all eye-witnesses of her marriage with the said Lee Martin, deceased. I separated these parties, and they severally made the following statement:

Martha stated that she was married to said Lee Martin at Memphis, Tennessee, in January, 1864, by a colored preacher by the name of Creuse. That Maddix, Kirkman, Falls, and Whitchell were all present and eye-witnesses of the marriage ceremony. Nelson Maddix and Shedrick Kirkman both stated upon examination that they had neither of them seen her married. Whitchell stated that he knew the woman one year and a half before she was married. She, however, states that she never saw Whitchell until about one month before she was married. James Falls and Whitchell were both positive that they saw her married.

Believing that the claim is a fraudulent one, and that Falls and Whitchell are not credible witnesses, I refused to allow her to sign the vouchers. Please inform me what disposition shall be made of them.

Very respectfully, your obedient servant,
FRED. S. PALMER,
Disbursing Officer of Claims.

Brevet Brigadier General GEO. W. BALLOCH,
Chief Disbursing Officer Bureau Refugees,
Freedmen and Abandoned Lands.

PALMER, E—CASE 9, No. 229.

BUREAU REFUGEES, FREEDMEN AND ABANDONED LANDS,
OFFICE DISBURSING OFFICER OF CLAIMS,
Memphis, Tennessee, March 29, 1869.

GENERAL: I have the honor to state that, in paying the bounties to widows and other relatives of deceased soldiers, I find cases in which the witnesses, through whom the identity of the claimant was established, had no personal knowledge of the facts to which they must have testified to have perfected the claim.

The following claims, which have been allowed, are of this character, to wit: Emily J. McCauley, widow of Burges McCauley, late private Company G Eleventh United States colored troops; Phillis Jeems, sister of Babe Smith, late private in Company F Sixty-first United States colored troops; Virginia Taylor, sister of Richard Taylor, late private Company C Eleventh United States colored troops.

In each of these cases I have carefully examined the claimants and original witnesses who swore through these claims, and their affidavits are herewith inclosed, and to which your attention is respectfully invited.

There is little doubt in my mind but that some of this class of claims are in reality good, that is, preferred by the proper parties, and could have been established by truthful witnesses; but claimant, rather than be at the trouble and delay of hunting up witnesses who really did know of the facts in the case, preferred to rely upon the testimony of parties who either knowingly or unknowingly committed perjury in perfecting the claim, which could be readily accomplished under the loose system of taking testimony as practiced by some of the claim agents of this city for some time past.

The position assumed by the claim agents appears to have been to look upon every applicant as a bona fide claimant, and that it was no part of their duty to detect fraud upon the government on the part of their client.

Will you please furnish me with instructions to govern my action in such cases? Shall I return the vouchers to you, or shall I permit the claimant to establish his identity by other and different witnesses who are really cognizant of the true relationship of the claimant to the deceased soldier?

I am, general, very respectfully, your obedient serqant,
FRED. S. PALMER,
Disbursing Officer of Claims.
Brevet Brigadier General GEO. W. BALLOCH,
Chief Disbursing Officer, Bureau Refugees, Freedmen and Abandoned Lands, Washington, D. C.

The above letter is indorsed as follows:

WAR DEPARTMENT, BUREAU REFUGEES, FREEDMEN
AND ABANDONED LANDS, CLAIM DIVISION,
Washington, D. C., December 7, 1869.

Respectfully referred to Hon. E. B. French, Second Auditor United States Treasury, for his information, and with request for instructions, to await which payment of these cases will be withheld.

By order of Brevet Major General O. O. Howard, Commissioner, &c.
WILLIAM P. DREW,
Chief of Claim Division.

PALMER, E—CASE $9\frac{1}{2}$.

SECOND AUDITOR'S OFFICE,
December 16, 1869.

Respectfully returned. I have carefully examined the within affidavits and cases referred to, and desire that you retain the funds and instruct your sub-agents to investigate. Undoubtedly many fraudulent claims are presented to this office, and it is almost impossible to ascertain who are the proper heirs without the aid of detectives or government officers stationed at the immediate vicinity where the parties reside. As your agents have facilities for this purpose, they should satisfy themselves before payment of the identity and honesty of claimants.

Respectfully,

E. B. FRENCH, *Auditor,*
By H. C. H.

I certify that the foregoing, as entered on pages numbered from seventeen to twenty-four, inclusive, are true copies as taken from the records of the agent and disbursing officer of claims, Bureau Refugees, Freedmen and Abandoned Lands, at Memphis, Tennessee, this day exhibited to me. Given under my hand and seal, at Memphis, Tennessee, this 25th day of January, 1870.

[SEAL.]
MARK EDWARDS,
U. S. Commissioner.

BOUNTIES TO COLORED SOLDIERS. 185

WAR DEPARTMENT, BUREAU REFUGEES, FREEDMEN
AND ABANDONED LANDS, CLAIM DIVISION,
Washington, December 17, 1869.

Respectfully returned to Lieutenant Colonel F. S. Palmer, disbursing officer, &c., Memphis, Tennessee, and attention invited to the indorsement of the honorable Second Auditor, with the terms of which Colonel Palmer will comply.

By order of Brevet Major General O. O. Howard, Commissioner, &c.
[SEAL.]
WILLIAM P. DREW,
Chief of Claim Division.

UNITED STATES OF AMERICA, *District of West Tennessee, ss :*

On this 25th day of March, 1869, before me, a United States commissioner in and for the district aforesaid, personally appeared Virginia Taylor, of Shelby County, State of Tennessee, who, being duly sworn according to law, deposes and says that she is the sister and next of kin of Richard Taylor, late a private in Company C, Eleventh United States colored troops; that her mother had five children, as follows : herself, Joseph, and Richard, and two other children who died in infancy. That a man by the name of Ed. Hughbank passed as the father of her two brothers, Joseph and Richard Taylor; that she saw her mother die in Marshall County, Mississippi, about two years before the war; that she saw the aforesaid Ed. Hughbank die in Memphis, Tennessee, in the summer of 1866; that she was informed that her brother, Joseph Taylor, died in Tunica County, Mississippi, about the commencement of the war; that she was also informed that her other brother, Richard Taylor, was drowned in Crittenden County, Arkansas, in the month of March, 1867; that in the month of May, 1868, she went to the office of Moyers & Dedrick and put in her claim for the bounty, &c., due on account of the services of her deceased brother, Richard Taylor, late private Company C, Eleventh regiment United States colored troops ; that the only witnesses she had to prove her identity and perfect her claim were Jetra White and David Laird ; that she never was acquainted with Jetra White until some time in the year 1864, and that she has no recollection of ever having seen David Laird previous to the day when he acted as her witness, when she put in her claim with Moyers & Dedrick.

her
VIRGINIA + TAYLOR.
mark.

Witnesses:
FRED. S. PALMER.
MARK EDWARDS.

Subscribed and sworn to on the day and year first above written ; and on the same day personally came Jetra White, of the county of Shelby and State of Tennessee, who, being duly sworn, deposes and says that he has been personally acquainted with Virginia Taylor, who signed the foregoing declaration, since some time in the year 1864; that he also became personally acquainted with Richard Taylor, who was a private in Company C Eleventh United States colored troops, at about the same time ; that he has heard the said Richard Taylor say that the said Virginia Taylor was his sister; that he has never been acquainted with the father, mother, brothers, or any other sister of said Richard Taylor, other than said Virginia Taylor ; that he knows that said Richard Taylor was drowned in Crittenden County, State of Arkansas, in the month of March, 1867; that he was present at the time, and an eye-witness of his death; that he and David Laird were witnesses for said Virginia Taylor when she put in her claim at the office of Moyers & Dedrick for the bounty due on account of the services of the said Richard Taylor, deceased; that he has been informed that David Laird, the other witness in the case, died at the county hospital, in the city of Memphis, State of Tennessee, on or about the 17th day of March, 1869.

JETRA WHITE.

Witnesses:
 FRED. S. PALMER.
 MARK EDWARDS.

Subscribed and sworn to before me this 25th day of March, 1869, at Memphis, Tennessee.
[SEAL.]
C. CANNING SMITH,
U. S. Commissioner.

To the foregoing affidavit is attached the following:

OFFICE COUNTY HOSPITAL, March 25, 1869.

David Laird died on the 17th instant, of consumption, after a lingering sickness.
G. GORDON HOGAN, Steward.

UNITED STATES OF AMERICA, *District of West Tennessee, ss* :

On this 10th day of March, 1869, before me, a United States commissioner for the district aforesaid, personally appeared Phillis Jeems, of the county of Tunica, State of Mississippi, who, being duly sworn according to law, deposes and says: That she is the sister of Babe Smith, who was a private in Company F Sixty-first regiment United States colored troops; that her father's name was Solomon Smith, and her mother's name was Phillis Smith; that her mother had the following children: Babe Smith, Phillis Jeems, John Smith, Tempe Smith, Harriet Smith, and several others who died when they were very young; that Babe Smith died in the service of the United States, in the State of Louisiana, in 1865; that she has been informed that John Smith died at La Grange, Tennessee, in 1863; that Tempe Smith died in Virginia several years before the war; that she has been informed that Harriet Smith died in Hardeman County, Tennessee, in 1867; that she has been informed that her father died at La Grange, Tennessee, in the summer of 1863, in the small-pox hospital; that her mother died in the fever hospital at Memphis, Tennessee, in 1864; that said Babe Smith cohabited with a woman by the name of Annie Rawlins for two years while in a state of slavery, and continued to live with said woman as man and wife up to the day of her reputed death; that she was informed by said Babe Smith that said Annie Rawlins died at La Grange, Tennessee, in the fall of the year 1863; that said Annie Rawlins never had any children by Babe Smith; that she put in the claim for bounty, back pay, &c., due on account of the services of her said brother, Babe Smith, who was a private in Company F Sixty-first regiment United States colored troops, with Moyers & Dedrick, claim agents of Memphis, Tennessee, in September, 1867; that the only witnesses she had to prove her identity and perfect her claim were Israel Harvey and Peter McCragin.

PHILLIS $\overset{\text{her}}{+}$ JEEMS.
mark.

Witnesses:
 MARK EDWARDS.
 A. T. CREGO.

Sworn to and subscribed before me on the day and year first above written; and on the same day personally came Peter McCragin, of the city of Memphis, county of Shelby and State of Tennessee, who, being duly sworn according to law, deposes and says that he was formerly a private in Company F Sixty-first regiment United States colored troops; that he was personally acquainted with Babe Smith, who was a private in Company F Sixty-first regiment United States colored troops; that he is also personally acquainted with Phillis Jeems, who made and subscribed to the foregoing declaration; that he was a witness for her at the office of Moyers & Dedrick, where she put in her claim for the bounty due on account of the services of Babe Smith aforesaid; that the first time he ever saw said Babe Smith and Phillis Jeems was at La Grange, Tennessee, in the summer of 1863, when the Sixty-first regiment was being organized; that he never was acquainted with Babe Smith's father, mother, or any of his brothers or sisters, except Phillis Jeems; that he heard Babe Smith say that Phillis was his sister.

his
PETER + McCRAGIN.
mark.

Witnesses:
MARK EDWARDS.
A. T. CREGO.

Sworn to and subscribed before me the day and year first above written; and on the same day personally came Israel Harvey, of the city of Memphis, county of Shelby and State of Tennessee, who, being duly sworn according to law, deposes and says that he was formerly a private in Company F of the Sixty-first regiment United States colored troops; that he was personally acquainted with Babe Smith, deceased, who was a private in Company F. Sixty-first regiment United States colored troops; that he is also personally acquainted with Phillis Jeems, who made and subscribed to the foregoing declaration; that he was a witness for said Phillis Jeems when she put in her claim at the office of Moyers & Dedrick for the bounty due on account of the services of the said Babe Smith; that the first time he ever saw said Babe Smith and Phillis Jeems was in 1862; they had first got free by going to the federal army; that he also got acquainted in the same year with a man whose name he does not remember, and a woman by the name of Phillis, who were acknowledged by Babe Smith to be his father and mother; that said father of Babe Smith died at La Grange, Tennessee, in the early part of the year 1863, and that he assisted to bury his dead body; that he heard said Babe Smith say that Phillis Jeems was his sister; that he never saw any other members of the family than the father, mother, Babe Smith, and Phillis Jeems; that said Babe Smith died in the service of the United States in the State of Louisiana, in the year 1865; that he has no personal knowledge of the death of the mother of said Babe Smith.

his
ISRAEL + HARVEY.
mark.

Witnesses:
MARK EDWARDS.
A. T. CREGO.

Subscribed and sworn to before me this 10th day of March, 1869, at Memphis, Tennessee.
[SEAL.]

ISAAC MORRISON,
U. S. Commissioner.

BOUNTIES TO COLORED SOLDIERS.

I certify that the foregoing, as entered on pages numbered from 25 to 34, inclusive, are true copies as taken from the records of the agent and disbursing officer of claims, Bureau Refugees, Freedmen and Abandoned Lands, at Memphis, Tennessee, this day exhibited to me. Given under my hand and seal at Memphis, Tennessee, this 25th day of January, 1870.

[SEAL.]   MARK EDWARDS,
                                          U. S. Commissioner.

UNITED STATES OF AMERICA, *District of West Tennessee, ss :*

On this 15th day of March, 1869, before me, a United States commissioner for the district aforesaid, personally appeared Emily J. McCauley, of the county of Mississippi, State of Arkansas, who, being duly sworn according to law, deposes and says that she is the widow and nearest of kin of Burges McCauley, who was a private in Company G Eleventh regiment United States colored troops; that she was married to said Burges McCauley by Chaplain Richardson, of the Eleventh regiment United States colored troops, at Memphis, in the year 1863; that she is certain it was in 1863, for the reason that she had one child by him that was born before the Fort Pillow fight, in 1864, and she lived with him as his wife up to the time of his supposed death, in the spring of 1866, when she was informed by his sister, Edith McCauley, that he was drowned at De Soto Front Landing, in Tunica County, Mississippi; that she put her claim in the hands of Moyers & Dedrick for collection in the month of March, 1868, and that the only witnesses she ever had to identify her in perfecting her claim were James Macklemore and Thomas Boon.

                                  EMILY J. + McCAULEY.
                                          mark.

Witnesses:
   WILLIAM H. WHITE.
   MARK EDWARDS.

Sworn to and subscribed before me the day and year first above written; and on the same day personally came Thomas Boon, who, being duly sworn according to law, deposes and says that he is personally acquainted with Emily J. McCauley, who signed the foregoing declaration; that he is also personally acquainted with Burges McCauley, who was a private in Company G Eleventh United States colored troops; that the said Burges McCauley and the said Emily J. McCauley were married at Memphis, Tennessee, by the Rev. Mr. Richardson, chaplain of the Eleventh regiment United States colored troops, in the year 1864; he is certain that it was after the Fort Pillow fight in that year; that the said parties lived together as man and wife from that time up to the day of the supposed death of the said Burges McCauley; that he was informed that the said Burges McCauley was drowned in the year 1866, but has no personal knowledge of his death; that he was a witness for said Emily J. McCauley when she put in her claim for collection in the hands of Moyers & Dedrick.

                                         THOMAS + BOON.
                                            mark.

Witnesses:
   MARK EDWARDS.
   WM. H. WHITE.

Sworn to and subscribed before me the day and year first above written; and on the same day personally appeared James Macklemore, who, being duly sworn according to law, deposes and says that he is personally acquainted with Emily J. McCauley, who signed the foregoing declaration; that he was a witness for her when she put in her claim with Moyers & Dedrick for the bounty due on account of the services of Burges McCauley, late private in Company G Eleventh United States colored troops; that he is personally acquainted with said Burges McCauley, and knows that said Burges McCauley and said Emily J. McCauley lived together as man and wife from on or about the month of June, 1864, to on or about the month of March, 1866; that he has no personal knowledge of the fact that they were ever married; that he was told that said Burges McCauley was drowned in the spring of 1866, but has no personal knowledge as to his death.

JAMES + MACKLEMORE.
his mark.

Witnesses:
MARK EDWARDS.
WM. H. WHITE.

Subscribed and sworn to before me this 15th day of March, 1869, at Memphis, Tennessee.
[SEAL.] ISAAC MORRISON,
U. S. Commissioner.

Mr. Drew to Colonel Palmer.

WAR DEPARTMENT, BUREAU REFUGEES, FREEDMEN
AND ABANDONED LANDS, CLAIM DIVISION,
Washington, D. C., December 7, 1869.

COLONEL: Referring to your letter of March 29, 1869, addressed to the chief disbursing officer of this bureau, inclosing affidavits of the claimants and witnesses taken after the receipt by you of vouchers in the cases of Phillis Jeems, as sister of Babe Smith, deceased, late private in Company F Sixty-first regiment United States colored troops; Virginia Taylor, as sister of Richard Taylor, deceased, late private in Company C One hundred and eleventh United States colored troops, and Emily J. McCauley, as widow of Reuben McCauley, late private in Company G One hundred and eleventh United States colored troops, I am directed by the Commissioner to state that the papers have been referred this day to the honorable Second Auditor of the Treasury, with a request for instructions, which, when received, will be duly communicated to you. Your action in reviewing the evidence upon which these claims were allowed, and declining accordingly to pay the amounts thus awarded, is fully approved.

The delay in attending to these cases has arisen from the fact that the papers by some oversight were not regularly referred to this office, and that after the receipt of the same at this office they were inadvertently placed with cases upon which action was necessarily deferred.

Very respectfully, &c.,
WILLIAM P. DREW,
Agent Bureau Refugees, Freedmen and Abandoned Lands,
Chief of Claim Division.

Lieutenant Colonel F. S. PALMER,
Agent and Disbursing Officer Bureau Refugees, Feeedmen
and Abandoned Lands, Memphis, Tennessee.

BOUNTIES TO COLORED SOLDIERS.

I certify that the foregoing, as entered on pages numbered from 35 to 40, are true copies as taken from the records of the agent and disbursing officer of claims, Bureau Refugees, Freedmen and Abandoned Lands, at Memphis, Tennessee, this day exhibited to me. Given under my hand and seal, at Memphis, Tennessee, this 25th day of January, 1870.

[SEAL.]   MARK EDWARDS,
              U. S. Commissioner.

PALMER, E—CASE 10, No. 449.

BUREAU REFUGEES, FREEDMEN AND ABANDONED LANDS,
  OFFICE DISBURSING OFFICER OF CLAIMS,
    Memphis, Tennessee, June 16, 1869.

GENERAL: I have the honor to call your attention to the claim of Albert Benson, brother of Henry Benson, deceased, late private Company E Forty-sixth United States colored troops. I inclose for, your information the affidavits of Alfred Benson, (evidently the identical person who put in the claim in the name of Albert Benson,) William Parker, Joseph Rice, and Sam. Benson. Alfred Benson, on the 22d of May, testified that Henry and himself had two half brothers by the name of Chill and Berry Benson, being children of his father by a previous wife, and that he had never seen any one who had any personal knowledge of the death of either of said half brothers; that his two witnesses when he put in his claim with Moyers & Dedrick were William Parker and Robert Thompson; that he had never seen Parker previous to his joining the army in 1863, but had seen Thompson some two or three times in slavery times; that he did not believe that Thompson ever saw or knew his father or mother. Yesterday, the 15th instant, he called at this office and stated that he has never known or seen Thompson previous to his enlisting in the Forty-sixth regiment United States colored troops.

William Parker, May 22, testifies that he was one of Alfred's witnesses when he put in his claim; that he never knew Alfred and Henry Benson's father, mother, or brothers; that he never knew Alfred or Henry until after they joined the army; that the only thing he knew about it was that Alfred and Henry passed for brothers in the regiment.

Sam. Benson, on same day, testifies that he knew the father and mother of Alfred Benson, who lived together as man and wife for about twenty years; that they had five children, as follows: Chill, Berry, Alfred, Henry, and another that died in infancy; that he saw Alfred's brother Chill alive in the fall of 1868, and that he also saw his other brother Berry alive in the spring of 1867; that he met these parties at or near Byhalia, Marshall County, Mississippi, at the time stated. He was certain that Chill and Berry were the full brothers of Alfred, and not his half brothers, as stated by him.

Joseph Rice, May 13, testifies as to Henry Benson having died at Helena, Arkansas, in April or May, 1867.

I have refused to permit Alfred to sign the vouchers in this case until I received further instructions from you. The certificate in this case, No. 507,603, was previously issued in favor of Henry Benson.

I am, general, very respectfully, your obedient servant,
          FRED. S. PALMER,
            Disbursing Officer of Claims.

Brevet Brigadier General GEO. W. BALLOCH,
  Chief Disbursing Officer, Washington, D. C.

I certify that the above is a true copy, as taken from the records of the agent and disbursing officer of claims, Bureau Refugees, Freedmen and Abandoned Lands, at Memphis, Tennessee, this day exhibited to me.

Given under my hand and seal, at Memphis, Tennessee, this 24th day of January, 1870.

[SEAL.]   MARK EDWARDS,
U. S. Commissioner.

PALMER, E—CASE 11, No. 840.

BUREAU REFUGEES, FREEDMEN AND ABANDONED LANDS,
OFFICE DISBURSING OFFICER OF CLAIMS,
Memphis, Tennessee, November 16, 1869.

GENERAL: I have the honor to call your attention to the claim of Adeline Maren and Aggie Parish, sisters of Pope Body, deceased, late musician Company F Third United States colored heavy artillery, whose vouchers were received from you December 16, 1868, number of certificate 484,861. I was satisfied, from the statement of the claimants and their witnesses, they were not the only heirs of the deceased soldier, and refused to allow them to sign the vouchers. Yesterday they brought me the inclosed power of attorney from Samuel and Coleman Body, whom they now say are their brothers, and that they are living in Sumner County, Tennessee. Please inform me what disposition shall be made of the vouchers.

Very respectfully, &c.,
         FRED. S. PALMER,
         Disbursing Officer of Claims.

Brevet Brigadier General GEO. W. BALLOCH,
   *Chief Disbursing Officer Bureau Refugees, Freedmen
     and Abandoned Lands, Washington, D. C.*

I certify that the above is a true copy as taken from the records of the agent and disbursing officer of claims, Bureau of Refugees, Freedmen and Abandoned Lands, at Memphis, Tennessee, this day exhibited to me.

Given under my hand and seal, at Memphis, Tennessee, this 24th day of January, 1870.

[SEAL.]   MARK EDWARDS,
U. S. Commissioner.

PALMER, E—CASE 12, No. 1023.

BUREAU REFUGEES, FREEDMEN AND ABANDONED LANDS,
OFFICE DISBURSING OFFICER OF CLAIMS,
Memphis, Tennessee, December 9, 1869.

GENERAL: Your attention is invited to the claim for bounty, &c., of Hannah Ross, sister of Philip Dickey, deceased, late private Company A, Third regiment United States colored heavy artillery, whose vouchers were forwarded by you October 1, 1868. From the inclosed affidavit of the aforesaid Hannah Ross, it would appear that the mother of said Philip Dickey had eleven children, as follows: Lucy, Stephen, Henry,

Fanny, Betty, George, Hannah, Joseph, Ned, Philip, and Ellinore; that the father of the soldier and the following children, Lucy, Joseph, Philip, and Ellinore, are dead; that she also heard that her mother died in August, 1869; that Stephen and Henry were taken to Arkansas before the war, and it is not known whether they are now alive or not; that Fanny, Betty, and Ned, at last accounts, some two years ago, were all living in McNairy County, Tennessee; and that George was alive and in this city in the month of May last. Also, that she had never seen any of the witnesses that swore her claim through until about the year 1863.

This is another one of those claims in which some "tall swearing" has been done. Her mother, two sisters, and two brothers, she admits, were alive when she filed her claim, with the possibility that her two other brothers, Stephen and Henry, were also alive.

I have refused to allow her to sign the vouchers until I receive further instructions from you.

I am, general, very respectfully, your obedient servant,
FRED. S. PALMER,
Disbursing Officer of Claims.
Brevet Brigadier General GEO. W. BALLOCH,
Chief Disbursing Officer Bureau Refugees, Freedmen and Abandoned Lands, Washington, D. C.

PALMER, E—CASE 13.

BUREAU REFUGEES, FREEDMEN AND ABANDONED LANDS,
OFFICE DISBURSING OFFICER OF CLAIMS,
Memphis, Tennessee, January 3, 1870.

GENERAL: I have the honor to invite your attention to the claim of Rebecca Harvey, sister of John Goode, late private Company F Sixty-first regiment United States colored troops, which has been allowed, per certificate 499,868, for $117 79, and the vouchers forwarded by you to this office November 10, 1869.

Rebecca called at this office to sign her vouchers, and stated that the only witnesses she had to prove her identity and perfect her claim when it was filed, were Israel Harvey and Thornton Gaylor; that Harvey was her brother-in-law, with whom she had been acquainted from childhood, and that she had known Gaylor since 1863. On the 31st ultimo she called again at this office, with these two witnesses, and your attention is invited to the inclosed affidavits of the claimant, Israel Harvey, and Thornton Gaylor. Rebecca swears that from the time of her earliest recollection she and her father, mother, and two brothers, being the entire family, always lived in the town of Augusta, Georgia, up to the time she was made free by the war in 1863, when she and her two brothers, John and Washington Goode, followed a detachment of cavalry from Augusta, Georgia, to Lagrange, Tennessee; that her mother and father both died at the residence of her owner, Charles Goode, who lived on Meeting street, in Augusta, Georgia, and were buried about one mile from town; that the former died about two years, and the latter about six years, before the war; that Israel Harvey was living in Augusta, Georgia, when the war commenced, and left there about one year before she did; that she has known him from childhood, and has cohabited with him from on or about the month of April, 1868.

Israel Harvey states under oath that he has known claimant about twenty years; that he lived near neighbor to her about eight years; that during that time she belonged to one Charles Goode, and lived with him on his plantation about three miles from Atlanta, Georgia; that he was acquainted with her family; that he knows that claimant's mother died on said plantation, and that he helped to bury her body; that at that time the father of the claimant was alive, and living on said plantation; that he was brought to Fayette County, Tennessee, eight or nine years before the war, and did not see claimant again until the year 1863, when he met her at Lagrange, Tennessee; that at the time claimant filed her claims, in which he is a witness, he was the lawful husband of claimant, having been regularly married to her in the fall of 1866, by the Rev. Morris Henderson, the pastor of the Beal street colored Baptist church, at Memphis, Tennessee, and has lived with her as man and wife ever since, and is so now living with her.

Thornton Gaylor states that he never saw claimant until the year 1863, after he was enlisted; that all he knows about her relationship to the deceased soldiers is that he heard them say she was their sister.

Attention is invited to the fact that this woman has filed another claim as the sister of Washington Goode, late private Company F Sixty-first United States colored troops.

There has been willful perjury in this case on the part of claimant and her husband, and I doubt not but that Gaylor was also a willing partner to the fraud. I do not believe that the woman is any kin to the soldier to whose bounty she lays claim. I would therefore recommend that payment in this case be stopped, as also in her claim as sister of Washington Goode, late private Company F Sixty-first United States colored troops. Such willful and open perjury ought to carry with it at least forfeiture of the claim. I will hold the vouchers subject to further instructions.

I am, general, very respectfully, your obedient servant,
FRED. S. PALMER,
Disbursing Officer of Claims.

Brevet Brigadier General GEO. W. BALLOCH,
*Chief Disbursing Officer Bureau Refugees, Freedmen
and Abandoned Lands, Washington, D. C.*

I certify that the foregoing, as entered on pages numbered from 47 to 52 inclusive, are true copies as taken from the records of the agent and disbursing officer of claims, Bureau Refugees, Freedmen and Abandoned Lands, at Memphis, Tennessee, this day examined to me.

Given under my hand and seal, at Memphis, Tennessee, this 25th day of January, 1870.

[SEAL.] MARK EDWARDS,
U. S. Commissioner.

PALMER, F.

BUREAU REFUGEES, FREEDMEN AND ABANDONED LANDS,
OFFICE DISBURSING OFFICER OF CLAIMS,
Memphis, Tennessee, January 22, 1870.

CAPTAIN: I have the honor, in accordance with the request made by the president of your commission, to transmit herewith copies of correspondence in regard to stoppages for advances in cases where the claimant denied having received the full amount claimed to have been advanced by the claim agent, as follows: Letters from this office, No. 457, March 6, 1868; No. 296, March 6, 1868; No. 437, April 3, 1868; No. 447, April 6, 1868; No. 552, April 24, 1868; No. 601, May 7, 1868; No. 695, May 28, 1868. Also, copies of letters received from Brevet Major General A. P. Howe, dated March 13, 1868, and April 16, 1868. I also inclose, as directed, a copy of my report to General Howard upon Captain Parkinson's letter to the Quartermaster General, No. 1403, December 5, 1868. I will forward the balance of the papers called for with as little delay as possible.

I am, captain, very respectfully, your obedient servant,
FRED. S. PALMER,
Disbursing Officer of Claims.

Captain J. A. SLADEN,
Recorder Military Commission, Bureau Refugees,
Freedmen and Abandoned Lands, Washington, D. C.

PALMER, F—CASE 1, No. 295.

BUREAU REFUGEES, FREEDMEN AND ABANDONED LANDS,
SUB-DISTRICT OF MEMPHIS,
Memphis, Tennessee, March 6, 1868.

GENERAL: I have the honor to state that on the 19th ultimo you forwarded to me the discharge papers of Frank Key, late private Company B Fifty-fifth United States colored infantry volunteers, whose claim for bounty has been allowed, as per United States Treasury certificate No. 380,510, amounting to $48 31, with an indorsement that "the amount due the claimant of the within discharge was advanced by his attorney, B. D. Hyam, of this city." I desire to state that said Key denies having ever received any advances from M. Coombs, jr., & Co., of this city, who prosecuted this claim through B. D. Hyam, of Washington City, and I inclose his affidavit to that effect. I also inclose a statement of A. T. Crego, one of my clerks, whom I sent to Coombs's office to see him in regard to the stoppage, from which it will be seen that Coombs admits that he never advanced said Key anything, and that he was only assisting one Brown, a third party, to collect an old debt. Key protests against said money being stopped against him, and requests that it be forwarded to him through this office.

Very respectfully, your obedient servant,
FRED. S. PALMER,
Lieutenant Colonel and Sub-Assistant Commissioner.

Brevet Brigadier General GEO. W. BALLOCH,
Chief Disbursing Officer, Washington, D. C.

PALMER, F—CASE 2.

WAR DEPARTMENT, BUREAU REFUGEES, FREEDMEN
AND ABANDONED LANDS, CLAIM DIVISION,
Washington, D. C., March 13, 1868.

COLONEL: I am directed to acknowledge the receipt of your letters of the 6th instant, with reference to alleged advances by attorneys to claim agents, and inclosing evidence implicating M. Combs, jr., & Co., agents of B. D. Hyam, in the matter of an advance alleged to have been made to Frank Key, late private Company B Fifty-fifth United States colored troops. Measures have been taken to recover the amount withheld from Key, and when recovered it will be forwarded to him through the disbursing office of the bureau at Memphis. The receipts of the following claimants for alleged advances made by M. Combs, jr., & Co., have been returned to B. D. Hyam, attorney of record, with statement that they must be certified to by you or by some officer designated by you, before the amounts thus represented can be allowed, viz: Alexander Smith, late corporal Company B Eleventh United States colored troops; David Weston, late sergeant Company D Eleventh United States colored troops; Ruthy Curtis, widow of Pleasant Curtis, late private Company G Eleventh United States colored troops; Edward Slocum, late private Company G Eleventh United States colored troops; David Allen, late sergeant Company D Fifty-fifth United States colored troops; Reuben Hogan, late private Company B Fifty-fifth United States colored troops; Reuben Sikes, late private Company K Eleventh United States colored troops; Abram Horton, late private Company K Eleventh United States colored troops; Adam Caruthers, late private Company F Eleventh United States colored troops; Henry Branch, late corporal Company E Eleventh United States colored troops; Mary Wood, mother of William Charles, late private Company M Third United States colored heavy artillery; John Hawkins, late private Company B Fifty-fifth United States colored troops; Tyler Hooker, late private Company F Eleventh United States colored troops; Shepard Waters, late private Company H Eleventh United States colored troops; William Horton, late private Company F Eleventh United States colored troops; John Ingerham, late private Company C Fifty-fifth United States colored troops; Moses Pedan, late private Company A Fifty-fifth United States colored troops; Isam Strong, late private Company K Eleventh United States colored troops.

Very respectfully,

A. P. HOWE,
Brevet Major General U. S. A. in charge of Division.

Lieutenant Colonel F. S. PALMER,
   Sub-Assistant Commissioner, &c.,
     Bureau R., F. and A. L., Memphis, Tenn.

BUREAU REFUGEES, FREEDMEN AND ABANDONED LANDS,
SUB-DISTRICT OF MEMPHIS,
Memphis, Tennessee, March 6, 1868.

GENERAL: I have the honor to call your attention to the extravagantly large sums of money which are being stopped at Washington, D. C., as advances made by claim agents of this city upon the bounty claims paid through this office. It is virtually, in many cases, permitting the claim agents to buy up the whole or part of said claims at from fifty to seventy-five cents on the dollar, and in other cases to collect old debts for third parties, contrary to the wishes and desires of the colored claimants. Cannot some means be taken to restrict the claim agents

BOUNTIES TO COLORED SOLDIERS.

in the amount of advances, thereby preventing them from obtaining, in many cases, the greater part of the bounty due the claimant?
Very respectfully, your obedient servant,
FRED. S. PALMER,
Lieutenant Colonel and Sub-Assistant Commissioner.
Brevet Brigadier General GEO. W. BALLOCH,
Chief Disbursing Officer, Washington, D. C.

PALMER, F—CASE 3, No. 437.

BUREAU REFUGEES, FREEDMEN AND ABANDONED LANDS,
SUB-DISTRICT OF MEMPHIS,
Memphis, Tennessee, April 3, 1868.

CAPTAIN: I have the honor, in accordance with Circular No. 13, series 1867, from the assistant commissioner's office for the State of Tennessee, to submit the following report of the number and kind of claims, and the amount collected and paid on each, paid at this office during the month of March, 1868.

No.	Date.	Name.	Rank.	Co.	Regiment and arm of service.	Kind of claims.	Amount.
1	Mar. 2, 1868	Henry Clayborn	Private	H	3d U. S. colored heavy artillery.	Arrears of pay and bounty.	$181 76
*	*	*	*	*	*	*	*
187	Mar. 31, 1868	Conger Houston	Private	A	110th U. S. colored troops	Arrears of pay and bounty.	239 10
	Total						38,046 03

* * * * * * * * *

I have collected from the firm of M. Combs, jr., & Co., claim agents, and paid over to the proper person, the sum of $463, which had been stopped from the bounties of said parties, at Washington, D. C., upon the misrepresentation that said sums of money had been actually advanced to them as follows:

No.	Date.	Name.	Rank.	Co.	Regiment and arm of service.	Kind of claims.	Am't.
1	Mar. 18, 1868	Ruthy Curtis, wid. of Pleasant Curtis.	Corporal.	G	11th U. S. colored troops.	Arrears of pay and bounty.	$55 00
2	Mar. 18, 1868	Simon Reynolds	Corporal.	E	55th U. S. colored troops.	......do......	40 00
3	Mar. 19, 1868	Wesley Simmons	Private.	C	......do......	......do......	30 00
4	Mar. 19, 1868	Reuben Hogan	Private.	B	......do......	......do......	56 00
5	Mar. 19, 1868	Washington Lyons	Private.	A	61st U. S. colored troops.	......do......	20 00
6	Mar. 19, 1868	George Holloway				......do......	28 00
7	Mar. 19, 1868	Abraham Horton	Private.	K	11th U. S. colored troops.	......do......	25 00
8	Mar. 20, 1868	David Weston	Sergeant.	D	......do......	......do......	68 00
9	Mar. 20, 1868	Henry Branch	Corporal.	E	......do......	......do......	25 00
10	Mar. 20, 1868	Lewis Horton	Private.	B	......do......	......do......	25 00
11	Mar. 20, 1868	William Horton	Private.	F	......do......	......do......	28 00
12	Mar. 31, 1868	Nelson Adams	Private.	I	61st U. S. colored troops	......do......	63 00
	Total						463 00

In addition to the above I have also caused the following claim agents to refund to the parties whose names are given below the sums set opposite their respective names, which had also been stopped by the authorities at Washington, D. C., from the bounties of the claimants, upon the misrepresentation that the amount had been actually advanced to said claimants, as follows:

No.	Name of claim ag't.	Name of claimant.	Kind of claims.	Am't.
1	Moyers & Dedrick.	Alexander Naison, private Co. C 11th U. S. colored troops.	Arrears of pay and bounty.	$45 00
2	......do	Pleasant Gilmore, pioneer corps, 16th army corps....	........do	130 00
3	M. Combs, jr., & Co.	David Allen, sergeant Co. D 55th U. S. colored troops	........do	30 00
4	......do	Ruben Sikes, private Co. K U. S. colored troops.....	........do	15 00
5	......do	Mary Wood, mother of Charles Wood, private Co. M 3d U. S. colored heavy artillery.	........do	33 00
6	......do	John Ingerham, private Co. C 55th U. S. colored troops	........do	30 00
7	......do	Moses Pedan, private Co. A 55th U. S. colored troops.	........do	65 00
8	......do	Isam Strong, private Co. K 11th U. S. colored troops.	........do	30 00

* * * * * * * * *

Very respectfully, your obedient servant,
FRED S. PALMER,
Lieutenant Colonel and Sub-Assistant Commissioner.

Brevet Captain SAMUEL WALKER,
Acting Assistant Adjutant General, Nashville, Tennessee.

PALMER, F—CASE 4, No. 447.

BUREAU REFUGEES, FREEDMEN AND ABANDONED LANDS,
SUB-DISTRICT OF MEMPHIS,
Memphis, Tennessee, April 6, 1868.

GENERAL: I have the honor to state that in paying the bounties due discharged colored soldiers I met with two classes of cases which are a source of continued annoyance. They are, first, when the claimants deny the correctness of the amount stopped against them for advances made by their attorneys; and second, when they inform me that the amount of the stoppage is in accordance with their agreement with their attorneys, and that they are willing and desirous that the attorney should receive it, but that they never actually received the amount of money charged as advances, but had to borrow from the claim agents certain sums of money, and agreed with them that they would pay from twenty-five to one hundred and fifty per cent. interest (without regard to time) for the money, and that they had authorized the claim agents to stop out of their bounties not only the actual advance but the additional sum which they had agreed to allow in the shape of interest.

It has been my habit, when a case of either of these classes was brought to my attention, to have the claim agents here rectify the error by paying over to the claimants the difference between the amounts actually received and the amounts stopped from the bounties as advances. Please furnish me with instructions upon the following points: First. Shall I continue to rectify the errors which are brought to my attention by calling upon the claim agents to refund the money to the claimants, or shall I forward all such cases to you for settlement? Second. When a claimant informs me that the amount stopped as advances is in strict accordance with the understanding he had with his attorney when he borrowed the money from them, and that the amount embraces not only the money which he actually received from them, but also the interest or bonus which he was to pay them, shall I pass the account as correct, or shall I call upon the claim agents to refund the difference between the amount actually received by the claimant and the amount stopped as advances from his bounty?

Very respectfully, your obedient servant,
FRED. S. PALMER,
Lieutenant Colonel and Sub-Assistant Commissioner.

Brevet Brigadier General GEO. W. BALLOCH,
Chief Disbursing Officer, Washington, D. C.

PALMER, F—CASE 5.

[Reply.]

WAR DEPARTMENT,
BUREAU REFUGEES, FREEDMEN AND ABANDONED LANDS,
Washington, April 16, 1868.

GENERAL: The communication of Lieutenant Colonel Palmer, sub-assistant commissioner, Memphis, Tennessee, referred by you to this office, has been received.

I recommend that you instruct your agents, whose duty it is to pay the amount due claimants on certificates, that, whenever the amount claimed by attorneys or agents for advances made in money is greater than the amount actually received by the claimant, the agent withhold the payment of the amount claimed for advances and forward to this office the affidavit of the claimant of the actual amount he has received from his agents or attorney, and the time when he received it, together with such other evidence as he may be able to obtain, to show the facts in the case.

I am, general, very respectfully, your obedient servant,
A. P. HOWE,
Brevet Major General, in charge Claim Division.

General BALLOCH,
Chief Disbursing Officer, Freedmen's Bureau.

[Indorsement.]

WAR DEPARTMENT,
BUREAU REFUGEES, FREEDMEN AND ABANDONED LANDS,
Washington, April 16, 1868.

Respectfully referred to Lieutenant Colonel Frederick S. Palmer, with instructions to carry out the suggestions contained in the within letter of Brevet Major General A. P. Howe.

By command of Major General O. O. Howard, Commissioner:
GEO. W. BALLOCH,
Brevet Brigadier General and Chief Disbursing Officer.

PALMER, F—CASE 6, No. 552.

BUREAU REFUGEES, FREEDMEN AND ABANDONED LANDS,
SUB-DISTRICT OF MEMPHIS,
Memphis, Tennessee, April 24, 1868.

GENERAL: I have the honor, in obedience to Brevet Brigadier General Balloch's indorsement of the 16th instant on your communication to him of the same date, in reference to advances made by claim agents to their clients, to transmit herewith the affidavits of the following parties in cases where the amount claimed by the attorneys or agents for ad-

BOUNTIES TO COLORED SOLDIERS. 199

vances made in money is greater than the amount actually received by the claimants, (as per their sworn statements,) to wit:

Claim agents.	Name.	Rank.	Co.	Regiment.	Amount stopped for advances.	Amount actually received by claimant.
Moyers & Dedrick.	William Moody	Private.	E	11th U. S. colored troops	$50 00	$20 00
Do	Wm. Dandridge	Q.M.Serg.	B	3d U. S. colored heavy art'y.	50 00	20 00
Do	Cyrus Kimball	Sergeant.	F	11th U. S. colored troops	25 00	10 00
Do	Green Johnson	Artificer.	B	3d U. S. colored heavy art'y.	172 00	100 00
Do	John Dilliworth	Private.	H	55th U. S. colored troops	60 00	30 00
Do	Martha Hilton, wid. of Mathew Hilton.	..do	B	11th U. S. colored troops	65 00	40 00
Do	Mary Warren, wid. of Jos. Warren.	..do	B	..........do..........	60 00	40 00

Please inform me if communications from this office of this nature should in future be sent direct or through the office of the general claim agent at Nashville, Tennessee.
    Very respectfully, your obedient servant,
                FRED. S. PALMER,
          Lieutenant Colonel and Sub-Assistant Commissioner.
Bvt. Maj. Gen. A. P. HOWE, *Claim Division, Washington, D. C.*

PALMER, F—CASE 7, No. 601.
BUREAU REFUGEES, FREEDMEN AND ABANDONED LANDS,
                SUB-DISTRICT OF MEMPHIS,
                Memphis, Tennessee, May 7, 1868.

GENERAL: I have the honor, in obedience to Brevet Brigadier General Balloch's indorsement of the 16th of April on your communication to him of the same date, in reference to advances made by claim agents to their clients, to transmit herewith the affidavits of the following parties in cases where the amount claimed by the attorneys or agents for advances made in money is greater that the amount actually received by the claimants, (as per their sworn statements,) to wit:

Claim agents.	Name.	Rank.	Co.	Regiment.	Amount stopped for advances and fees.	Amount actually received by claimant.
M.Coombs,jr.& Co.	Alexander Alston	Private.	B	55th U. S. colored troops	$116 00	$58 00
Moyers & Dedrick	Warren Brown	Q.M.Sarg.	G	3d U. S. colored heavy art'y.	138 50	75 00
Do	John Buchanan	Private.	G	11th U. S. colored troops	38 50	10 00
M.Coombs,jr.& Co.	Humphrey Means	..do	E	61st U. S. colored troops	164 00	50 00
Do	Abraham Marsh	Corporal.	L	3d U. S. colored heavy art'y.	95 50	4 00
Do	Abraham Polk	Private.	G	11th U. S. colored troops	116 50	30 00
Moyers & Dedrick	Daniel Persons	..do	F	..........do..........	123 50	60 00
Do	Nice Ann Tansel, wid. of Moses Tansel.	Sergeant.	B	..........do..........	164 50	100 00

    Very respectfully, your obedient servant,
                FRED. S. PALMER,
          Lieutenant Colonel and Sub-Assistant Commissioner.
Bvt. Maj. Gen. A. P. HOWE, *Claim Division, Washington, D. C.*

BOUNTIES TO COLORED SOLDIERS.

PALMER, F—CASE 8, No. 695.

BUREAU REFUGEES, FREEDMEN AND ABANDONED LANDS,
SUB-DISTRICT OF MEMPHIS,
Memphis, Tennessee, May 28, 1868.

GENERAL: I have the honor, in obedience to Brevet Brigadier General Balloch's indorsement of the 11th of April, in your communication to him of the same date, in reference to advances made by claim agents to their clients, to transmit herewith the affidavits of the following parties in cases when the amount claimed by the attorneys or agents for advances made in money is greater than the amount actually received by the claimants, (as per their sworn statements,) to wit:

Claim agents.	Claimant's name.	Rank.	Co.	Regiment.	Amount stopped for advances and fees.	Amount actually received by claimant.
Frank Bras	Samuel Robinson	Private.	C	55th U. S. colored troops	$163 50	$50 00
Moyers & Dedrick	Peter Canady	Corporal.	H	11th U. S. colored troops	63 50	20 00
Frank Bras	Washington Conly	Private.	K	63d U. S. colored troops	53 00	25 00

Very respectfully, your obedient servant,
FRED. S. PALMER,
Lieutenant Colonel and Sub-Assistant Commissioner.
Brevet Major General A. P. HOWE,
Claim Division, Washington, D. C.

I certify the foregoing, as entered on pages numbered from 1 to 16 inclusive, are true copies, as taken from the records of the agent and disbursing officers of claims, Bureau of Refugees, Freedmen and Abandoned Lands, at Memphis, Tennessee, this day exhibited to me.

Given under my hand and seal at Memphis, Tennessee, this 22d day of January, 1870.
[SEAL.]
MARK J. EDWARDS,
U. S. Commissioner.

BUREAU REFUGEES, FREEDMEN AND ABANDONED LANDS,
Memphis, Tennessee, December 5, 1868.

GENERAL: I have the honor to submit the following report, in obedience to your indorsement of the 16th ultimo, upon Captain Parkinson's letter of September 28, 1868, to Brevet Major General M. C. Meigs, Quartermaster General United States Army, relative to frauds perpetrated upon the government and colored claimants for bounty and pension by claim agents of this city.

For the purpose of making my report as thorough as possible, I have divided the subject and considerations into three classes, as follows: 1st. Frauds upon the government in perfecting the claims for pension and bounty; 2d. Advances to claimants; and 3d. Pension claims for widows and orphans.

1st. *Frauds.*—There is no doubt in my mind but that a large number of claims for bounty are prosecuted and perfected by parties who have no legal right to the same, and especially is this the case where the applicants represent themselves to be the heirs of deceased soldiers. My attention has been called to this subject by the great difficulties which some of this class meet with in endeavoring to establish their identity as the heir of the deceased soldier, and in some cases their utter inability to do so when they present themselves at this office for the payment of the bounties which have been allowed them. In my opinion, during the first year or so after the bounty acts went into effect, the claims forwarded were, with perhaps a few exceptions, genuine. The claim agents, however, realizing what an immense field they had to operate in, making, of course, the most strenuous efforts to expand and increase their business generally, adopted the plan of paying hand money, of from one to five dollars, to parties who would bring to their office applicants for pension or bounty. Under this arrangement a corps of runners or solicitors for claims sprung into existence, some of whom soon discovered that, as their compensation depended altogether upon the number of claimants secured, it made but little difference to them whether the claim was a lawful one or not, provided they could produce the necessary witnesses to testify as to the identity of the claimant.

During the last year or two of the war, many companies had gotten up what were termed company records. These records embrace, among other things, the names and date of death of each soldier who died in the service from the date of the organization of the company up to the printing of the record. The runners referred to above, taking these records, set themselves to work hunting up parties who would file claims as the wives, children, fathers, mothers, brothers, or sisters of the deceased soldiers. This, of course, opened up comparatively a new field of operation for them, and their success can be judged from the fact that Mr. Reuben Daily, who I have been informed prosecutes his claims through the office of Tucker & Sells, of Washington, D. C., informs me that he went into the claim business on the 25th day of June, 1868, and that he has already forwarded over fourteen hundred claims, as follows: About five hundred claims for widows' bounties; four hundred claims for fathers, brothers, and sisters' bounty, and five hundred claims for widows' pensions, and less than one hundred claims filed by the soldiers themselves. Mr. Dailey has been in the habit of paying $1 50 hand money to the runners who brought the claimants to his office. He has undoubtedly done a larger business in this line, since he commenced operations, than any other claim agent in the city, yet I believe nearly every one has been engaged in it to a greater or less extent. Whether it was the deliberate intention of the claim agents to be parties to these frauds upon the government I am unable to state, but I do believe that they exhibited a carelessness in taking some classes of claims which justly lay them open to suspicions. I have been informed by the deputy clerk of the law court of Memphis, that a runner for Moyers & Dedrick had brought to his office parties to be sworn in widows' claims, in which the widows had forgotten the names of their deceased husbands, and that in consequence thereof he had refused to administer the oath. Mr. Frank Bras, a United States commissioner, also informs me that he met with similar cases. These parties who pick up this class of claims are never at a loss to find witnesses who will readily testify to any circumstance which may be necessary to make out the claims. In regard to the mode of taking the affidavits of claimants, as practiced at the office of Moyers & Dedrick, I would state that on the 23d day of March, 1868, Mr. Thomas L. Dean, a clerk in their office, was appointed a special deputy clerk of the circuit court of Shelby County, by M. D. L. Stewart, clerk of said court, "to administer oaths to applicants and witnesses to claims against the government of the United States, and all other oaths necessary in and about the collection of the same." A copy of said appointment is herewith inclosed. This appointment has never as yet been revoked. The manner of administering oaths under it was, for Mr. Dean to swear the parties at the office of Moyers & Dedrick, and then for Mr. Stewart to sign the certificates, certifying that the parties had personally appeared before him, Stewart, whereas, in fact, in many instances he had not seen the parties at all. Mr. Dedrick, of the firm of Moyers & Dedrick, informed me that for some time past Mr. Dean had only administered the oath to applicants in exceptional cases, when it was inconvenient for them to appear before Mr. Stewart.

2. *Advances.*—This has been and is a source of immense revenue to claim agents, and I have but little faith in the ability of any one to entirely correct the abuse. My observation has led me to believe that a large majority of claimants will borrow money on their claims, and pay from fifty to one hundred and fifty per cent. interest for the use of it, without any reference as to the length of time they have had the money. In the payment of bounties, in which advances had been stopped on the affidavit of the attorneys of record, as required by circular No. 19, Commissioner's office, series 1867, it was found that claim agents were not only having the money actually advanced to claimants stopped from the bounties, but an additional sum for interest, in some cases as high as one hundred and fifty per cent. on money which had been loaned thirty or sixty days. For instance, when ten dollars had been advanced, twenty-five had been collected through the bureau at Washington. And again, instances had occurred where sums of money had been stopped as advances, amounting to one and two hundred dollars, when in fact no advance had been made whatever. Circular No. 1, Commissioner's office, current series, requiring the claimant to appear before an agent of the bureau, and acknowledge the receipt of the advance, was for a time an improvement on the other system; yet I am satisfied that at the present time it is more objectionable than the other. So anxious are claimants to borrow money on their claims that many of them have, in my opinion, called at this office and informed me that they had larger sums of money advanced to them than they had actually received, thereby assisting the claim agents to collect large sums through the bureau for interest on the money advanced. Moyers & Dedrick are advancing heavily to their clients, and part of such advances are made in the following manner: A person by the name of G. C. Moyers, a brother of Mr. Moyers of the firm of Moyers & Dedrick, claim agents, is the ostensible proprietor of a clothing store, located on the floor underneath their office. When a claimant desires to receive an advance of clothing he makes his purchase at this store; goes up stairs, receiving the amount of the bill in cash from Moyers & Dedrick, and after paying the same to the storekeeper below, calls at my office and acknowledges to have received from Moyers & Dedrick so much money as an advance on his bounty. I have been of the opinion that Moyers & Dedrick were partners in this store, which, however, they deny. They evidently are interested either in the store itself, or receive a per cent. for the collections which are thus made through the bureau. The most objectionable feature, however, to claimants acknowledging the receipt of advances from their attorneys before an agent of the bureau is that it offers to a dishonest agent a rare opportunity and great inducement, by collusion with the claim agents, to swindle the claimants; while an honest person will always be subjected to the suspicion of being interested in the advances certified to by him.

The amount of advances certified to by me under circular No. 1, Circular Orders, current series, from April 21st to date, amounts to over $13,000, of which amount $7,801 was certified to in the months of October and November. In addition to the advances collected at Washington, claim agents and others loan money to claimants at large rates of interest, from fifty to one hundred per cent., and collect it from them after they have been paid their bounties. Daily a large number of persons hover around my office for the purpose of making such collections as soon as the parties are paid off and fairly outside. Under the present system of the claim agents retaining the discharge papers when they return the certificates to General Howard, they are, of course, duly notified when the claimants are to be paid by my sending to their offices for the discharge, which is necessary for me to have in identifying the soldiers.

3d. *Pension claims.*—I have from time to time been called upon by widows for assistance in obtaining from claim agents their pension certificates, which they inform me the claim agents refuse to give up. My demands have always been complied with, except in a few instances, where the claimant had received an advance, and the agent objected to surrendering the certificate until the advance had been refunded. I am satisfied that gross frauds are sometimes perpetrated by claim agents upon the pension clients. It is in some cases almost impossible for a pensioner to get her money from her attorney until months after he has received it from the pension agent. The fees sometimes charged are exorbitant, and especially is this the case with the firm of M. Coombs, jr., & Co. Two cases of this class have been brought to my knowledge. That of Julia Ann Granberry, and Margaret Granberry, two widows' claims for pension, in which Coombs charged each of these parties $69 13 for collecting their pension certificates, $10 of which he claimed as his legal fee, and the other $59 13 as the costs of the affidavits which were taken in the case. (?) I never knew of a single case in which Coombs did not, to a greater or less extent, swindle the pensioner out of some of the money which passed through his hands. In fact, I have but very little confidence in the entire set of claim agents, and do not believe that any of them handle the pensioner's money simply for the fee allowed by law. In regard to the number of pension certificates in the hands of Moyers & Dedrick, I would state that Mr. Dedrick informed me that they had in their office the certificates of ninety-two colored pensioners, which had been left with them for safe keeping, and on which they collected the semi-annual payments for the pensioners. That the total number of pension certificates collected by them was two hundred and forty-nine, of which one hundred and fifty-one were collected through their office in this city, and the balance through their offices at Vicksburg, Natchez, and New Orleans. They offered to let me look over the books of their house for the purpose of verifying their statement, but as it would have necessitated the looking over a list of nine or ten thousand claims, I did not deem it necessary.

I do not believe that the abuses referred to in the foregoing can be completely eradicated, but I do believe that they could, by taking the proper action, be somewhat abated, and would respectfully suggest the following plan to accomplish that object:

First. By the employment of able counsel to prosecute all parties connected with the frauds referred to above.

Second. By the bureau refusing to further acknowledge advances made by claim agents to their clients.

Third. By requiring claim agents to return to General Howard with certificates the discharge paper of the soldier, and,

Fourth. By an act of Congress requiring the pension certificates to be delivered to the pensioners through the bureau, in the same manner as bounty money is now paid.

The communication of Captain Parkinson, referred by you to me, is returned herewith.

I am, general, very respectfully, your obedient servant,
FRED. S. PALMER,
Disbursing Officer of Claims.

Brevet Brigadier General F. D. SEWELL,
Acting Assistant Adjutant General, Washington, D. C.

I certify the foregoing, as entered on pages numbered from 1 to 12, inclusive, are true copies, as taken from the records of the agent and disbursing officer of claims, Bureau Refugees, Freedmen and Abandoned Lands, at Memphis, Tennessee, this day exhibited to me.

Given under my hand and seal at Memphis, Tennessee, this 22d day of January, 1870.

[SEAL.] MARK EDWARDS,
U. S. Commissioner.

PALMER, G.

BUREAU REFUGEES, FREEDMEN AND ABANDONED LANDS,
OFFICE DISBURSING OFFICER OF CLAIMS,
Memphis, Tennessee, January 27, 1870.

CAPTAIN: I have the honor, in accordance with the request made by the president of your commission, to transmit herewith copies of papers relating to the following cases, in which claim agents received advanced fees from claimants when they put in their claims, and afterward again collected full fees when the claim was allowed, viz: Lisha Robinson, private Company C Sixty-first United States colored troops; George Holland, sergeant Company G Fifty-fifth United States colored troops; Frederick Towles, private Company D Fifty-ninth United States colored troops. I also send, as directed, copies of my letter and the affidavit in the case of Emily Stanley, a fraudulent pension claim.

This completes, I believe, the list of copies from the records of this office asked for by your commission.

Very respectfully, your obedient servant,
FRED. S. PALMER,
Disbursing Officer of Claims.

Captain J. A. SLADEN,
Recorder Military Commission,
Bureau R., F. and A. L., Washington, D. C.

PALMER, G—CASE 1, No. 496.

BUREAU REFUGEES, FREEDMEN AND ABANDONED LANDS,
SUB-DISTRICT OF MEMPHIS,
Memphis, Tennessee, April 13, 1868.

GENERAL: I have the honor to state that on the 18th day of March I paid Lisha Robinson, late private Company C Sixty-first United States colored troops, his bounty money. There was stopped for fees

and advances the sum of $75 50. Inclosed you will find the affidavit of Robinson, together with that of James Falls, late private Company C Sixty-first United States colored troops, in which they state that Robinson paid his attorney, M. Coombs, jr., & Co., $11 in the month of January, 1866, and $5 in January, 1867, as his fees for the prosecuting of his claim. Can not M. Coombs, jr., be made to refund this money?
Very respectfully, your obedient servant,
FRED. S. PALMER,
Lieutenant Colonel and Sub-Assistant Commissioner.
Brevet Brigadier General GEO. W. BALLOCH,
Chief Disbursing Officer, Washington, D. C.

I certify that the above is a true copy, as taken from the records of the agent and disbursing officer of claims Bureau Refugees, Freedmen and Abandoned Lands, at Memphis, Tennessee, this day exhibited to me.

Given under my hand and seal at Memphis, Tennessee, this 24th day of January, 1870.

[SEAL.] MARK EDWARDS,
U. S. Commissioner.

BUREAU REFUGEES, FREEDMEN AND ABANDONED LANDS,
Memphis, Tennessee, January 26, 1870.

In the case of Lisha Robinson, private Company C Sixty-first United States colored troops, I received May 13, 1868, of M. Coombs, jr., & Co., the sum of $11. Coombs stated that his books showed that he had received but $11 from Robinson, and therefore refused to refund the other $5 claimed by Robinson.

FRED. S. PALMER,
Disbursing Officer of Claims.

PALMER, G—CASE 2, No. 1054.

BUREAU REFUGEES, FREEDMEN AND ABANDONED LANDS,
SUB-DISTRICT OF MEMPHIS,
Memphis, Tennessee, August 27, 1868.

GENERAL: I have the honor to state that on the 26th instant I paid the bounty money due George Holland, late a sergeant in Company G Fifty-fifth United States colored troops, amounting to $231 50. There had been stopped for attorney's fees the sum of $14. Holland states that he paid his attorneys, M. Coombs, jr., & Co., of this city, the sum of $12 when he put his claim in their hands for collection, June 13, 1866, as advanced fees. Inclosed you will find Holland's affidavit to that effect; also the affidavits of Alvin Drissel and George Lane, who claim to have been present at the time. I directed Holland to call on Mr. Coombs and ask him to refund that money, which he stated he did, but that Coombs refused.

Cannot Coombs be compelled to refund the amount through the department at Washington?

Very respectfully, your obedient servant,
FRED. S. PALMER,
Lieutenant Colonel and Sub-Assistant Commissioner.
Brevet Brigadier General GEO. W. BALLOCH,
Chief Disbursing Officer, Washington, D. C.

I certify that the above is a true copy as taken from the records of the agent and disbursing officer of claims, Bureau Refugees, Freedmen and Abandoned Lands, at Memphis, Tennessee, exhibited to me this day.

Given under my hand and seal at Memphis, Tennessee, this 24th day of January, 1870.

[SEAL.]   MARK EDWARDS,
U. S. Commissioner.

BUREAU REFUGEES, FREEDMEN AND ABANDONED LANDS,
Memphis, Tennessee January 26, 1870.

In the case of George Holland, sergeant Company G Fifty-fifth United States colored troops, I received from William P. Drew, esq., chief claim division, Washington, D. C., October 6, 1868, the sum of $12, refunded by B. D. Hyam, the Washington agent of M. Coombs, jr., & Co., of this city.

                               FRED. S. PALMER,
Disbursing Officer of Claims.

PALMER, G—CASE 3, No. 415.

BUREAU REFUGEES, FREEDMEN AND ABANDONED LANDS,
OFFICE DISBURSING OFFICER OF CLAIMS,
Memphis, Tennessee, June 4, 1869.

SIR: I have the honor to state that Frederick Towles, late private Company D Fifty-ninth United States colored troops, called at this office yesterday and signed the vouchers for his claim, which was allowed per certificate No. 510,629 for $75 26. There was stopped for attorney fees $7 50, and for notarial fees $7 50; total $15. Towles states that when he put in his claim with his attorneys, Messrs. M. Coombs, jr., & Co., in 1865, he paid them advanced fees amounting to $8, and that he also paid at the same time $1 75 notarial fees. Inclosed please find his affidavit corroborated by that of Henry Harris, of the same regiment, who swears that he was present and saw Towles pay the money as claimed by him. I would respectfully recommend that the attorney be made to refund the advance obtained from Towles.

I am, sir, very respectfully, your obedient servant,

                               FRED. S. PALMER,
Disbursing Officer of Claims.

WILLIAM P. DREW, Esq.,
Chief Claim Division, Washington, D. C.

I certify that the above is a true copy as taken from the records of the office of the agent and disbursing officer of claims, Bureau Refugees, Freedmen and Abandoned Lands, this day exhibited to me at Memphis, Tennessee.

Given under my hand and seal at Memphis, Tennessee, this 27th day of January, 1870.

[SEAL.]   MARK EDWARDS,
U. S. Commissioner.

BUREAU REFUGEES, FREEDMEN AND ABANDONED LANDS,
Memphis, Tennessee, January 27, 1870.

In the case of Frederick Towles, private Company D Fifty-ninth United States colored troops, I received June 26, 1869, from William

P. Drew, esq., chief claim division, Washington, D. C., the sum of $9 75, refunded by B. D. Hyam, the Washington attorney of M. Coombs, jr., & Co., of this city.

FRED. S. PALMER,
Disbursing Officer of Claims.

PALMER, G—CASE 4.

BUREAU REFUGEES, FREEDMEN AND ABANDONED LANDS,
OFFICE DISBURSING OFFICER OF CLAIMS,
Memphis, Tennessee, April 1, 1869.

GENERAL: I have the honor to state that on the 13th day of March, A. D. 1869, I paid Emily, widow of Jacob Stanley, late private Company D Fifty-ninth United States colored troops, the bounty which had been allowed him, amounting to $242 46, and that yesterday she called again at this office for another bounty which she claims is due her as the widow of Granville Elliott, late private Company A Fifty-ninth United States colored troops. She also stated that she had made application for pension as the widow of said Jacob Stanley; that Stanley was her first husband, and died in the service, and that about six months after his death she married said Elliott; that John Ingalls, the claim agent who got her to apply for said pension, knew at the time that she had been living with the said Elliott as his wife; in fact she herself told him that said Elliott was her husband, and that she had applied for bounty as his widow.

Your attention is invited to the inclosed statement of the case, sworn to before a United States commissioner. There is undoubtedly fraud in this claim, and the evidence goes to show that the claim agent must have been cognizant of it. Emily has identified herself at this office as the widow of said Jacob Stanley, but undoubtedly ignored her subsequent marriage with Granville Elliott in her application for pension money, but the records of the Freedmen's Bank here show that Ingalls has collected through it two of her pension checks, as follows: March 17, 1868, $53 47; September 14, 1868, $47 60.

Very respectfully, your obedient servant,

FRED. S. PALMER,
Disbursing Officer of Claims.

Brevet Brigadier General GEO. W. BALLOCH,
*Chief Disbursing Officer Bureau of R., F.
and A. L., Washington, D. C.*

UNITED STATES OF AMERICA, *District of West Tennessee, ss:*

On this 31st day of March, 1869, before me, a United States commissioner in and for the district aforesaid, personally appeared Emily Elliott, of the city of Memphis, State of Tennessee, who, being duly sworn according to law, deposes and says that she was married to Jacob Stanley, late private Company D Fifty-ninth regiment United States colored troops, on the plantation of her former owner, John Stanley, in Fayette County, Tennessee, about fifteen years before Jacob Stanley went into the army; that she lived with him in slavery times as his wife from the time she was married until he left the plantation and went to the federal army; that she was informed that said Jacob Stanley died at Corinth, Illinois, in the fall of 1863; that in the month of April, 1864, she was again married at Memphis, Tennessee, by the chaplain of the Fifty-ninth United States colored troops, to a man by the name of Granville

Elliott, who was a private in Company A of the Fifty-ninth United States colored troops; that she lived with said Granville Elliott as his wife from that time up to the date of his death, in September, 1866; that in the month of March, 1867, she put in with McAllister & Punnell, claim agents, her claim for bounty as the widow of said Granville Elliott, deceased; that in the month of July, 1867, she put in with Dr. John Ingalls, claim agent, her claim for bounty as the widow of said Jacob Stanley, deceased; that on the 13th day of March, 1869, she was paid by Fred. S. Palmer, disbursing officer of claims Bureau of Refugees, Freedmen and Abandoned Lands, the bounty due on account of the services of her husband, Jacob Stanley, deceased, late private Company D Fifty-ninth United States colored troops, amounting to $242 46; that in the month of July, 1867, at the time she put in her claim with Dr. Ingalls for bounty, she also put in with him her claim for pension as the widow of said Jacob Stanley, late private Company D Fifty-ninth United States colored troops; that she has never been paid by said Ingalls any money on account of her pension, and that the only money that she ever received from him was $2, which he loaned her last fall; that the said John Ingalls was surgeon of the Fifty-ninth regiment United States colored troops; that she was well acquainted with him in the regiment; that she was said Ingalls's washerwoman for about one year during the war, and that said Ingalls was her family physician after said Granville Elliott was mustered out of service; that she is certain that said Ingalls must have known that Granville Elliott was her husband; that she is certain that she has told him that she and said Granville Elliott had been married before she put in her claim for the pension as widow of said Jacob Stanley; that she put in her claim for pension at the advice of said Ingalls.

her
EMILY + ELLIOTT.
mark.

Witnesses:
  FRED. S. PALMER,
  A. T. CREGER.

Subscribed and sworn to before me this 31st day of March, 1869, at Memphis, Tennessee.
  [SEAL.]   ISAAC MORRISON,
                         U. S. Commissioner.

I certify that the above is a true copy of the original affidavit exhibited to me this day. Given under my hand and seal, at Memphis, Tennessee, this 26th day of January, 1870.
  [SEAL.]   MARK EDWARDS,
                         U. S. Commissioner.

DEPARTMENT OF THE INTERIOR,
Pension Office, Washington, D. C., April 14, 1869.

SIR: I have before me a paper purporting to be the statement under oath of Emily Elliott, who, as Emily Stanley, has been granted a pension. The paper demonstrates that fraud upon this office has been committed, and with the knowledge of John Ingalls, in whose handwriting the claim, and evidence in support thereof, really is. The allegations therefore are, that John Ingalls has allowed Emily Elliott to apply for and receive a pension, as widow of Jacob Stanley, which is untrue. Another allegation is that the same attorney has received $96 on vouchers signed by Emily Stanley, and has retained the money. I therefore submit all the inclosed papers, the claim itself, and the statement of the person pensioned, and ask that you at once cause the arrest of John Ingalls, charging him with fraud upon the government. I invite your attention to the act of April 5, 1866, page 12, chapter 24, section 1, Statutes at Large, first session thirty-ninth Congress, taking cognizance of the false claim, and papers in support of the same.

I also invite your attention to the twelfth and thirteenth sections of the act of July 4, 1864, page 389, punishing any agent or attorney wrongfully retaining a part or the whole of any money due a pensioner.

I ask that you bring to bear, in the prosecution of the party accused, all that ability and zeal for which I am advised you are in no small degree entitled to credit, to the end that the interests of the government may secure complete and speedy protection in the premises.

Any aid I may be able to render you in pursuing the legal proceedings referred to be pleased to command at pleasure.

I have the honor to be very respectfully,

CHAS. C. COX,
Commissioner.

Hon. J. W. PURVEYANCE,
United States Attorney, Memphis, Tennessee.

BUREAU REFUGEES, FREEDMEN AND ABANDONED LANDS,
OFFICE DISBURSING OFFICER OF CLAIMS,
Memphis, Tennessee, April 1, 1869.

GENERAL: I have the honor to state that on the 13th day of March, 1869, I paid Emily, widow of Jacob Stanley, late private Company D Fifty-ninth United States colored troops, the bounty which had been allowed her, amounting to $242 46, and that yesterday she called again at this office for another bounty, which she claims is due her as the widow of Granville Elliot, late Company H Fifty-ninth United States colored troops. She also stated that she had made application for pension as the widow of said Jacob Stanley; that Stanley was her first husband and died in the service, and that about six months after his death she married said Elliot; that John Ingalls, the claim agent, who got her to apply for said pension, knew at the time that she had been living with said Elliot as his wife; in fact, that she herself told him that said Elliot was her husband, and that she had applied for bounty as his widow. Your attention is invited to inclosed statement of the case, sworn to by her before a United States commissioner. There is undoubtedly fraud in this claim for pension, and the evidence goes to show that the claim agent must have been cognizant of it. Emily has identified herself at this office as the widow of said Jacob Stanley, but undoubtedly ignored her subsequent marriage with Granville Elliot in her application for pension. The pensioner swears that she has never received any pension money, but the records of the Freedmen's Bank here show that Ingalls has collected through it two of her pension checks, as follows: March 17, 1868, $53 47; September 14, 1868, $47 60.

Very respectfully, your obedient servant,

FRED. S. PALMER,
Disbursing Officer of Claims.

Brevet Brigadier General GEO. W. BALLOCH,
*Chief Disbursing Officer, Bureau R., F.
and A. L., Washington, D. C.*

BOUNTIES TO COLORED SOLDIERS.

I certify that the within, and indorsements hereon, is a true copy of the original this day exhibited to me by Fred. S. Palmer, agent and disbursing officer of claims, Bureau Refugees, Freedmen and Abandoned Lands.

Given under my hand and seal at Memphis, Tennessee, this 26th day of January, 1870.

[SEAL.]   MARK EDWARDS,
U. S. Commissioner.

[Indorsements.]

APRIL 5, 1869.

Respectfully referred to Mr. Drew, chief of the claim division.
GEO. W. BALLOCH,
Brevet Brigadier General and Chief Disbursing Officer.

WAR DEPARTMENT, BUREAU REFUGEES, FREEDMEN
AND ABANDONED LANDS, CLAIM DIVISION,
Washington, D. C., April 10, 1869.

Respectfully forwarded to Hon. C. C. Cox, Commissioner of Pensions, for his information.

By order of Brevet Major General O. O. Howard, Commissioner &c.
WILLIAM P. DREW,
Agent Bureau Refugees, Freedmen, and Abandoned Lands,
Chief of Claim Division.

VARIOUS COMMUNICATIONS REFERRED TO THE COMMISSION FROM THE BUREAU REFUGEES, FREEDMEN AND ABANDONED LANDS.

FAYETTEVILLE, TENNESSEE,
April 25, 1869.

SIR: The inclosed slip was cut from the Lincoln County News, of yesterday's date, a newspaper printed in this place. On last evening the inquiry was made in my presence of the clerk of the county court, if he had seen the article in the newspaper, and if so, was it correct. He said the statement was correctly stated; that the editor of the News had submitted the article to him before it was put in type. He said that Cloon had requested him to sign and affix his official (?) to a number of blanks, to be filled up by him, Cloon, as he pleased, and that he, Cloon, would pay for them all. Cloon, as I understand, is here proposing to purchase claims, principally of negroes against the United States, for bounty, back pay, and pensions, and all other claims against the government. If you desire you can address E. P. Reynolds, clerk of the county court, who is a radical republican of the strictest sect.

Very respectfully,
G. W. JONES.

General M. C. MEIGS,
Quartermaster General.

True copy:

JAMES A. EKIN,
Deputy Quartermaster General, United States Army.

[Indorsement.]

ADJUTANT GENERAL'S OFFICE,
Washington, May 12, 1869.

Official copy respectfully referred to Brevet Major General O. O. Howard, Commissioner Freedmen's Bureau, for his information.

E. D. TOWNSEND,
Adjutant General.

[Extract from local column of the Lincoln County News, of Saturday morning, April 24, 1869.]

DECIDEDLY COOL.

A rumor that has caused no little indignation with the citizens of our town, has been current upon the streets for a day or two past, to the effect that an effort had been made to bribe our county clerk to issue a lot of blank government claims, with his signature and county seal attached.

We called upon Mr. Reynolds to get the facts, and learn that a Mr. Cloon, a claim agent, who has located here, did call upon and propose to him to sign and seal some sixty or eighty blank government claims, and turn them over to be filled as he (Mr. Cloon) should see fit, proposing to pay the fees on them at once. It was decidedly a cool proposition, and one that justly deserves and calls forth the indignation of every honest, law-abiding man.

The times for such games have "played," and if Mr. Cloon desires to ply his vocation among us, let him do it in an honorable way.

For the present we would advise our friends to place their claims in the hands of Captain J. W. Newman, who is a regular claim agent, fully prepared, a resident of our town, and a responsible man.

[Indorsements.]

WASHINGTON, D. C., *May 12, 1869.*

E. D. Townsend, Adjutant General, refers copy of communication of G. W. Jones, of Fayetteville, Tennessee, to Quartermaster General, inclosing copy of newspaper slip, stating that a Mr. Cloon, claim agent, tried to induce the county clerk to sign and seal sixty or eighty government claims, to be filled at his (Cloon's) pleasure, evidently an attempt at fraud. States that this man has been purchasing bounty claims from negroes in that vicinity, &c., &c.

WAR DEPARTMENT,
BUREAU REFUGEES, FREEDMEN AND ABANDONED LANDS,
Washington, May 15, 1869.

Respectfully referred to William P. Drew, chief of claim division.
By order of Brevet Major General Howard.

E. WHITTLESEY,
Assistant Acting Adjutant General.

OFFICE AGENT AND DISBURSING OFFICER,
BUREAU REFUGEES, FREEDMEN AND ABANDONED LANDS,
Huntsville, Alabama, May 18, 1869.

GENERAL: Do I send my vouchers to you direct or to Colonel Beecher? What reports will I have to make out? I suppose that I will have the same duties with the schools.

There is a claim agent, M. M. Cloon, whose headquarters are at Pulaski, Tennessee; he is doing a land office business; has flaming circulars out; now is at Athens, Alabama, where he is calling the colored people, saying that he can get their money in three or five weeks, and they are going to him from all parts of the country. Some who have made application through this office have been here to have their claims transferred into his hands, saying he can get it sooner.

Some parties in Athens write me that he says he is an agent of the government, and can get claims paid sooner than any one else; has the inside track; receives a salary of two hundred dollars per month from the government. I wrote to the agent in Nashville about him and he says that he thinks he is one who wants watching.

He wrote me to send him some discharges I had. I replied I would not surrender them but to the parties on their personal application, and he wrote an insolent reply.

He is doing great damage to the colored people, so parties report, by calling them to him as he does.

I would like to have his status, so I can satisfy the parties whose claims were forwarded through this office.

I send you his circular, just received.

Respectfully, your obedient servant,
JOHN H. WAGER,
Agent and Disbursing Officer.

Brevet Brigadier General GEO. W. BALLOCH,
Chief Disbursing Officer, Washington, D. C.

[Indorsements.]

OFFICE CHIEF DISBURSING OFFICER,
BUREAU REFUGEES, FREEDMEN AND ABANDONED LANDS,
May 21, 1869.

Respectfully referred to Mr. W. P. Drew, chief of claim division.
GEO. W. BALLOCH,
Brevet Brigadier General and Chief Disbursing Officer.

WAR DEPARTMENT, BUREAU REFUGEES, FREEDMEN
AND ABANDONED LANDS, CLAIM DIVISION,
Washington, May 24, 1869.

Respectfully referred to Hon. E. B. French, Second Auditor United States Treasury, (in connection with a communication from the Adjutant General United States Army, in regard to the same person,) with request for his advice and co-operation, in order if possible to effectually prevent further mischief by Mr. Cloon. He is believed to be a correspondent of Messrs. O'Neill and Dufour, and of other attorneys of record.

Please return these papers with advice.

By order of Brevet Major General O. O. Howard, Commissioner, &c.
WILLIAM P. DREW,
Agent Bureau Refugees, Freedmen and Abandoned Lands,
Chief of Claim Division.

SECOND AUDITOR'S OFFICE, *May 26, 1869.*

Respectfully returned to William P. Drew, esq., chief claim division. M. M. Cloon is not a licensed agent. He will be suspended from the time he files his license, in case he ever files one.

E. B. FRENCH, *Auditor,*
By C. H. M.

BOUNTIES TO COLORED SOLDIERS.

M. M. CLOON'S CLAIM AGENCY AND UNITED STATES COLLECTING OFFICE.

I hereby inform the public generally that I will have open, for a few months, an office in this town, (the county seat of this county,) where all persons, both white and colored, having claims of any kind against the United States government, are requested to appear, and I will promptly collect for them all such legitimate claims; and also I will use every effort to procure the speedy settlement of all unsettled claims which have been filed through other agents or attorneys.

Having given my whole attention to the claim business for several years past, I flatter myself that my experience enables me to judge as to the practicability of collecting any claim offered, and, if just, to collect it in the shortest possible time. *And furthermore, from a personal and very intimate acquaintance with several of the accounting officers in the respective departments where these claims are settled, combined with other matters, gives me all the facilities necessary to insure a speedy and prompt settlement of all claims intrusted to my care.*

The collection of all legitimate claims upon the government is not only of importance to the individual parties directly interested, but it is of vital importance to the county at large where such parties reside, because it brings money into the county, to be spent with the merchant, the mechanic, the farmer, and people of all other branches of business, and thereby it revives trade, rewards industry, and promotes prosperity, which is beneficial to all classes; and whereas the wealthier the county the more prosperous are its citizens, therefore everybody should be more or less interested in this matter, and should advise all persons having claims on the government to come to our office. I would here respectfully remark that some of the more enlightened portion of the community often inform the uneducated that their claims cannot be collected, or that the government will not pay them. Such remarks are not only unjustifiable and injurious to the legitimate claimant, but it is also injurious to the party who gives such information, and to the county at large, for reasons as above specified, and because the government is daily paying just claims, and will so continue until all are paid; therefore please say not to your neighbors that their claims cannot be collected, but rather urge them to come to our office and let us be the judges as to the genuineness of their claims. The want of confidence in the government by those who conceive that their claims will not be paid, has arisen from the fact that they trusted their claims for collection to men who knew little or nothing of claim business; consequently the claims were presented incomplete, and are now suspended for some additional evidence, or correction of some paper, in the departments; hence the government cannot pay such claims until the required evidence is furnished. We are ready to furnish such evidence and secure the prompt payment of all such claims.

I annex hereto a few of the many claims we are daily collecting:

Bounty and arrears of pay for discharged soldiers, both white and colored.

Extra bounty for soldiers who served two or three years, or were discharged on account of wounds received, or disease contracted, in the army.

Bounty for veteran soldiers who served three years, and were mustered in as "recruits," they having previously served for nine months or more in some other organization, and have received less than four hundred dollars bounty for their last service.

Veteran bounty for non-commissioned officers who were mustered out as supernumeraries, on consolidation.

Bounty for soldiers discharged for disability, or otherwise honorably discharged, without bounty.

Commutation for rations for soldiers who were prisoners of war.

Claims for quartermaster and commissary stores, such as horses, mules, hogs, corn, fodder, &c., which were taken or destroyed by the army, whether receipted for or not.

Claims for reimbursement for subsistence and transportation of recruits prior to their being mustered in, and other necessary expenses incident to the recruiting service.

Certificates of non-indebtedness procured for officers in a short time, on which they can draw their arrears of pay.

Pay will be had for horses and equipage lost in the service.

Pay collected for officers who were not properly mustered; will procure their muster back, and collect pay from the date on which they received their commission and went on duty in new grade.

Extra pay (three months) collected for officers who were in the service April 9, 1865, and in commission on or before March 3, 1865.

The following classes of claims are very important:

Pensions procured for officers and soldiers generally who were disabled by wounds or disease contracted in the service.

Pensions procured for widows whose husbands died of wounds or of disease contracted in the service; also, a pension of two dollars a month for each child surviving, under sixteen years of age, of the deceased soldier.

Pensions procured for the father or mother of any deceased soldier who, previous to his death, contributed to their support.

Pensions procured for the brothers and sisters of a deceased soldier who were dependent on him, partly or wholly, for support, before his death.

By recent acts of Congress, increased rates of pensions are granted to all persons who have been previously pensioned; and the widows of revolutionary soldiers and others, drawing a pension of less than eight dollars a month, are now entitled to that amount, and are also entitled to a pension of two dollars a month for each of the surviving children under sixteen years of age of the person on whose account the pension was granted.

Loyal pensioners who, by reason of the late war, were dropped from the pension rolls, can now be restored by calling at our office.

Premiums collected for presenting recruits at general rendezvous in 1864. Soldiers and others who presented recruits early in 1864, and have not been paid premiums therefor, will do well to address us, stating names, &c., of recruits.

Land warrants for one hundred and sixty acres of land will be procured for any person (or their heirs, if they be dead) who served in the United States service fifteen days or more previous to 1856, or were engaged in one battle (even without being mustered in) in any of the revolutionary wars; that is to say, any war from the Revolution to the Mexican. Those, or their heirs, who have got eighty acres, are entitled to eighty more.

Many claims of the above class are suspended for one thing or another. We attend to the completion of such claims, as well as to procuring those not yet presented. Disloyalty does not debar anybody of a right to a land warrant, provided they are otherwise entitled to it.

Bounty and other allowances are paid to the heirs of deceased soldiers in the following order: First, to his widow; if no widow survives, then

BOUNTIES TO COLORED SOLDIERS.

to his children; if no children, then to his father and mother; if no father or mother, then to his brothers and sisters. The children of deceased soldiers, whose mothers have died or remarried, will have to procure a guardian, who will draw for them their bounty and pension. Those widows of deceased soldiers who have remarried may have whom they please appointed guardians for their children; a widow may have herself appointed guardian, or any other person, provided they are otherwise qualified. It is always more economical to have, if possible, some member of the family appointed guardian, as the pension and any other moneys which the widow deprived herself of by having remarried, is paid to her children through their appointed guardian; however, the guardian is always firmly bound for the safety of the money. A widow does not deprive herself of bounty by having remarried, whether she has again married or not since the death of her husband on whose account the bounty is granted; she is still entitled to all the original bounty, and if she did not remarry prior to the 28th of July, 1866, she is also entitled to the additional bounty; and furthermore she is entitled to a pension of eight dollars a month from the date of her husband's death up to the date of her remarriage, providing no legitimate children of theirs under sixteen years of age are living. What a widow loses by her death or remarriage, is paid her minor children through their guardian.

Soldiers, and the widows, fathers and mothers, and brothers and sisters of deceased soldiers, together with all persons having claims on the government, of any of the above-described classes, or claims not herein named, should come to our office forthwith, as the sooner all claims are filed the sooner will they be paid; and furthermore, if you lose the present opportunity you may lose the best and only opportunity you will ever have again of having your claims collected. Whatever work you may be at when you receive this information, lay it aside, and come and have your claims attended to. Your work cannot be so very important that you cannot absent yourself from it for a few hours, and in those few hours you may make more money, by having your claims attended to, than if you worked at your regular business for twenty years. Particularly the colored soldiers, and the widows of deceased colored soldiers, are very slow about having such matters attended to. Such persons need what the government owes them much more than any others, and therefore they should be more eager to have their claims attended to; besides, if a widow, or any other person entitled to a pension, does not apply for it within five years from the date of the death of the person on whose account the pension is granted, then, when allowed, it only commences from the date of making the application; thereby the pensioner loses nearly five hundred dollars through their negligence. Some try to excuse themselves for not being more punctual about such matters by saying that they have tried, and tried in vain, to get their money. That is no excuse. As I have herein previously stated, it is the fault of the incompetent agent who received your claim, and not the fault of the government.

The reader will please make known the contents of this circular to his friends and neighbors generally, and urge on them the importance of attending to the matters herein referred to without delay. Teachers of public and private schools, and ministers and preachers of the gospel, are also requested to make known explicitly the contents of this circular at their meetings. Favorable arrangements made with attorneys and others throughout the State relative to the collection of government claims; also, attorneys and others who have filed claims, whether in their own names or through other agents, can sell their interest therein at our office. Full instructions and particulars can be had by calling at our office in this town (the county seat of this county;) also, any letters addressed to me here, or at my headquarters in Pulaski, Giles County, Tennessee, will be promptly answered.

The highest prices paid for land warrants at our office.

Very respectfully,

M. M. CLOON.

WAR DEPARTMENT, BUREAU OF REFUGEES, FREEDMEN
AND ABANDONED LANDS, CLAIM DIVISION,
Washington, July 26, 1869.

SIR: Having read your letter of the 6th instant, addressed to Brevet Brigadier General George W. Balloch, chief disbursing officer, and referring to M. M. Cloon, esq., I have thought it might not be unedifying, and possibly serve a good purpose, to forward for your perusal certain correspondence which has passed between Mr. Cloon and myself. My letter to him of the 25th ultimo was intended to be "sarcastic," but, judging from his answer thereto, it would seem that he interpreted it as "complimentary" and as in some sort approving his course.

I agree with you entirely in your opinions concerning the conduct of Mr. Cloon, and trust that some measures may be adopted at an early day to bring him to an account, or, at least, to prevent him from doing further mischief.

Any efforts which you may be able to make to secure that end will be actively seconded by this office. Please return the inclosed papers after examination, with such remarks and suggestions as your position and knowledge may enable you to make.

Very respectfully, your obedient servant,

WILLIAM P. DREW,
Agent Bureau Refugees, Freedmen and Abandoned Lands,
Chief of Claim Division.

J. B. COONS, Esq.,
Agent and Disbursing Officer, Bureau Refugees, Freedmen and Abandoned Lands, Nashville, Tennessee.

[Indorsement.]

NASHVILLE, TENNESSEE, *August* 4, 1869.

Respectfully returned with original inclosures. The correspondence is indeed "Cloonish!" Cloon is constitutionally a rogue of considerable ability, has faith in himself, and having no moral parts whatever, believes in Cloon, and makes no mean opponent in a contest where he holds a few points. Without these, however, he is bombastic, bluffish, and amounts to nothing. I have long believed that the bureau had rotten spots about Columbia and Pulaski, caused by acts of former agents, and that just such men as Cloon would find them out and use them. This belief was engendered by the thousand and one little inklings which go to make up a belief, but which do not constitute a proof. I have expected that Cloon, or some of the Noah's might, for some purpose, open upon and make this institution trouble in that way. His letter to yourself, however, show that he is not dangerous—that if he attempts anything, it will be a *mere* attempt to intimidate, in order that *he* may be let alone. I have always repulsed him here, and as a sequence he is not known in Nashville. I have no doubt but that I could get on his track, and, in a few weeks, run him down. My idea, however, is to let

Wilson, of whom he now has a mortal terror, fight him with his own weapons. Wilson is a physical giant—a whole-souled fellow with no politics. The clannish pistol-carriers of Giles and Maury counties admire him, and detest Cloon, and no doubt, at a hint from the former, would drive the latter from the country—maybe into "God's country"—literally. Any extended official notice of Cloon by the bureau would delight him. A slow consuming correspondence, or a direct cut, with Wilson to look after him in person, would, I think, finish the gentlemen, and be the proper course to pursue in the premises.

J. B. COONS,
Agent Bureau Refugees, Freedmen and Abandoned Lands.

WASHINGTON, D. C., *August 26*, 1869.

SIR: We have yours of the 25th instant, referring to the matter of the claim for commutation for rations of Pink Leatherman, asking what disposition has been made of the amount allowed him; in answer, have to state that check No. 6084, for $54 75 to his order, was received from the office of Colonel George Bell, on the 19th of May, 1869, and on the same day forwarded to M. M. Cloon, Pulaski, Tennessee, (our agent from whom we received the claim,) said check and discharge. Our fee charged was $2 75.

Your letter is herewith returned; we hold no receipt from claimant for the money, as our transaction was with the agent and not with claimant.

Very respectfully,

O'NEILL & DUFOUR,
Per MILLER.

WM. P. DREW,
*Agent Bureau Refugees, Freedmen
and Abandoned Lands, Washington, D. C.*

[Indorsements.]

WAR DEPARTMENT, BUREAU REFUGEES, FREEDMEN
AND ABANDONED LANDS, CLAIM DIVISION,
Washington, August 28, 1869.

Respectfully referred to J. B. Coons, esq., agent and disbursing officer, Nashville, Tennessee, who will please ascertain, if practicable, what disposition has been made of the check within referred to, returning these papers with report.

Mr. Coons will also please inform the claimant of the result of the investigation thus far.

By order of Brevet Major General O. O. Howard, Commissioner, &c.

WILLIAM P. DREW,
*Agent Bureau Refugees, Freedmen and Abandoned Lands,
Chief of Claim Division.*

BUREAU REFUGEES, FREEDMEN AND ABANDONED LANDS,
OFFICE DISBURSING AGENT CLAIMS,
Nashville, Tennessee, Sept. 13, 1869.

Respectfully returned to William P. Drew, esq., chief claim division, &c. Attention invited to accompanying letter of John L. Wilson, agent at Columbia, Tennessee. We will not relinquish this case, but keep you advised as to future developments.

J. B. COONS,
Agent, &c.

DISBURSING OFFICE OF CLAIM BUREAU, &C,
Columbia, Tennessee, September 10, 1869.

DEAR SIR: In the case of Pink Leatherman, which you sent me to investigate, I have the honor to state that I did not find the man. After a great deal of inquiry I found that man lived nine or ten miles from Pulaski, and I telegraphed to a man there to send for him and I would be down on the morning train. I knew that Cloon was in Pulaski. I am satisfied how the case stands, and I am working up five or six more of them. I don't know whether O'Niell at Washington is engaged in it or not, but Cloon is charged with forging powers of attorney in favor of O'Niell & Dufour, authorizing them to sign all papers for him; as in the case at hand, the check is sent to Cloon, and the claimants have had such confidence in him that they do and sign anything he wants them. A colored man told me yesterday that Cloon told three claimants to go to Huntsville, Alabama, and he would pay them. Now if O'Niell & Dufour can sign vouchers and certificates in Washington, and sends checks to such men as M. M. Cloon, what chance has the claimant got. O'Niell may act in good faith, but he is aiding a grand rascal. I have a case in which Cloon told a man he had his money; amount, $300, Calvin Word, Company H Twelfth Infantry, but he had no orders to pay him. In eight or ten days the man went again, when Cloon told him his claim was on hand for $200, and finally offered the man $15, and told him if he did not take that he would drive him out of the office. This can be sworn to and proved by two witnesses. Now, if the claim is paid through power of attorney, it is easily known how their plan has been. You, no doubt, have seen Leatherman, and, if he has not got his money, you can make what report of the case you may, with the information contained in this, or send me word to do it. *I will keep no copy of this letter.*

Respectfully yours,

J. L. WILSON.

OFFICE AGENT BUREAU REFUGEES,
FREEDMEN AND ABANDONED LANDS,
Huntsville, Alabama, Nov. 26, 1869.

GENERAL: I have the honor to state that Anderson Sloss, late private Company B One hundred and eleventh United States colored infantry, states that he gave his claim for bounty to Captain Judd, in Pulaski, Tennessee, and that M. M. Cloon sent for him and took up the receipt given him by Captain Judd, and paid him $100, saying "This is for your bounty," about middle of October, 1868. He does not know whether it was for bounty commutation of rations or for pension, as he had claims in for all three. Will you please see to it? He is living near Pulaski, Tennessee.

I am, general, very respectfully, your obedient servant,

JOHN H. WAGER, *Agent.*

Major General O. O. HOWARD,
*Commissioner Bureau Refugees Freedmen and
Abandoned Lands, Washington, D. C.*

[Indorsement.]

WAR DEPARTMENT, BUREAU REFUGEES, FREEDMEN
AND ABANDONED LANDS, CLAIM DIVISION,
Washington, November 30, 1869.

Respectfully referred to John L. Wilson, esq., agent and disbursing officer, Columbia, Tennessee, inclosing check No. 571, of George W.

Balloch, chief disbursing officer, dated June 5, 1868, for $301, payable to the order of Anderson Sloss, and purporting to be indorsed by said Sloss, witnessed by "M. M. Cloon." The check was forwarded to Charles R. Simpson, esq., at that time disbursing officer of this bureau at Pulaski, Tennessee.

Mr. Wilson will please make full investigation, returning these papers with report. Mr. Wager has been notified of this reference.

By order of Brevet Major General O. O. Howard, Commissioner, &c.

WILLIAM P. DREW,
Chief of Claim Division.

TREASURY DEPARTMENT, SECOND AUDITOR'S OFFICE,
December 20, 1869.

SIR: I have the honor to acknowledge the receipt of your letter of the 18th instant, in relation to the appointment of a commission for investigating complaints against officers and agents of the Freedmen's Bureau, and requesting that any such complaints filed in this office may be sent to you.

There are at present no such complaints in this office, the last and only one received for a long time being that of James Cloon, of Huntsville, Alabama, which I had the honor to refer to you several days since.

I am, sir, very respectfully,

E. B. FRENCH, *Auditor.*

Brevet Major General O. O. HOWARD,
Commissioner, &c.

[Indorsement.]

WAR DEPARTMENT, BUREAU REFUGEES,
FREEDMEN AND ABANDONED LANDS,
Washington, December 22, 1869.

Respectfully referred to commission appointed to investigate charges preferred against parties concerned in the payment of bounties to colored soldiers, &c.

By order of Brevet Major General O. O. Howard.

HENRY M. WHITTLESEY,
Acting Asst. Adjt. General.

DEPARTMENT OF THE INTERIOR, PENSION OFFICE,
Washington, D. C., December 21, 1869.

SIR: I have the honor to acknowledge the receipt of your favor of the 18th instant, asking for such complaints as have been filed with me against the officers and agents of your bureau, and in reply I have to state that no complaints have been filed in this office against such officers or agents.

I will, however, add that in the recent investigation made in the State of Tennessee by special agents of this bureau, certain charges came to the knowledge of the commission against Mr. Wilson, of Columbia. The charges however had been the subject of a judicial investigation before the United States commissioner at Nashville, from whom the information was derived, and which have probably come to your knowledge.

I am, sir, very respectfully, your obedient servant,

H. VAN AERNAM,
Commissioner.

General O. O. HOWARD, *Washington, D. C.*

[Indorsement.]

WAR DEPARTMENT,
BUREAU REFUGEES, FREEDMEN AND ABANDONED LANDS,
Washington, December 22, 1869.

Respectfully referred to the commission appointed to investigate charges preferred against certain persons connected with the payment of bounties to colored soldiers, &c.

By order of Brevet Major General O. O. Howard.

HENRY M. WHITTLESEY,
Acting Asst. Adjt. General.

COMMUNICATIONS FROM CLOON (M. M., JAS., AND JAS. M. M.,) REFERRED TO THE COMMISSION BY THE BUREAU REFUGEES, FREEDMEN AND ABANDONED LANDS.

CLOON No. 1.

PULASKI, TENNESSEE, *June* 15, 1869.

SIR: I have learned from some parties at Washington that, in your office on several occasions, very harsh and unbecoming language has been made use of, tending to stigmatize my character, and otherwise to destroy my business relations in the different departments in your city, the immediate cause of which I can't very well comprehend, other than that I suppose it had its origin in the report of some functionary of the Bureau of Freedmen, &c., and in supposing that it originated as herein suggested, I can't conceive why it is that you would be guilty of such imprudence as to denounce me, of whom you know nothing, on the simple report of an illiterate puppy who perchance obtained the office of disbursing agent, and whose corruption and public swindling has been unearthed by me in every place I have gone to. Such are these men that make reports detrimental to my feelings of honor—men whom I know have made thousands of dollars out of the ignorant blacks whose bounty and pay they have the disbursement of—men who would not be admitted into any kind of decent society, and who are too cowardly to make such reports in the districts wherein they operate, or even to suggest the slightest intimation of the matter to those whose characters they seek to defame. If I was guilty of such conduct as they are wont to report, then why not take me before a United States court and there made to answer the charges for which I am arraigned? No, they will not do that, knowing that such proof could not be established, sufficient to make it even the shadow of a crime, and the consequences would be that a cowhide, quick and hot, would be laid on their defamed forms of corruption for such proceedings. It is not their love for honesty and affection for the colored people that causes them to make such reports, but it is a hatred and jealousy which they are possessed of, in common with all other thieves, at the prosperity and general welfare of their imaginary enemy. I have never known a thief yet (that is, of the class of whom I write) but rejoiced at the downfall of his neighbor, and was jealous and indignant at their prosperity and welfare. The truth of the matter is this: I have more influence among the negroes of Middle Tennessee and North Alabama than any other man, I dare say, in this country; and they generally come to me for advice in case of necessity, which I have given and continue to do so, which has devel6ped a great many frauds on the negroes entitled to bounty, &c., by some of those functionaries. Hence this bitterness for forcing such men to remain honest. While in North Alabama last month I took the depositions of several persons of respectability, charging a certain official of that section with petty frauds of the character herein alluded to. I took such depositions to please the people who gave them, and not for the purpose of using them in scandalizing the person for whose benefit they were made. No gentleman will be guilty of making reports tending to defile or injure the character of his neighbor. Hence I am possessed of more decency and honor than report such men, notwithstanding that they are continually reporting me. I always make it a rule that if a man does me an injury intentionally I hold him personally responsible for it, and accordingly seek satisfaction in that way. So I am not much in reporting "*bureau agents*," providing it is in my power not to do so. However, I am called upon now to prosecute *one*, of bar-room notoriety, for swindling the colored people, and am now taking the depositions of those whom he robbed; so, in a week or ten days you will hear of one of your brethren being in *limbo;* and, if I am not mistaken, after him will go others. Running up as far as your city, I have not forgotten the big swindling arrangement entered into some time ago between Chipman, Hosmer & Co. and some of "*you gentlemen*" who figure rather conspicuously in the *bureau* at Washington. I have not forgotten the conduct of "*Mann,*" who came down here some time ago on a swindling expedition, and I suppose that *you* have not forgotten it. Then why don't you use your influence with Second Auditor, and try and have Chipman, Hosmer & Co. suspended, whose rascality is known all over the *United States?* But remember, the *people* have become tired of reporting the conduct of officers to each other, owing to the unfair manner in which such reports were received; to wit: if the party was friendly to the officers to whom he was reported, then the matter would be quashed; but if the party reported was not friendly to such official, then a big hubbub was made about his swindling, and steps were immediately taken for his suspension and general proscription, as in my case. Now, sir, the people have determined to arraign all of that class of officials herein alluded to before the United States courts, and there expose them to the condemnation of all decent people, thereby doing away with this matter of reporting one thief to another. When this plan is adopted, it will have a tendency of making those roguish "*bureau agents*" now in this country attend to their own business and let claim agents and correspondents alone, knowing as they will that the matter will be disposed of by the United States court instead of a bureau agent or commissioner. Now, sir, whereas this letter has already grown tolerably long, then I will close by asking you a few questions, or, in other words, by making a few suggestions for your consideration.

Under the present laws regulating the payment of bounties to both whites and blacks, how can a claim agent swindle, as bureau agents are wont to style it? You know that all money now being paid by the United States Treasurer for said purpose is paid through disbursing agents appointed for that purpose. Then, where does the swindling come in? Why, you know as well as other decent men that a claim agent can't swindle without the co-operation of a bureau agent, as the time has past when he could do without. It's true a claim agent may be thief enough to present false claims, or charge usurious interest on advanced money, or collect more money than what he really advanced to a claimant, and the like; and then, if those *bureau agents* find such men who are guilty of such crimes, then why not make it known to the claim agent and give him a chance to defend himself? Now, as far as I am concerned, I care not how many times I may be reported by such men, but I can assure you that the next report of the kind will cause me to bring to light such *"facts"* in regard to bureau agents as will startle *"people"* beside the *"sensational."* I hope you will consider this a letter of information and facts and not one of resentment, as it is not intended for anything other than your information.

Very respectfully, &c.,

M. M. CLOON.

WILLIAM P. DREW, Esq.,
    *Agent of Bureau of Refugees, Freedmen and
     Abandoned Lands, Washington, D. C.*

CLOON No. 2.

PULASKI, TENNESSEE, *July* 3, 1869.

SIR: Yours of the 25th ultimo is received. I am much pleased with the kind expressions contained therein, and hope that a more friendly relationship, reciprocated on all sides, may in future mark our conduct. Nothing good can be achieved by a vindictive course on our part. If more prudence was used on the part of sub-bureau agents stationed in the country, we would be better off on all sides. While I must acknowledge that claim agents, with few exceptions, would cheat and swindle when opportunity would permit, yet I can assure you that it was in very few cases that claim agents alone done the cheating, as they were always associated with bureau agents, as you know yourself that their chances for making money without being associated with bureau agents was too slim to be indulged in by those of good sense. The bounty having to pass through the hands of the bureau officers, they could advise the colored man not to pay any body a cent of it unless he was pleased to do so; and the negro is a genius who will pay you his debts if you happen on him when he has the money, but he will never approach you for that purpose himself; hence claim agents and bureau agents, in a great measure, work together in the premises. As far as I am concerned I have no objections to the acts of disbursing agents, or others, providing they don't interfere with me. However, if I am called upon to prosecute them, as attorney-at-law, for any misdemeanors, I always do so. I was called upon to prosecute John L. Wilson, your representative in this section, on yesterday; he was arrested by the United States marshal, on affidavits sworn out for him by negroes who claim to be swindled by him at the time of paying them their bounty. There are seven distinct charges against him, which, if established, will go heavy on his displeasure. He will have a hearing on Monday before the United States commissioner. I have learned, a few days ago, that Mr. Wager, your representative at Huntsville, Alabama, reported me through headquarters, which has affected a friend of mine, named James Cloon, who has nothing to do with me nor I with him. Of course, as far as I am concerned, I would just as soon be reported as not, had it not been for its effects upon my feelings of honor. But what this man Wager reported me for I know not, as God knows I have not been guilty of anything for which I could be reported, unless it was because I went into Alabama to take up claims for collection against the United States government. Therefore, I know that his report was fraught with maliciousness, and nothing more. This man Wager has been guilty of some of the most petit swindling imaginable; and while I was in Alabama, several parties wanted that I should have him arrested for such rascality; but I simply took their depositions, and told them that I would have the matter investigated. Therefore, I suppose that, on learning of such proceedings, he made the confounded complaint alluded to herein, and I think the consequence was that James Cloon was perhaps suspended. Now, if the heads of departments at Washington are such persons as to believe that they can deprive an attorney, who has been guilty of nothing dishonorable, of a practice in their departments, as easily as they can one who has been guilty of imprudence, there they are badly mistaken. No member of a department has a right to deprive an attorney of practice in his department by way of suspending him, without it is clearly shown to him that such attorney or agent has been guilty of some misdemeanor; and of course it cannot be shown on the simple report of a bureau agent, because the party against whom complaint is made should have a right to make a defense. Therefore, the party aggrieved can bring suit for damages against such heads of departments as may deprive him of such practice. So, if I or my friend Cloon have been unjustly injured by the report of Wager, I shall not only prosecute him for swindling, but I shall get after French, Van Aernam, and others, for suspending him without showing cause, and I will show to the world, if they are just in their suspension, that they should first begin at home, as it is *there* they want the attention of such honest men as Mr. French and Van Aernam.

Very respectfully, &c.,

M. M. CLOON.

WM. P. DREW, Esq.,
 Agent of Bureau of Refugees, Freedmen and
  AbandonedLands, Washington.

CLOON No. 3.

FLORENCE, ALABAMA, *August* 2, 1869.

GENERAL: I have the honor to inclose herewith a copy of the decision of United States Commissioner L. J. Noah, in the case of the United States *vs.* John L. Wilson, your representative and disbursing agent for the counties of Maury, Giles, Marshall, and others, of Middle Tennessee, together with a letter received from J. T. Fisher, a highly respectable colored citizen of Pulaski, Tennessee, complaining that Wilson is still committing, with impunity, the same offenses for which he had been arraigned and committed, as shown by the inclosed paper. Said letter and decision will explain themselves, both of which are respectfully transmitted for your information and action.

I am already apprised of the fact that this matter has already been brought to your notice, without action. Yet, I cannot conceive for a moment that *you*, whose character is spotless, and for which you have acquired such prominence in position as well as mind, could allow such a matter to pass unnoticed. I hope it is not possible that a criminal, found guilty before an impartial judge, will still be allowed to commit, daily, the offenses for which he has been found guilty. Can it be possible that such a felon will still be intrusted with thousands of dollars of the poor widow and orphan to rob and fleece them of the same by his coadjutors? Can it be possible that such an officer will be allowed to jeopardize the honor, integrity, and uprightness of your department? If so, let us know it, that we may be better able to judge of the immediate circumstances by which the matter is surrounded. Yes, that we may be able to bring the matter before the world in its true light, and show up to the contempt of all honest people the supporters of such a villainous scheme.

Very respectfully, &c.,

M. M. CLOON.

GENERAL O. O. HOWARD,
*Chief Commissioner of Bureau Refugees,
Freedmen and Abandoned Lands, Washington, D. C.*

THE UNITED STATES } Before L. J. Noah, United States circuit court
against } commissioner, middle district of Tennessee.
JOHN L. WILSON. }

Copy judgment and opinion.

The defendant, John L. Wilson, is a disbursing agent of the government, under supervision of the Bureau of Refugees, Freedmen and Abandoned Lands, and it appears that upon him devolves the duty in the counties of Maury and Giles, State of Tennessee, of disbursing and paying to discharged colored soldiers, or to the heirs and representatives of deceased colored soldiers, such sums of money as under the laws of Congress may be found due to them for bounties or otherwise, by the accounting officers of the Treasury. He stands charged with "illegally depriving certain colored soldiers of portions of their bounty money due them from the United States government, contrary to law."

It appears, in view of the fact that these colored soldiers, or the heirs of deceased colored soldiers, were not educated, or used to the ordinary transaction of business, and hence were liable to be imposed upon or deprived of a portion or the whole of their bounty or pay by designing parties, it was directed that the proper government officials should adjust and retain in their hands the legal fees of claim agents, and pay or cause to be paid the entire balance to the party entitled to receive the same.

In order that these wise and beneficent regulations should be carried into complete effect, officers have been designated and appointed in different localities, charged with the responsibility of personally superintending the exact payment of bounty moneys to the proper claimants. The sphere of such duty undoubtedly was to impose upon such disbursing officer a most religious and rigid scrutiny of all attending circumstances of such payment, to protect the ignorant and uneducated from being wronged, fleeced, or bled, by claim agents or other designing parties.

It appears, also, that the intention of Congress, in rewarding these soldiers or their heirs with certain bounty moneys, was that they *should receive all of such sums*, except the legal deductions for fees and notarial expenses, which are limited by law. Hence the proper officers of the government, recognizing the intention of the law-making power, sought, by official orders, to surround the payment of these bounties with such safeguards as would insure their honest and exact liquidation.

The evidence in this case clearly shows that certain colored soldiers, entitled to bounties, and their claims therefor adjusted, and legal fees of attorneys and notaries duly deducted, were mulcted of ten per centum of their adjusted bounties by certain parties, who claimed this percentage for attorney fees other than those allowed by law, and that this was permitted and done with the full knowledge of the defendant, without restraint, remonstrance, or interference. It also appears that these malpractices were brought, time and time again to the notice of the defendant, Wilson, by the injured parties, and that he refused to interpose in their behalf, or declined to discharge any of the functions or duties imposed upon him by law as the agent of the government, or as the friend of the colored soldier, for which he was employed and paid. In fact there can be no doubt whatever from the evidence that he personally knew the wrongs that were going on, and winked at them.

The proof shows that, while the defendant paid the whole amount to the parties entitled to receive the same, yet it was a mere form or pretence of payment, and was not such a payment as is contemplated by law and required by the rules and orders of the Treasury Department.

There can be no duty performed when the result of that performance is *quasi*, and the same amounts only to a subtle trick of avoidance. This avoidance was in my judgment criminal, and clearly shows that the defendant aided and abetted in, and was consenting to, the illegal depriving of these bounties from the colored soldiers, and he is therefore liable as a principal offender under the law. It is high time that some steps were taken to check these frauds, the perpetration of which tends to lower the dignity of the nation in the estimation of the people. The testimony shows conclusively that the defendant avoided the especial trust reposed upon him by the government, and that the duty imposed upon him of caring for these colored soldiers was wantonly neglected, through which neglect these soldiers were in fact "deprived of a portion of their bounty money."

I feel constrained to send this case before the grand jury of the United States circuit court. Let the defendant, Wilson, be held to bail in the sum of $1,000 to appear and answer an indictment accordingly.

[SEAL.]
         L. J. NOAH,
      U. S. Circuit Court Commissioner,
        Middle District of Tennessee.

NASHVILLE, *Tennessee, July* 7, 1869.

UNITED STATES OF AMERICA,
    Middle District of Tennessee.

I, L. J. Noah, United States circuit court commissioner for the middle district of Tennessee, do hereby certify that the foregoing is a true and correct copy of the judgment and opinion rendered by him in the case of the United States against John L. Wilson, on a charge of "illegally depriving certain colored soldiers of portions of their bounty money."

In testimony whereof, I have hereunto set my hand and official seal, at office at Nashville, this 22d day of July, 1869, and of the independence of the United States the 94th year.

[SEAL.]
         L. J. NOAH,
      U. S. Circuit Court Commissioner,
        Middle District of Tennessee.

          PULASKI, TENNESSEE,
            July 29, 1869.

DEAR SIR: Mr. Wilson was here to-day, and was here also last Thursday, carrying on the same game as before, and abusing you and me before every claimant, and asking them if they owe anything; and if they say they do, he advises them not to pay me. And Wilson tells the colored people that you have nothing to do with claims; that the government has taken the business from you; and all parties that will not give up your receipt to Jones he will not. He tells them to go to you and get their money. Jones charges every one ten per cent. Albert Harvey's check called for $214 23; they gave him $87.

When do you expect to come to Pulaski?

Yours, truly,

J. T. FISHER.

Dr. M. M. CLOON,
   Florence, Alabama.

TREASURY DEPARTMENT,
SECOND AUDITOR'S OFFICE,
December 13, 1869.

DEAR SIR: As the accompanying document makes grave charges against some of your subordinates, I have taken the liberty to inclose it to you personally.

Very respectfully,

E. B. FRENCH.

Major General O. O. HOWARD.

[This should be carefully read by the Auditor personally.]

HUNTSVILLE, ALABAMA,
November 29, 1869.

SIR: I have the honor to inform you that I have indirectly learned that evidence prejudicial to my character is on file in your office, causing doubts in your mind as to my good faith and honesty as claim agent. If such be the case, I most respectfully ask that you inform me of the nature and character of such charges, that I may refute the same, and show to your satisfaction that they are groundless, and are fraught with malice and envy, calculated only to destroy my reputation in the departments, and to otherwise defame me personally.

The only source from whence I have anticipated a tirade of abuse is from bureau officials, whose public swindling and dishonest transactions have been unearthed by me in the States of Tennessee and Alabama, and for which I had such men arraigned before United States courts, and there punished for such nefarious practices. Notwithstanding that subordinates of the bureau in the States named have been found guilty of such crimes by impartial courts of justice, and General O. O. Howard, Chief Commissioner of the Bureau, at your city, having been duly notified of the same by forwarding to him copies of the decisions of the courts in each case, yet, to the mortification of the poor widow and ex-colored soldier, he has failed to notice such matters, and still allows such officers to rob and fleece the poor and almost destitute negro out of a portion of that bounty which, by the goodness of the government, he is entitled to. Yes, he allows such men to disgrace the dignity of the government which they claim to represent. It is not the subordinates of which I write that are guilty of all the dishonest transactions committed by the bureau, but we can trace it to the very feet of some of the highest officials connected with the bureau in your city. This I write not from hearsay, but can bring the testimony of over one hundred highly respectable Union men to show that the highest officials in Washington who are connected with the bureau are guilty of crimes so dishonest in their transactions as to make honesty and decency blush. Therefore, whereas I am the only person that has at the solicitations of the victimized shown up to the contempt of all honest people the unholy and disgraceful doings of such officials, hence their wrath and malice is directly aimed at me, and their object is to break, if possible, my reputation in the departments, so as to lessen the weight of my charges. Again, they know that I intend bringing the matter before the next Congress in all its disgraceful aspects, and show that body that the bureau as it now is conducted is the source of all swindling and rascality being perpetrated on the colored claimants. This can be easily shown, as follows: All certificates for bounty and back pay issued in favor of colored claimants from your office are made payable to General O. O. Howard, who is, by an act of Congress, held responsible for the faithful disbursement of the money thus intrusted to his care; and, in order that matters might be facilitated in the honest discharge of the duty thus involving on him, he is authorized to appoint subordinate officers to be stationed at different points in the lately insurgent States, whose duty it is from time to time to pay over, or cause to be paid, to the legitimate claimants all bounties, &c., received by such officers for disbursement, if the claimant be found within their districts. Now, it is well known that a colored claimant living in any of the lately rebellious States does not, nor have they ever since March 30, 1867, received a cent in bounty or pay, only through the agents of the bureau. Every claimant has to come to their office to draw his money in person, even though he may live two hundred miles distant, they always taking good care not to send it in the care of anybody nor to the care of anybody. Now, I ask you, if those people are swindled out of their bounty and pay, how is it done without a bureau agent? The answer must be that they cannot be cheated only through the bureau agents being directly associated with claim agents or others, who do the work of the bad man. It might be said that the money is extracted from them after they have received it. That would not stand, as persons guilty of such offenses would be held amenable to the law for such conduct, and besides the colored people have become too intelligent to have themselves fleeced of their just dues after getting it into their hands. No; the way most generally resorted to by agents of the bureau for swindling the colored claimant is about as follows: They have an accomplice, who is notified of the receipt by them of the bounty of such a person, at the same time making known the amount of the same. The accomplice then seeks the claimant and purchases his or her claim for a trivial sum, or if they can't succeed in buying the same, they generally advance money at enormous and usurious interest, and after the elapse of a few weeks the claimant is taken into the agent's office, where a check is given to the claimant in the presence of the accomplice who has advanced the money or bought the claim, as the case may be, and who immediately lays hold of the bounty check, giving to the claimant the amount of the same, less principal or money advanced with interest. If the claim had been previously bought, the claimant in that case is ordered off without a cent, notwithstanding that the party had been swindled out of twenty-five per cent. or more of his or her bounty. After each day's transactions the agent of the bureau and his coadjutor in the misdemeanor divide spoils, and live fat on the expense of others. So you may see that it is an impossibility for claim agents or others to swindle colored claimants without the co-operation of agents of the bureau. Therefore you must come to the conclusion that bureau agents are responsible for every cent of money (bounty) out of which colored claimants have been cheated since the passage of the act making such claims payable through General Howard. Now, it is a well-known fact that all reports received at bureau headquarters relative to such swindling, wherein the names of bureau agents who are connected with the "bureau ring" are named as the guilty parties in such cases, there is nothing more heard of it, it being referred to the agent complained of, who is ordered to settle the matter quietly and to have the matter quashed. On the contrary, if a report is received at bureau headquarters complaining of a claim agent or other person, then the bureau officials howl and cry thief, and immediately report him to the heads of bureaus of the War Department, with a recommendation for his suspension if he be a claim agent, and, if not, they let the matter go by the board, the object of attacking persons not directly connected with their thieving ring being to hide their own damnable rascality, and to pretend that they are guarding the interests of the colored man. It is alarming in the extreme to know the amount of bounty money out of which colored claimants have been swindled; in fact, they have not, on an average, received fifty per cent. of the amount of the treasury certificates issued in their favor from your office. They are complaining of such wrongs all over the southern States, and more particularly in Tennessee and Alabama, and they being ignorant of the *modus operandi* of the collection and payment of this bounty, hence they know not who are the immediate cause of those high-handed outrages, and hence do often charge their claim agents with the offense, when they are entirely innocent of the crime. Again, the negroes know not who to complain to for redress against such outrages, as all the complaints made by them to sub-agents have proved futile and have no effect whatever; such bureau agents being the persons of whose acts the negro complains, hence they tell the victimized that they will investigate the case and have the guilty ones punished, &c., they knowing that the negro never suspects them as the guilty ones. Again, some negroes get tired of the fair promises of their bureau friends, and, in such cases, they get some one to write to Washington in regard to it; the letter gets into the bureau there, the contents being that he gave his discharge to such a claim agent, and has not received more than half the bounty to which he is entitled, and believes that the claim agent has swindled him, &c. The bureau at Washington immediately refers the letter to the departments, showing that the claim agent named therein has been guilty of fraud and should be reprimanded, &c., said bureau agents knowing at the same time that the agent named in the letter of complaint was not nor could not be guilty of the offense named without the aid of the bureau agent located in his section, the object of reporting the claim agent being, of course, to shield themselves from the reproach which it might bring upon them.

Again, when bureau agents have operated rather extensively in a neighborhood, and have brought condemnation of the citizens on themselves by their theory, in such cases they are removed into some other locality, and their place is taken by another gentleman whose devotion to the colored man is very great for a few months; during which time the negroes flock to him in hundreds, complaining of their wrongs in the payment of their bounty, and asking that they be indemnified—the negroes telling him that they filed their claims with such claim agents and have not received half their legitimate dues, and do believe that the claim agent cheated them, as he would not pay them the bounty himself, but turned it over to the bureau agent to pay it; and that he did not turn over half the money received for them, &c. Now, the foregoing will give you an idea of the manner in which the negroes complain, they all thinking, and you can't make them believe differently, but that the claim agent who received their claim for collection is the one who receives the bounty. Now the late arrival; he listens to their stories very carefully, and after he hears all he makes a strong report against claim agents, and forwards the same to the bureau at Washington, where it is examined and referred to the departments. Yet not a word is said about the bureau agent, notwithstanding that they know that he was the source of all the rascality complained of, and that if any of the claim agents complained of were guilty of any part in the crime they were simply aiding the bureau agent. Now, it must not be understood that I claim that all bureau agents are dishonest and that all claim agents are honorable and honest. I know a great many bureau agents who are honorable gentlemen and would scorn to be guilty of any of the offenses above alluded to. Again, I know the majority of claim agents to be public thieves and men whom I would not trust as far as I could see them. But it does not follow that if some are bad all should be bad. The same rule applies to bureau agents.

Ask General O. O. Howard what he done with Mr. Eastman, formerly bureau agent at Columbia, Tennessee, who robbed the colored people of over $25,000 of bounty money. Ask him what he has done with John L. Wilson, who is now bureau agent for the counties of Maury, Giles, Marshall, Lincoln, and others of Middle Tennessee, whose swindling is open and above-board, and tells the people that he will do as he damn pleases. Wilson has been arrested, and is now under heavy bonds for his swindling, but is still swindling with impunity. Copies of the decisions of the courts in the Wilson case, and in other cases against bureau agents, had been forwarded to General Howard, with recommendations for their removal. Yet, although the decisions of the courts showed the most disgraceful swindling and usurpation of the duties devolving on them as agents of the bureau, yet Howard has done nothing toward any of their removals, but rather writes them encouraging them in their villainy. Again, we will ask Howard what he done with Carlin Simpson and others of Tennessee, whose swindling was enormous. I can name for you a hundred cases in which bureau agents have been guilty of such theft, and in each case will furnish you copies of the decisions of the United States district courts before whom those men were formerly arraigned for such offenses. Some of them had their indictments quashed through their money, others of them have their cases yet pending, and so on. Again, we will ask Howard what he has done with the affidavits gotten up by John Mills, formerly bureau agent at Athens, Alabama, and those gotten up by John W. Wager, now bureau agent at this place; said affidavits being sworn to by colored claimants and were forwarded to General Howard by said sub-agents, showing that a firm of agents at Washington, with whom some of the bureau agents were co-operating, were guilty of some scandalous thieving, it being done by the aid of the bureau at Washington and through the bureau. Are said firm of claim agents suspended, or were they reported? No, indeed; they are to-day the largest and the strongest firm of that kind in Washington, and boast that they can do as much in the departments as the heads of the same can, and that they can direct and instruct clerks to do as they choose. Again, four correspondents of the said firm, namely, J. M. Hickey and A. M. Hickey, of Columbia, Tennessee, and Calvin and Charles A. Jones, of Pulaski, Tennessee, are associated with the aforesaid John L. Wilson, the bureau agent for several counties of Middle Tennessee, previously named in his swindling scheme, which

BOUNTIES TO COLORED SOLDIERS.

is carried on as follows: The claimant goes to the office of the said Wilson and asks if his claim is ready for settlement. Wilson says, "No." The claimant tells him that his claim agent told him that it was settled. Wilson says, "If you depend upon your claim agent you will never get it;" in the meantime telling claimant to go and see the Hickeys, or the Joneses, assuring him that they will promptly receive his money. The claimant complies, and goes forthwith to said parties, who tell him that they must get fifteen per cent. for getting his bounty. Of course the poor, illiterate negro would give twenty-five or fifty per cent. as quick as he would fifteen, and complies at once to their proposition, when he is ordered to report at their office in about ten days, at which time he will get his money. Claimant accordingly appears back at the appointed time and is taken to Wilson's office, after which Wilson goes to the bank with claimant's check for bounty, it having been previously indorsed by the claimant, and draws the amount of said check, returns and pays to the claimant the amount of the same in the presence of the Hickeys, who take the money out of the claimants hands and deducts his fifteen per cent., and the balance he returns to the claimant. Now, when that poor claimant first went to Wilson he had his check in his possession, but denies it that the Hickeys or Joneses, who are his coadjutors, may rob him out of fifteen per cent. of it, and who, of course, divide with Wilson. Now, though I have not shown you half the rascality committed by the bureau, yet I have shown you enough to convince you that it is the source of all the black swindling committed on the colored claimant. That you may be convinced of the truth of my statement, I ask you to call upon Mr. Trevitt, Mr. Strecker, or any of the other gentlemen who constituted the commission sent out by the Pension Bureau a short time ago. Although they were not looking after bounty frauds, yet they could not shut their eyes and ears to the hundreds of complaints made daily to them by colored people, citing the wrongs imposed on them in the payment of their bounty. Now, in view of all this, will I stand by and allow such miscreants to abuse my character and charge me with offenses of which I know nothing? Can I stand by and allow myself to be charged with the offenses of others? No, I will not, but I will shift the responsibility where it belongs, and show to the world the villainy in its true light, and bring the odium and scorn of all honest and decent people down upon perpetrators of such foul deeds. If I am guilty, let me be punished according to the extent of my crimes, but I will never allow myself to sustain a loss personally nor financially for an imagined offense without resisting to the last. It may be asked why am I not arrested and arraigned before United States courts the same as bureau agents, and there punished for my offenses. It may be easily answered by saying that they cannot prove anything against me. Notwithstanding that I have had over twenty bureau agents arrested in Tennessee and Alabama, and had them arraigned for fraudulently retaining portions of bounty money from colored claimants, and some of them severely punished, yet although they claim that I am cheating and swindling the ex-soldiers, yet none of them ever had me arrested for the offense, knowing, of course, that they could not establish the charge, and hence they prefer to attack me in Washington, where they need not substantiate their statements by the testimony of anybody; but I think they will find themselves mistaken; let claim agents who are guilty of the offenses charged against them keep their mouths closed and say not a word in their own defense; but I, who am innocent, will vindicate my honor to the utmost extreme, if necessary. So if any evidence prejudicial to my character has been filed in your office, please let me know its nature and character, that I may vindicate myself in the premises, and if I cannot, then let me be suspended and my name stricken from the rolls as a practicing agent. This I write not in a spirit of vindictiveness, but simply to help you to lay the blame where it belongs, and that I may be able to exonerate myself from any charges that may be preferred against me. The rebels of this country being very bitterly opposed to Union men, and more particularly to claim agents who may have dealings with the negroes, hence they don't feel conscientiously affected if they tell a lie on such. Allowance should be made for their statements, if any be made. Watch the bureau agents and you will receive no complaint of swindling from the South. Ninety-nine colored men out of one hundred will substantiate the foregoing statement, and will acknowledge my fidelity to them in every way since I have come among them. I have upheld their cause, vindicated their rights, and protected their liberties all over Tennessee and Alabama, and they will acknowledge the same and will deprecate the idea of my trying to swindle them. Please excuse this long letter.

Very respectfully, your very obedient servant,

JAS. CLOON.

Hon. E. B. FRENCH,
   Second Auditor, Washington, D. C.

HUNTSVILLE, ALABAMA, *November* 20, 1869.

SIR : I have the honor to call your attention to a letter dated at your office on the 16th instant, and addressed to Jacob T. Noah, of your city, in which you say that evidence prejudicial to my character is on file in you office. This is the first intimation I have had that any such evidence was presented against me, and therefore respectfully ask that you inform me of the nature and character of the same, that I may refute such charges, and show to your satisfaction, and to the satisfaction of all interested, that they are groundless, and are fraught with malice and envy, calculated only to destroy my reputation in the department, and otherwise to defame me personally.

The only source from whence I have anticipated a tirade of abuse is from bureau officials, whose public swindling and dishonest transactions I have unearthed in the States of Tennessee and Alabama, and for which, at the solicitations of those thus fleeced and robbed, I have had such men arraigned before United States courts, and there made answer such charges, after which they were punished according to their offenses in such case.

Immediately after such parties had been found guilty of appropriating to their own personal purposes the money intrusted to them for payment to the poor widow and orphan and others, I notified General O. O. Howard of the same, yet, to the mortification of those whose matters he is paid to attend to, he still allows such men to disgrace the dignity of the United States government, by still holding them in the positions which by right they forfeited by dishonesty.

Again, sir, I can show you that it is not the subordinates who represent the bureau in the States that are guilty of nefarious practices exclusively, but that the very highest official next to Howard himself in the bureau has been guilty of frauds so gross in their nature as to make decency and honesty blush. This I speak not from hearsay, but on the contrary I can bring the testimony of more than one hundred persons to substantiate the same.

232 BOUNTIES TO COLORED SOLDIERS.

Therefore, my belief is that they, knowing that I intend bringing the matter before the next Congress in all its disgraceful aspects—their object was hence to destroy my reputation, and thereby weaken the weight of my charges.

If I am guilty of any offenses, contrary to the rulings of your or any other department in Washington, let me be treated as such offenses deserve, but I beg that no testimony prejudicial to my character will be received to the exclusion of mine. I would impress on your mind that the greatest prejudices exist in all the Southern States against anybody having anything to do with the ex-colored soldier, by those lately in rebellion against the United States government, hence that class of people are always anxious to add to anything detrimental to the honor and character of claim agents, wherefore allowance should be made for any statements they may make in such cases.

I some time ago wrote you, requesting that you send me information in relation to some claims filed in your office by me, yet you failed to reply. I hope that you will make known the cause of such non-recognition, that I may exonerate myself fully in the premises.

Very respectfully, your obedient servant,
JAMES M. M. CLOON.

Hon. SAMUEL BRECK,
Assistant Adjutant General, Washington, D. C.

[Indorsement.]

ADJUTANT GENERAL'S OFFICE,
November 20, 1869.

Respectfully referred to Brevet Major General O. O. Howard, in charge of Bureau Refugees, Freedmen and Abandoned Lands, who will please furnish this office with such information as may be in his possession relative to the writer of the within communication.

This paper to be returned.
E. D. TOWNSEND,
Adjutant General.

WAR DEPARTMENT,
BUREAU REFUGEES, FREEDMEN AND ABANDONED LANDS,
Washington, December 3, 1869.

Respectfully referred to W. P. Drew, esq., chief of claim division, for report.

By order of Brevet Major General Howard:
E. WHITTLESEY,
Acting Assistant Adjutant General.

WAR DEPARTMENT, BUREAU REFUGEES, FREEDMEN
AND ABANDONED LANDS, CLAIM DIVISION,
Washington, December 18, 1869.

Respectfully returned to Brevet Brigadier General E. Whittlesey, acting assistant adjutant general, transmitting all papers (fourteen inclosures) received at this office from and respecting M. M. Cloon.

This office has no information concerning James M. M. Cloon, further than that he is reported to be a brother of M. M. Cloon.

Attention is invited to similarity of their handwriting.

Please return inclosures.
WILLIAM P. DREW,
Agent Bureau Refugees, Freedmen and Abandoned Lands,
Chief of Claim Division.

PULASKI, TENNESSEE, *January* 3, 1870.

GENTLEMEN : I have the honor to inform you that, if not wholly, it was partially through my suggestions to the honorable Second Auditor of the Treasury that your honorable body was convened to investigate the cause of the many complaints forwarded to the departments from this and other sections of the State by the colored people through me and others—citing the many wrongs to which they had been subjected to by bureau agents and others in the payment of their bounties and other allowances due them for their services in our late war; and believing that many obstacles will be thrown in the way of a fair and impartial investigation of such frauds by those who were foremost in the perpetration of the same, therefore I tender my services and testimony, tending to throw as much light on the matter as possible, that the immediate cause of such frauds may be easily discovered, and that the blame of the same may be laid upon the shoulders of those who are guilty in the premises.

In Maury County, great frauds have been committed by second parties—coadjutors of bureau agents—by charging from ten to twenty per cent. of the bounty for a pretended collection of the same, which fee was not only fraudulent if services were rendered, but was doubly so, inasmuch as that no such services as claimed had been rendered, as the claim for the collection of which the fee was obtained had been previously collected by another agent, and such was not only known by the party demanding the fee, but was known to the bureau agent, who sanctioned it, and who was already possessed of the bounty for the collection of which a fee was demanded by his coadjutors in crime. Not wishing to annoy you, I will hence refrain from giving you any further information in regard to the matter until called upon.

Very respectfully, your obedient servant,

M. M. CLOON.

Generals RUNKLE, LEWIS, and others,
Special Commissioners on Bounty Frauds,
Nashville, Tennessee.

PULASKI, TENNESSEE, *November* 5, 1867.

Received the claim of Peter Wright, of Company H Thirteenth regiment of colored infantry, for the purpose of collecting his bounty.
Advancements $1 75.

M. M. CLOON.

PULASKI, TENNESSEE, *September* 24, 1867.

Received the claim of Sophia Paul, on account of her husband, Sergeant Paul, of Company C Forty-fourth regiment United States colored infantry, for the purpose of collecting his bounty, &c.
Advancements, 50 cents.

M. M. CLOON.

HUNTSVILLE, ALABAMA, *August* 28, 1869.

I have filed claims for bounty in favor of Milly Wall, on account of the services of her deceased son.

M. M. CLOON.

(Had two witnesses.)

HUNTSVILLE, ALABAMA, *July* 13, 1869.

Received from Sergeant Jerry Billip his discharge, for the purpose of collecting the commutation of rations due him.

M. M. CLOON,
Pulaski, Tennessee,
Per ADAM.

COMMUNICATION OF M. M. CLOON TO O'NEIL AND DUFOUR.

HUNTSVILLE, ALABAMA, *September* 25, 1869.

GENTLEMEN: On my return from Tennessee, I received yours from Vevay, Indiana, of the 20th instant, per Mr. Dufour. It was gratifying to me to learn therefrom that the delay in the adjustment of our accounts was not wrought with any dishonest practices, and that a settlement would be effected on the first proximo. I am sorry, and do protest, that you have filed any certificates belonging to my claimants before consulting me in the matter, and hope that reoccurrence of the same may never again happen. It is useless to state now what damage I have sustained in the premises, but must say that you have done me great injustice and injury, whether intentionally or not, in doing so.

In regard to my character in the bureau office, I suppose that it is below par, simply because I don't allow his *pets* to rob and fleece the blacks in the payment of their bounties, &c. All their commissioners who were recently sent out to investigate matters in Tennessee, have returned, and found nothing to blow on against Cloon. In fact, they must acknowledge that the colored people all over Middle Tennessee told them that had it not been for me they would never have received half their legitimate dues; and that, whereas the investigation was seemingly solely directed against me, that it was hence a farce, tending only to deceive the colored people into the belief that they were trying to shield them from the swindling hand, thereby passing over the conduct of Howard's appointees, who had been arraigned before United States courts for their thievery, and yet disgrace the offices which they are allowed to fill.

I scorn the idea of cheating a man out of any part of his dues. 'Tis true that I have had some dealings with both white and black soldiers, but it was, as it will be, honorable. My letter of the 13th instant was written while a little excited. I hope that you will overlook its vulgarity, and hope for more consoling times.

Truly,

M. M. CLOON.

Messrs. O'NEILL & DUFOUR,
Washington, D. C.

NASHVILLE, TENNESSEE, *October* 7, 1869.

GENTLEMEN: I am here looking after the interests of our pensioners and applicants for pension who are called before the commissions appointed by the Commissioner of Pensions. The commissions are tolerable strict, and make quite a howl over any discrepancy that may show itself. You will be kind enough, and I most respectfully ask, that you furnish me immediately with the names of the different witnesses used in the pension certificates that have been issued through us so far; that is to say, you will give the names of the witnesses in all the original applications, showing what each of said witnesses has proven, and also, if additional evidence was called for in any of the cases, show what it was, and give the names of the witnesses who proved the same. I presume that you cannot give the names in the original cases, but if possible give the names in all the cases. Again, I say, show what the different witnesses have proven. Give the names of the witnesses proving death, names of witnesses proving births of children, proof of marriage, &c. Address me at Huntsville, as usual. My cases will be examined on the 19th instant.

Truly yours,

M. M. CLOON.

Messrs. O'NEILL & DUFOUR,
Washington, D. C.

HUNTSVILLE, ALABAMA, *October* 11, 1869.

I have yours of the 6th instant, through Mr. Miller. I know that you are mistaken in your belief that General Balloch requires the filing of an oath as to the amount of notarial fees advanced, except in cases where it exceeds $5, and then he requires it of all except Chipman, Hosmer & Co., who collect $6 50 in each case. The notarial fees in White's case are $3 50, and the notarial fees in Masser's case are $1. If Balloch refuses to pay the same without a sworn statement let me know it and I shall send it; which will make it $1 more. The day is not far distant when the bureau will get fits. We have all the necessary dispositions taken necessary.

Yours truly,

M. M. CLOON.

Messrs. O'NEILL & DUFOUR.

HUNTSVILLE, ALABAMA, *November* 2, 1869.

GENTLEMEN: I have yours of the 29th ultimo. I have this day written a personal letter to Van Aernam in relation to his demands. You will be out of the contest and you had better stay out and let me handle the matter and do with it as is necessary. I feel quite confident that I will show him that his demands are rather premature and untimely. You are the only agents that such a demand had been made on. I presently know the reason. I will give all things in the premises my personal attention, and keep you fully acquainted with my action.

Truly yours,

M. M. CLOON.

Messrs. O'NEILL & DUFOUR,
Washington, D. C.

HUNTSVILLE, ALABAMA, *November* 6, 1869.

GENTLEMEN: I have yours of the 2d instant. It is well that Foster is in Washington and I in Huntsville while trying to degrade me by saying that I have drawn money on forged papers and powers of attorney. I, nor any one of my name connected with me, has never drawn any money at any pension agency in Tennessee.

I learned from Stokes, the pension agent at Nashville, that the Ingersolls had drawn several hundred dollars of pension money at his agency, and only a portion had been paid to the pensioners. They claim, very correctly too, that a portion was drawn for my pensioners, and was turned over to me. I, however, can show that all the pension money received by me was paid the pensioners, less fees, by vouchers which were signed and acknowledged before the county court clerk, and which I hold in my possession. You say that if you are suspended on my account you hence would hold me responsible. This seems to me a very foolish expression. Reason alone can teach you that you are not responsible for my acts. Should I violate any of the rulings of any of the bureaus of the War Department, then do you do it? You have nothing to do with me, nor I with you, only in a foreign official manner. That is, I commission you to attend to my matters in Washington, and hence you don't direct, order, nor command me; if any such had to be done, I should in point of reason be the dictator. Now, if I was an agent of yours, regularly constituted and paid by you, then you very probably would be held to account for my acts, simply because you had the supervision and direction of my business in your hands. But as it is you have no such authority. You should have corrected the heads of departments when they speak of me as being your agent. Why not tell them that I am correspondent, and not your agent. However, it is useless to dwell on this matter. It is only a malice they have in store for me, and they can't get a more suitable time to let it come.

I shall say very little upon the matter till after I interview the commission again, which will be in a few days. Whereas it is essential that I should know what is going on in the departments, that I may move accordingly, you will therefore keep me posted. I will make things come all right by the 20th instant. I am sorry that you will not presently remit my fees. However, although I need it, you can hold it till things are amicably fixed. You can tell that blowhard, French, that I am the only Cloon from whom you received claims.

Very respectfully,

M. M. CLOON.

Messrs. O'NEILL & DUFOUR.

HUNTSVILLE, ALABAMA, *November* 12, 1869.

GENTLEMEN: I have yours of the 6th instant with inclosures. I have just returned from Tennessee, after investigating the cause of General Foster's remarks. I found that the Ingersoll Brothers have acted rather imprudently and unwise in having drawn pension money of several colored pensioners, and having appropriated the whole or the greater portion of it to their own interests. I had the misfortune of having prepared the papers necessary to drawing such moneys—whereas, the parties resided in Giles County, and hence, having been asked by said parties to prepare papers and forward the same to them, I could not very well refuse and hence done so. Some persons have attempted to implicate me as a party to such proceedings, and I have, seemingly, been reported to the departments in such a position. I can show, however, to the satisfaction of all persons, that I am entirely innocent of any complicity whatever in the matter. W. W. Ingersoll has been indicted by grand jury now in session in the federal court-room, at Nash-

ville; so far there has been four true bills brought in against him by that body. This, however, I say confidentially, as nobody knows it but me, outside of the jurors. They have attempted to indict me as accomplice, but have failed so far. I don't know what they may do before adjourning, however. As I told you in my last, I want that I have the handling of this trouble and let you be out of it. I know what I can do in the premises.
Truly yours,

M. M. CLOON.

Messrs. O'NEILL & DUFOUR,
  Washington, D. C.

HUNTSVILLE, ALABAMA, *November* 18, 1869.

GENTLEMEN: I interviewed the pension commissioners on yesterday and the day prior, in relation to our matters. I will not at present give you an account of our conversations. Suffice it to say that the same was satisfactory to all parties, and that I will be fully exonerated from any complicity with the swindling and other depredations committed in Tennessee. Furthermore, I will say (notwithstanding that the subject was not mentioned between the commissioners and I) that Foster will, before the middle of January next, retract and fully excuse himself from the charges made to you against me, not only to myself, but he must also do it to you. God knows, if others don't, that it is not my intention to swindle neither individuals nor the government, and hence, I never shall allow persons to scandalize me in such an odious manner.
Truly yours,

M. M. CLOON.

O'NEILL & DUFOUR,
  Washington, D. C.

HUNTSVILLE, ALABAMA, *September* 30, 1869.

GENTLEMEN: I have yours of the 27th instant, with a partial, and, as I think, an inaccurate statement of the present status of our accounts. I wish that you will prepare a full and complete statement of the same, embracing our entire business from the time that you last received a remittance from me. This is essential that we may clearly see how we stand; the names of each and everybody whose claim was settled should be given; the amount of notarial advancements collected, as directed by me in my letter directing you to file the certificates at one time held by my orders. The amounts of notarial fees collected by you in the last cases fall far behind the amounts advanced by me for such purposes; therefore I deem it only just and right that I hold you responsible for the *deficit*, in view of the fact that you filed the certificates without consulting me, which I think was very wrong. I have advanced as much as $3 in cases where only $1 is collected, besides being deprived of my money for a long time. I will therefore hold you responsible for $52 50, notarial advancements in the last cases settled, which amount was advanced by me, as I can show by the certificate of the clerk before whom the papers were executed, and who received the same (fees.) Whereas I don't intend filing all my claims hereafter through you, I therefore don't hold you to the $1 fee in any case, but I would suggest

$2 50 in each case, providing you keep a record. Under this rule, you can get a good number of cases from me. Make known your intention in the matter as early as practicable, as I have a goodly number which I must file forthwith.

Truly yours,

M. M. CLOON.

Messrs. O'NEILL & DUFOUR.

PULASKI, TENNESSEE, *December* 28, 1869.

GENTLEMEN : I have yours of the 24th instant. I find no records of the claims of Susan Cruser and Abraham Cruser. It may be that they were forwarded from me and that no record was kept of them. You can be your own judge as to what you will do in the premises. I hope by this time that you are fully impressed with the belief that you will not be suspended on my account, and hence I respectfully ask an immediate settlement of our matters. You will remember that some time ago I wrote you, assuring you that the charges made against me by General Foster, of the Pension Bureau, would be retracted, and that I would be exonerated. Again I assure you that such will be the case as soon as I deem it advisable to make such demands; but presently I think it impracticable to do so, for the following reasons: Whereas I was the party who prepared the vouchers of the colored pensioners whose money was by Ingersoll drawn, and a portion of the same appropriated to his own purposes, so on the first investigation Mr. Trevitt, the chief of the commission making the examination, reported without having examined the records of the Pension Office to ascertain to whom was said pension money paid, thinking of course that the money was paid to me; but having had the records of the Pension Office afterward examined, then discovered that no money at all was paid to me, and excused himself to me at Huntsville, Alabama. Now, whereas I promised Trevitt that I would see that those pensioners whose vouchers I prepared would get their money, and whereas Ingersoll has promised that he would give their money, therefore I am awaiting the payment of said money to said pensioners before I make a peremptory demand on General Foster for a retraction.

The second reason is that I think that the fighting of one department at the same time is sufficient, and having just terminated a fierce attack with General Howard and Mr. French, which resulted in my exoneration by Mr. French, and the crime of odium and the most disgraceful swindling left at the door of Howard and his subordinates, he has already cleaned out his subordinate at this point, and I think has removed them at Huntsville, and at other points.

I hold in my possession a personal letter from Mr. French, which is very complimentary, and, as I have said, exonerates me from all prejudicial evidence filed in his office.

Now I have just opened a big row with the assistant adjutant general, which bids fair to be quite spicy, and as others, he will have to act with justice toward me, for I never will stand undeserved censure and abuse detrimental to my honor. They may suspend agents whose acts called for it without resistance; but with the assistance of God, I never will allow such an imposition on my rights without resistance, first by exhausting all gentlemanly, just, and legitimate means, and if such avail nothing, then I will make the matter personal with the trespasser. It is astonishing to me that you have failed to send me any information about my commission claims. What about them; are they suspended, or have they been settled? Inquire into the matter and make known all about them. The last notice received of the settlement of a claim through you was in the case of Moses Musser, and Hiram and Rachel White, parents of William. The companies, ranks, and regiments, together with the numbers of certificates in each case, should be given, and always notification should be immediately sent on the settlement of a claim, and the amount of my notarial fees ascertained; thereby we can get along amicably and without contention. I now receive the Daily Globe regularly. Hoping that you will, without delay, attend to matters herein alluded to, I remain respectfully,

M. M. CLOON.

Messrs. O'NEILL & DUFOUR,
   Washington, D. C.

I inclose Emeline Brewer's vouchers.

PULASKI, TENNESSEE, *January* 18, 1870.

GENTLEMEN: I have yours of 14th instant inclosing copy of letter from Pension Office. Such information was unexpected from that source, as I had anticipated that all matters were satisfactorily arranged. It is a direct insult to honor and decency, and I assure you I am at a loss to know how to treat it. I surmise that it had its origin in a written demand made by me on the 4th instant on General Foster, of the Pension Bureau, demanding a retraction of the charges brought against me by that functionary, which he made known to you. If God permits he will have to retract or do something else, or have his name published as a liar and "ruffian."

If Mr. Van Aernam has the power, "right or wrong," to so illy abuse me and suspend my operations in his office, then I must succumb; but so long as I have a mind to think and a motive power to urge, I will oppose it. It all has originated in malice, black and deep, and only is calculated to do me wrong and to gratify their spirit of revenge. I have been for the past six months trying to break down the swindling of General Balloch and others of the Freedmen's Bureau, and have been continually complaining of their conduct to General Howard, all to no avail. I brought the matter to the notice of the Secretary of War and Adjutant General of the army, without effect. I finally prepared a full history of the whole matter and sent it to the Second Auditor, and in about three weeks thereafter a military commission was sent here to investigate the nature of the charges. It was composed of Generals Lewis and Runkle and Captain Sladen, by brevet rank. They came into town without giving any notice of their intention to come, nor their object. Of course their object was to have as few as possible go before them, and hence they did not wish it to be known, fearing that the victims of bureau corruption would be there in force to recite their wrongs inflicted by their bureau guardians. They sat here on the 10th and 11th instant. They refused to hear any complaints against bureau agents, and conducted the most corrupt farce in the form of an investigation that has ever been seen or heard of. They got up a big string of evidence against claim agents, and more particularly against Chipman, Hosmer & Co. They were either ignorant of or entirely ignored the common rulings of courts of justice. I having been present, a feeling of disgust and indignation pervaded my whole system. After listening for awhile to their mockery, and all of a sudden, when I no longer could stand such proceedings, I gave vent to my pent-up indignation by protesting against their ridiculous proceedings. They attempted to motion me into awe by the waving of their hands and stamping of their feet, but it prevailed not. I overcame them, and during the balance of the day things were kept straight, during which time we hurled it at bureau agents. However, the next day came with a less brighter aspect. Things were changed from the course pursued the day previous. The commission put on a bold front and were determined to do as they were directed, I suppose, to hide the enormity of the bureau ring. So in a few words I on the next day, the 11th instant, my words not prevailing, cleaned the court-room and put Mr. Generals to flight. They were glad to get out of town with their coat-tails unharmed, after assuring me that they would direct the Secretary of War to attend to me. Now what do I expect from the Adjutant General, the Secretary of the Interior, the Commissioner of Pensions, or any other head of a department, when a set of round-heads with shoulder straps, indicative of general's rank on their coats, can't conduct an impartial investigation in favor of the deluded negro? I expect nothing from such officials. Hence, as I have already said, I know not how to take matters. I can only frown on them with derision. Men who resort to the lowest depths of meanness and lying to degrade a supposed enemy will not permit me to exonerate myself from their foul slanders and calumny. Truth will live forever, while falsehoods will triumph only for awhile. Then be ye patient. In regard to the instructions of Mr. Van Aernam, wherein he orders you not to correspond with me in relation to pension claims, nor forward to me any certificates, this is absurd beyond precedence. What right has Van Aernam in saying that you shall not correspond with only such as he directs? Is he governor of your business? Does he preside over the destinies of yours, as well as the Pension Office? He has the power to suspend you if he can clearly show that the welfare of the government and applicants for pension demand it. We must not submit silently to a known wrong upon our rights. How can he legitimately demand, nor can you comply with, such an absurd request without my consent? I designated you as the attorneys, and not the claimants; hence, regularly speaking, the power on which you operate is null—as in only a few instances were the claimants aware that you were the attorneys named. You, then, in obedience to the behests of Foster, Van Aernam, and others, tell me that I must have no say so in such claims. Please pause on the matter for a little and see if you can reconcile it as being legitimate, before you add insult to injury—before you attempt to be a party to my proscription. Claim business is the smallest part of my business. I care not ever again to file another claim; but can I stand by and see my character, honor, and all that is worth living for trampled under foot basely, without resisting such proceedings? Not I. It is contrary to my temperament and ideas. If it is better for our mutual interests that I have no say-so in matters, then I will be only happy to remain reticent; but I can't stuff Van Aernam's suggestions. I want, as I have already said, a list of all my settled claims and an immediate settlement of our accounts. Gentlemen, I want nothing but justice. That I must have, else it will not be my fault. This hurried letter I have written in good faith and not for the purpose of abusing anybody; so you will please to so consider it.

Respectfully, &c.,

M. M. CLOON.

Messrs. O'NEILL & DUFOUR,
    Washington, D. C.

BOUNTIES TO COLORED SOLDIERS.

FIFTIETH DAY'S PROCEEDINGS.

The commission met at 10 a. m. Friday, March 4, 1870, and continued examining the records and making out the report. At 4 p. m. the commission adjourned.

BEN. P. RUNKLE,
Brevet Colonel United States Army.
J. R. LEWIS,
Brevet Colonel United States Army.
J. A. SLADEN,
Brevet Captain United States Army, Recorder.

FIFTY-FIRST DAY'S PROCEEDINGS.

The commission met at 10 a. m. Saturday, March 5, 1870, finishing and signing reports. At 12 m. the commission adjourned *sine die.*

BEN. P. RUNKLE,
Brevet Colonel United States Army.
J. R. LEWIS,
Brevet Colonel United States Army.
J. A. SLADEN,
Brevet Captain United States Army, Recorder.

PENSION OFFICE, A.

DEPARTMENT OF THE INTERIOR, PENSION OFFICE,
Washington, D. C., February 11, 1870.

GENTLEMEN: In compliance with your request I transmit herewith a statement giving the condition and payments made in some of the cases enumerated in your list.

Of the other cases mentioned in your list this office has no record.

As to the names of the attorneys to whom payments have been made in the admitted cases, you will have to apply to the Third Auditor for information, as this office has no evidence on that point.

Respectfully,

C. S. TREVITT,
Chief Clerk, for Commissioner.

SPECIAL AGENTS, *Investigating Complaints Against Officers, &c., Room 7, Plant's Building, Bureau Refugees, Freedmen and Abandoned Lands.*

Adaline Williams, mother of Isum, No. 158,630. Claim pending. Witnesses to original application, Columbus Gordon and Milton Gordon.

Julia Tucker, widow of Congo, No. 168,851, claim for pension pending. Witnesses to original application, Eliza Smith and Katy Glenn.

Nancy Johnson, widow of Benjamin, No. 169,981. Claim for pension pending. Witnesses, Izra Potter and Henry Johnson.

Stephen Sloss, No. 130,548. Claim pending. Witnesses, Anderson Sloss and Henry Everly.

H. Ex. Doc. 241——16

BOUNTIES TO COLORED SOLDIERS.

Mary Buford, widow of Solomon, No. 103,678. Pension certificate was issued and sent to B. D. Hyam, of this city, November 26, 1867; rate, $8 per month from March 13, 1864, and $2 additional for one child from July 25, 1866. Paid to September 4, 1868. Nashville agency.

Sophia Parkeson, widow of Berry, No. 115,913. Pension certificate was issued and sent to O'Neill & Dufour of this city October 5, 1868; rate $8 per month from January 18, 1865, and $2 additional for each of three children from July 25, 1866. Paid to September 4, 1868, to W. W. Ingersoll, attorney. Nashville agency.

Winnie Roberts, widow of Henry, No. 119,091. Pension certificate was issued and sent to J. O'Neill of this city, September 21, 1868; rate $8 per month from January 3, 1866, and $2 additional for each of two children from July 25, 1866. Paid to September 4, 1868, (to W. W. Ingersoll, attorney, $357 47.) Nashville agency.

Hannah Booker, widow of Archibald, No. 112,220. Pension certificate was issued April 25, 1868; rate $8 per month, commencing April 11, 1864. Paid to September 4, 1868. Nashville agency.

Mary Edwards, widow of John, application No. 181,345. Pension allowed in January, 1870. The other cases mentioned in your list cannot be found on the records or files of this office.

PENSION OFFICE, B.

DEPARTMENT OF THE INTERIOR, PENSION OFFICE,
Washington, D. C., February 15, 1870.

SIR: In compliance with your request of the 11th instant, I give herewith a statement showing the status of pension cases called for in your letter, viz:

Rachel Crofford, widow of Henderson. Pension certificate No. 130,571 was issued and sent to O'Neill & Dufour of this city, June 17, 1869, payable at Nashville, rate $8 per month, commencing December 17, 1864, and $2 additional for one child from July 25, 1866. No payments made.

Bidda J. English, widow of Franklin. Pension certificate No. 129,441 was issued and sent to O'Neill & Dufour May 21, 1869, payable at Nashville, rate $8, from March 13, 1864. No payments.

Amanda Grimes, widow of Alfred. Pension certificate No. 129,443 was issued and sent to O'Neill & Dufour May 21, 1869, payable at Nashville, rate $8 from April 6, 1865, and additional $2 for each of two children from July 25, 1866. No payments.

Rhoda Jones, widow of Nelson. Pension certificate No. 131,748 was issued and sent to J. J. McCarty of this city July 14, 1869, payable at Nashville, rate $8 from July 29, 1865, and $2 additional for one child from July 25, 1866. No payments.

Mary Rountree, widow of Albert. Pension certificate No. 131,535 was issued and sent to O'Neill & Dufour July 9, 1869, payable at Nashville, rate $8 from April 8, 1864, and $2 additional for each of three children from July 25, 1866. No payments.

The case of Ruthie Fox, widow of Benjamin, was admitted September 4, 1869. No payments.

Respectfully,

H. VAN AERNAM,
Commissioner.

Captain J. A. SLADEN,
Room No. 7, Plant's Building, Present.

BOUNTIES TO COLORED SOLDIERS. 243

War Department, Bureau of Refugees,
Freedmen and Abandoned Lands, Claim Division,
Washington, D. C., February 8, 1870.

Captain: In accordance with your letters of the 2d and 3d instants, forwarding lists of names of colored soldiers, with request for information respecting the settlement or condition of their claims for bounty, &c., I am directed to inclose herewith a report covering such cases comprised in the lists referred to as have been settled and adjusted through this office.

The other names included in your lists have been forwarded to the honorable Second Auditor, from whom an immediate report is expected as to the condition of the respective claims, if filed in his office, which will be furnished the commission promptly upon its receipt.

Very respectfully, your obedient servant,
WILLIAM P. DREW,
Agent Bureau Refugees, Freedmen and Abandoned Lands,
Chief of Claim Division.

Brevet Captain J. A. Sladen, U. S. A.,
Recorder for Military Commission, Bureau Refugees,
Freedmen and Abandoned Lands, Washington, D. C.

War Department, Bureau of Refugees,
Freedmen and Abandoned Lands, Claim Division,
Washington, D. C., February 9, 1870.

Captain: In accordance with your letters of the 4th and 5th instant, forwarding lists of names of colored soldiers, with request for information respecting the settlement or condition of their claims for bounty, &c., I am directed to inclose herewith a report covering all the cases comprised in the lists referred to.

The attorney of record in the claim of Orrin Harris, late of Company C Sixty-first United States colored troops, is Mr. B. D. Hyam, of this city, who received the claim from his correspondents, Messrs. M. Combs, jr. & Co., of Memphis, Tennessee.

Concerning Mr. D. H. Evans, nothing is known at this office further than that his name appears as an assignee of the certificate of Orrin Harris, as above.

Very respectfully, your obedient servant,
WILLIAM P. DREW,
Agent Bureau Refugees, Freedmen and Abandoned Lands,
Chief of Claim Division.

Brevet Captain J. A. Sladen, U. S. A.,
Recorder for Military Commission, Bureau Refugees,
Freedmen and Abandoned Lands, Washington, D. C.

244   BOUNTIES TO COLORED SOLDIERS.

A.—Drew's

Name of soldier.	Company and regim't.	Certificate issued in favor of—	No. of certificate.	Attorney.	Amount of certificate.
Good, John a	F, 61st c'd tr.	Rebecca Harvey, sister.	499, 868	Moyers & Dedrick, (suspended.)	$117 79
Gordon, Thomas	A, 13th	Soldier	445, 787	S. H. Ingersoll	127 80
Gilmore, Washington.	D, 14th	Mattie Gilmore, wid	468, 110	J. Jay Buck	261 73
Hargroves, Henry b..	K, 110th	Soldier	366, 706	Chipman, Hosmer & Co.	203 20
Hines, Henry c	H, 110th	Soldier	363, 225	Chipman, Hosmer & Co.	204 20
Harney, Albert	K, 110th	Soldier	366, 704	Chipman, Hosmer & Co.	203 20
Jackson, Peter d	D, 13th	Soldier	545, 932	G. H. Zeigler, attorney in fact for D. H. Prunk.	124 05
Jenkins, Jerry e	K, 110th	Soldier	366, 730	Chipman, Hosmer & Co.	203 20
Key, Elois	F, 14th	Soldier	463, 368	Moyers & Dedrick	176 00
Lansden, Thomas	F, 17th	Soldier	324, 984	S. H. Ingersoll, (suspended.)	206 20
Clay, Henry, corp'l	A, 61st	Soldier	300, 883	B. D. Hyam	300 00
Young, William	A, 55th	Soldier	361, 726	B. D. Hyam	248 97
Smith, Albert f	F, 55th	Soldier	373, 174	Moyers & Dedrick	247 87
Robinson, Edward g	B, 3d h'y art	Soldier		Moyers & Dedrick	
Bellamy, Henry	G, 61st	Soldier	338, 045	B. D. Hyam	225 56
Mooney, Alfred	F, 2d l't art	Felix Mooney, father	446, 505	C. C. Tucker	131 36
Mooney, Alfred	F, 2d l't art	Felix and Annie, par's.	446, 506	C. C. Tucker	100 00
Garner, Albert h	F, 3d h'y art	Queen Garner, widow	491, 045	Tucker & Sells	143 08
Martin, Lee h	E, 61st	Martha Martin, wid	489, 758	J. J. McCarty	295 25
McCauley, Burgess i	G, 11th	Emily J. McCauley, widow.	504, 559	Moyers & Dedrick	300 00
Smith, Babe i	F, 61st	Phillis Jeemes, sister	499, 867	Moyers & Dedrick	250 89
Taylor, Richard j	C, 11th	Virginia Taylor, sister.	480, 269	Moyers & Dedrick	100 00
Benson, Henry k	E, 46th	Soldier	507, 603	Moyers & Dedrick	255 20
Scales, John	F, 2d l't art	Emily Scales, widow	546, 908	Tucker & Sells	256 12
Lundy, Joseph k	E, 3d h'y art	Jane Lundy, widow	484, 833	Tucker & Sells	222 46
Lewis, James l	C, 11th	Hattie Davis, sister	416, 029	Moyers & Dedrick	128 80
Watkins, Daniel	F, 13th	Soldier	451, 269	A. M. Hughes	113 92
Sloss, Stephen	B, 111th	Soldier	517, 624	Jno. O'Neill, (through O'Neill and Dufour.)	301 00
Sloss, Anderson	B, 111th	Soldier	441, 561	Major Wm. Fowler	301 00
Thomas, Wm	B, 17th	Soldier	324, 934	S. H. Ingersoll, (suspended.)	208 20
Tompkins, Thomas	K, 13th	Soldier	457, 226	Chipman, Hosmer & Co.	213 21
Upshur, Thomas	K, 110th	Soldier	366, 726	Chipman, Hosmer & Co.	203 20
Vance, James	I, 110th	Soldier	366, 681	Chipman, Hosmer & Co.	300 29
Ashwood, Charles	A, 110th	Soldier	346, 678	D. C. Rugg	248 00
Blackburn, William	G, 17th	Soldier	467, 655	S. B. Brown & Son	206 20
Bailey, Paldo	K, 110th	Soldier	366, 693	Chipman, Hosmer & Co.	203 20
Brown, James	I, 110th	Soldier	366, 665	Chipman, Hosmer & Co.	300 20

a Payment suspended.   b Funds in office of C. S. O.   c Attorney paid February 28, 1868.   d Funds sent to Memphis, Tenn., January 15, 1868, not yet returned.   g Suspended in claim division December by order of Second Auditor.   i Vouchers sent to Memphis, Tenn., February 18, 1869, not returned. of Second Auditor.   l Amount returned to treasury November, 1868.

BOUNTIES TO COLORED SOLDIERS. 245

statement.

When.	Where.	Paid. By whom.	Legal fee.	Advances.	Notarial expenses.	Date of blue-letter.
			$10 00	$54 00	$4 00	Oct. 30, 1868, amount paid J. L. Hodge, P. M., U. S. A., Feb. 20, 1870, by order of Second Auditor.
June 22, 1869	Columbia, Tenn...	John L. Wilson, bureau agent.	10 00		1 50	May 21, 1868.
Nov. 6, 1868	Clarksville, Tenn.	J. C. McMullen, bureau agent.	10 00		1 00	July 3, 1868.
			10 00	100 00	6 50	February 10, 1867.
			10 00	188 20	6 00	December 7, 1867..
July 27, 1869	Columbia, Tenn...	John L. Wilson, bureau agent.	10 00	100 00	6 50	December 10, 1867.
			10 00		1 00	November 2, 1869.
			10 00	40 00	7 50	December 10, 1867.
Oct. 13, 1868	Memphis, Tenn...	Col. F. S. Palmer, bureau agent.	10 00		2 50	July 7, 1868. Paid by J. B. Coons. See letter of Feb. 11, 1870, to Wm. T. Drew.
Apr. 9, 1868	Nashville, Tenn ..	J. B. Coons, bureau agent.				April 10, 1867.
Aug. 19, 1867	Memphis, Tenn...	Col. F. S. Palmer, bureau agent.	10 00	100 00	3 00	No blue letter received, C. D. O.
Sept, 21, 1868	Memphis, Tenn...	Col. F. S. Palmer, bureau agent.	10 00	200 00	3 50	January 4, 1868.
			10 00	200 00	3 50	December 14, 1867.
Mar. 30, 1868	Memphis, Tenn...	Col. F. S. Palmer, bureau agent.	10 00	100 00	8 50	October 7, 1867.
Aug. 24, 1868	Memphis, Tenn...	Col. F. S. Palmer, bureau agent.	10 00		4 50	June 13, 1868.
Aug. 24, 1868	Memphis, Tenn...	Col. F. S. Palmer, bureau agent.	10 00		2 00	June 13, 1868.
			10 00		5 50	October 23, 1868.
			10 00		3 00	October 28, 1868.
			10 00		4 00	January 12, 1869.
			10 00		4 00	October 30, 1868.
			10 00		3 50	December 2, 1868.
			10 00		2 50	December 29, 1868.
Aug. 24, 1868	Memphis, Tenn...	Col. F. S. Palmer, bureau agent.	10 00		3 50	June 13, 1868.
						August 29, 1868.
			10 00		2 50	February 28, 1868.
Nov. 23, 1869	Xenia, Ohio......	Warren Anderson, mayor of Xenia.	10 00		2 50	May 26, 1869.
June 8, 1869	Columbia, Tenn...	John L. Wilson, bureau agent.	1 20		2 50	March 18, 1869.
June 6, 1868	Pulaski, Tenn	Lt. George E. Judd, bureau agent.			♦..	April 27, 1868.
Oct. 4, 1869	Nashville, Tenn...	J. B. Coons, bureau agent.				August 5, 1867.
Feb. 3, 1870	Nashville, Tenn...	J. B. Coons, bureau agent.	10 00		6 00	May 25, 1868.
Apr. 4, 1868	Pulaski, Tenn	Lt. George E. Judd, bureau agent.	10 00	50 00	7 50	December 10, 1867..
Oct. 26, 1869	Pulaski, Tenn	By John L. Wilson, bureau agent at Columbia, Tenn.	10 00	150 00	6 50	December 9, 1867.
Feb. 15, 1868	Huntsville, Ala...	D. C. Rugg........	10 00	20 00	1 00	November 12 1867.
Sept. 15, 1868	Nashville, Tenn...	J. B. Coons, bureau agent.	10 00			June 8, 1868.
July 27, 1868	Athens, Ala	J. H. W. Mills, bureau agent.	10 00	100 00	6 50	December 10, 1867.
Apr. 13, 1868	Pulaski, Tenn.....	Lt. George E. Judd, bureau agent.	10 00	80 00	7 00	December 9, 1867.

in office C. D. O. *e* Vouchers sent to Nashville, Tenn., January 11, 1870, not yet returned. *f* Vouchers 14, 1868, the soldier being reported dead, without heirs. *h* Amount returned to treasury, April 28, 1869, *j* Vouchers sent to Memphis, Tenn., January 21, 1869, not returned. *k* Payment suspended by order

BOUNTIES TO COLORED SOLDIERS.

A.—Drew's state

Name of soldier.	Company and regim't.	Certificate issued in favor of—	No. of certificate.	Attorney.	Amount of certificate.
Booker, Archer	I, 53d col. tr.	Hannah Booker, wid	491, 178	B. D. Hyam	$287 70
Conner, Robert, serg't.	F, 56th	Soldier	541, 038	Chipman, Hosmer & Co.	52 03
Finley, Alexander a.	D, 15th	Soldier	437, 754	Major Wm. Fowler	300 20
Dickey, Philip	A, 3d h'y art.	Hannah Ross, sister	477, 092	Moyers & Dedrick	154 60
Webster, Dallas	F, 13th	Soldier	451, 270	McQuitley & Alden, (suspended.)	218 20
MEMPHIS CASES.					
Cartman, Madison, sergeant.	G, 3d h'y art.	Soldier	491, 091	Moyers & Dedrick	240 56
Fogg, Alfred	F, 11th	Soldier	504, 542	Moyers & Dedrick	300 00
Key, Frank b	B, 55th	Soldier	320, 518	B. D. Hyam	48 31
McKinney, John	D, 64th	Soldier	509, 429	Moyers & Dedrick	206 79
Thompson, Henderson.	B, 3d h'y art.	Soldier	345, 370	Moyers & Dedrick	244 63
Young, John	F, 111th	Soldier	491, 316	W. P. Drew	100 00
Redus, Burrell, 1st sergeant.	I, 110th	Soldier	363, 256	Jno. O'Neill	316 33
Redus, Burrell, 2d sergeant.	I, 110th	Soldier	366, 678	Jno. O'Neill	300 20

a Vouchers sent to Huntsville, Ala., August 8, 1868, not returned.

B.—Drew's

Name of soldier.	Company and regim't.	Certificate issued to—	No. of certificate.	Attorney.	Amount of certificate.
Black, William, serg't.	E, 55th col. tr.	Soldier	364, 409	William Walker	$247 87
Barnett, Edward, (Edmund. not Edward, by bureau records.)	C, 55th	Soldier	364, 354	William Walker	252 00
Clay, Henry	A, 61st	See report furnished the commission by claim div'n Bureau Refugees, Freedmen and Abandoned Lands, Feb. 8, 1870.			
Young, William	A. 55th				
Smith, Albert	C, 55th				
Robinson, Edw	B, 3d, h'y art.				
Bellamy, Henry	G, 61st				
Naison, Alexander	C, 11th	Soldier	400, 318	Tucker & Sells	225 20
Gilmore, Pleasant	Pion'r corps, 16th A. C.	Soldier	369, 314	Tucker & Sells	200 00
Allen, David, serg't	D, 55th	Soldier	364, 366	B. D. Hyam	247 66
Sikes, Reuben	K, 11th	Soldier	400, 283	B. D. Hyam	300 00
Wood, Charles, (Mary Wood, as mother of. William Charles, Mary Wood, as mother of William Charles, not Charles Wood.)	M, 3d heavy artillery.		391, 368	B. D. Hyam	94 20
Ingerham, John	C, 55th	Soldier	380, 516	B. D. Hyam	252 00
Pedan, Moses *a*	A, 55th	Soldier	364, 335	B. D. Hyam	73 97
Strong, Isam	K, 11th	Soldier	400, 282	B. D. Hyam	300 00

a Amount paid attorney

BOUNTIES TO COLORED SOLDIERS. 247

ment—Continued.

When.	Where.	By whom. (Paid)	Legal fee.	Advances.	Notarial expenses.	Date of blue letter.
Mar. 22, 1869	Memphis, Tenn...	Col. F. S. Palmer, bureau agent.	$10 00	....	$6 50	December 9, 1868.
Oct. 14, 1869	Nashville, Tenn...	J. B. Coons, bureau agent.	7 50	....	3 00	September 7, 1869.
Dec. 22, 1869	Memphis, Tenn...	Col. F. S. Palmer, bureau agent.	10 00	....	4 00	April 17, 1868. August 22, 1868.
June 26, 1868	Columbia, Tenn...	John L. Wilson, bureau agent.	....	....	....	May 21, 1868.
Dec. 11, 1869	Memphis, Tenn...	Col. F. S. Palmer, bureau agent.	10 00	$104 00	2 50	Blue letter misplaced.
Dec. 22, 1869	Memphis, Tenn...	Col. F. S. Palmer, bureau agent.	10 00	80 00	3 50	January 9, 1869.
....	....	....	5 00	38 81	4 50	January 24, 1868.
Dec. 11, 1869	Memphis, Tenn...	Col. F. S. Palmer, bureau agent.	10 00	89 00	2 50	January 16, 1869.
Jan. 17, 1868	Memphis, Tenn...	Col. F. S. Palmer, bureau agent.	10 00	....	2 50	November 5, 1867.
June 16, 1869	Columbia, Tenn...	John L. Wilson, bureau agent.	....	....	....	March 9, 1869.
Jan. 16, 1868	Pulaski, Tenn.....	Lt. George E. Judd, bureau agent.	10 00	....	50	December, 9, 1867.
Jan. 16, 1868	Pulaski, Tenn	Lt. George E. Judd, bureau agent.	10 00	....	50	December 9, 1867.

b Amount paid to attorney February 18, 1868.

statement.

When.	Where.	By whom. (Paid)	Legal fee.	Advances.	Notarial expenses.	Date of blue-letter.
Apr. 13, 1868	Memphis, Tenn...	Col. F. S. Palmer, bureau agent.	$10 00	$46 75	......	December 14, 1867.
Apr. 7, 1868	Memphis, Tenn...	Col. F. S. Palmer, bureau agent.	10 00	46 75	......	December 13, 1867.
Mar. 20, 1868	Memphis, Tenn...	Col. F. S. Palmer, bureau agent.	10 00	75 00	$3 00	B. L. misplaced.
Feb. 28, 1868	Memphis, Tenn...	Col. F. S. Palmer, bureau agent.	10 00	178 00	3 00	December 27, 1867.
Aug. 1, 1868	Memphis, Tenn...	Col. F. S. Palmer, bureau agent.	10 00	40 00	3 50	December 13, 1867.
Sept. 29, 1868	Memphis, Tenn...	Col. F. S. Palmer, bureau agent.	10 00	20 00	3 50	February 12, 1868.
Sept. 11, 1868	Memphis, Tenn...	Col. F. S. Palmer, bureau agent.	7 50	50 00	6 50	February 7, 1868.
May 18, 1868	Memphis, Tenn...	Col. F. S. Palmer, bureau agent.	10 00	100 00	6 50	January 24, 1868.
....	....	....	7 50	60 97	5 50	February 14, 1868.
Aug. 17, 1868	Memphis, Tenn ..	Col. F. S. Palmer, bureau agent.	10 00	40 00	3 50	February 12 1868.
July 19, 1868.						

248   BOUNTIES TO COLORED SOLDIERS.

B.—*Drew's state*

Name of soldier.	Company and regim't.	Certificate issued to—	No. of certificate.	Attorney.	Amount of certificate.
Moody, William	E, 11th col. tr.	Soldier	391,156	Moyers & Dedrick	$206 60
Dandridge, William, Q. M. S.	B, 3d h'y art.	Soldier	345,353	Moyers & Dedrick	272 09
Kimball, Cyrus, sg't, (private, by bureau records.)	F, 11th	Soldier	391,187	Moyers & Dedrick	300 00
Johnson, Green	B, 3d h'y art.	Soldier	345,361	Moyers & Dedrick	244 63
Dillworth, John, (John Dillworth, by bureau records.)	H, 55th	Soldier	373,213	Moyers & Dedrick	244 85
Hilton, Mathew	B, 11th	Martha Hilton, as wid.	402,941	Tucker & Sells	279 60
Warren, Joseph, (jr., as shown by bureau records.)	B, 11th	Mary Warren, as wid.	402,963	Tucker & Sells	279 60
Alston, Alexander, (Alexandria Alston, by bureau records.)	B, 55th	Soldier	361,737	B. D. Hyam	248 31
Brown, Warren, Q. M. S.	G, 3d h'y art.	Soldier	345,312	Moyers & Dedrick	262 53
Buchanan, John	G, 11th	Soldier	396,280	Moyers & Dedrick	300 00
Means, Humphrey	E, 61st	Soldier	337,993	D. B. Hyam	227 51
Morse, Abraham, corpor'l, (Abraham Marsh, by bureau records.)	L, 3d h'y art.	Soldier	345,336	D. B. Hyam	204 76
Polk, Abraham	G, 11th	Soldier	396,311	D. B. Hyam	300 00
Persons, Daniel	F, 11th	Soldier	396,269	Moyers & Dedrick	300 00
Tausel, Moses, serg't, (Moses Tausell, by bureau records.)	B, 11th	Nice Ann Tausell, as widow.	402,956	Tucker & Sells	312 06
Robinson, Samuel	C, 55th	Soldier	364,369	Frank Bras	252 00
Canady, Peter, corp'l, (Peter Cannady, by bureau records.)	H, 11th	Soldier	396,329	Moyers & Dedrick	300 00
Coney Washington, (Washington Conley, by bu. records.)	K, 63d	Soldier	366,427	Frank Bras	106 00

BOUNTIES TO COLORED SOLDIERS. 249

ment—Continued.

When.	Paid.		Am'ts paid attorney.			Date of blue letter.
	Where.	By whom.	Legal fee.	Advances.	Notarial expenses.	
Mar. 24, 1868	Memphis, Tenn...	Col. F. S. Palmer, bureau agent.	$10 00	$50 00	$3 50	February 6, 1868.
Apr. 10, 1868	Memphis, Tenn...	Col. F. S. Palmer, bureau agent.	10 00	50 00	3 50	February 27, 1868.
Mar. 30, 1868	Memphis, Tenn...	Col. F. S. Palmer, bureau agent.	10 00	25 00	3 50	February 8, 1868.
May 4, 1868	Memphis, Tenn...	Col. F. S. Palmer, bureau agent.	10 00	172 50	3 50	February 27, 1868.
Mar. 16, 1868	Memphis, Tenn...	Col. F. S. Palmer, bureau agent.	10 00	60 00	3 50	December 16, 1867.
Apr. 18, 1868	Memphis, Tenn...	Col. F. S. Palmer, bureau agent.	10 00	65 00	4 00	February 25, 1868.
Apr. 20, 1868	Memphis, Tenn...	Col. F. S. Palmer, bureau agent.	10 00	60 00	6 00	February 25, 1868.
Mar. 9, 1868	Memphis, Tenn...	Col. F. S. Palmer, bureau agent.	10 00	100 00	6 00	December 12, 1867.
Apr. 27, 1868	Memphis, Tenn...	Col. F. S. Palmer, bureau agent.	10 00	125 00	3 50	February 27, 1868.
May 14, 1868	Memphis, Tenn...	Col. F. S. Palmer, bureau agent.	10 00	25 00	3 50	February 10, 1868.
May 9, 1868	Memphis, Tenn...	Col. F. S. Palmer, bureau agent.	10 00	150 00	4 00	October 16, 1867.
Mar. 20, 1868	Memphis, Tenn...	Col. F. S. Palmer, bureau agent.	10 00	80 00	5 50	November 5, 1867.
Mar. 30, 1868	Memphis, Tenn...	Col. F. S. Palmer, bureau agent.	10 00	100 00	6 50	February 10, 1868.
May 9, 1868	Memphis, Tenn...	Col. F. S. Palmer, bureau agent.	10 00	110 00	3 50	February 8, 1868.
Apr. 20, 1868	Memphis, Tenn...	Col. F. S. Palmer, bureau agent.	10 00	150 00	4 50	February 25, 1868.
June 1, 1868	Memphis, Tenn...	Col. F. S. Palmer, bureau agent.	10 00	150 00	3 00	January 31, 1868.
May 5, 1868	Memphis, Tenn...	Col. F. S. Palmer, bureau agent.	10 00	50 00	3 50	February 10, 1867.
May 19, 1868	Memphis, Tenn...	Col. F. S. Palmer, bureau agent.	10 00	40 00	3 00	December 18, 1867.

DREW'S STATEMENT C.

WAR DEPARTMENT, BUREAU OF REFUGEES, FREEDMEN
AND ABANDONED LANDS, CLAIM DIVISION,
Washington, D. C., February 11, 1870.

CAPTAIN: In answer to your request of the 8th instant, for information concerning settlement and payment of the claim of Elvis Key, late private Company F 14th United States colored troops, I am directed to state that a re-examination of the records of this bureau shows the claim to have been settled by Second Auditor's certificate, No. 463,368, for $176, (being $100 original bounty, act of July 22, 1861, and $100 additional bounty, act of July 28, 1866, less $24 overpaid on company rolls,) and the amount (less $12 50 attorney's fee and notarial expenses) paid by check No. 1,381 of the chief disbursing officer of this bureau, for $163 50, sent October 13, 1868, to J. B. Coons, esq., agent and disbursing officer at Nashville, Tennessee.

The mistake in report of the 8th instant, from this office, arose from erroneous statement forwarded from the office of the chief disbursing officer that the claim was paid through Lieutenant Colonel F. S. Palmer, agent and disbursing officer at Memphis, Tennessee.

Very respectfully, &c.,
WILLIAM P. DREW,
Agent Bureau Refugees, Freedmen and Abandoned Lands,
Chief of Claim Division.

Brevet Captain J. A. SLADEN, *U. S. A.,*
Recorder for Military Commission Bureau Refugees,
Freedmen and Abandoned Lands, Washington, D. C.

DREW'S STATEMENT D.

WAR DEPARTMENT, BUREAU OF REFUGEES, FREEDMEN
AND ABANDONED LANDS, CLAIM DIVISION,
Washington, February 12, 1870.

CAPTAIN: In answer to your letter of the 11th instant for information concerning the settlement and payment of the claim of William Redus, first, late corporal Company I One hundred and tenth United States colored troops, I am directed to state that the records of this bureau show the claim to have been settled by certificate No. 366,677, (received at this office January 7, 1868,) for $300 20, of which $215 50 ($10 legal fee, $5 50 notarial expenses, and $200 advances) was paid on the same date to Messrs. Chipman, Hosmer & Co., attorneys in the claim, by check No. 57 of the chief disbursing officer of this bureau on United States treasury.

The advance appears to have been made October 23, 1867, by Daniel S. Mann, as agent of Messrs. Chipman, Hosmer & Co., and is sworn to by them by affidavit dated January 3, 1868.

Vouchers for the payment of the balance ($84 70) to the claimant were sent by the chief disbursing officer, November 12, 1868, to J. H. Wager, agent and disbursing officer at Athens, Alabama.

These vouchers were returned to this office December 4, 1868, by Mr. Wager, with affidavit of Redus that he received but $100 advances.

On December 10, 1868, this affidavit was inclosed to Messrs. Chipman, Hosmer & Co., with request for their report in the case.

The vouchers on which the advance of $200 had been allowed by this office having been forwarded by the chief disbursing officer with his accounts to the honorable Second Auditor, it became necessary to recall the same for examination, which was done by letter of February 19, 1869, from this office.

No receipts of the claimant being returned with these vouchers, another search was made by request of this office, with report, dated May 20, 1869, that no receipts were received with the accounts.

A certificate (No. 493,411) having been received at this office, May 1, 1869, in favor of Toliver Redus, as brother of William Redus, deceased, late corporal Company I One hundred and tenth United States colored troops, investigation as to the alleged advances in the case of William Redus was suspended, on suspicion that either his claim, or that of his brother, or both, were fraudulent. It was finally ascertained, however, that the claim of Toliver Redus was genuine, as brother of William Redus, second, deceased.

It is but just to add that Messrs. Chipman, Hosmer & Co. have repeatedly acknowledged themselves responsible for any errors in this and similar cases, and willing to refund whenever called upon by this office, after satisfactory investigation.

Mr. Wager, of this bureau, has been kept informed concerning this case by letters from this office.

I have ventured to be thus full and explicit in this case, as it is one of a number which have been under investigation by this office for several months, among them the cases of Henry Hines, Company H One hundred and tenth; Alexander Brooks, Company F One hundred and tenth; Benjamin Luder, Company K One hundred and tenth; Paldo Bailey, Company K One hundred and tenth; Charles Kemp, Company E Forty-fourth; John Jackson, Company I One hundred and tenth, and others; all of which it is believed will be eventually adjusted by this office without loss to the claimants.

Very respectfully, your obedient servant,
WILLIAM P. DREW,
Agent Bureau Refugees, Freedmen and Abandoned Lands,
Chief of Claim Division.

Brevet Captain J. A. SLADEN, *U. S. A.*,
Recorder for Military Commission Bureau of Refugees,
Freedmen and Abandoned Lands, Washington, D. C.

WAR DEPARTMENT, BUREAU OF REFUGEES, FREEDMEN
AND ABANDONED LANDS, CLAIM DIVISION,
Washington, D. C., February 23, 1870.

CAPTAIN: In further answer to your letters of the 2d and 3d instant, inclosing lists of names of colored soldiers, with request for information respecting the settlement or condition of their claims for bounty, &c., I am directed to inclose herewith a report covering such (unsettled) cases comprised in the lists referred to as were not included in reports forwarded to you from this office on the 8th and 9th instant, respectively.

The information contained in the inclosed report has been obtained from the office of the honorable Second Auditor of the Treasury.

Very respectfully, your obedient servant,
WILLIAM P. DREW,
Agent Bureau of Refugees, Freedmen and Abandoned Lands,
Chief of Claim Division.

Brevet Captain J. A. SLADEN, *U. S. A.*,
Recorder for Military Commission Bureau of Refugees,
Freedmen and Abandoned Lands, Washington, D. C.

BOUNTIES TO COLORED SOLDIERS.

E.—Drew's statement.

Name.	Company and regiment.	Attorney.	Remarks.
Body, Pope, (Adeline Warren and Aggie Parish, sisters, claimants.)	F, 3d U. S. col. h. art...	Moyers & Dedrick, Memphis, Tenn.	Settled October 22, 1868, and certificate No. 484,861 for $146 40, sent to attorneys. T. L. Dean and C. E. Bent, witnesses.
Barlow, George	I, 13th U. S. col. tr'ps..	John O'Neill, Washington, D. C.	Suspended for information from Adjutant General's Office. Discharge not on file.
Cook, Silas	D, 101st U. S. col. tr'ps..	J. C. McMullen, Clarksville, Tenn.	Disallowed July 28, 1867. Paid $100 bounty, act July 4, 1864, all he was entitled to. Discharge sent to attorney.
Dickerson, Edward	A, 13th U. S. col. tr'ps		No claim registered in case as stated.
Diggs, James R.	M, 9th Tenn. cavalry..		No claim.
Drake, Lafayette, (Martha Drake, mother, claimant, Huntsville, Ala.)	G, 101st U. S. col. tr'ps.	James Cloon	Suspended for proof of heirship by persons who can write, &c., giving the circumstances under which they knew the parties, length of time, place, &c. Identifying witnesses, Peter and Philip Ackland, who sign by mark; attesting witnesses, A. P. McIntyre and B. J. Sheridan.
Elliott, Silas	K, 101st U. S. col. tr'ps.	B. D. Hyam, Washington, D. C.	Disallowed April 8, 1868. Paid $100 bounty, act July 4, 1864, all that was due. Discharge sent to attorney.
Fusill, Johnson	I, 55th U. S. col. tr'ps..	R. McAllister, Washington, D. C.	Settled April 8, 1867, and certificate No. 294,426 for $265 sent to attorney.
Finley, Alexander	D, 15th U. S. col. tr'ps		Witnesses T. U. Green and John W. Rames.
Freeman, Sandy	I, 12th U. S. col. tr'ps..	Bunts & Lindsley, Nashville, Tenn.	Settled August 23, 1866; certificate No. 264,369, for $98 77, sent to attorneys.
Frierson, Columbus, (Abby Frierson, Nashville, Ten., claims as mother, and Sallie Frierson, Columbia, Tenn., also claims as mother.)	B, 17th U. S. col. tr'ps..	Freedmen's Bureau.	Contested claim. No settlement. Soldier belonged to 14th U. S. colored troops, not 17th.
Fogg, Alfred	F, 110th U. S. col. tr'ps.		No claim registered in case as stated.
Grier, Henry	B, 55th U. S. col. tr'ps..	B. D. Hyam, Washington, D. C.	Settled March 25, 1867, and certificate No. 293,704, for $248 31 sent to attorney.
Goodman, Lucas	I, 15th U. S. col. tr'ps..	Beant Noah, Columbia, Tenn.	Disallowed June 19, 1869; paid $200 bounty act July 4, 1864, all he was entitled to. Discharge on file in claim division, Bureau Refugees, Freedmen, and Abandoned Lands.
Greed, T. M	I, 110th U. S. col. tr'ps		No claim on file as stated.
Green, Joseph W	K, 110th U. S. col. tr'ps		No claim on file as stated.
Gallegher, Mack	C, 12th U. S. col. h. a	W. A. Lord, Nashville, Tenn.	Awaiting information from Adjutant General's Office, called for Feb. 9, 1870.
Goff, Sorrow	C, 101st U. S. col. tr'ps.		Out for settlement, and will be disposed of very soon.
Goode, John, (Rebecca Harvey, sister, claimant.)	F, 61st U. S. col. tr'ps..	Moyers & Dedrick, Memphis, Tenn.	Settled October 29, 1868, and certificate No. 490,868, for $117 79, sent to attorneys. Witnesses, Israel Harvey and Thornton Gaylor; residence, Memphis, Tenn.
Goode, Washington, (Rebecca Harvey, sister, cl'mant.)	F, 61st U. S. col. tr'ps..		Claim contested. In hands of Col. Palmer. Witnesses, Israel Harvey and Thornton Gaylor.
Harris, Orrin	C, 61st U. S. col. tr'ps..	B. D. Hyam, Washington, D. C.	Settled January 23, 1867, and certificate No. 285,264. for $300, sent to attorney,

BOUNTIES TO COLORED SOLDIERS. 253

E.—*Drew's statement*—Continued.

Name.	Company and regiment.	Attorney.	Remarks.
Harney, Simon............	D, 12th U. S. col. tr'ps.	....	No claim on file as stated.
Jordan, Daniel.............	F, 44th U. S. col. tr'ps.	Chipman, Hosmer & Co., Washington, D. C.	Disallowed May 18, 1868; paid $200 bounty, act July 4, 1864, all he was entitled to.
Johnson, Benjamin.......	D, 110th U. S. col. tr'ps.	....	Under examination.
Japper, William C.........	E, 39th U. S. col. tr'ps	....	No claim registered in case as stated.
Kimber, Thomas...........	A, 14th U. S. col. tr'ps.	S. H. Ingersoll, Nashville, Tenn.	Suspended for statement of correct service. Adjutant General reports name not borne on rolls.
Killick, Logan, (Marshall Johnson, brother, claimant.)	A, 55th U. S. col. tr'ps.	....	Fraudulent claim filed; now under investigation.
Killick, Richard, (Marshall Johnson, claimant.)	A, 55th U. S. col. tr'ps.	....	Fraudulent claim filed; no settlement.
Luper, Joseph	D, 3d U. S. col. h. art..	Chipman, Hosmer & Co., Washington, D. C.	Disallowed June 13, 1868, paid $100 bounty, act July 4, 1864, all he was entitled to. Discharge sent to attorneys.
Luper, Joseph	C, 3d U. S. col. h. art...	....	No claim registered in case as stated.
Love, William	B, 101st U. S. col. tr'ps.	....	No claim registered in case as stated.
Martin, Joseph M., (Ann McClenahan, Cedar st., Nashville, Tennessee, claimant.)	D, 14th U. S. col. tr'ps.	A. M. Hughes, Tennessee military State agent, Washington, D. C.	Disallowed March 15, 1869, soldier slave April 19, 1861; brothers and sister not entitled to bounty, act July 28, 1866. Discharge sent to attorney.
McSwan, Alexander......	E, 1st U. S. col. h. art..	....	No claim registered in case as stated.
McClure, Jackson..........	E, 1st U. S. col. h. art..	Wolf, Hart & Co., Washington, D. C.	Settled. Amount recovered by this office and paid to claimant.
McKay, Henry	A, 12th U. S. col. tr'ps	....	No claim registered in case as stated.
Miller, Henry...............	F, 3d U. S. col. troops..	Geo. Cragg & Bro., Philadelphia, Pa.	Claim disallowed October 12, 1868. Soldier was a substitute and not entitled to bounty. Was paid all dues on muster-out. Discharge was sent to attorneys.
McClellan, Elias	D, 12th U. S. col. tr'ps..	....	No claim in case registered as stated.
Nickerson, Ellis	H, 101st U. S. col. tr'ps.	....	No claim in case registered as stated.
Roberson, George, (Harry Roberson, father, claimant.)	E, 101st U. S. col. tr'ps.	....	No claim on file as stated.
Silkin, Michael, (Eliza Silkin, widow, claimant,)	E, 101st U. S. col. tr'ps.	....	No claim on file as stated,
Sumners, Abraham	I, 46th U. S. col. tr'ps..	....	No claim on file as stated.
Smith, Jacob,(Emmy Smith, mother, claimant.)	A, 40th U. S. col. tr'ps .	....	Mother has not filed an application. Applications of soldier and of reputed widow are on file. Soldiers post office address, Memphis, Tenn, widow's, Murfreesboro, Tenn.
Stevine, William	F, 44th U. S. col. tr'ps..	Moyers & Dedrick, Memphis, Tenn,	Disallowed May 18, 1868. Paid $200 bounty, act July 4, 1864, all that he was entitled to. Discharge sent to attorneys.
Stevenson, Henry..........	K, 11th U. S. col. tr'ps .	....	No claim registered in the case as stated.
Suggs, Prince...............	D, 12th U. S. col. tr'ps..	....	No claim registered in the case as stated.
Steel, William	C, 14th U. S. col. tr'ps..	....	No claim registered in the case as stated.
Turner, Green	A, 1st U. S. col. h. art..	....	No claim registered in case as stated.
Tynham, Culvin	110th U. S. col. troops..	....	No claim registered in case as stated.

BOUNTIES TO COLORED SOLDIERS.

E.—*Drew's statement*—Continued.

Name.	Company and regiment.	Attorney.	Remarks.
Tucker, Conger, (Julia Tucker, wid., claimant.)	A, 59th U. S. col. tr'ps..	B. D. Hyam, Washington, D. C.	Settled January 12, 1867, and certificate No. 283,917, for $142 67, sent to attorney.
Tillman, Shenold..........	G, 12th U. S. col. h. art.	....	No claim on file in case.
Townsend, Israel	B, 101st U. S. col. tr'ps..	....	Out for settlement and will be disposed of soon.
Upshaw, Thomas..........	K, 110th U. S. col. tr'ps.	Chipman, Hosmer & Co., Washington, D. C.	Settled December 10, 1867, and certificate No.336,726, for $203 20, sent to attorneys.
Vance, Lewis, (Nancy Dailey, widow, claimant.)	I, 110th U. S. col. tr'ps.	....	No claim registered.
Warren, London, (Frances Warren, wid., claimant.)	F, 40th U. S. col. tr'ps..	....	No claim registered.
Woodfolk, Meridith........	C, 5th Ohio cavalry....	....	No claim on file.
Ware, Alfred..............	A, 44th U. S. col. tr'ps..	....	Out for settlement and will be disposed of soon.
Williams, John............	I, 55th U. S. col. tr'ps.	R. McAllister, Washington, D, C.	Settled March 27, 1867, and certificate No. 294,430, for $271 50, sent to attorney.

WAR DEPARTMENT, BUREAU OF REFUGEES, FREEDMEN
AND ABANDONED LANDS, CLAIM DIVISION,
Washington, D. C., February 28, 1870.

CAPTAIN: In further answer to your letters of the 2d and 3d instant, requesting information as to the condition of certain claims therein mentioned, I am directed to inclose herewith a supplementary schedule, showing the condition of the claims of William Jones, late of Company I One hundredth United States colored troops; Parker Fry, late of Company I Sixth United States colored heavy artillery; Isaac Maxwell, late of Company H Fifteenth United States colored troops; and Katie Gardner, mother of Alexander Smith, deceased, late of Company D Tenth United States colored troops.

It would seem that in the last-named case an error in statement has been made, as the records of this office show the claim of Katie Gardner, as mother of Aleck Gardner, deceased, late of Company B Twelfth United States colored troops, settled by certificate No. 476,368, (O'Neill & Dufour, attorneys,) for $306 34, and paid July 6, 1869, by John L. Wilson, agent and disbursing officer at Columbia, Tennessee.

The inclosed schedule, with that forwarded to the commission on the 23d instant, comprises all the cases concerning which information was requested, except those of Conger Tucker, late of Company E Fifty-ninth United States colored troops, and Julia Tucker, widow of Conger Tucker, late of Company E Eleventh United States colored troops, reports in which were omitted by inadvertence at the Auditor's office. These are, however, probably identical.

Very respectfully, your obedient servant,
WILLIAM P. DREW,
Agent Bureau of Refugees, Freedmen and Abandoned Lands,
Chief of Claim Division.

Brevet Captain J. A. SLADEN, *U. S. A.*,
Recorder for Military Commission Bureau of Refugees,
Freedmen and Abandoned Lands, Washington, D. C.

BOUNTIES TO COLORED SOLDIERS.

Drew's Statement F.

CLAIM DIVISION, BUREAU OF REFUGEES, FREEDMEN
AND ABANDONED LANDS, *February* 28, 1870.

1. Alexander Gardner, Company D Tenth regiment United States colored troops; Katie Gardner, mother, claimant. No claim registered in case as stated.

2. William Jones, Company I One hundredth regiment United States colored troops; Justus J. McCarty, Washington, D. C., attorney. Disallowed June 11, 1868; $100 bounty, act July 4, 1864; all due him was paid at time of muster out of service; discharge sent to attorney.

3. Parker Fry, Company I Sixth regiment United States colored heavy artillery; McQuithy & Alden, attorneys. Suspended for information from the Adjutant General United States Army, in reply to letter of date January 22, 1870, requesting same.

4. Isaac Maxwell, Company H Fifteenth regiment United States colored troops; McQuithy & Alden, attorneys. Rejected August 22, 1868, and discharge returned to Chipman, Hosmer & Co. This man received $100 bounty, all he was entitled to by terms of his enlistment.